GROWING OLD IN AMERICA

ISSN 1538-6686

GROWING OLD IN AMERICA

Barbara Wexler

INFORMATION PLUS® REFERENCE SERIES
Formerly Published by Information Plus, Wylie, Texas

GALE
CENGAGE Learning®

Detroit • New York • San Francisco • New Haven, Conn • Waterville, Maine • London

GALE
CENGAGE Learning®

Growing Old in America

Barbara Wexler

Kepos Media, Inc.: Paula Kepos and Janice Jorgensen, Series Editors

Project Editors: Elizabeth Manar, Kathleen J. Edgar, Kimberley McGrath

Rights Acquisition and Management: Bill Jentzen, Kimberly Potvin, Sheila R. Spencer

Composition: Evi Abou-El-Seoud, Mary Beth Trimper

Manufacturing: Cynde Lentz

Cover photograph: Image copyright Cassiede Alain, 2011. Used under license from Shutterstock.com.

Gale
27500 Drake Rd.
Farmington Hills, MI 48331-3535

ISBN-13: 978-0-7876-5103-9 (set)   ISBN-10: 0-7876-5103-6 (set)
ISBN-13: 978-1-4144-8142-5   ISBN-10: 1-4144-8142-X

ISSN 1538-6686

This title is also available as an e-book.
ISBN-13: 978-1-4144-9632-0 (set)
ISBN-10: 1-4144-9632-X (set)
Contact your Gale sales representative for ordering information.

Printed in the United States of America
1 2 3 4 5 6 7 16 15 14 13 12

305.26
WEXLER

TABLE OF CONTENTS

Medicaid, are presented in this chapter. The challenges of long-term care are discussed along with in-home services that enable older adults to remain in the community.

delves into the types of frauds that are perpetrated against the older population, domestic and institutional abuse, and mistreatment.

PREFACE

Growing Old in America is part of the *Information Plus Reference Series*. The purpose of each volume of the series is to present the latest facts on a topic of pressing concern in modern American life. These topics include the most controversial and studied social issues of the 21st century: abortion, capital punishment, crime, the environment, health care, immigration, minorities, national security, social welfare, sports, women, youth, and many more. Even though this series is written especially for high school and undergraduate students, it is an excellent resource for anyone in need of factual information on current affairs.

By presenting the facts, it is the intention of Gale, Cengage Learning to provide its readers with everything they need to reach an informed opinion on current issues. To that end, there is a particular emphasis in this series on the presentation of scientific studies, surveys, and statistics. These data are generally presented in the form of tables, charts, and other graphics placed within the text of each book. Every graphic is directly referred to and carefully explained in the text. The source of each graphic is presented within the graphic itself. The data used in these graphics are drawn from the most reputable and reliable sources, such as from the various branches of the U.S. government and from private organizations and associations. Every effort has been made to secure the most recent information available. Readers should bear in mind that many major studies take years to conduct and that additional years often pass before the data from these studies are made available to the public. Therefore, in many cases the most recent information available in 2012 is dated from 2009 or 2010. Older statistics are sometimes presented as well if they are landmark studies or of particular interest and no more-recent data are available.

Even though statistics are a major focus of the *Information Plus Reference Series*, they are by no means its only content. Each book also presents the widely held positions and important ideas that shape how the book's subject is discussed in the United States. These positions are explained in detail and, where possible, in the words of their proponents. Some of the other material to be found in these books includes historical background, descriptions of major events related to the subject, relevant laws and court cases, and examples of how these issues play out in American life. Some books also feature primary documents or have pro and con debate sections that provide the words and opinions of prominent Americans on both sides of a controversial topic. All material is presented in an even-handed and unbiased manner; readers will never be encouraged to accept one view of an issue over another.

HOW TO USE THIS BOOK

The percentage of Americans over the age of 65 years has increased over the past century, and it will continue to increase as the children born during the mid-20th-century baby boom age. This book explores the current condition of growing old in the United States. Included is a general overview on growing old in the United States; the economic status of older people; the Social Security program; Medicare and Medicaid; the living arrangements of older adults; working and retirement; and the education levels, voting trends, and political behavior of older Americans. Physical and mental health problems, drug and alcohol abuse, care for older adults, and crime and victimization of older adults are also covered.

Growing Old in America consists of 11 chapters and three appendixes. Each chapter is devoted to a particular aspect of aging. For a summary of the information that is covered in each chapter, please see the synopses provided in the Table of Contents. Chapters generally begin with an overview of the basic facts and background information on the chapter's topic, then proceed to examine subtopics of particular interest. For example, Chapter 6: On the Road: Older Adult Drivers, observes that the ability to drive often determines whether an older adult is able to live independently. It then goes on to detail the modes of transportation that are available to older adults. This is followed by a discussion of transportation initiatives to address the needs of older adults, including innovative transportation solutions, especially for rural areas. Even though older Americans have high fatality rates on a per-mile-driven basis, older drivers are less likely to hurt others—older drivers pose more of a danger to themselves. Readers can find their way through a chapter by looking for the section and subsection headings, which are clearly set off from the text. They can also refer to the book's extensive Index if they already know what they are looking for.

Statistical Information

The tables and figures featured throughout *Growing Old in America* will be of particular use to readers in learning about this issue. These tables and figures represent an extensive collection of the most recent and important statistics on growing old and related issues—for example, graphics cover the living arrangements of older adults, the marital status of older Americans, chronic health conditions, crimes against older Americans, health care costs paid by Medicare and Medicaid, health insurance coverage, and how older adults are redefining retirement. Gale, Cengage Learning believes that making this information available to readers is the most important way to fulfill the goal of this book: to help readers understand the issues and controversies surrounding growing old in the United States and to reach their own conclusions.

Each table or figure has a unique identifier appearing above it for ease of identification and reference. Titles for the tables and figures explain their purpose. At the end of each table or figure, the original source of the data is provided.

To help readers understand these often complicated statistics, all tables and figures are explained in the text. References in the text direct readers to the relevant statistics. Furthermore, the contents of all tables and figures are fully indexed. Please see the opening section of the Index at the back of this volume for a description of how to find tables and figures within it.

Appendixes

Besides the main body text and images, *Growing Old in America* has three appendixes. The first is the Important Names and Addresses directory. Here, readers will find contact information for a number of government and private organizations that can provide further information on growing old. The second appendix is the Resources section, which can also assist readers in conducting their own research. In this section, the author and editors of *Growing Old in America* describe some of the sources that were most useful during the compilation of this book. The final appendix is the detailed Index. It has been greatly expanded from previous editions and should make it even easier to find specific topics in this book.

ADVISORY BOARD CONTRIBUTIONS

The staff of Information Plus would like to extend their heartfelt appreciation to the Information Plus Advisory Board. This dedicated group of media professionals provides feedback on the series on an ongoing basis. Their comments allow the editorial staff who work on the project to make the series better and more user-friendly. The staff's top priority is to produce the highest-quality and most useful books possible, and the Information Plus Advisory Board's contributions to this process are invaluable.

The members of the Information Plus Advisory Board are:

- Kathleen R. Bonn, Librarian, Newbury Park High School, Newbury Park, California

- Madelyn Garner, Librarian, San Jacinto College, North Campus, Houston, Texas

- Anne Oxenrider, Media Specialist, Dundee High School, Dundee, Michigan

- Charles R. Rodgers, Director of Libraries, Pasco-Hernando Community College, Dade City, Florida

- James N. Zitzelsberger, Library Media Department Chairman, Oshkosh West High School, Oshkosh, Wisconsin

COMMENTS AND SUGGESTIONS

The editors of the *Information Plus Reference Series* welcome your feedback on *Growing Old in America*. Please direct all correspondence to:

Editors
Information Plus Reference Series
27500 Drake Rd.
Farmington Hills, MI 48331-3535

CHAPTER 1

OLDER AMERICANS: A DIVERSE AND GROWING POPULATION

Old age is the most unexpected of all the things that happen to a man.

—Leon Trotsky

THE UNITED STATES GROWS OLDER

The United States is aging. Throughout the second half of the 20th century and the first two decades of the 21st century the country's older population—adults aged 65 years and older—increased significantly. According to Saadia Greenberg of the Administration on Aging, in *A Profile of Older Americans: 2010* (2011, http://www .aoa.gov/aoaroot/aging_statistics/Profile/2010/docs/2010 profile.pdf), the number of older adults grew from 35.3 million in 1999 to 39.6 million in 2009 (the most recent year for which comprehensive data, as opposed to estimates or projections, were available as of June 2011), which represented 12.9% of the total U.S. population. In *The Next Four Decades—The Older Population in the United States: 2010 to 2050* (May 2010, http://www.cen sus.gov/prod/2010pubs/p25-1138.pdf), Grayson K. Vincent and Victoria A. Velkoff of the U.S. Census Bureau project that by 2030 one out of five U.S. residents will be aged 65 years and older and that by 2050 the population of people aged 65 years and older will number 88.5 million. Table 1.1 shows projections of the growth in the population of older adults between 2010 and 2050. It also shows how older adults will make up an increasing percentage of the total U.S. population, growing from 13% in 2010 to 20.2% in 2050.

The Census Bureau reports in the press release "Older Americans Month: May 2011" (March 23, 2011, http:// www.census.gov/newsroom/releases/pdf/cb11-ff08_older americans.pdf) that in 2011 there were 545 million people aged 65 years and older worldwide and that this population will grow to nearly 1.6 billion in 2050. The percentage of people aged 65 years and older worldwide will rise from about 8% in 2011 to 17% in 2050. Throughout the

world, the growth in the population of older adults will outpace the growth of any other segment of the population. Figure 1.1 compares the percentages of young children (aged five years and younger) and adults aged 65 years and older of the global population between 1950 and 2050; it reveals a steady decline in the percentage of children and a sharp increase in the percentage of older adults between 2000 and 2050. Figure 1.2 shows how the percentage of the oldest older adults (people aged 80 years and older) is expected to increase. For example, in the United States the percentage of older adults aged 80 years and older is projected to increase by six percentage points between 2008 and 2040, from 29.5% to 35.5%. In Japan the percentage of people aged 80 years and older is projected to grow by nearly 12 percentage points during the same period, from 26.4% to 38%.

Fewer children per family and longer life spans have shifted the proportion of older adults in the population. Growth in the population segment of older adults in the United States, often called "the graying of America," is considered one of the most significant issues facing the country in the 21st century. The swelling population of people aged 65 years and older affects every aspect of society—challenging policy makers, health care providers, employers, families, and others to meet the needs of older Americans.

Many of the findings and statistics cited in this chapter, as well as a number of the tables and figures presented, are drawn from *Older Americans 2010: Key Indicators of Well-Being* (July 2011, http://www.agingstats.gov/ agingstatsdotnet/Main_Site/Data/2010_Documents/Docs/ OA_2010.pdf), a report prepared by the Federal Interagency Forum on Aging-Related Statistics. This forum consists of 15 federal entities—the Administration on Aging, the Agency for Healthcare Research and Quality, the Centers for Medicare and Medicaid Services, the Census Bureau, the Employee Benefits Security

TABLE 1.1

Projected U.S. population by age, 2010–50

[Number in thousands]

Age	2010	2020	2030	2040	2050
Number					
Total	**310,233**	**341,387**	**373,504**	**405,655**	**439,010**
Under 20 years	84,150	90,703	97,682	104,616	112,940
20 to 64 years	185,854	195,880	203,729	219,801	237,523
65 years and over	40,229	54,804	72,092	81,238	88,547
65 to 69 years	12,261	17,861	20,381	18,989	21,543
70 to 74 years	9,202	14,452	18,404	17,906	18,570
75 to 79 years	7,282	9,656	14,390	16,771	15,964
80 to 84 years	5,733	6,239	10,173	13,375	13,429
85 to 89 years	3,650	3,817	5,383	8,450	10,303
90 years and over	2,101	2,780	3,362	5,748	8,738
Percent					
Total	**100.0**	**100.0**	**100.0**	**100.0**	**100.0**
Under 20 years	27.1	26.6	26.2	25.8	25.7
20 to 64 years	59.9	57.4	54.5	54.2	54.1
65 years and over	13.0	16.1	19.3	20.0	20.2
65 to 69 years	4.0	5.2	5.5	4.7	4.9
70 to 74 years	3.0	4.2	4.9	4.4	4.2
75 to 79 years	2.3	2.8	3.9	4.1	3.6
80 to 84 years	1.8	1.8	2.7	3.3	3.1
85 to 89 years	1.2	1.1	1.4	2.1	2.3
90 years and over	0.7	0.8	0.9	1.4	2.0

SOURCE: Grayson K. Vincent and Victoria A. Velkoff, "Appendix Table A-1. Projections and Distribution of the Total Population by Age for the United States: 2010 to 2050," in *The Next Four Decades—The Older Population in the United States: 2010 to 2050*, U.S. Census Bureau, May 2010, http://www.census.gov/prod/2010pubs/p25-1138.pdf (accessed April 2, 2011).

FIGURE 1.1

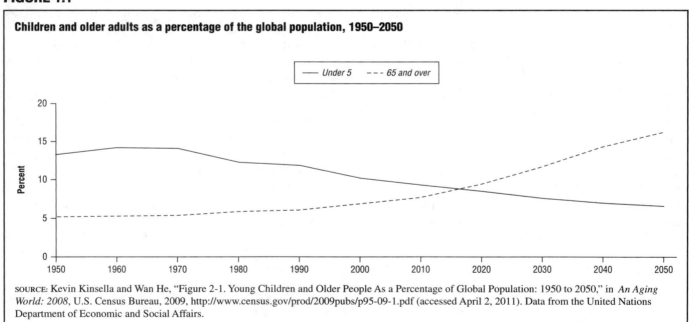

Children and older adults as a percentage of the global population, 1950–2050

SOURCE: Kevin Kinsella and Wan He, "Figure 2-1. Young Children and Older People As a Percentage of Global Population: 1950 to 2050," in *An Aging World: 2008*, U.S. Census Bureau, 2009, http://www.census.gov/prod/2009pubs/p95-09-1.pdf (accessed April 2, 2011). Data from the United Nations Department of Economic and Social Affairs.

Administration, the U.S. Bureau of Labor Statistics, the U.S. Department of Housing and Urban Development, the U.S. Department of Veterans Affairs, the U.S. Environmental Protection Agency, the National Center for Health Statistics, the National Institute on Aging, the Office of Statistical and Science Policy, the Office of the Assistant Secretary for Planning and Evaluation (U.S. Department of Health and Human Services), the Office of Research, Evaluation, and Statistics, and the Substance Abuse and Mental Health Services Administration—that are dedicated to encouraging cooperation and collaboration among federal agencies to improve the quality and utility of data on the aging population. Other data are drawn from Greenberg's *Profile of Older Americans*.

FIGURE 1.2

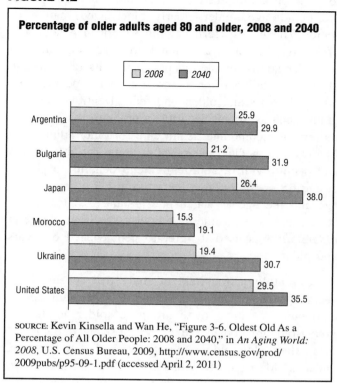

Percentage of older adults aged 80 and older, 2008 and 2040

Legend: ☐ 2008 ■ 2040

Country	2008	2040
Argentina	25.9	29.9
Bulgaria	21.2	31.9
Japan	26.4	38.0
Morocco	15.3	19.1
Ukraine	19.4	30.7
United States	29.5	35.5

SOURCE: Kevin Kinsella and Wan He, "Figure 3-6. Oldest Old As a Percentage of All Older People: 2008 and 2040," in *An Aging World: 2008*, U.S. Census Bureau, 2009, http://www.census.gov/prod/2009pubs/p95-09-1.pdf (accessed April 2, 2011)

To understand the aging of the United States, it is important to not only consider the current population of older adults but also to look at how the older population will fare over time. To anticipate the needs of this growing segment of society, policy makers, planners, and researchers rely on projections and population estimates. Population estimates and projections are made at different times and are based on different assumptions. Therefore, it is not surprising to find considerable variation in the statistics cited by different agencies and investigators. This chapter contains estimates and projections of demographic changes from several different sources, and as a result there is some variability in the data presented.

HOW DO POPULATIONS AGE?

Unlike people, populations can age or become younger. There are key indicators of the age structure of a given population. Populations age or grow younger because of changes in fertility (birth rates expressed as the number of births per 1,000 population per year) and/or mortality (death rates expressed as the number of deaths per 1,000 population per year) or in response to migration—people entering or leaving the population.

The aging of the United States in the early 21st century resulted from changes in fertility and mortality that occurred over the past century. Such shifts in birth and death rates are called demographic transitions. Generally, population aging is primarily a response to long-term declines in fertility, and declining fertility is the

basic cause of the aging of the U.S. population. Reduced infant and child mortality, chiefly as a result of public health measures, fueled the decline in the fertility rate; that is, the increased survival of children prompted families to have fewer offspring. The birth of fewer babies resulted in fewer young people.

According to the Central Intelligence Agency (CIA), in *The World Factbook: United States* (May 26, 2011, https://www.cia.gov/library/publications/the-world-factbook/geos/us.html), in 2011 the total fertility rate in the United States was two children born per woman. This rate, which has not changed significantly since the mid-1980s, is sharply lower than the fertility rates between 1946 and 1964, following the end of World War II (1939–1945). Victorious U.S. soldiers returning home after the war were eager to start families, and this was facilitated by the relatively prosperous postwar economy.

Census Bureau statistics indicate that during this period, which came to be known as the baby boom, U.S. fertility rates exploded, at one point approaching four children born per woman. Children born during the baby boom became known as baby boomers, and it is this huge cohort (a group of individuals that shares a common characteristic such as birth years and is studied over time) that is responsible for the tremendous increase projected in the number of people aged 65 years and older, and especially aged 65 to 74 years. The older adult segment of the population is expected to swell until 2030, as the baby boom cohort completes its transition from middle age to old age.

The decline in death rates, especially at the older ages, has also contributed to the increase in the number of older adults. The death rates of older adults began to decrease during the late 1960s and continued to decline through the first decade of the 21st century. Advances in medical care have produced declining death rates for all three of the leading causes of death: heart disease, malignancies (cancer), and cerebrovascular diseases that cause strokes. The Centers for Disease Control and Prevention reveals in the press release "US Death Rate Falls for 10th Straight Year" (March 16, 2011, http://www.cdc.gov/media/releases/2011/p0316_deathrate.html) that the age-adjusted death rate in the United States reached an all-time low in 2009 of 741 deaths per 100,000 population, down from 799 deaths per 100,000 in 2005.

Projections of an increasing proportion of older adults between 2012 and 2030 are based on three assumptions: historic low fertility and the prospect of continuing low fertility until 2030, aging of the baby boom cohort, and continued declines in mortality at older ages and low mortality until 2030. Demographers (those who study population statistics) expect that when the entire baby boom generation has attained age 65 (or older) in 2030, the proportion of older people in the U.S. population will stabilize. (See Figure 1.3.)

DEFINING OLD AGE

Forty is the old age of youth; fifty the youth of old age.

—Victor Hugo

When does old age begin? The challenge of defining old age is reflected in the terminology that is used to describe adults aged 50 years and older: for example, middle aged, elder, elderly, older, aged, mature, or senior. The AARP (formerly the American Association of Retired Persons), a national advocacy organization for older adults, invites people to join its ranks at age 50. Many retailers offer senior discounts to people aged 50 or 55 years and older, and federal entitlement programs such as Social Security (a program that provides retirement income and health care for older adults) and Medicare (a medical insurance program for older adults and people with disabilities) extend benefits to people at age 65 or 67. Despite the varying definitions of old age and the age at which one assumes "older adult" status, in this text, unless otherwise specified, the term *older adults* is used to refer to people aged 65 years and older.

Gerontology (the field of study that considers the social, psychological, and biological aspects of aging) distinguishes among three groups of older adults: the young-old are considered to be those aged 65 to 74 years, the middle-old includes those aged 75 to 84 years, and the oldest-old are those aged 85 years and older. Figure 1.4 shows that the oldest segment of older adults, the oldest-old, grew from just over 100,000 in 1900 to 5.7 million in 2008 and is projected to steadily increase to 19 million by 2050.

FIGURE 1.3

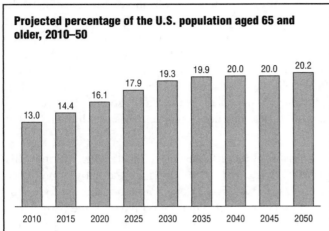

Projected percentage of the U.S. population aged 65 and older, 2010–50

SOURCE: "Projected Percent of the U.S. Population Aged 65 and Older: 2010 to 2050," in *2008 National Population Projections Tables and Charts*, U.S. Census Bureau, Population Division, August 2008, http://www.census.gov/population/www/projections/tablesandcharts/chart_6.pdf (accessed April 2, 2011)

FIGURE 1.4

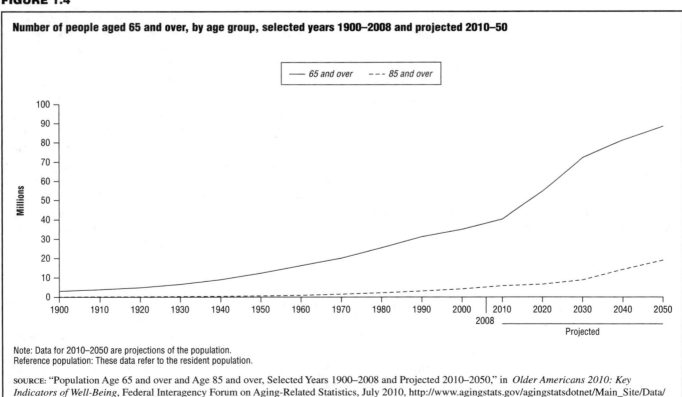

Number of people aged 65 and over, by age group, selected years 1900–2008 and projected 2010–50

Note: Data for 2010–2050 are projections of the population.
Reference population: These data refer to the resident population.

SOURCE: "Population Age 65 and over and Age 85 and over, Selected Years 1900–2008 and Projected 2010–2050," in *Older Americans 2010: Key Indicators of Well-Being*, Federal Interagency Forum on Aging-Related Statistics, July 2010, http://www.agingstats.gov/agingstatsdotnet/Main_Site/Data/2010_Documents/Docs/OA_2010.pdf (accessed April 2, 2011)

LIFE EXPECTANCY

In *Health, United States, 2010* (February 2011, http://www.cdc.gov/nchs/data/hus/hus10.pdf), the National Center for Health Statistics indicates that life expectancy (the anticipated average length of life) has increased dramatically since 1900, when the average age of death for men and women combined was 47.3 years. Between 2000 and 2007 life expectancy increased by 1.3 years for males and by 1.1 years for females. Most projections see life expectancy continuing to rise; according to the CIA, in *World Factbook*, the life expectancy of a baby born in the United States in 2011 was 75.9 years for males and 80.9 years for females.

However, some researchers caution that the historic trend of increasing longevity has ended, with life expectancy at birth beginning to decline by as much as five years as a direct result of the obesity epidemic in the United States. Nancy E. Adler and Judith Stewart of the University of California, San Francisco, suggest in "Reducing Obesity: Motivating Action While Not Blaming the Victim" (*Milbank Quarterly*, vol. 87, no. 1, March 2009) that the rise in obesity in the United States may slow or even reverse the long-term trend of increasing life expectancy.

Adler and Stewart base their projections on an analysis of the body mass index (a number that shows body weight adjusted for height) and on other factors that could potentially affect the health and well-being of the current generation of children and young adults. They observe that obesity currently reduces life expectancy at age 18 by 7.2 years for obese women and by 4.4 years for obese men. The researchers assert that unless individual and society-wide actions taken to address the obesity epidemic are effective, younger Americans will likely face a greater risk of mortality throughout life than previous generations.

Obesity has an impact not only on life expectancy but also on the health of older adults because obese older adults are more likely than their healthy-weight peers to experience obesity-related conditions such as heart disease, diabetes, arthritis, and some cancers. In "Obesity and Excess Mortality among the Elderly in the United States and Mexico" (*Demography*, vol. 47, no. 1, February 2010), Malena Monteverde et al. suggest that increasing rates of obesity may jeopardize life expectancy in developing countries as well as in the United States. The researchers compare the rates of obesity, obesity-related chronic diseases, and deaths attributable to obesity in the United States and Mexico. They find that even though the effect of obesity on mortality of older adults is greater in Mexico than in the United States, the likelihood of developing obesity-related chronic diseases is higher in the United States and caution that these findings suggest that "longevity among older individuals may be compromised in the future."

Global Life Expectancy

The more developed regions of the world have lower death rates than the less developed regions and, as such, have higher life expectancies. In *World Factbook*, the CIA observes that some nations more than doubled their life expectancy during the 20th century. In 2011 the projected life expectancy at birth in Monaco was 89.7 years, and it was at least 79 years in many developed countries. (See Table 1.2.) Many less developed countries have also seen a steady increase in life expectancy, except for countries in Africa that have been hard hit by the human immunodeficiency virus (HIV)/acquired immunodeficiency syndrome

TABLE 1.2

Estimated life expectancy at birth by country, 2011

1	Monaco	89.73
2	Macau	84.41
3	San Marino	83.01
4	Andorra	82.43
5	Japan	82.25
6	Guernsey	82.16
7	Singapore	82.14
8	Hong Kong	82.04
9	Australia	81.81
10	Italy	81.77
11	Canada	81.38
12	Jersey	81.38
13	France	81.19
14	Spain	81.17
15	Sweden	81.07
16	Switzerland	81.07
17	Israel	80.96
18	Iceland	80.90
19	Anguilla	80.87
20	Bermuda	80.71
21	Cayman Islands	80.68
22	Isle of Man	80.64
23	New Zealand	80.59
24	Liechtenstein	80.31
25	Norway	80.20
26	Ireland	80.19
27	Germany	80.07
28	Jordan	80.05
29	United Kingdom	80.05
30	Greece	79.92
31	Saint Pierre and Miquelon	79.87
32	Austria	79.78
33	Faroe Islands	79.72
34	Malta	79.72
35	Netherlands	79.68
36	Luxembourg	79.61
37	Belgium	79.51
38	Virgin Islands	79.33
39	Finland	79.27
40	Turks and Caicos Islands	79.11
41	Korea, South	79.05
42	Wallis and Futuna	78.98
43	Puerto Rico	78.92
44	European Union	78.82
45	Bosnia and Herzegovina	78.81
46	Saint Helena, Ascension, and Tristan da Cunha	78.76
47	Gibraltar	78.68
48	Denmark	78.63
49	Portugal	78.54
50	United States	78.37

SOURCE: Adapted from "Country Comparison: Life Expectancy at Birth," in *The World Factbook*, Central Intelligence Agency, April 2011, https://www.cia.gov/library/publications/the-world-factbook/rankorder/2102 rank.html (accessed April 2, 2011)

TABLE 1.3

Countries with lowest estimated life expectancy at birth, 2011

198	Sierra Leone	56.13
199	Sudan	55.42
200	Congo, Democratic Republic of the	55.33
201	Congo, Republic of the	54.91
202	Cameroon	54.39
203	Burkina Faso	53.70
204	Niger	53.40
205	Uganda	53.24
206	Tanzania	52.85
207	Mali	52.61
208	Gabon	52.49
209	Zambia	52.36
210	Namibia	52.19
211	Mozambique	51.78
212	Malawi	51.70
213	Lesotho	51.63
214	Somalia	50.40
215	Central African Republic	50.07
216	Zimbabwe	49.64
217	South Africa	49.33
218	Guinea-Bissau	48.70
219	Swaziland	48.66
220	Chad	48.33
221	Nigeria	47.56
222	Afghanistan	45.02
223	Angola	38.76

SOURCE: Adapted from "Country Comparison: Life Expectancy at Birth," in *The World Factbook*, Central Intelligence Agency, April 2011, https://www.cia.gov/library/publications/the-world-factbook/rankorder/2102rank.html (accessed April 2, 2011)

(AIDS) epidemic. Table 1.2 shows ranks of the top 50 countries in terms of life expectancy in 2011.

Even though the United Nations' Department of Economic and Social Affairs predicts in *World Population Prospects: The 2008 Revision* (2009, http://www.un.org/esa/population/publications/wpp2008/wpp2008_highlights.pdf) that the gap in life expectancy will narrow during the first half of the 21st century, the developed world will still be far ahead. Between 2045 and 2050 the more developed regions will have a life expectancy of 83 years, compared to 74 years for the less developed regions. Table 1.3 shows the ranks of the 25 countries with the lowest estimates of life expectancy in 2011. Angola and Afghanistan had the lowest life expectancy at 38.8 and 45 years, respectively.

OLDER ADULTS IN THE UNITED STATES

According to U.S. census estimates, in 2015 there will be an estimated 46.8 million people aged 65 years and older living in the United States. (See Table 1.4.) The young-old bracket (aged 65 to 74 years) will account for 58% (27 million) of the 65 and older population. Twenty-nine percent (13.6 million) of the older adult population will be in the middle-old bracket (aged 75 to 84 years), and 13% (6.3 million) will make up the oldest-old bracket (aged 85 years and older).

By 2020 the number of young-old is projected to rise to 32.3 million, the middle-old will be nearing 15.9 million, and the oldest-old will be 6.6 million. (See Table 1.4.) Older women are expected to outnumber men in all three age brackets. Greenberg indicates that in 2009 the female-to-male sex ratio increased with advancing age, from about 114 for the young-old to 216 for the oldest-old. Figure 1.5 shows the increasing percentages of females in the older adult population in 2010, 2030, and 2050. Longer female life expectancy, combined with the fact that men often marry younger women, contributes to a higher proportion of older women living alone—widowed or unmarried.

The Oldest-Old

Greenberg states that in 2007 adults who reached "age 65 had an average life expectancy of an additional 18.6 years (19.9 years for females and 17.2 years for males)." The 85 and older population will grow from 5.7 million in 2010 to 6.6 million in 2020, an increase of 15% for that decade.

In *Older Americans 2010*, the Federal Interagency Forum on Aging-Related Statistics notes that some researchers believe death rates at older ages will decline more rapidly than is reflected in Census Bureau projections, which will result in even faster growth of this population segment. The Census Bureau reports that among the oldest-old, women dramatically outnumber men—in 2015 there will be nearly twice as many women aged 85 years and older than men. (See Table 1.4.) Because it is anticipated that women will continue to live longer into the middle of the 21st century, they will make up an even larger proportion of the older population and the overall U.S. population in the future.

THE WORLD'S 80-PLUS POPULATION. According to Kevin Kinsella and Wan He of the Census Bureau, in *An Aging World: 2008* (June 2009, http://www.census.gov/prod/2009pubs/p95-09-1.pdf), in 2008 the United States was second only to China in terms of the number of people aged 80 years and older. The United States contained just 5% of the world's population but 13% of the U.S. population was aged 80 years and older. Furthermore, people aged 85 years and older made up the fastest-growing population segment in the world. In "Older Americans Month: May 2011," the Census Bureau indicates that in the United States the 85 and older population grew from just over 100,000 in 1900 to 5.6 million in 2009. The U.S. population aged 80 years and older is estimated to reach 12 million by 2015. (See Table 1.4.)

Centenarians

During the first half of the 21st century the United States will experience a centenarian boom. Living to age 100 and older is no longer a rarity. The chances of living to age 100 have increased by 40% since 1900. The centenarian population more than doubled during the 1980s, and the

TABLE 1.4

Projections of the population by age and sex, 2015–50

[Resident population as of July 1. Numbers in thousands.]

Sex and age	2015	2020	2025	2030	2035	2040	2045	2050
Both sexes	**325,540**	**341,387**	**357,452**	**373,504**	**389,531**	**405,655**	**422,059**	**439,010**
Under 5 years	22,076	22,846	23,484	24,161	25,056	26,117	27,171	28,148
5 to 9 years	21,707	22,732	23,548	24,232	24,953	25,893	26,998	28,096
10 to 14 years	21,658	22,571	23,677	24,567	25,319	26,105	27,108	28,274
15 to 19 years	21,209	22,554	23,545	24,723	25,682	26,501	27,354	28,422
20 to 24 years	22,342	21,799	23,168	24,191	25,408	26,408	27,272	28,171
25 to 29 years	22,400	22,949	22,417	23,804	24,855	26,102	27,138	28,039
30 to 34 years	22,099	23,112	23,699	23,216	24,647	25,745	27,040	28,126
35 to 39 years	20,841	22,586	23,645	24,279	23,848	25,321	26,462	27,799
40 to 44 years	20,460	21,078	22,851	23,944	24,612	24,224	25,726	26,897
45 to 49 years	21,001	20,502	21,154	22,943	24,061	24,759	24,411	25,933
50 to 54 years	22,367	20,852	20,404	21,087	22,884	24,025	24,750	24,445
55 to 59 years	21,682	21,994	20,575	20,186	20,903	22,703	23,867	24,621
60 to 64 years	18,861	21,009	21,377	20,080	19,760	20,513	22,305	23,490
65 to 69 years	15,812	17,861	19,957	20,381	19,230	18,989	19,776	21,543
70 to 74 years	11,155	14,452	16,399	18,404	18,879	17,906	17,754	18,570
75 to 79 years	7,901	9,656	12,598	14,390	16,249	16,771	16,016	15,964
80 to 84 years	5,676	6,239	7,715	10,173	11,735	13,375	13,925	13,429
85 to 89 years	3,786	3,817	4,278	5,383	7,215	8,450	9,767	10,303
90 to 94 years	1,856	1,976	2,047	2,360	3,044	4,180	5,007	5,909
95 to 99 years	546	669	739	795	952	1,270	1,803	2,229
100 years and over	105	135	175	208	239	298	409	601
Median age (years)	37.1	37.7	38.2	38.7	39.0	38.9	38.9	39.0
Male	**160,424**	**168,258**	**176,102**	**183,870**	**191,609**	**199,434**	**207,465**	**215,825**
Under 5 years	11,278	11,671	11,996	12,341	12,797	13,338	13,876	14,374
5 to 9 years	11,074	11,596	12,011	12,358	12,724	13,202	13,764	14,322
10 to 14 years	11,049	11,514	12,076	12,527	12,906	13,304	13,811	14,403
15 to 19 years	10,844	11,513	12,016	12,612	13,095	13,506	13,934	14,472
20 to 24 years	11,378	11,072	11,749	12,266	12,878	13,379	13,810	14,259
25 to 29 years	11,353	11,624	11,321	12,004	12,531	13,154	13,669	14,115
30 to 34 years	11,182	11,674	11,962	11,682	12,384	12,930	13,574	14,110
35 to 39 years	10,506	11,399	11,913	12,223	11,969	12,689	13,255	13,918
40 to 44 years	10,247	10,581	11,486	12,014	12,340	12,107	12,840	13,420
45 to 49 years	10,447	10,210	10,560	11,469	12,009	12,348	12,136	12,878
50 to 54 years	10,977	10,302	10,091	10,456	11,364	11,915	12,267	12,079
55 to 59 years	10,524	10,700	10,078	9,898	10,278	11,184	11,745	12,111
60 to 64 years	9,023	10,079	10,283	9,727	9,584	9,981	10,878	11,448
65 to 69 years	7,449	8,412	9,434	9,665	9,189	9,090	9,502	10,380
70 to 74 years	5,109	6,660	7,564	8,529	8,787	8,406	8,356	8,782
75 to 79 years	3,480	4,285	5,635	6,452	7,331	7,610	7,341	7,345
80 to 84 years	2,342	2,622	3,275	4,363	5,056	5,810	6,096	5,952
85 to 89 years	1,409	1,466	1,681	2,144	2,913	3,437	4,017	4,282
90 to 94 years	591	663	713	844	1,110	1,551	1,879	2,251
95 to 99 years	142	186	218	244	302	413	599	753
100 years and over	21	29	40	51	62	81	114	172
Median age (years)	35.9	36.5	37.0	37.5	37.7	37.7	37.7	37.8
Female	**165,116**	**173,128**	**181,349**	**189,634**	**197,922**	**206,221**	**214,594**	**223,185**
Under 5 years	10,798	11,175	11,488	11,820	12,259	12,779	13,296	13,775
5 to 9 years	10,633	11,136	11,537	11,874	12,229	12,691	13,234	13,773
10 to 14 years	10,609	11,057	11,601	12,040	12,412	12,802	13,297	13,872
15 to 19 years	10,365	11,041	11,529	12,112	12,587	12,995	13,420	13,950
20 to 24 years	10,963	10,728	11,419	11,926	12,530	13,029	13,462	13,913
25 to 29 years	11,048	11,325	11,096	11,800	12,324	12,948	13,469	13,925
30 to 34 years	10,917	11,438	11,737	11,534	12,263	12,814	13,466	14,015
35 to 39 years	10,335	11,186	11,732	12,056	11,879	12,632	13,206	13,881
40 to 44 years	10,214	10,497	11,365	11,929	12,272	12,117	12,886	13,477
45 to 49 years	10,553	10,292	10,594	11,474	12,052	12,411	12,275	13,056
50 to 54 years	11,390	10,550	10,313	10,632	11,520	12,111	12,483	12,366
55 to 59 years	11,158	11,293	10,497	10,288	10,625	11,519	12,122	12,509
60 to 64 years	9,838	10,929	11,094	10,353	10,176	10,532	11,428	12,043
65 to 69 years	8,364	9,449	10,524	10,715	10,041	9,899	10,273	11,163

Census Bureau estimates in "Older Americans Month: May 2011" that in December 2010 the country had 71,991 centenarians. By 2050 the number of centenarians will increase more than eightfold to 601,000. (See Table 1.4.)

The National Centenarian Awareness Project (NCAP; February 2011, http://www.adlercentenarians.org/), a nonprofit advocacy organization for older adults, observes that the number of centenarians is growing steadily and is

TABLE 1.4

Projections of the population by age and sex, 2015–50 [CONTINUED]

[Resident population as of July 1. Numbers in thousands.]

Sex and age	2015	2020	2025	2030	2035	2040	2045	2050
70 to 74 years	6,046	7,791	8,835	9,875	10,092	9,500	9,398	9,788
75 to 79 years	4,421	5,371	6,962	7,937	8,918	9,161	8,674	8,619
80 to 84 years	3,334	3,618	4,440	5,810	6,679	7,565	7,830	7,477
85 to 89 years	2,376	2,351	2,598	3,239	4,302	5,013	5,750	6,021
90 to 94 years	1,265	1,312	1,334	1,515	1,934	2,629	3,128	3,657
95 to 99 years	404	484	521	551	650	857	1,203	1,476
100 years and over	84	106	134	156	177	217	295	429
Median age (years)	38.4	38.9	39.4	39.9	40.2	40.2	40.2	40.2

SOURCE: Adapted from "Table 12. Projections of the Population by Age and Sex for the United States: 2010 to 2050," in *2008 National Population Projections Summary Tables*, U.S. Census Bureau, Population Division, August 2008, http://www.census.gov/population/www/projections/summarytables.html (accessed April 25, 2011)

FIGURE 1.5

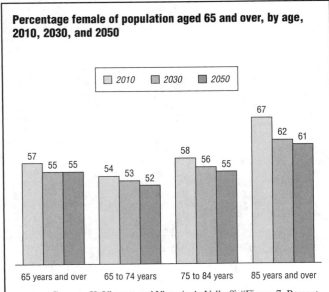

Percentage female of population aged 65 and over, by age, 2010, 2030, and 2050

☐ 2010 ▨ 2030 ■ 2050

SOURCE: Grayson K. Vincent and Victoria A. Velkoff, "Figure 7. Percent Female for the Older Population by Age for the United States: 2010, 2030, and 2050," in *The Next Four Decades—The Older Population in the United States: 2010 to 2050*, U.S. Census Bureau, May 2010, http://www.census.gov/prod/2010pubs/p25-1138.pdf (accessed April 2, 2011)

According to the Guinness World Records (2011, http://www.guinnessworldrecords.com/Search/Details/Oldestperson/64353.htm), the oldest verified age attained by a human is 122 years and 164 days. The Guinness World Records relies on the Gerontology Research Group (GRG, http://www.grg.org/calment.html), which tracks supercentenarians (people aged 110 years and older). The GRG reports that as of June 2011, it had validated 90 living supercentenarians: 85 women and 5 men.

On April 14, 2011, Walter Breuning, the oldest man in the world, died at age 114. In "World's Oldest Man dies in Montana at 114" (Associated Press, April 15, 2011), Matt Volz recounts Breuning's advice about how to live a long life:

- Embrace change, even when the change slaps you in the face. ("Every change is good.")

- Eat two meals a day. ("That's all you need.")

- Work as long as you can. ("That money's going to come in handy.")

- Help others. ("The more you do for others, the better shape you're in.")

- Accept death. ("We're going to die. Some people are scared of dying. Never be afraid to die. Because you're born to die.")

Racial and Ethnic Diversity

The older population is becoming more ethnically and racially diverse, although at a slower pace than the overall population of the United States. In 2008 the older population was made up by approximately 80% of non-Hispanic whites, 9% of African-Americans, 7% of Hispanics, and 3% of Asian-Americans. (See Figure 1.7.) By 2050 the composition of the older population is projected to be more racially and ethnically diverse: 59% will be non-Hispanic white, 20% Hispanic, 12% African-American, and 9% will be Asian-American.

"predicted to more than quadruple by 2030, reaching 1.15 million by 2050." The NCAP also asserts that "at least one out of three women age 50 today will reach 90" and that "high school students of today have a good chance of reaching the century mark."

As the numbers and percentages of all older adults increase, the shape of the U.S. population pyramid (also called the age-sex pyramid and the age structure diagram), which graphically displays the projected population by age, will change. Figure 1.6 shows how the projected population distribution in 2030 and 2050 differs from the distribution in 2010. By 2050 all age groups are projected to be larger than they were in 2010.

FIGURE 1.6

Projected population by age and sex, 2010, 2030, and 2050

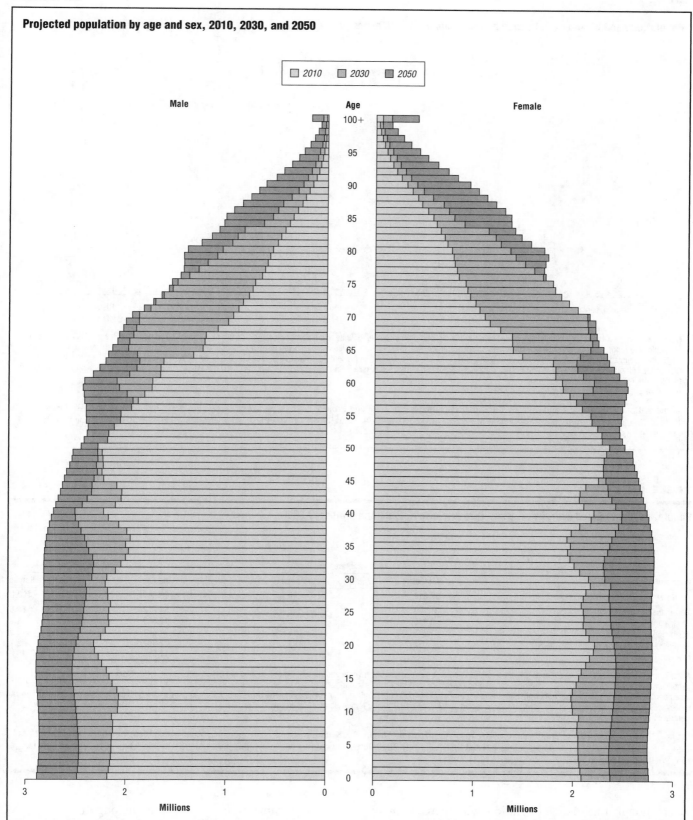

SOURCE: Grayson K. Vincent and Victoria A. Velkoff, "Figure 1. Age and Sex Structure of the Population for the United States: 2010, 2030, and 2050," in *The Next Four Decades—The Older Population in the United States: 2010 to 2050*, U.S. Census Bureau, May 2010, http://www.census.gov/prod/2010pubs/p25-1138.pdf (accessed April 2, 2011)

FIGURE 1.7

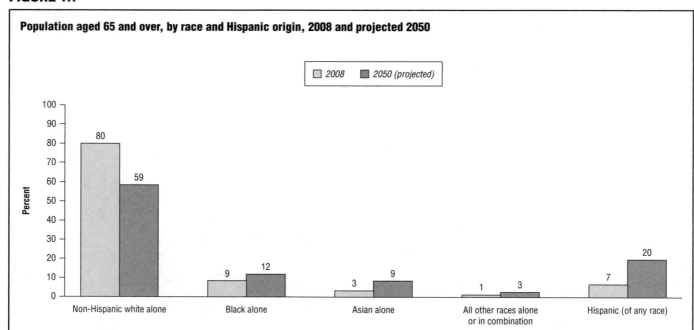

Population aged 65 and over, by race and Hispanic origin, 2008 and projected 2050

Note: The term "non-Hispanic white alone" is used to refer to people who reported being white and no other race and who are not Hispanic. The term "black alone" is used to refer to people who reported being black or African American and no other race, and the term "Asian alone" is used to refer to people who reported only Asian as their race. The use of single-race populations in this report does not imply that this is the preferred method of presenting or analyzing data. The U.S. Census Bureau uses a variety of approaches. The race group "All other races alone or in combination" includes American Indian and Alaska Native alone; Native Hawaiian and Other Pacific Islander alone; and all people who reported two or more races.
Reference population: These data refer to the resident population.

SOURCE: "Population Age 65 and over, by Race and Hispanic Origin, 2008 and Projected 2050," in *Older Americans 2010: Key Indicators of Well-Being*, Federal Interagency Forum on Aging-Related Statistics, July 2010, http://www.agingstats.gov/agingstatsdotnet/Main_Site/Data/2010_Documents/Docs/OA_2010.pdf (accessed April 2, 2011)

TABLE 1.5

Population aged 65 and over, by race and Hispanic origin, 2008 and projected 2050

[In thousands]

Race and Hispanic origin	2008 estimates		2050 projections	
	Number	Percent	Number	Percent
Total	**38,870**	**100.0**	**88,547**	**100.0**
Non-Hispanic white alone	31,238	80.4	51,772	58.5
Black alone	3,315	8.5	10,553	11.9
Asian alone	1,295	3.3	7,541	8.5
All other races alone or in combination	522	1.3	2,397	2.7
Hispanic (of any race)	2,661	6.8	17,515	19.8

Note: The term "non-Hispanic white alone" is used to refer to people who reported being white and no other race and who are not Hispanic. The term "black alone" is used to refer to people who reported being black or african American and no other race, and the term "Asian alone" is used to refer to people who reported only Asian as their race. The use of single-race populations in this report does not imply that this is the preferred method of presenting or analyzing data. The U.S. Census Bureau uses a variety of approaches. The race group "All other races alone or in combination" includes American Indian and Alaska Native alone; Native Hawaiian and other Pacific Islander alone; and all people who reported two or more races.
Reference population: These data refer to the resident population.

SOURCE: "Table 2. Population Age 65 and over, by Race and Hispanic Origin, 2008 and Projected 2050," in *Older Americans 2010: Key Indicators of Well-Being*, Federal Interagency Forum on Aging-Related Statistics, July 2010, http://www.agingstats.gov/agingstatsdotnet/Main_Site/Data/2010_Documents/Docs/OA_2010.pdf (accessed April 2, 2011)

Even though the older population will increase among African-Americans, Asian-Americans, and Hispanics, the older Hispanic population will grow the most dramatically, from 2.7 million (6.8%) in 2008 to 17.5 million (19.8%) in 2050. (See Table 1.5.) During this same period non-Hispanic whites will decline from 80.4% to 58.5%.

The same trend is apparent among the oldest-old adults; however, the rate of change is less dramatic. The population of people aged 85 years and older will be increasingly diverse in 2030 and 2050. (See Table 1.6.) For example, 10.4% will be African-American and 6% will be Asian-American in 2050.

TABLE 1.6

Distribution of population aged 85 and older by race, 2010, 2030, and 2050

[Numbers in thousands]

Race	2010 Number	2010 Percent	2030 Number	2030 Percent	2050 Number	2050 Percent
85 years and over	**5,751**	**100.0**	**8,745**	**100.0**	**19,041**	**100.0**
White alone	5,189	90.2	7,542	86.2	15,491	81.4
Black alone	397	6.9	701	8.0	1,982	10.4
American Indian and Alaska Native alone	20	0.4	62	0.7	180	0.9
Asian alone	113	2.0	356	4.1	1,145	6.0
Native Hawaiian and other Pacific Islander alone	3	0.1	11	0.1	35	0.2
Two or more races	29	0.5	74	0.8	208	1.1

SOURCE: Grayson K. Vincent and Victoria A. Velkoff, "Table 1. Projections and Distribution of the Population Aged 85 and over by Race for the United States: 2010, 2030, and 2050," in *The Next Four Decades—The Older Population in the United States: 2010 to 2050*, U.S. Census Bureau, May 2010, http://www.census.gov/prod/2010pubs/p25-1138.pdf (accessed April 2, 2011)

FIGURE 1.8

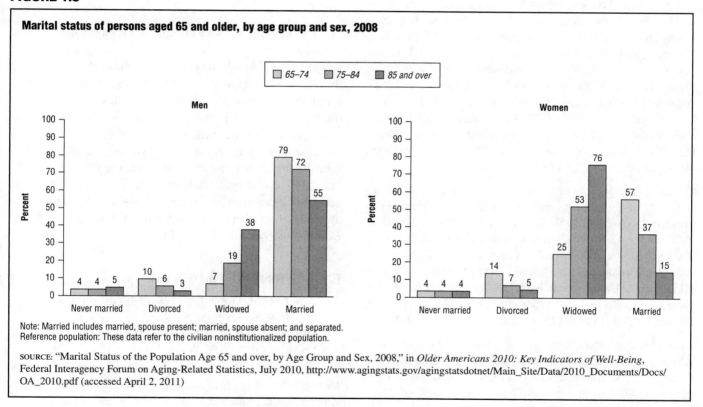

Marital status of persons aged 65 and older, by age group and sex, 2008

Note: Married includes married, spouse present; married, spouse absent; and separated.
Reference population: These data refer to the civilian noninstitutionalized population.

SOURCE: "Marital Status of the Population Age 65 and over, by Age Group and Sex, 2008," in *Older Americans 2010: Key Indicators of Well-Being*, Federal Interagency Forum on Aging-Related Statistics, July 2010, http://www.agingstats.gov/agingstatsdotnet/Main_Site/Data/2010_Documents/Docs/OA_2010.pdf (accessed April 2, 2011)

Marital Status

As in previous years, in 2008 older men were much more likely than older women to be married. Nearly eight out of 10 (79%) men aged 64 to 75 years were married, compared to 57% of women in the same age group. (See Figure 1.8.) The proportion married decreases with advancing age. In 2008, 37% of women aged 75 to 84 and 15% of women aged 85 years and older were married. Among men the proportion that were married decreased with advancing age but not as sharply. Even among the oldest-old, most men (55%) were married.

As older women outnumber older men in all age groups, it is not surprising that there are more widows than widowers. In 2008 more than three times as many women as men aged 65 to 74 years were widowed—25% of women, compared to 7% of men. (See Figure 1.8.) Even though the gap narrows in the older age groups, there were twice as many women as men aged 85 years and older who were widowed—76% of women as opposed to 38% of men. A fairly small proportion of older adults were divorced, whereas an even smaller proportion had never married.

Foreign-Born Older Adults

Elizabeth M. Grieco and Edward N. Trevelyan of the Census Bureau report in "Place of Birth of the Foreign-Born Population: 2009" (October 2010, http://www.census.gov/prod/2010pubs/acsbr09-15.pdf) that in 2009 the nation's foreign-born population numbered 38.5 million, accounting for an estimated 12.5% of the total U.S. population. Of this foreign-born population, 4.4 million were older adults: 1.6 million came from Latin America, 1.2 million from Europe, 1.3 million from Asia, and the balance from other areas. (See Table 1.7.)

WHERE OLDER AMERICANS LIVE

Greenberg reports that in 2009 adults aged 65 years and older accounted for 14% or more of the population in 13 states. The proportion of the population aged 65 years and older varied by state. In Florida the older adult population was 17.2%, followed by West Virginia with 15.8%; Maine with 15.6%; Pennsylvania with 15.4%; Iowa with 14.8%; North Dakota with 14.7%; Montana with 14.6%; Hawaii, Vermont, and South Dakota with 14.5% each; and Arkansas, Delaware, and Rhode Island with 14.3% each. (See Figure 1.9.) In 11 states—Alaska (52.1%), Nevada (47.9%), Arizona (37.9%), Utah (35.3%), Georgia (33.3%), Idaho (32%), South Carolina (31.7%), Colorado (30.9%), New Mexico (30.7%), Delaware (29.1%), and Texas (25.9%)—the 65 and older population grew by 25% or more between 1999 and 2009. (See Figure 1.10.)

In 2010, 17.8% of Florida's population was composed of older adults, and by 2030 that percentage is projected to rise to 27.1%. (See Table 1.8.) Five other states in which the older population is predicted to exceed 25% by 2030 are Maine and Wyoming (26.5% each), New Mexico (26.4%), Montana (25.8%), and North Dakota (25.1%). In 2030 the states in which older adults will constitute the lowest percentage of the population are Utah (13.2%), Alaska (14.7%), Texas (15.6%), and Georgia (15.9%).

Greenberg indicates that in 2009, 80.6% of older adults lived in metropolitan areas. Nearly three-quarters (72%) of these lived outside of cities and more than one-quarter (28%) were city dwellers. About 19% of older adults lived in nonmetropolitan areas. Greenberg also observes that older adults relocate less often than any other age group. Of the scant 3.4% of older adults who changed residence between 2008 and 2009, just 16.3% moved out of state; the vast majority (83.7%) remained in the same state and nearly two-thirds (62.7%) stayed in the same county.

Older Americans Are More Religious

In "The Social Connectedness of Older Adults: A National Profile" (*American Sociological Review*, vol. 73, no. 2, April 2008), Benjamin Cornwell, Edward O. Laumann, and L. Philip Schumm of the University of Chicago report the results of an analysis of data from the National Social Life, Health, and Aging Project, a population-based study of noninstitutionalized older Americans (people who are not in the U.S. military, school, jail, or mental health facilities) aged 57 to 85 years that was conducted between 2005 and 2006. One of their findings is that age was positively related to religious participation. About half of adults in their 70s and 80s attended religious services weekly, compared to 40% of people in their 50s and 60s. Older adults in their 70s were twice as likely to attend religious services weekly as people in their late 50s, and those in their 80s were nearly 50% more likely to attend religious services than middle-aged adults. The researchers observe that older adults were more frequently involved with religious activities than people of other ages, that increased religious participation may be one way older adults compensate for social losses, and that religious participation has been linked to improved health of older adults.

The Pew Forum on Religion and Public Life states in "Religion among the Millennials" (February 2010, http://pewforum.org/Age/Religion-Among-the-Millennials.aspx) that "it is well-known that older Americans are the most religious." Consistent with this observation is the fact that older adults are also more likely to say they believe in God. Survey data from the latter half of the first decade of the 21st century reveal that 71% of older adults (people born before 1928) and 68% of those born between 1928 and 1945 said they believe in God, compared to 65% of boomers (born between 1946 and 1964), 61% of Generation X (born between 1965 and 1980), and 53% of Millennials (born in 1981 or later).

ENJOYMENT OF OLDER AGE

Getting old isn't nearly as bad as people think it will be. Nor is it quite as good.

—Pew Research Center, "Growing Old in America: Expectations vs. Reality" (June 29, 2009)

In view of the myriad difficulties and challenges facing older adults, including ill health, inadequate financial resources, and the loss of friends and loved ones, it seems natural to assume that advancing age will be associated with less overall happiness and more worry. However, several studies refute this premise. Researchers find less worry among older adults than anticipated and a remarkable ability of older adults to adapt to their changing life conditions.

In "Growing Old in America: Expectations vs. Reality" (June 29, 2009, http://pewresearch.org/pubs/1269/aging-survey-expectations-versus-reality), the Pew Research Center reports the results of a survey of 2,969 young, middle-aged, and older adults about a range of experiences, positive and negative, that are associated with

TABLE 1.7

Foreign-born population by sex, age, and region of birth, 2009

							World region of birth							
	Total		Asia		Europe		Latin America						Other areas[b]	
							Total Latin America		Mexico		Other Latin America[a]			
Sex and age	Number	Percent	Number	Percent	Number	Percent	Number	Percent	Number	Percent	Number	Percent	Number	Percent
Both sexes	**36,750**	**100.0**	**9,925**	**100.0**	**4,572**	**100.0**	**19,882**	**100.0**	**11,615**	**100.0**	**8,267**	**100.0**	**2,371**	**100.0**
0 to 4 years	263	0.7	100	1.0	27	0.6	110	0.6	75	0.6	34	0.4	26	1.1
5 to 9 years	638	1.7	178	1.8	64	1.4	334	1.7	245	2.1	89	1.1	62	2.6
10 to 14 years	964	2.6	255	2.6	103	2.3	550	2.8	375	3.2	176	2.1	55	2.3
15 to 19 years	1,355	3.7	319	3.2	107	2.3	835	4.2	529	4.6	306	3.7	94	4.0
20 to 24 years	2,379	6.5	485	4.9	191	4.2	1,506	7.6	981	8.4	525	6.4	196	8.3
25 to 29 years	3,684	10.0	837	8.4	263	5.7	2,357	11.9	1,491	12.8	866	10.5	227	9.6
30 to 34 years	3,916	10.7	988	10.0	311	6.8	2,376	12.0	1,517	13.1	859	10.4	241	10.2
35 to 39 years	4,381	11.9	1,201	12.1	334	7.3	2,584	13.0	1,655	14.2	930	11.2	262	11.0
40 to 44 years	3,878	10.6	1,028	10.4	412	9.0	2,179	11.0	1,286	11.1	892	10.8	259	10.9
45 to 49 years	3,623	9.9	1,052	10.6	411	9.0	1,914	9.6	1,051	9.0	862	10.4	247	10.4
50 to 54 years	3,036	8.3	874	8.8	368	8.0	1,574	7.9	802	6.9	772	9.3	220	9.3
55 to 59 years	2,340	6.4	738	7.4	353	7.7	1,142	5.7	566	4.9	576	7.0	107	4.5
60 to 64 years	1,856	5.1	585	5.9	393	8.6	774	3.9	365	3.1	409	4.9	104	4.4
65 to 69 years	1,425	3.9	475	4.8	271	5.9	589	3.0	270	2.3	318	3.9	90	3.8
70 to 74 years	1,079	2.9	304	3.1	300	6.6	421	2.1	184	1.6	237	2.9	54	2.3
75 to 79 years	853	2.3	251	2.5	251	5.5	309	1.6	115	1.0	194	2.3	41	1.8
80 to 84 years	605	1.6	165	1.7	210	4.6	200	1.0	71	0.6	129	1.6	30	1.3
85 years and over	475	1.3	89	0.9	202	4.4	129	0.7	37	0.3	92	1.1	55	2.3
Under 15 years	1,865	5.1	533	5.4	195	4.3	994	5.0	695	6.0	299	3.6	143	6.0
15 years and over	34,885	94.9	9,392	94.6	4,377	95.7	18,888	95.0	10,920	94.0	7,968	96.4	2,228	94.0
Under 16 years	2,091	5.7	586	5.9	207	4.5	1,137	5.7	778	6.7	359	4.3	162	6.8
16 years and over	34,659	94.3	9,339	94.1	4,365	95.5	18,745	94.3	10,838	93.3	7,908	95.7	2,209	93.2
Under 18 years	2,638	7.2	723	7.3	251	5.5	1,467	7.4	979	8.4	488	5.9	197	8.3
18 years and over	34,111	92.8	9,201	92.7	4,321	94.5	18,415	92.6	10,636	91.6	7,779	94.1	2,174	91.7
Under 21 years	3,597	9.8	933	9.4	339	7.4	2,061	10.4	1,360	11.7	702	8.5	262	11.1
21 years and over	33,153	90.2	8,991	90.6	4,233	92.6	17,821	89.6	10,256	88.3	7,565	91.5	2,109	88.9
Under 55 years	28,116	76.5	7,318	73.7	2,590	56.7	16,319	82.1	10,007	86.2	6,312	76.4	1,889	79.7
55 years and over	8,634	23.5	2,607	26.3	1,982	43.3	3,563	17.9	1,608	13.8	1,955	23.6	482	20.3
Under 65 years	32,313	87.9	8,641	87.1	3,337	73.0	18,234	91.7	10,938	94.2	7,296	88.3	2,101	88.6
65 years and over	4,437	12.1	1,284	12.9	1,235	27.0	1,648	8.3	677	5.8	970	11.7	270	11.4
Median age (years)	41.00	(X)	42.90	(X)	50.90	(X)	38.60	(X)	36.80	(X)	42.00	(X)	40.40	(X)
Male	**18,285**	**100.0**	**4,681**	**100.0**	**2,058**	**100.0**	**10,342**	**100.0**	**6,393**	**100.0**	**3,949**	**100.0**	**1,204**	**100.0**
0 to 4 years	141	0.8	55	1.2	19	0.9	50	0.5	37	0.6	14	0.3	16	1.3
5 to 9 years	306	1.7	89	1.9	32	1.6	153	1.5	112	1.7	41	1.0	32	2.7
10 to 14 years	501	2.7	122	2.6	71	3.5	276	2.7	188	2.9	88	2.2	32	2.7
15 to 19 years	669	3.7	152	3.3	40	1.9	429	4.2	278	4.3	151	3.8	48	4.0
20 to 24 years	1,294	7.1	231	4.9	82	4.0	891	8.6	592	9.3	299	7.6	90	7.5
25 to 29 years	2,006	11.0	420	9.0	101	4.9	1,368	13.2	874	13.7	493	12.5	117	9.8
30 to 34 years	2,013	11.0	447	9.6	157	7.6	1,277	12.3	831	13.0	446	11.3	133	11.0
35 to 39 years	2,333	12.8	618	13.2	147	7.1	1,415	13.7	923	14.4	492	12.5	153	12.7
40 to 44 years	1,987	10.9	483	10.3	235	11.4	1,133	11.0	727	11.4	405	10.3	136	11.3
45 to 49 years	1,760	9.6	488	10.4	199	9.7	947	9.2	564	8.8	383	9.7	126	10.5

TABLE 1.7

Foreign-born population by sex, age, and region of birth, 2009 [CONTINUED]

					World region of birth								
							Latin America						
	Total		Asia		Europe		Total Latin America		Mexico		Other Latin America[a]		Other areas[b]	
Sex and age	Number	Percent	Number	Percent	Number	Percent	Number	Percent	Number	Percent	Number	Percent	Number	Percent
50 to 54 years	1,547	8.5	443	9.5	169	8.2	803	7.8	444	6.9	360	9.1	132	10.9
55 to 59 years	1,114	6.1	333	7.1	154	7.5	568	5.5	314	4.9	254	6.4	59	4.9
60 to 64 years	840	4.6	273	5.8	175	8.5	360	3.5	193	3.0	166	4.2	33	2.7
65 to 69 years	615	3.4	220	4.7	92	4.5	250	2.4	127	2.0	124	3.1	52	4.4
70 to 74 years	426	2.3	112	2.4	121	5.9	175	1.7	85	1.3	90	2.3	18	1.5
75 to 79 years	343	1.9	107	2.3	98	4.7	132	1.3	54	0.8	78	2.0	6	0.5
80 to 84 years	220	1.2	49	1.0	91	4.4	74	0.7	39	0.6	35	0.9	7	0.6
85 years and over	171	0.9	37	0.8	76	3.7	42	0.4	12	0.2	30	0.8	15	1.3
Under 15 years	948	5.2	266	5.7	123	6.0	479	4.6	337	5.3	143	3.6	80	6.6
15 years and over	17,337	94.8	4,415	94.3	1,935	94.0	9,863	95.4	6,056	94.7	3,807	96.4	1,124	93.4
Under 16 years	1,061	5.8	288	6.1	124	6.0	561	5.4	386	6.0	174	4.4	89	7.4
16 years and over	17,224	94.2	4,393	93.9	1,934	94.0	9,782	94.6	6,007	94.0	3,775	95.6	1,115	92.6
Under 18 years	1,329	7.3	347	7.4	143	7.0	727	7.0	493	7.7	235	5.9	112	9.3
18 years and over	16,955	92.7	4,333	92.6	1,915	93.0	9,615	93.0	5,900	92.3	3,715	94.1	1,092	90.7
Under 21 years	1,820	10.0	465	9.9	172	8.3	1,046	10.1	698	10.9	348	8.8	136	11.3
21 years and over	16,465	90.0	4,215	90.1	1,886	91.7	9,296	89.9	5,695	89.1	3,601	91.2	1,068	88.7
Under 55 years	14,557	79.6	3,549	75.8	1,252	60.8	8,741	84.5	5,569	87.1	3,172	80.3	1,014	84.2
55 years and over	3,728	20.4	1,131	24.2	806	39.2	1,601	15.5	824	12.9	777	19.7	190	15.8
Under 65 years	16,510	90.3	4,155	88.8	1,580	76.8	9,670	93.5	6,076	95.0	3,593	91.0	1,106	91.8
65 years and over	1,775	9.7	526	11.2	477	23.2	673	6.5	316	5.0	356	9.0	98	8.2
Median age (years)	39.70	(X)	42.10	(X)	48.70	(X)	37.60	(X)	36.50	(X)	39.50	(X)	39.40	(X)
Female	**18,465**	**100.0**	**5,244**	**100.0**	**2,514**	**100.0**	**9,540**	**100.0**	**5,222**	**100.0**	**4,317**	**100.0**	**1,167**	**100.0**
0 to 4 years	122	0.7	45	0.9	8	0.3	59	0.6	39	0.7	20	0.5	10	0.8
5 to 9 years	332	1.8	89	1.7	31	1.3	182	1.9	133	2.6	48	1.1	30	2.6
10 to 14 years	462	2.5	133	2.5	32	1.3	274	2.9	186	3.6	88	2.0	23	2.0
15 to 19 years	686	3.7	167	3.2	67	2.7	406	4.3	251	4.8	155	3.6	47	4.0
20 to 24 years	1,085	5.9	255	4.9	109	4.3	615	6.5	389	7.5	226	5.2	106	9.1
25 to 29 years	1,678	9.1	417	8.0	162	6.4	989	10.4	617	11.8	373	8.6	110	9.4
30 to 34 years	1,902	10.3	541	10.3	154	6.1	1,100	11.5	686	13.1	414	9.6	108	9.3
35 to 39 years	2,049	11.1	583	11.1	188	7.5	1,169	12.3	731	14.0	438	10.1	109	9.3
40 to 44 years	1,891	10.2	545	10.4	177	7.0	1,046	11.0	559	10.7	487	11.3	123	10.6
45 to 49 years	1,863	10.1	564	10.8	212	8.4	967	10.1	488	9.3	479	11.1	121	10.3
50 to 54 years	1,489	8.1	431	8.2	199	7.9	770	8.1	358	6.9	412	9.5	89	7.6
55 to 59 years	1,227	6.6	405	7.7	199	7.9	574	6.0	252	4.8	322	7.4	49	4.2
60 to 64 years	1,016	5.5	312	6.0	219	8.7	414	4.3	172	3.3	242	5.6	72	6.2
65 to 69 years	810	4.4	255	4.9	179	7.1	339	3.5	144	2.8	195	4.5	38	3.2
70 to 74 years	653	3.5	192	3.7	179	7.1	246	2.6	99	1.9	147	3.4	36	3.1
75 to 79 years	510	2.8	144	2.7	154	6.1	177	1.9	61	1.2	116	2.7	35	3.0
80 to 84 years	385	2.1	116	2.2	120	4.8	126	1.3	32	0.6	94	2.2	23	2.0
85 years and over	305	1.6	52	1.0	126	5.0	87	0.9	25	0.5	62	1.4	39	3.4

TABLE 1.7

Foreign-born population by sex, age, and region of birth, 2009 [CONTINUED]

| | Total | | World region of birth | | | | Latin America | | | | | | Other areas[b] | |
| | | | Asia | | Europe | | Total Latin America | | Mexico | | Other Latin America[a] | | | |
Sex and age	Number	Percent	Number	Percent	Number	Percent	Number	Percent	Number	Percent	Number	Percent	Number	Percent
Under 15 years	917	5.0	267	5.1	72	2.9	515	5.4	359	6.9	156	3.6	63	5.4
15 years and over	17,548	95.0	4,977	94.9	2,442	97.1	9,025	94.6	4,864	93.1	4,161	96.4	1,104	94.6
Under 16 years	1,030	5.6	299	5.7	83	3.3	576	6.0	392	7.5	185	4.3	73	6.2
16 years and over	17,435	94.4	4,946	94.3	2,432	96.7	8,964	94.0	4,831	92.5	4,133	95.7	1,094	93.8
Under 18 years	1,309	7.1	376	7.2	108	4.3	740	7.8	487	9.3	253	5.9	85	7.3
18 years and over	17,156	92.9	4,868	92.8	2,407	95.7	8,800	92.2	4,736	90.7	4,064	94.1	1,082	92.7
Under 21 years	1,777	9.6	468	8.9	168	6.7	1,015	10.6	662	12.7	353	8.2	126	10.8
21 years and over	16,688	90.4	4,776	91.1	2,347	93.3	8,525	89.4	4,561	87.3	3,964	91.8	1,040	89.2
Under 55 years	13,559	73.4	3,769	71.9	1,339	53.2	7,577	79.4	4,438	85.0	3,139	72.7	875	75.0
55 years and over	4,905	26.6	1,475	28.1	1,176	46.8	1,963	20.6	785	15.0	1,178	27.3	292	25.0
Under 65 years	15,802	85.6	4,486	85.5	1,756	69.9	8,565	89.8	4,861	93.1	3,703	85.8	995	85.3
65 years and over	2,662	14.4	758	14.5	758	30.1	975	10.2	361	6.9	614	14.2	171	14.7
Median age (years)	42.40	(X)	43.60	(X)	52.90	(X)	39.90	(X)	37.10	(X)	44.10	(X)	41.70	(X)

(X) Not applicable.

[a]Those born in 'Other Latin America' are from all sub-regions of Latin America (Central America, South America, and the Caribbean), excluding Mexico.

[b]Those born in 'Other areas' are from Africa, Oceania, Northern America,or were born at sea.

Notes: Numbers in thousands. Universe is the civilian noninstitutionalized population of the United States, plus armed forces living off post or with their families on post.

SOURCE: "Table 3.1. Foreign-Born Population by Sex, Age, and World Region of Birth: 2009," in *Foreign-Born Population of the United States Current Population Survey–March 2009 Detailed Tables*, U.S. Census Bureau, Population Division, October 2010, http://www.census.gov/population/www/socdemo/foreign/cps2009.html (accessed April 4, 2011)

FIGURE 1.9

Persons aged 65 and older as a percentage of total population, 2009

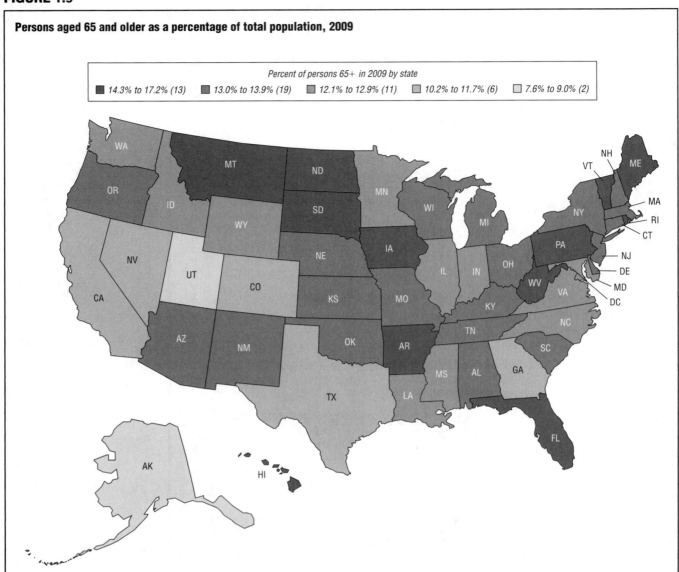

Percent of persons 65+ in 2009 by state

■ 14.3% to 17.2% (13)   ▨ 13.0% to 13.9% (19)   ▨ 12.1% to 12.9% (11)   ▨ 10.2% to 11.7% (6)   □ 7.6% to 9.0% (2)

SOURCE: Saadia Greenberg, "Figure 4. Persons 65+ As a Percentage of Total Population, 2009," in *A Profile of Older Americans: 2010*, U.S. Department of Health and Human Services, Administration on Aging, 2011, http://www.aoa.gov/aoaroot/aging_statistics/Profile/2010/docs/2010profile.pdf (accessed April 2, 2011)

aging. Pew finds that younger adults associated aging with health and financial problems, memory loss, loneliness, and depression far more than older adults. By contrast, older adults reported fewer of the benefits that are associated with aging, such as more time to spend with family, traveling, and on hobbies than the younger adults anticipated. Furthermore, older adults said they have greater financial security than they did when they were younger.

Even though reports of happiness decline with advancing age, the Pew Research Center notes that older adults still report considerable happiness. Among survey respondents aged 65 to 74 years, 32% described themselves as "very happy" and an additional 44% said they

are "pretty happy." The percentages decline slightly among respondents aged 75 years and older—28% said they are "very happy" and 43% are "pretty happy." Six out of 10 said they feel younger than their age and feel less stress than they felt earlier in their life. The youngest survey respondents, aged 18 to 29 years, report the highest levels of happiness—37% said they are "very happy" and 53% are "pretty happy," but said they feel about their chronological age. In contrast, about half of the respondents aged 50 years and older report feeling at least 10 years younger than their age. Of the older adult respondents, those aged 65 to 74 years, one-third said they feel 10 to 19 years younger than their age, and one out of six feels at least 20 years younger than their chronological age.

FIGURE 1.10

Percentage increase in population aged 65 and older, 1999–2009

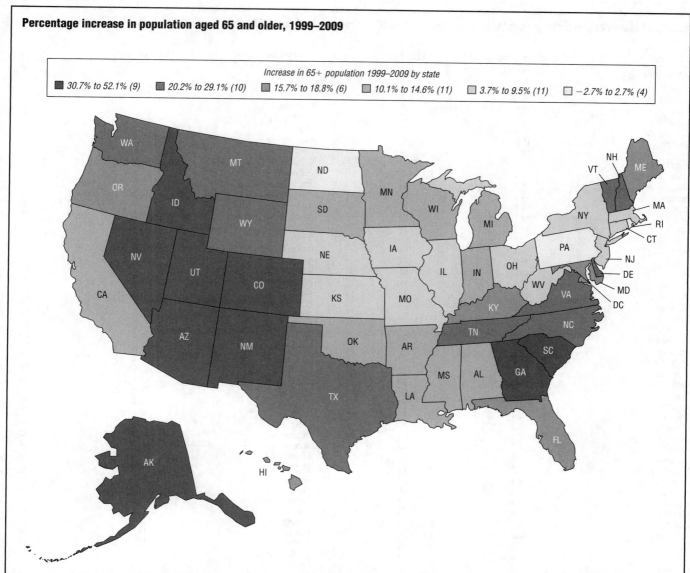

Increase in 65+ population 1999–2009 by state

■ 30.7% to 52.1% (9) ■ 20.2% to 29.1% (10) ■ 15.7% to 18.8% (6) ■ 10.1% to 14.6% (11) ■ 3.7% to 9.5% (11) □ −2.7% to 2.7% (4)

SOURCE: Saadia Greenberg, "Figure 5. Percent Increase in Population Age 65+, 1999 to 2009," in *A Profile of Older Americans: 2008*, U.S. Department of Health and Human Services, Administration on Aging, 2011, http://www.aoa.gov/aoaroot/aging_statistics/Profile/2010/docs/2010profile.pdf (accessed April 2, 2011)

David G. Blanchflower and Andrew J. Oswald assert in "Is Well-Being U-shaped over the Life Cycle?" (*Social Science and Medicine*, vol. 66, no. 8, April 2008) that psychological well-being is U-shaped through life. After analyzing several data sets including data from 500,000 Americans and Europeans, the researchers conclude that happiness typically declines as people age, reaching its lowest point during middle age but then rising again throughout later life. Their finding supports other studies that have found higher levels of happiness and life satisfaction among older adults than middle-aged people.

Lewis Wolpert of the University College London reviews in *You're Looking Very Well: The Surprising Nature of Getting Old* (2011) several studies conducted during the first decade of the 21st century that focused on happiness throughout life and confirms the observation that for most people it declines at midlife but then resurges. In "Happiness Peaks in Our Eighties" (*Telegraph* [London], March 28, 2011), Nick Collins quotes Wolpert as explaining that "from the mid-forties, people tend to become ever more cheerful and optimistic, perhaps reaching a maximum in their late seventies or eighties."

Positive Perceptions of Aging Influence Longevity and Happiness

Becca R. Levy et al. report in the landmark study "Longevity Increased by Positive Self-Perceptions of Aging" (*Journal of Personality and Social Psychology*, vol. 83, no. 2, August 2002) that older people with more

TABLE 1.8

Ranking of states by projected percentage of population aged 65 and older, 2010 and 2030

2010 state	2010 percent	2010 rank	2030 state	2030 percent	2030 rank
United States	13.0	(x)	**United States**	19.7	(x)
Florida	17.8	1	Florida	27.1	1
West Virginia	16.0	2	Maine	26.5	2
Maine	15.6	3	Wyoming	26.5	3
Pennsylvania	15.5	4	New Mexico	26.4	4
North Dakota	15.3	5	Montana	25.8	5
Montana	15.0	6	North Dakota	25.1	6
Iowa	14.9	7	West Virginia	24.8	7
South Dakota	14.6	8	Vermont	24.4	8
Connecticut	14.4	9	Delaware	23.5	9
Arkansas	14.3	10	South Dakota	23.1	10
Vermont	14.3	11	Pennsylvania	22.6	11
Hawaii	14.3	12	Iowa	22.4	12
Delaware	14.1	13	Hawaii	22.3	13
Alabama	14.1	14	Arizona	22.1	14
Rhode Island	14.1	15	South Carolina	22.0	15
New Mexico	14.1	16	Connecticut	21.5	16
Wyoming	14.0	17	New Hampshire	21.4	17
Arizona	13.9	18	Rhode Island	21.4	18
Missouri	13.9	19	Wisconsin	21.3	19
Oklahoma	13.8	20	Alabama	21.3	20
Nebraska	13.8	21	Massachusetts	20.9	21
Ohio	13.7	22	Nebraska	20.6	22
Massachusetts	13.7	23	Mississippi	20.5	23
New Jersey	13.7	24	Ohio	20.4	24
New York	13.6	25	Arkansas	20.3	25
South Carolina	13.6	26	Missouri	20.2	26
Wisconsin	13.5	27	Kansas	20.2	27
Kansas	13.4	28	New York	20.1	28
Tennessee	13.3	29	New Jersey	20.0	29
Kentucky	13.1	30	Kentucky	19.8	30
Oregon	13.0	31	Louisiana	19.7	31
Michigan	12.8	32	Michigan	19.5	32
Mississippi	12.8	33	Oklahoma	19.4	33
Indiana	12.7	34	Tennessee	19.2	34
Louisiana	12.6	35	Minnesota	18.9	35
New Hampshire	12.6	36	Virginia	18.8	36
North Carolina	12.4	37	Nevada	18.6	37
Virginia	12.4	38	Idaho	18.3	38
Illinois	12.4	39	Oregon	18.2	39
Minnesota	12.4	40	Washington	18.1	40
Nevada	12.3	41	Indiana	18.1	41
Washington	12.2	42	Illinois	18.0	42
Maryland	12.2	43	California	17.8	43
Idaho	12.0	44	North Carolina	17.8	44
California	11.5	45	Maryland	17.6	45
District of Columbia	11.5	46	Colorado	16.5	46
Colorado	10.7	47	Georgia	15.9	47
Texas	10.5	48	Texas	15.6	48
Georgia	10.2	49	Alaska	14.7	49
Utah	9.0	50	District of Columbia	13.4	50
Alaska	8.1	51	Utah	13.2	51

SOURCE: Adapted from "Table 3. Interim Projections: Ranking of States by Projected Percent of Population Age 65 and Older: 2000, 2010, and 2030," in *State Interim Population Projections by Age and Sex: 2004–2030*, U.S. Census Bureau, Population Division, April 21, 2005, http://www.census.gov/population/www/projections/projectionsagesex.html (accessed April 2, 2011)

positive self-perceptions of aging lived 7.5 years longer than those with less positive self-perceptions of aging, even after taking into account other factors, including age, gender, socioeconomic status, loneliness, and overall health. Analyzing data from the 660 participants aged 50 years and older in the Ohio Longitudinal Study of Aging and Retirement, Levy et al. compared mortality rates with responses made 23 years earlier by the participants (338 men and 322 women). The responses included agreeing or disagreeing with statements such as "As you get older, you are less useful."

Levy et al. assert that "the effect of more positive self-perceptions of aging on survival is greater than the physiological measures of low systolic blood pressure and cholesterol, each of which is associated with a longer life span of 4 years or less.... [It] is also greater than the independent contribution of lower body mass index, no history of smoking, and a tendency to exercise; each of these factors has been found to contribute between 1 and 3 years of added life." They conclude that negative self-perceptions can diminish life expectancy, whereas positive self-perceptions can prolong it.

According to Jennifer Reichstadt et al., in "Building Blocks of Successful Aging: A Focus Group Study of Older Adults' Perceived Contributors to Successful Aging" (*American Journal of Geriatric Psychiatry*, vol. 15, no. 3, March 2007), older adults themselves believe that a positive attitude about life and aging and having the ability to adapt to change are associated with successful aging and a long, happy life. The researchers interviewed 72 older adults living in the community (as opposed to people living in institutions) and identified the factors that older adults feel contribute to successful aging. The interviewees named psychosocial factors such as a sense of engagement, pursuit of continued stimulation, learning, feeling a sense of purpose in life, and being useful to others and to society as more important for successful aging than factors such as freedom from illness and disability.

In "The Power of Positive Emotions: It's a Matter of Life or Death—Subjective Well-Being and Longevity over 28 Years in a General Population" (*Health Psychology*, vol. 29, no. 1, January 2010), Jingping Xu and Robert E. Roberts analyze 28 years of data from 6,856 subjects to determine whether happiness and life satisfaction are related to longevity. The researchers find that the subjective assessment of well-being, which includes positive feelings and life satisfaction, predicted a lower risk of mortality in the population. Xu and Roberts explain that "positive emotions broaden our attention and action span, down-regulate ('undo') what negative feelings do to us, and build enduring psychological, physical, and social resources that we can draw upon when needed, thus promote health and longevity."

ATTITUDES ABOUT AGING

People of all ages hold beliefs and attitudes about aging and older adults. Even young children can distinguish age differences, and they display attitudes that appear to be characteristic of their generation. Because attitudes strongly influence behavior and because more Americans reach older ages than ever before, interaction with older people and deeply held beliefs about growing old are likely influenced by cultural and societal attitudes about aging and older adults. The availability, accessibility, adequacy, and acceptability of health care and other services intended to meet the needs of older people are similarly influenced by the attitudes of younger people. The prevailing attitudes and opinions of political leaders, decision makers, health and human services personnel, and taxpayers are particularly important in shaping policies, programs, services, and public sentiment.

In nonindustrialized countries older people are often held in high esteem. Older adults are respected because they often have endured and persevered in harsh living conditions and because they have accumulated wisdom

and knowledge that younger generations need to survive and carry on the traditions of their culture. In many industrialized societies, including the United States, a person's worth may be measured in terms of income (the flow of money earned through employment, interest on investments, and other sources) and the amount of accumulated wealth. When older adults retire from full-time employment, they may lose status because they are no longer working, earning money, and "contributing" to society. When an individual's sense of self-worth and identity is closely bound to employment or occupation, retirement from the workforce can make him or her feel worthless.

Stereotypes Fuel Worries of Older Adults

Even though people of all ages worry about the future, for older adults aging may signify a future threat to their health and well-being, diminished social status, a loss of power, and the possibility of a loss of control over their life. Researchers posit that social stereotypes, such as media portrayals of older adults as weak and helpless and of old age as a time of hardship, loss, and pain, have a powerful influence on attitudes and may be another source of worry for older adults. They contend that the image of a tragic old age can create worries about having a tragic old age. Worse still, the negative image of old age can become a self-fulfilling prophecy, thereby confirming negative stereotypes and promoting ageism (discrimination or unfair treatment based on age).

For example, in "Expectations about Memory Change across the Life Span Are Impacted by Aging Stereotypes" (*Psychology and Aging*, vol. 24, no. 1, March 2009), Tara T. Lineweaver, Andrea K. Berger, and Christopher Hertzog interviewed 373 people, in three different age groups, to find out what they thought about memory throughout the adult lifespan. They were asked to rate the memory of different older adults, who were described as having positive or negative personality traits. Consistent with previous research, the study subjects believed that memory declines with advancing age. Furthermore, they rated adults described as having positive personality traits with having better memory ability and less age-related memory loss than those described as having negative personality traits. Another important finding was that the older subjects were more strongly influenced by the personality descriptions than the younger subjects.

Gabriel A. Radvansky, Nicholas A. Lynchard, and William von Hippel confirm in "Aging and Stereotype Suppression" (*Aging, Neuropsychology, and Cognition*, vol. 16, no. 1, January 2009) that older adults are more likely than younger adults to believe and use stereotypic information, even when they do not intend to judge people based on stereotypes. Furthermore, older adults have trouble changing or modifying their interpretation of a situation, even when it becomes apparent that their initial interpretation was incorrect. The researchers aver that even though older adults may be more susceptible to the influence of stereotypes, this effect can be prevented, or minimized, by providing them with clear information that contradicts stereotypical information.

Baby Boomers and Centenarians Challenge Stereotypes

Since their inception, baby boomers have left their mark on every U.S. institution. As teenagers and young adults, they created and championed a unique blend of music, pop culture, and political activism. They have witnessed remarkable technological and medical advancements during their lifetime and have come to expect, and even loudly demand, solutions to health and social problems.

As the baby boomers begin to join the ranks of older Americans, they are fomenting a cultural revolution. The almost 80 million boomers approaching age 65 are not content to be regarded as "old." Accustomed to freedom and independence, they want to be recognized and treated as individuals rather than as stereotypes. The aging boomers are healthier, better educated, and wealthier than any other older adult cohort in history. They are redefining old age by reinventing retirement, continuing to pursue health, and challenging the public's perception of what it is to be old.

In "Aging America and the Boomer Wars" (*Gerontologist*, vol. 48, no. 6, December 2008), Harry R. Moody, the director of the Office of Academic Affairs for the AARP, describes the polarizing stereotypes of the baby boomers. On one side are people who characterize boomers as selfish, materialistic, whining, and greedy—people who will consume all available resources with no thought to future generations. On the other side are those who view boomers as idealistic advocates of social activism and community service. Moody cautions that these opposing stereotypes should be avoided to prevent "over-simplified polarities and to appreciate the power that public discourse and media images can have in shaping our thinking about generational change in an aging society."

Edward S. Potkanowicz, Paula Hartman-Stein, and Jeanette S. Biermann suggest in "Behavioral Determinants of Health Aging Revisited: An Update on the Good News for the Baby Boomer Generation" (*Online Journal of Issues in Nursing*, vol. 14, no 3, September 2009) that the key to healthy aging for baby boomers will be to remain physically and mentally active. The researchers assert that boomers "will want more out of life in their later years compared to their predecessors" and that new understanding of ways to slow physical and mental decline "make it an exciting time to contemplate the future of aging, a time when older adults can be fully functioning without the prevalence of some of the declines and deficits that we have here-to-fore accepted as an unavoidable side effect of getting older."

CHAPTER 2
THE ECONOMICS OF GROWING OLD
IN THE UNITED STATES

Security was attained in the earlier days through the interdependence of members of families upon each other and of the families within a small community upon each other. The complexities of great communities and of organized industry make less real these simple means of security. Therefore, we are compelled to employ the active interest of the Nation as a whole through government in order to encourage a greater security for each individual who composes it.... This seeking for a greater measure of welfare and happiness does not indicate a change in values. It is rather a return to values lost in the course of our economic development and expansion.

—Franklin D. Roosevelt, Message of the President to Congress, June 8, 1934

The economic status of older Americans is more varied than that of any other age group. Even though a few older adults are well off, most have limited resources. As a whole, historically the older U.S. population has a lower economic status than the overall adult population. During retirement most people rely on Social Security and are supplemented by pensions and assets. Some must also depend on Supplemental Security Income (SSI), a federal assistance program administered by the U.S. Social Security Administration (SSA) that guarantees a minimum level of income for needy older adults, blind, or disabled individuals. It acts as a safety net for individuals who have little or no Social Security or other income and limited resources.

With fixed incomes and sharply limited potential to improve their incomes through employment, many older people become vulnerable to circumstances such as the loss of a spouse, prolonged illness, or even economic variations such as inflation or recession that further compromise their financial well-being, sometimes plunging them into poverty. One common scenario is a couple that has planned well for retirement but then runs through all their assets to pay the health care costs of a long-term illness. When the ill partner dies, the surviving spouse is

left impoverished. Another example is retirees who discover, as many people did during the latter half of the first decade of the 21st century, that their retirement accounts have lost more than half of their value.

The economic recession that lasted from late 2007 to mid-2009 had far-reaching effects for older adults. In "The Magic Numbers of Retirement Planning?" (*U.S. News & World Report*, March 28, 2011), Emily Brandon reports that after dramatic declines, it took an average of three years for most retirement accounts to return to their 2007 amounts. For example, an account with $69,200 in 2007 that fell to $50,200 in 2008 eventually rebounded to $71,500 by the close of 2010. Brandon observes that retirees and those nearing retirement were harder hit than workers with many years until retirement, who presumably have time to recover. Older adults have little time to recover the value of their homes, 401(k) plans, and individual retirement accounts—the key elements of financially secure retirement. Brandon asserts that to counteract the effects of the recession early baby boomers (people born between 1946 and 1954) need to save at least 4.3% of their annual salary to recoup their losses; later boomers have a little more time so they only need to save an additional 1.2% to restore their retirement nest eggs.

Even though some older adults may want to return to work, their prospects may be bleak. Widespread layoffs and economic uncertainty have produced increasing rates of unemployment across all age groups. The U.S. Bureau of Labor Statistics (June 3, 2011, http://www.bls.gov/news .release/empsit.t06.htm) reports that the unemployment rate for older workers aged 65 years and older was 5.8% in May 2011 (this is out of the approximately 20 percent of those over 65 who are still in the workforce). Sara E. Rix of the AARP observes in "The Employment Situation, April 2011: Average Duration of Unemployment for Older Job-seekers Exceeds One Year" (May 2011, http://assets.aarp .org/rgcenter/ppi/econ-sec/fs225-employment.pdf) that in

TABLE 2.1

Duration of unemployment as of October 2010

	Percent distribution of duration						
	Fewer than 5 weeks	5 to 14 weeks	15 to 26 weeks	27 to 51 weeks	52+ weeks	Average in weeks	Median in weeks
All unemployed							
Age 25 to 54	17%	20%	16%	14%	34%	37	25
Age 55 and older	12%	16%	16%	15%	41%	44	35
Men							
Age 25 to 54	17%	19%	15%	14%	36%	39	28
Age 55 and older	13%	15%	16%	14%	42%	45	37
Women							
Age 25 to 54	16%	21%	17%	13%	32%	36	23
Age 55 and older	11%	17%	17%	16%	40%	44	33

SOURCE: Janemarie Mulvey, "Table 2. Duration of Unemployment," in *Older Unemployed Workers Following the Recent Economic Recession*, Congressional Research Service, January 5, 2011, http://aging.senate.gov/crs/pension42.pdf (accessed April 4, 2011)

April 2011 unemployment among adults aged 55 years and older was 6.5%, compared to 9% in the overall population. Among older men, the unemployment rate was nearly 7% during April 2011, comparable to the rate at the end of the recession in June 2009. In "Older Unemployed Workers Following the Recent Economic Recession" (January 5, 2011, http://aging.senate.gov/crs/pension42.pdf), Janemarie Mulvey of the Congressional Research Service observes that unemployed older workers suffer longer periods of unemployment than younger job seekers; on average they are unemployed five weeks longer than younger workers. Older workers are also more likely to be unemployed for more than one year—41% are unemployed for longer durations, compared to 34% of younger workers. (See Table 2.1.)

THE ECONOMIC WELL-BEING OF OLDER ADULTS

There are two important measures of an individual's or household's economic well-being. One is income (the flow of money earned through employment, interest on investments, and other sources) and the other is asset accumulation or wealth (the economic resources—property or other material possessions—owned by an individual or household).

Income Distribution

According to the Federal Interagency Forum on Aging-Related Statistics, in *Older Americans 2010: Key Indicators of Well-Being* (July 2011, http://www.agingstats.gov/agingstatsdotnet/Main_Site/Data/2010_Documents/Docs/OA_2010.pdf), the trend in median (the middle value—half are higher and half are lower) household income of the older population has been positive, and fewer older adults are living in poverty. Between 1974 and 2007 the proportion of older adults living in poverty declined. Figure 2.1 shows that since the late 1970s poverty rates have been comparable among people aged 18 to 64 years and 65 years and older.

In 2007 about 11% of the older population lived below the poverty threshold, compared to about 14% in 1974. (See Figure 2.1.) The proportion of the older population in the low-income bracket also fell, from 50% in 1974 to 36% in 2007. (See Figure 2.2.)

According to Saadia Greenberg of the Administration on Aging, in *A Profile of Older Americans: 2010* (2011, http://www.aoa.gov/aoaroot/aging_statistics/Profile/2010/docs/2010profile.pdf), the median reported income for all older adults in 2009 was $25,877 for males and $15,282 for females. Figure 2.3 shows the distribution of income among older adults. Households headed by people aged 65 years and older had a median income of $43,702 in 2009, whereas the individual median income for older adults that year was $19,167. Nearly two-thirds (62.6%) of households headed by an older adult had incomes of $35,000 or more, and 6.3% had incomes less than $15,000. Greenberg indicates that the median household income for older adults was highest for Asian-Americans ($47,319), followed by non-Hispanic whites ($45,400), African-Americans ($35,049), and Hispanics ($32,820).

Sources of Income

Unlike younger adults, who derive most of their income from employment, older adults rely on a variety of sources of income to meet their expenses. Since the 1960s Social Security has provided the largest share of income for older Americans. In 2008 Social Security benefits were a major source of income—providing at least 50% of total income—reported for 52% of older couples and 73% of unmarried older adult beneficiaries. (See Figure 2.4.) For 43% of unmarried Americans and 21% of couples over the age of 65 years in 2008, Social Security accounted for 90% of total income.

FIGURE 2.1

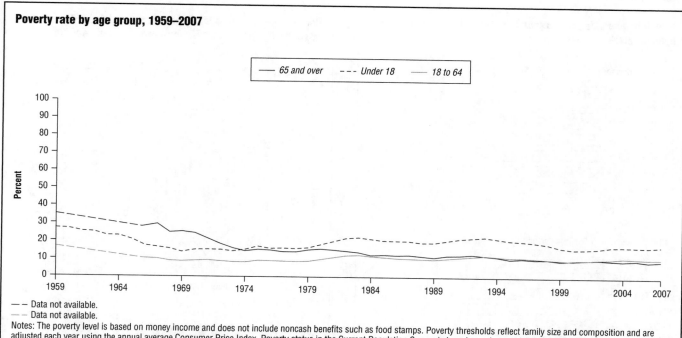

Poverty rate by age group, 1959–2007

— 65 and over   - - - Under 18   ⋯⋯ 18 to 64

— — Data not available.
— — Data not available.

Notes: The poverty level is based on money income and does not include noncash benefits such as food stamps. Poverty thresholds reflect family size and composition and are adjusted each year using the annual average Consumer Price Index. Poverty status in the Current Population Survey is based on prior year income.
Reference population: These data refer to the civilian noninstitutionalized population.

SOURCE: "Poverty Rate of the Population, by Age Group, 1959–2007," in *Older Americans 2010: Key Indicators of Well-Being*, Federal Interagency Forum on Aging-Related Statistics, July 2010, http://www.agingstats.gov/agingstatsdotnet/Main_Site/Data/2010_Documents/Docs/OA_2010.pdf (accessed April 2, 2011)

FIGURE 2.2

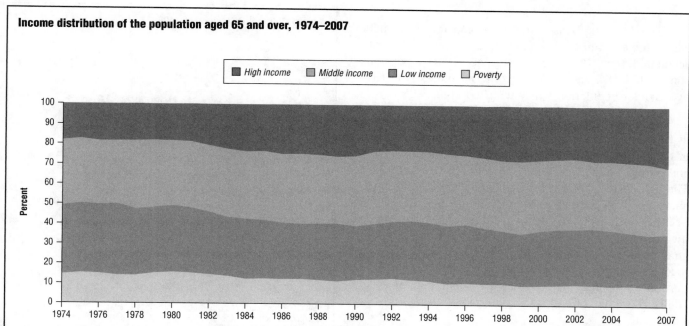

Income distribution of the population aged 65 and over, 1974–2007

■ High income   ■ Middle income   ■ Low income   □ Poverty

Notes: The income categories are derived from the ratio of the family's income (or an unrelated individual's income) to the corresponding poverty threshold. Being in poverty is measured as income less than 100 percent of the poverty threshold. Low income is between 100 percent and 199 percent of the poverty threshold. Middle income is between 200 percent and 399 percent of the poverty threshold. High income is 400 percent or more of the poverty threshold.
Reference population: These data refer to the civilian noninstitutionalized population.

SOURCE: "Income Distribution of the Population Age 65 and over, 1974–2007," in *Older Americans 2010: Key Indicators of Well-Being*, Federal Interagency Forum on Aging-Related Statistics, July 2010, http://www.agingstats.gov/agingstatsdotnet/Main_Site/Data/2010_Documents/Docs/OA_2010.pdf (accessed April 2, 2011)

FIGURE 2.3

FIGURE 2.4

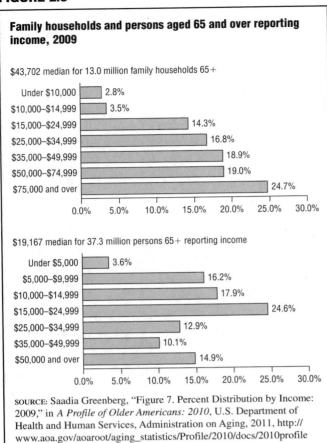

Family households and persons aged 65 and over reporting income, 2009

$43,702 median for 13.0 million family households 65+

Income	Percent
Under $10,000	2.8%
$10,000–$14,999	3.5%
$15,000–$24,999	14.3%
$25,000–$34,999	16.8%
$35,000–$49,999	18.9%
$50,000–$74,999	19.0%
$75,000 and over	24.7%

$19,167 median for 37.3 million persons 65+ reporting income

Income	Percent
Under $5,000	3.6%
$5,000–$9,999	16.2%
$10,000–$14,999	17.9%
$15,000–$24,999	24.6%
$25,000–$34,999	12.9%
$35,000–$49,999	10.1%
$50,000 and over	14.9%

SOURCE: Saadia Greenberg, "Figure 7. Percent Distribution by Income: 2009," in *A Profile of Older Americans: 2010*, U.S. Department of Health and Human Services, Administration on Aging, 2011, http://www.aoa.gov/aoaroot/aging_statistics/Profile/2010/docs/2010profile.pdf (accessed April 2, 2011).

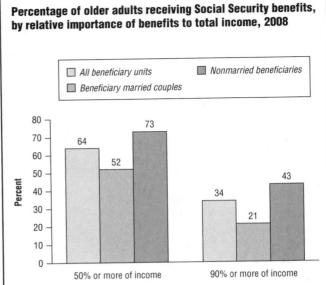

Percentage of older adults receiving Social Security benefits, by relative importance of benefits to total income, 2008

- All beneficiary units
- Beneficiary married couples
- Nonmarried beneficiaries

50% or more of income: 64, 52, 73
90% or more of income: 34, 21, 43

Note: An aged unit is a married couple living together or a nonmarried person, which also includes persons who are separated or married but not living together.

SOURCE: "Percentage of Aged Units Receiving Social Security Benefits, by Relative Importance of Benefits to Total Income," in *Fast Facts and Figures about Social Security, 2010*, U.S. Social Security Administration, Office of Retirement and Disability Policy, August 2010, http://www.ssa.gov/policy/docs/chartbooks/fast_facts/2010/fast_facts10.pdf (accessed April 4, 2011)

Greenberg explains that the income for most older adults comes from four sources. In 2008 Social Security accounted for 37%, earnings provided 30%, pensions contributed 18%, and asset income accounted for 13% of the older population's income. (See Figure 2.5.)

For older Americans in the lowest fifth of the income distribution in 2008, Social Security accounted for 83% of their aggregate income (total income from all sources) and public assistance for another 9%. (See Figure 2.6.) The aggregate income for high-income older adults was about one-fifth each of pension, asset income, and Social Security, and about two-fifths were derived from earned income. Among people aged 80 years and older, aggregate income largely consisted of Social Security and asset income, with earnings contributing a much smaller proportion, compared to the youngest population of older adults, those aged 65 to 69 years. (See Table 2.2.)

Pension Funds

Many large employers, along with most local and state governments and the federal government, offer pension plans for retirement. In the United States American Express established the first private pension plan (an employer-run retirement program) in 1875. General

FIGURE 2.5

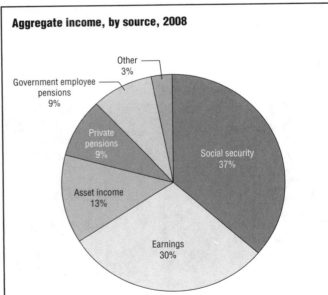

Aggregate income, by source, 2008

- Other 3%
- Government employee pensions 9%
- Private pensions 9%
- Asset income 13%
- Earnings 30%
- Social security 37%

Notes: The unit of analysis is the aged unit, defined as a married couple living together or a nonmarried person, which also includes persons who are separated or married but not living together.
Totals do not necessarily equal the sum of rounded components.

SOURCE: "Aggregate Income, by Source," in *Fast Facts and Figures about Social Security, 2010*, U.S. Social Security Administration, Office of Retirement and Disability Policy, August 2010, http://www.ssa.gov/policy/docs/chartbooks/fast_facts/2010/fast_facts10.pdf (accessed April 4, 2011)

FIGURE 2.6

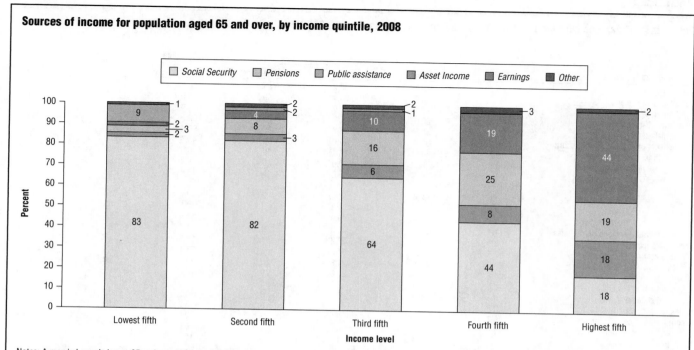

Sources of income for population aged 65 and over, by income quintile, 2008

Notes: A married couple is age 65 and over if the husband is age 65 and over or the husband is younger than age 55 and the wife is age 65 and over. The definition of "other" includes, but is not limited to, public assistance, unemployment compensation, worker's compensation, alimony, child support, and personal contributions. Quintile limits are $12,082, $19,877, $31,303, and $55,889 for all units; $23,637, $35,794, $53,180, and $86,988 for married couples; and $9,929, $14,265, $20,187, and $32,937 for nonmarried persons.
Reference population: These data refer to the civilian noninstitutionalized population.

SOURCE: "Sources of Income for Married Couples and Nonmarried People Who Are Age 65 and over, by Income Quintile, 2008," in *Older Americans 2010: Key Indicators of Well-Being*, Federal Interagency Forum on Aging-Related Statistics, July 2010, http://www.agingstats.gov/agingstatsdotnet/Main_Site/Data/2010_Documents/Docs/OA_2010.pdf (accessed April 2, 2011).

Motors Corporation provided the first modern plan during the 1940s.

Employers are not required to provide pensions, and pension plans do not have to include all workers; they may exclude certain jobs and/or individuals. Before 1976 pension plans could require an employee to work a lifetime for one company before becoming eligible for pension benefits. As required by the Employee Retirement Income Security Act (ERISA) of 1974, starting in 1976 an employee became eligible after 10 years of service. By 2000 most plans required five years of work before an employee became vested (eligible for benefits). In companies that offer pension plans, employees are eligible to begin receiving benefits when they retire or leave the company if they have worked for the requisite number of years and/or have reached the specified eligibility age.

DEFINED BENEFIT PLANS AND DEFINED CONTRIBUTION PLANS. There are two principal types of pension plans: defined benefit plans and defined contribution plans. Traditionally, employers offered defined benefit plans that promised employees a specified monthly benefit at retirement. A defined benefit plan may stipulate the promised benefit as an exact dollar amount, such as $100 per month at retirement. More often, however, benefits are calculated using a plan formula that considers both salary and service—for example, 1% of the average salary for the last five years of employment multiplied by every year of service with the employer.

A defined contribution plan does not promise employees a specific amount of benefits at retirement. Instead, the employee and/or employer contribute to a plan account, sometimes at a set rate, such as 5% of earnings annually. Generally, these contributions are invested on the employee's behalf, and the amount of future benefits varies depending on investment earnings.

An example of a defined contribution plan is the 401(k) plan. This plan allows employees to defer receiving a portion of their salary, which is contributed on their behalf to the plan. Income taxes are deferred until the money is withdrawn at retirement. In some instances employers match employee contributions. Created in 1978, these plans were named for section 401(k) of the Internal Revenue Code.

The Urban Institute (2011, http://www.urban.org/retirement_policy/pensions.cfm) reports that about half of U.S. workers are covered by an employer pension plan that provides a defined benefit or more commonly a defined contribution plan that grows in response to

TABLE 2.2

Percentage of persons with income from specified sources, by age group, 2008

Source of family income	55–61	62–64	Aged 65 or older				
			Total	65–69	70–74	75–79	80 or older
Earnings	85.7	72.3	38.2	55.2	40.5	30.0	22.0
Wages and salaries	82.1	68.2	35.1	50.9	36.9	27.2	20.6
Self-employment	12.6	11.3	5.9	9.2	6.4	4.7	2.5
Retirement benefits	33.0	62.0	91.3	86.6	92.9	93.4	94.1
Social Security	20.5	51.6	88.7	83.0	90.4	91.4	91.9
Benefits other than Social Security	19.8	33.8	44.0	43.0	44.9	45.1	43.8
Other public pensions	9.2	14.9	16.1	15.7	16.8	16.2	16.0
Railroad retirement	0.3	0.5	0.6	0.4	0.4	0.6	1.0
Government employee pensions	8.9	14.3	15.6	15.3	16.4	15.7	15.1
Military	1.9	2.4	2.2	2.0	2.7	2.5	1.7
Federal	2.0	3.3	4.3	3.8	4.2	4.3	5.0
State or local	5.3	9.4	9.9	10.3	10.4	10.1	8.9
Private pensions or annuities	11.4	20.6	30.9	30.0	31.2	32.1	30.7
Income from assets	59.6	60.8	59.2	61.0	58.3	59.7	57.4
Interest	57.7	58.3	57.2	59.0	57.1	57.4	55.0
Other income from assets	25.7	27.8	24.8	26.8	24.5	25.4	22.4
Dividends	21.8	23.4	20.6	22.2	20.4	21.2	18.5
Rent or royalties	8.5	9.2	7.9	8.9	7.8	7.8	6.8
Estates or trusts	0.3	0.2	0.2	0.2	0.2	0.2	0.4
Veterans' benefits	3.8	4.4	4.2	3.5	3.7	4.8	5.1
Unemployment compensation	6.7	4.9	2.5	3.4	2.8	2.2	1.4
Workers' compensation	1.5	1.3	0.6	0.9	0.6	0.7	0.3
Cash public assistance and noncash benefits	10.3	10.4	11.7	10.2	12.4	11.8	12.7
Cash public assistance	5.8	5.4	4.8	4.1	5.9	4.8	4.6
Supplemental Security Income	5.2	4.8	4.5	3.8	5.6	4.5	4.4
Other	0.8	0.8	0.4	0.4	0.5	0.3	0.3
Noncash benefits	7.0	7.1	9.1	8.0	9.4	9.2	9.9
Food	5.0	4.5	4.5	4.6	5.1	4.4	4.0
Energy	2.1	2.6	2.8	2.6	2.9	2.7	3.2
Housing	2.4	2.5	4.3	3.4	4.3	4.5	5.3
Personal contributions	2.5	1.8	1.4	1.7	1.4	1.1	1.4
Number (thousands)	25,796	8,493	37,788	11,825	8,579	7,329	10,054

Reference population: These data refer to the civilian noninstitutionalized population.

SOURCE: "Table 9c. Percentage of People Age 55 and over with Family Income from Specified Sources, by Age Group, 2008," in *Older Americans 2010: Key Indicators of Well-Being*, Federal Interagency Forum on Aging-Related Statistics, July 2010, http://www.agingstats.gov/agingstatsdotnet/Main_Site/Data/2010_Documents/Docs/OA_2010.pdf (accessed April 2, 2011)

employer and worker contributions. Participation in defined benefit plans has declined, whereas participation in defined contribution plans has increased. The Bureau of Labor Statistics reports in "Six Ways to Save for Retirement" (*Program Perspectives*, vol. 3, no. 3, March 2011) that in 2010, 41% of workers in the private sector participated in defined contribution plans. (See Figure 2.7.) Since the mid-1990s many employers have converted their defined benefit plans to hybrid plans that incorporate elements of both defined benefit and defined contribution plans. For example, cash balance plans are based on defined contributions of pay credits (based on an employee's compensation rate) and interest credits that are deposited annually by the employer into an account, the balance of which serves as the defined benefit.

PRIVATE AND PUBLIC PENSIONS. The SSA reports in *Fast Facts and Figures about Social Security, 2010* (August 2010, http://www.ssa.gov/policy/docs/chartbooks/fast_facts/2010/fast_facts10.pdf) that the proportion of older adults' income from pensions grew rapidly during the 1960s, with private pensions more than tripling by 2008. (See Figure 2.8.) During the same period the proportion of people receiving government employee pensions increased by 56%, from 9% in 1962 to 14% in 2008. The proportion of older adults with income from assets—the second-most common source of income after Social Security—in 2008 (54%) was identical to 1962. In contrast, the proportion of older adults with earned income declined by 28%, from 36% in 1962 to 26% in 2008.

Unlike Social Security and many public plans, most private pension plans do not provide automatic cost-of-living adjustments. Without these adjustments many retirees' incomes and purchasing power erode. Military, government, and Railroad Retirement pensioners were more likely to receive cost-of-living increases than were pensioners in the private sector.

FEDERAL PENSION LAWS. Pension plan funds are often invested in stocks and bonds, much as banks invest their depositors' money. When the investment choice is a good one, the company makes a profit on the money in the fund; bad investments result in losses. During the early 1970s several major plans were terminated before they accumulated sufficient assets to pay employees and their beneficiaries retirement benefits. These asset-poor plans were unable to make good on their promises, leaving retirees without benefits despite their years of service.

To protect retirement plan participants and their beneficiaries from these catastrophic losses, ERISA was passed in 1974. ERISA established a new set of rules for participation, added mandatory and quicker vesting schedules, fixed minimum funding standards, and set standards of conduct for administering plans and handling plan assets. It also required the disclosure of plan information, established a system for insuring the payment of pension benefits, and created the Pension Benefit Guaranty Corporation, a federal corporation, to provide uninterrupted benefit payments when pension plans are terminated.

The Retirement Equity Act of 1984 requires pension plans to pay a survivor's benefit to the spouse of a deceased vested plan participant. Before 1984 some spouses received no benefits unless the employee was near retirement age at the time of death. Under the 1984 law, pension vesting begins at age 21, or after five years of being on the job, and employees who have a break in employment for reasons such as maternity leave do not lose any time already accumulated.

PENSION FUNDS DECLINE. Because both private and public pension funds are invested in the stock market, many suffered serious losses in response to the recession.

FIGURE 2.7

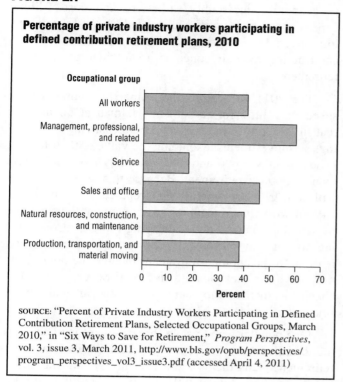

Percentage of private industry workers participating in defined contribution retirement plans, 2010

SOURCE: "Percent of Private Industry Workers Participating in Defined Contribution Retirement Plans, Selected Occupational Groups, March 2010," in "Six Ways to Save for Retirement," *Program Perspectives*, vol. 3, issue 3, March 2011, http://www.bls.gov/opub/perspectives/program_perspectives_vol3_issue3.pdf (accessed April 4, 2011)

FIGURE 2.8

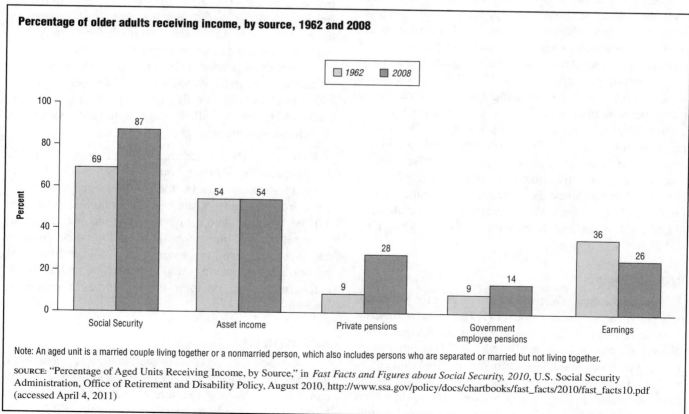

Percentage of older adults receiving income, by source, 1962 and 2008

Note: An aged unit is a married couple living together or a nonmarried person, which also includes persons who are separated or married but not living together.

SOURCE: "Percentage of Aged Units Receiving Income, by Source," in *Fast Facts and Figures about Social Security, 2010*, U.S. Social Security Administration, Office of Retirement and Disability Policy, August 2010, http://www.ssa.gov/policy/docs/chartbooks/fast_facts/2010/fast_facts10.pdf (accessed April 4, 2011)

According to John W. Ehrhardt and Paul C. Morgan, in "Modest Increase in 2010 Funded Status as a Result of Record Employer Contributions" (March 2011, http://publications.milliman.com/publications/eb-published/pdfs/2011-pension-funding-study.pdf), the 100 largest corporate (defined benefit) pension plans suffered a record $300 billion loss of funded status in 2008. Five years of pension gains were lost in 2008 and losses continued in early 2009.

The losses in funding sustained during the recession, along with the funding requirements by the Pension Protection Act (PPA) of 2006, which provides significant tax incentives to enhance and protect retirement savings for millions of Americans, combined to create a growing pension fund deficit. Ehrhardt and Morgan note that the act increased employer contributions to $59.4 billion for 2010. Many companies were expected to make increased contributions in 2011 to avoid benefit restrictions of the PPA. These record contributions resulted in a modest increase in pension funding.

There have also been many instances of alleged pension fraud. For example, Mary Williams Walsh and Louise Story report in "U.S. Inquiry Said to Focus on California Pension Fund" (*New York Times*, January 7, 2011) that the California Public Employees' Retirement System—the nation's largest public pension fund—not only lost 27% of its value in 2008 but also may have misled investors about the risk in its pension fund. There were two issues that concerned investigators: one was whether conflicts of interest occurred when specific investments were made and the other involved transparency and questions whether the fund should have disclosed the risk profile of its investments. Other instances of pension fraud include an investigator in the Warren County, New York, district attorney's office, and a New Jersey investment adviser who admitted defrauding investors, including a union pension plan. The Warren County case involved an individual who defrauded the pension fund by collecting a pension while he was still employed, an illegal practice that is called "double dipping." The New Jersey case involved an investment adviser who admitted to defrauding many investors, including the United Marine Division, International Longshoreman's Association, a union for tugboat and ferry workers in the New York and New Jersey waterways.

Personal Savings

One of the most effective ways to prepare for retirement is to save for it. In the issue brief *The 2011 Retirement Confidence Survey: Confidence Drops to Record Lows, Reflecting "the New Normal"* (March 2011, http://www.ebri.org/publications/ib/index.cfm?fa=ibDisp&content_id=4772), Ruth Helman et al. report on the results of the 2011 Retirement Confidence Survey (RCS) that was cosponsored by the Employee Benefit Research Institute

and Matthew Greenwald & Associates. Helman et al. report that a record low number of Americans—just 13%—said they are confident of having enough money to live comfortably in retirement. Even though this loss of confidence is largely attributable to universal issues such as economic uncertainty, inflation, and cost-of-living expenses, surveyed workers also cited job losses, pay cuts, loss of retirement savings, and increased debt as factors contributing to their concerns about their prospects in retirement.

The 2011 RCS finds that American workers have saved very little for retirement. Helman et al. indicate that in 2011, 56% of workers reported having total savings and investments, excluding the value of their homes, of less than $25,000 and 29% said they have saved less than $1,000 for retirement. Because this level of savings will render them woefully unprepared for retirement, 74% of workers are planning to supplement their income by working longer—either delaying retirement or working for pay in retirement. The most frequently cited reasons for postponing retirement include the poor economy (36%), a lack of faith in Social Security (16%), a change in their employment (15%), and an inability to finance retirement (13%).

One popular way to save for retirement is to contribute to individual retirement plans. Individuals fund these retirement plans themselves. The money that they contribute can be tax deductible, the plans' earnings are not taxed, and contributors determine how the money is invested. Since 1974 one of the major types of individual retirement plans has been the individual retirement account (IRA). IRAs fall into several different categories, but the two most common types are traditional IRAs (deductible and nondeductible) and Roth IRAs; a variety of factors determine which kind of IRA best serves an individual's needs. Profit-sharing plans for the self-employed (formerly called Keogh plans) are another type of individual retirement plan.

The 2011 RCS finds that 68% of retirees consider Social Security a major source of retirement income, whereas workers believe their retirement income will come from a variety of sources: 33% said Social Security will be a major source of retirement income, 29% said their retirement income will primarily come from an employer-sponsored retirement plan, 26% said they will rely on personal savings and investments, and 24% said employment will be their major source of retirement income.

NET WORTH

Because the economic well-being of households depends on both income and wealth, assessment of income alone is not the best measure of older adults' financial health. To draw a more complete economic profile of the older population, it is necessary to evaluate older households in terms of measures of wealth, such as home equity, savings, and other assets and liabilities. For example, a household may be in the top one-fifth of the income distribution but be saddled with a large amount of debt.

Net worth is a measure of economic valuation and an indicator of financial security that is obtained by subtracting total liabilities from total assets. Greater net worth enables individuals and households to weather financial challenges such as illness, disability, job loss, divorce, widowhood, or general economic downturns.

In *Older Americans 2010*, the Federal Interagency Forum on Aging-Related Statistics states that the median net worth of households headed by white older adults increased by 112%, from $131,000 in 1984 to $280,000 in 2007. During this period the increase in net worth was substantially greater for older white adults than for older African-American adults. (See Figure 2.9.) The median net worth of households headed by older African-American adults aged 65 years and older grew just 55%, from $29,700 in 1984 to $46,000 in 2007. In 2007 the median net worth of households headed by older white adults was six times greater than that of older African-American adults.

The median net worth of households headed by college-educated older adults rose from $114,900 in 1984 to $237,000 in 2007, a 106% increase, whereas households headed by an older adult without a high school diploma remained relatively unchanged in terms of net worth—$60,900 in 1984 and $78,000 in 2007. (See Figure 2.10.) In 2007 the median net worth of households headed by older adults with some college education was more than five times greater than that of households headed by older adults without a high school diploma.

It is important to observe that the net worth of many older Americans declined significantly between 2008 and 2009, at least in part because home equity, which is a primary source of wealth for older Americans, declined sharply. Older adults are at a disadvantage compared to other age groups because unlike younger workers, they do not have the time to recoup their losses.

Older Adults Are Hard Hit by the Mortgage Crisis and Low Interest Rates

According to the AARP Public Policy Institute, in *The Mortgage Crisis: Older Americans Are Feeling the Pain* (February 4, 2009, http://www.aarp.org/money/credit-loans-debt/info-02-2009/the_mortgage_crisis_older_americans_are_feeling_the_pain.html), at the close of 2007 more

FIGURE 2.9

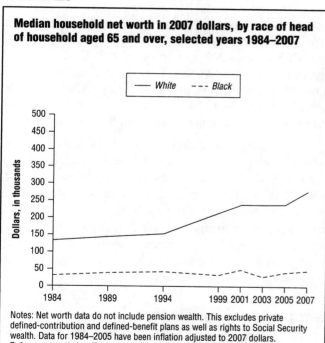

Median household net worth in 2007 dollars, by race of head of household aged 65 and over, selected years 1984–2007

Notes: Net worth data do not include pension wealth. This excludes private defined-contribution and defined-benefit plans as well as rights to Social Security wealth. Data for 1984–2005 have been inflation adjusted to 2007 dollars. Reference population: These data refer to the civilian noninstitutionalized population.

SOURCE: "Median Household Net Worth in 2007 Dollars, by Race of Head of Household Age 65 and over, in 2005 Dollars, Selected Years 1984–2007," in *Older Americans 2010: Key Indicators of Well-Being*, Federal Interagency Forum on Aging-Related Statistics, July 2010, http://www.agingstats.gov/agingstatsdotnet/Main_Site/Data/2010_Documents/Docs/OA_2010.pdf (accessed April 2, 2011)

FIGURE 2.10

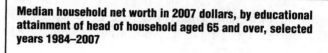
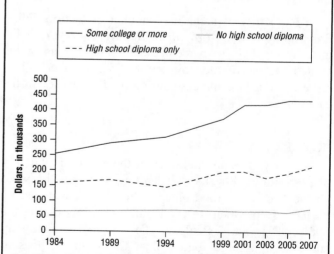

Median household net worth in 2007 dollars, by educational attainment of head of household aged 65 and over, selected years 1984–2007

Notes: Net worth data do not include pension wealth. This excludes private defined-contribution and defined-benefit plans as well as rights to Social Security wealth. Data for 1984–2005 have been inflation adjusted to 2007 dollars. Reference population: These data refer to the civilian noninstitutionalized population.

SOURCE: "Median Household Net Worth in 2007 dollars, by Educational Attainment of Head of Household Age 65 and over, in 2005 Dollars, Selected Years, 1984–2007," in *Older Americans 2010: Key Indicators of Well-Being*, Federal Interagency Forum on Aging-Related Statistics, July 2010, http://www.agingstats.gov/agingstatsdotnet/Main_Site/Data/2010_Documents/Docs/OA_2010.pdf (accessed April 2, 2011)

than 700,000 homeowners aged 50 years and older were either delinquent in mortgage payments or in foreclosure, and older adults represented 28% of all foreclosures. The rate of foreclosures for older adults continued through 2011 as property values declined, limiting the ability of older homeowners to refinance their mortgages.

In "Fed's Low Interest Rates Crack Retirees' Nest Eggs" (*Wall Street Journal*, April 4, 2011), Mark White-house observes that low interest rates intended to avert economic disaster and spur economic recovery following the downturn in 2007 have hurt retirees counting on the interest income from their savings. Whitehouse reports that in 2011 the average interest paid on savings and money market accounts was just 0.2%—one-tenth the rate in late 2007 and the lowest rate on record since 1959.

Bankruptcies Increase among Older Adults

According to Bob Calandra, in "Bankruptcies up for Older Adults: Filers Cite Lost Jobs, Credit Card Debt, and Empty Retirement Accounts" (January 6, 2011, http://www.aarp.org/money/credit-loans-debt/info-01-2011/bankruptcies_up_for_older_americans_.html), older adults make up a growing proportion of the bankruptcy filers. In 2009, 27% of bankruptcy filers were aged 45 to 54 years, up two percentage points from 2006. Seventeen percent of filers were aged 55 to 64 years in 2009, up from 14% in 2006, and during the same period the rate rose among adults aged 65 years and older, from 7.8% to 8.3%. Two-thirds (67%) of older adults who filed for bankruptcy in 2009 attributed their financial problems to mounting credit card interest and fees.

Rina Miller explains in "Number of Seniors Filing Bankruptcy Rising" (*Michigan Radio*, January 7, 2011) that "more than 20 percent of all bankruptcies in the United States are filed by people 55 and older." This represented a 12% increase during the first decade of the 21st century.

POVERTY

Poverty rates are measures of the economic viability of populations. Poverty standards were originally based on the "economy food plan," which was developed by the U.S. Department of Agriculture (USDA) during the 1960s. The plan calculated the cost of a minimally adequate household food budget for different types of households by age of householder. Because USDA surveys showed that the average family spent one-third of its income on food, it was decided that a household with an income three times the amount needed for food was living fairly comfortably. In 1963 the poverty level was calculated by simply multiplying the cost of a minimally adequate food budget by three. Later, the U.S. Census Bureau began comparing family income before taxes with a set of poverty thresholds that vary based on family size and composition and are adjusted annually for inflation using the Consumer Price Index (CPI; a measure of the average change in consumer prices over time in a fixed market basket of goods and services).

According to Table 2.3, the poverty rate of adults aged 65 years and older (8.9%) in 2009 was slightly lower than the previous year (9.7%) and represented 3.4 million older adults living in poverty. The rates recorded in 2009 for 18- to 64-year-olds (12.9%) and children under the age of 18 years (20.7%) both exceeded that of older adults. Census Bureau data reveal that in 1959 the poverty rate for people aged 65 years and older was 35%, well above the rates for the other age groups. (See Figure 2.11.) The lowest level of poverty in the older population occurred in 2009, when the rate fell to 8.9%.

Poverty Thresholds Are Lower for Older Adults

The Census Bureau measures need for assistance using poverty thresholds (specific dollar amounts that determine poverty status). Each individual or family is assigned one of 48 possible poverty thresholds. Thresholds vary according to family size and the ages of the members. The thresholds do not vary geographically, and they are updated annually for inflation using the CPI.

One assumption used to determine poverty thresholds is that healthy older adults have lower nutritional requirements than younger people, so they require less money for food. This assumption has resulted in different poverty thresholds for both the young and old. For example, in 2010 the poverty threshold for a single person under the age of 65 was $11,369, as opposed to $10,481 for a person aged 65 years or older. (See Table 2.4.) The 2010 poverty threshold for two people including a householder under the age of 65 was $14,634, compared to $13,209 for two people including a householder aged 65 years or older.

This method of defining poverty fails to take into account the special financial and health challenges that older adults may face. For example, no household costs other than food are counted, even though older adults spend a much greater percentage of their income on health care than younger people do. Also, the dollars allocated for food only consider the nutritional needs of healthy older adults; many are in poor health and may require more costly special diets or nutritional supplements.

WELL-OFF OLDER ADULTS

More older Americans live comfortably in the 21st century than at any other time in history. Many of those in their mid-70s to 80s were born during the Great Depression (1929–1939). The enforced Depression-era frugality taught their families to economize and save. During the 1950s and 1960s, their peak earning years, they enjoyed a period of unprecedented economic expansion. Since then, many have raised their children, paid off

TABLE 2.3

People and families in poverty, by selected characteristics, 2008 and 2009

[Numbers in thousands. Percentage points as appropriate. People as of March of the following year.]

Characteristic	2008 Total	2008 Below poverty Number	2008 Below poverty Percent	2009 Total	2009 Below poverty Number	2009 Below poverty Percent	Change in poverty[a] Number	Change in poverty[a] Percent
People								
Total	301,041	39,829	13.2	303,820	43,569	14.3	3,740	1.1
Family status								
In families	248,301	28,564	11.5	249,384	31,197	12.5	2,634	1.0
Householder	78,874	8,147	10.3	78,867	8,792	11.1	644	0.8
Related children under 18	72,980	13,507	18.5	73,410	14,774	20.1	1,267	1.6
Related children under 6	24,884	5,295	21.3	25,104	5,983	23.8	688	2.6
In unrelated subfamilies	1,207	555	46.0	1,357	693	51.1	138	5.1
Reference person	452	207	45.7	521	253	48.7	47	2.9
Children under 18	712	341	47.8	747	423	56.6	82	8.7
Unrelated individuals	51,534	10,710	20.8	53,079	11,678	22.0	968	1.2
Male	25,240	4,759	18.9	26,269	5,255	20.0	496	1.1
Female	26,293	5,951	22.6	26,811	6,424	24.0	473	1.3
Race[b] and Hispanic Origin								
White	240,548	26,990	11.2	242,047	29,830	12.3	2,841	1.1
White, not Hispanic	196,940	17,024	8.6	197,164	18,530	9.4	1,506	0.8
Black	37,966	9,379	24.7	38,556	9,944	25.8	565	1.1
Asian	13,310	1,576	11.8	14,005	1,746	12.5	169	0.6
Hispanic (any race)	47,398	10,987	23.2	48,811	12,350	25.3	1,363	2.1
Age								
Under 18 years	74,068	14,068	19.0	74,579	15,451	20.7	1,383	1.7
18 to 64 years	189,185	22,105	11.7	190,627	24,684	12.9	2,579	1.3
65 years and older	37,788	3,656	9.7	38,613	3,433	8.9	−223	−0.8
Nativity								
Native born	264,314	33,293	12.6	266,223	36,407	13.7	3,114	1.1
Foreign born	36,727	6,536	17.8	37,597	7,162	19.0	626	1.3
Naturalized citizen	15,470	1,577	10.2	16,024	1,736	10.8	160	0.6
Not a citizen	21,257	4,959	23.3	21,573	5,425	25.1	466	1.8
Region								
Northeast	54,123	6,295	11.6	54,571	6,650	12.2	355	0.6
Midwest	65,589	8,120	12.4	65,980	8,768	13.3	648	0.9
South	110,666	15,862	14.3	112,165	17,609	15.7	1,747	1.4
West	70,663	9,552	13.5	71,103	10,542	14.8	990	1.3
Residence								
Inside metropolitan statistical areas	253,048	32,570	12.9	256,028	35,655	13.9	3,085	1.1
Inside principal cities	97,217	17,222	17.7	97,725	18,261	18.7	1,039	1.0
Outside principal cities	155,831	15,348	9.8	158,302	17,394	11.0	2,046	1.1
Outside metropolitan statistical areas[c]	47,993	7,259	15.1	47,792	7,914	16.6	656	1.4
Work experience								
Total, 16 years and older	236,024	27,216	11.5	238,095	29,625	12.4	2,409	0.9
All workers	158,317	10,085	6.4	154,772	10,680	6.9	595	0.5
Worked full-time, year-round	104,023	2,754	2.6	99,306	2,641	2.7	−113	—
Less than full-time, year-round	54,294	7,331	13.5	55,466	8,039	14.5	708	1.0
Did not work at least 1 week	77,707	17,131	22.0	83,323	18,944	22.7	1,814	0.7

their home mortgages, invested wisely, and become eligible to receive Social Security payments that are larger than ever.

Even though these factors have contributed to a more favorable economic status for this cohort (a group of individuals that shares a common characteristic such as birth years and is studied over time) of older adults than they would have otherwise enjoyed, most older people are not wealthy. Figure 2.3 shows that in 2009, 24.7% of households headed by older adults had total incomes of $75,000 or more and 19% of households headed by older adults reported incomes ranging from $50,000 to $74,999.

It should also be noted that even well-off older adults were affected by the recession. Mauricio Soto of the Urban Institute explains in the fact sheet "How Is the Financial Crisis Affecting Retirement Savings?" (March 9, 2009, http://www.urban.org/UploadedPDF/411847_update-3-09-2009-pr.pdf) that between September 2007 and March 2009 the stock market lost an estimated $13 trillion. This loss devastated the retirement savings of many Americans, and even though older adults typically have fewer funds

TABLE 2.3

People and families in poverty, by selected characteristics, 2008 and 2009 [CONTINUED]

[Numbers in thousands. Percentage points as appropriate. People as of March of the following year.]

Characteristic	2008 Total	2008 Below poverty Number	2008 Below poverty Percent	2009 Total	2009 Below poverty Number	2009 Below poverty Percent	Change in poverty[a] Number	Change in poverty[a] Percent
Families								
Total	78,874	8,147	10.3	78.867	8,792	11.1	644	0.8
Type of family								
Married-couple	59,137	3,261	5.5	58,428	3,409	5.8	147	0.3
Female householder, no husband present	14,482	4,163	28.7	14,857	4,441	29.9	278	1.1
Male householder, no wife present	5,255	723	13.8	5,582	942	16.9	219	3.1

—Represents or rounds to zero.
[a]Details may not sum to totals because of rounding.
[b]Federal surveys now give respondents the option of reporting more than one race. Therefore, two basic ways of defining a race group are possible. A group such as Asian may be defined as those who reported Asian and no other race (the race-alone or single-race concept) or as those who reported Asian regardless of whether they also reported another race (the race-alone-or-in-combination concept). This table shows data using the first approach (race alone). The use of the single-race population does not imply that it is the preferred method of presenting or analyzing data. About 2.6 percent of people reported more than one race in Census 2000. Data for American Indians and Alaska Natives, Native Hawaiians and other Pacific Islanders, and those reporting two or more races are not shown separately.
[c]The "Outside metropolitan statistical areas" category includes both micropolitan statistical areas and territory outside of metropolitan and micropolitan statistical areas.

SOURCE: Carmen DeNavas-Walt, Bernadette D. Proctor, and Jessica C. Smith, "Table 4. People and Families in Poverty by Selected Characteristics: 2008 and 2009," in *Income, Poverty and Health Insurance Coverage in the United States: 2009*, U.S. Census Bureau, September 2010, http://www.census.gov/prod/2010pubs/p60-238.pdf (accessed April 4, 2011)

FIGURE 2.11

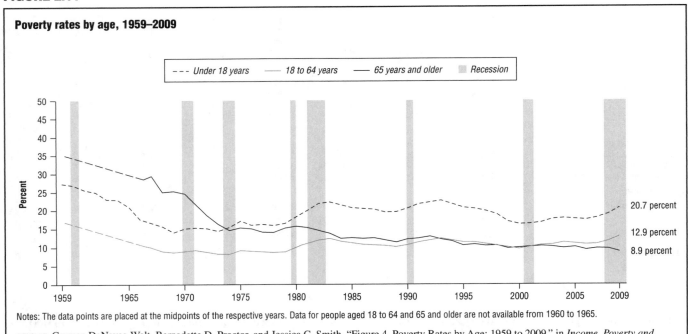

Poverty rates by age, 1959–2009

Notes: The data points are placed at the midpoints of the respective years. Data for people aged 18 to 64 and 65 and older are not available from 1960 to 1965.

SOURCE: Carmen DeNavas-Walt, Bernadette D. Proctor, and Jessica C. Smith, "Figure 4. Poverty Rates by Age: 1959 to 2009," in *Income, Poverty and Health Insurance Coverage in the United States, 2009*, U.S. Census Bureau, September 2010, http://www.census.gov/prod/2010pubs/p60-238.pdf (accessed April 4, 2011)

invested in stocks than younger adults, many endured substantial losses. However, by 2011 many of these losses had been reversed. In "Retirement Account Balances" (April 2011, http://www.urban.org/UploadedPDF/411976_retirement_account_balances.pdf), Barbara A. Butrica and Philip Issa of the Urban Institute note that retirement account assets (defined contribution plans and IRAs) totaled an estimated $8.7 trillion during the third quarter of 2007 and by the first quarter of 2009 they had dropped to $6 trillion, a decrease of 31%. By the first quarter of 2011, however, retirement account assets had risen to $8.7 trillion.

TABLE 2.4

Poverty thresholds, by size of family and number of related children under 18, 2010

Size of family unit	Related children under 18 years								
	None	One	Two	Three	Four	Five	Six	Seven	Eight or more
One person (unrelated individual)									
Under 65 years	11,369								
65 years and over	10,481								
Two people									
Householder under 65 years	14,634	15,063							
Householder 65 years and over	13,209	15,006							
Three people	17,094	17,590	17,607						
Four people	22,541	22,910	22,162	22,239					
Five people	27,183	27,579	26,734	26,080	25,681				
Six people	31,266	31,390	30,743	30,123	29,201	28,654			
Seven people	35,975	36,199	35,425	34,885	33,880	32,707	31,420		
Eight people	40,235	40,590	39,860	39,219	38,311	37,158	35,958	35,653	
Nine people or more	48,400	48,635	47,988	47,445	46,553	45,326	44,217	43,942	42,249

SOURCE: "Poverty Thresholds for 2010 by Size of Family and Number of Related Children under 18 Years," in *Poverty Thresholds*, U.S. Census Bureau, 2011, http://www.census.gov/hhes/www/poverty/data/threshld/index.html (accessed April 4, 2011)

Older adults' responses to economic uncertainty vary. The article "Living, Working, and Saving Together in a Recessed Economy" (*AARP Bulletin Today*, April 7, 2009) opines that many older adults, having previously experienced times of economic uncertainty, are able to offer a long-range and measured perspective about economic upheaval and may be able to provide insight based on their experiences about how best to cope with the effects of the recession. In *Assessing the Impact of Severe Economic Recession on the Elderly: Summary of a Workshop* (2011), Malay Majmundar observes that older adults who reduced their consumption and spending in response to the economic downturn, especially those who vividly remember the toll of the Great Depression, may remain fearful even when the economy recovers and may continue to limit their spending.

CONSUMER EXPENSES

On average, older households spend less than younger households because they generally have less money to spend, fewer dependents to support, and different needs and values. The Bureau of Labor Statistics reports that in 2009 the annual per capita expenditure for people aged 65 to 74 years was $42,957, whereas those aged 75 years and older spent just $31,676. (See Table 2.5.) Those under the age of 25 years were the only group with a smaller expenditure, spending $28,119 per capita annually. The greatest amounts were spent on housing (including utilities), food, transportation, and health care. Not surprisingly, older adults spent more on health care than any other age group, both in actual dollars and as a percentage of expenditures. Older adults spent less on tobacco and smoking products, alcoholic beverages, apparel, and food away from home than other age groups.

Smaller Households Are More Expensive to Run

Most older adult households contain fewer people than younger households. Even though larger households, in general, cost more to feed, operate, and maintain, they are less expensive on a per capita basis.

Home maintenance, such as replacing a roof or major appliance, costs the same for any household, but in larger households the per capita cost is lower. Purchasing small quantities of food for one or two people may be almost as costly as buying in bulk for a larger household. Because older adults often have limited transportation and mobility, they may be forced to buy food and other necessities at small neighborhood stores that generally charge more than supermarkets and warehouse stores. Larger households may also benefit from multiple incomes.

High energy costs also cause older adults physical and financial hardship, prompting some to suffer extreme heat and cold in their homes. Programs such as the Low Income Home Energy Assistance Program (LIHEAP; June 6, 2011, http://www.acf.hhs.gov/programs/ocs/liheap/), which is operated by the U.S. Department of Health and Human Services' Administration for Children and Families, attempt to prevent older adults from suffering from a lack of heat in their home. LIHEAP assists eligible households to meet their home energy needs.

AGING CONSUMERS: A GROWING MARKET

Older adults have proven to be a lucrative market for many products. Marianne Wilson states in "Top Consumer Trends for 2011" (October 21, 2010, http://www.chainstoreage.com/article/top-consumer-trends-2011) that "people are working beyond retirement—either due to financial need, or because they have grown attached to a lifestyle of leisure and pleasure. The number of over 65s working will reach nearly 20% by 2014.... This group may prove an untapped market for advertisers, affecting a number of consumer sectors." Older adults are redefining aging—only a minority of Americans expects to retire as their parents did. Older adults are

TABLE 2.5

Average annual expenditures and characteristics, by age, 2009

Item	All consumer units	Under 25 years	25–34 years	35–44 years	45–54 years	55–64 years	65 years and older	65–74 years	75 years and older
Number of consumer units (in thousands)	120,847	7,875	20,044	22,199	25,440	20,731	24,557	12,848	11,709
Consumer unit characteristics:									
Income before taxes	$62,857	$25,695	$58,946	$77,005	$80,976	$70,609	$39,862	$47,286	$31,715
Income after taxes	60,753	25,522	57,239	74,900	77,460	67,586	39,054	46,147	31,272
Age of reference person	49.4	21.4	29.7	39.7	49.5	59.1	75.0	68.9	81.6
Average number in consumer unit:									
Persons	2.5	2.0	2.8	3.3	2.8	2.1	1.7	1.9	1.6
Children under 18	0.6	0.4	1.1	1.3	0.6	0.2	0.1	0.1	a
Persons 65 and older	0.3	a	a	a	a	0.1	1.4	1.4	1.4
Earners	1.3	1.3	1.5	1.6	1.7	1.3	0.5	0.6	0.2
Vehicles	2.0	1.2	1.7	2.1	2.4	2.2	1.6	1.9	1.3
Percent distribution:									
Sex of reference person:									
Male	47	47	48	49	49	48	43	46	39
Female	53	53	52	51	51	52	57	54	61
Housing tenure:									
Homeowner	66	14	46	65	74	81	79	81	77
With mortgage	41	10	39	56	55	47	22	31	12
Without mortgage	25	4	7	9	20	34	58	51	65
Renter	34	86	54	35	26	19	21	19	23
Race of reference person:									
Black or African-American	12	13	14	14	12	11	10	11	8
White, Asian, and all other races	88	87	86	86	88	89	90	89	92
Hispanic or Latino origin of reference person:									
Hispanic or Latino	12	14	17	17	11	8	6	7	4
Not Hispanic or Latino	88	86	83	83	89	92	94	93	96
Education of reference person:									
Elementary (1–8)	5	1	4	4	3	5	10	8	12
High school (9–12)	34	32	29	30	34	33	45	42	48
College	61	66	67	66	62	62	45	50	40
Never attended and other	b	b	b	b	b	b	b	b	b
At least one vehicle owned or leased	88	69	89	91	92	92	84	88	79
Average annual expenditures	**$49,067**	**$28,119**	**$46,494**	**$57,301**	**$58,708**	**$52,463**	**$37,562**	**$42,957**	**$31,676**
Food	6,372	4,179	6,169	7,760	7,445	6,303	4,901	5,561	4,189
Food at home	3,753	2,449	3,478	4,446	4,343	3,678	3,222	3,567	2,851
Cereals and bakery products	506	307	473	629	586	465	439	463	414
Cereals and cereal products	173	124	177	223	188	152	138	151	124
Bakery products	334	183	296	406	397	313	301	312	290
Meats, poultry, fish, and eggs	841	571	757	983	978	849	720	849	581
Beef	226	146	196	263	263	242	192	246	133
Pork	168	130	147	198	196	166	145	168	120
Other meats	114	68	102	139	129	110	101	114	87
Poultry	154	120	160	188	177	147	111	121	100
Fish and seafood	135	75	111	145	166	142	129	153	104
Eggs	44	33	40	50	47	43	42	48	37
Dairy products	406	281	376	495	465	386	346	381	308
Fresh milk and cream	144	110	144	179	155	127	125	136	113
Other dairy products	262	171	232	315	310	259	221	244	195
Fruits and vegetables	656	398	593	739	750	663	618	684	546
Fresh fruits	220	116	189	249	249	227	215	244	185
Fresh vegetables	209	130	184	229	247	219	192	220	161
Processed fruits	118	86	114	135	136	105	109	107	110
Processed vegetables	110	67	106	126	118	111	102	113	91
Other food at home	1,343	891	1,280	1,600	1,564	1,314	1,100	1,190	1,002
Sugar and other sweets	141	88	112	162	170	147	127	138	115
Fats and oils	102	63	94	116	117	106	91	104	77
Miscellaneous foods	715	495	729	869	810	664	576	584	568
Nonalcoholic beverages	337	232	315	401	405	329	264	309	216
Food prepared by consumer unit on out-of-town trips	49	13	31	51	62	68	42	56	27
Food away from home	2,619	1,731	2,691	3,314	3,102	2,626	1,679	1,994	1,338
Alcoholic beverages	435	344	481	498	502	440	292	389	188
Housing	16,895	9,735	17,258	20,705	19,004	16,991	13,196	14,462	11,811
Shelter	10,075	6,306	10,856	12,753	11,356	9,749	7,173	7,828	6,454
Owned dwellings	6,543	1,245	5,581	8,832	8,093	7,149	4,838	5,802	3,781
Mortgage interest and charges	3,594	783	3,843	5,863	4,677	3,352	1,322	1,976	603
Property taxes	1,811	324	1,130	2,022	2,296	2,234	1,793	1,950	1,622
Maintenance, repairs, insurance, other expenses	1,138	139	608	947	1,120	1,563	1,723	1,876	1,556

TABLE 2.5

Average annual expenditures and characteristics, by age, 2009 [CONTINUED]

Item	All consumer units	Under 25 years	25–34 years	35–44 years	45–54 years	55–64 years	65 years and older	65–74 years	75 years and older
Rented dwellings	$2,860	$4,885	$4,877	$3,328	$2,369	$1,570	$1,741	$1,320	$2,202
Other lodging	672	176	398	593	894	1,031	594	706	471
Utilities, fuels, and public services	3,645	1,821	3,249	4,093	4,275	3,896	3,282	3,568	2,967
Natural gas	483	188	405	524	552	530	494	485	504
Electricity	1,377	696	1,232	1,529	1,596	1,481	1,261	1,386	1,123
Fuel oil and other fuels	141	16	62	131	179	177	186	192	179
Telephone services	1,162	758	1,142	1,372	1,398	1,179	858	1,003	700
Water and other public services	481	163	409	537	550	528	483	503	461
Household operations	1,011	370	1,231	1,377	964	871	876	801	957
Personal services	389	156	786	753	253	103	194	111	285
Other household expenses	622	214	445	623	711	767	681	690	672
Housekeeping supplies	659	309	506	698	703	825	682	773	584
Laundry and cleaning supplies	156	91	148	187	172	157	137	161	112
Other household products	360	168	247	372	380	490	377	443	306
Postage and stationery	143	49	111	139	152	178	167	169	166
Household furnishings and equipment	1,506	929	1,416	1,786	1,705	1,651	1,184	1,491	850
Household textiles	124	43	99	154	135	154	107	125	88
Furniture	343	336	432	391	375	330	209	252	163
Floor coverings	30	5	17	28	39	36	37	49	25
Major appliances	194	79	164	216	199	278	159	197	117
Small appliances, miscellaneous housewares	93	39	88	96	103	110	90	121	57
Miscellaneous household equipment	721	427	616	901	855	743	581	747	401
Apparel and services	1,725	1,396	1,871	2,346	1,885	1,591	1,068	1,322	793
Men and boys	383	256	407	562	443	335	215	277	148
Men, 16 and over	304	228	291	405	360	301	190	244	132
Boys, 2 to 15	79	28	116	156	83	34	25	33	16
Women and girls	678	545	677	871	772	664	456	541	364
Women, 16 and over	561	480	533	624	652	596	427	503	346
Girls, 2 to 15	118	65	144	248	120	69	29	38	18
Children under 2	91	153	198	109	50	66	26	39	12
Footwear	323	278	336	449	351	269	223	262	181
Other apparel products and services	249	163	253	355	270	256	149	204	88
Transportation	7,658	5,334	7,671	8,364	9,409	8,323	5,409	7,033	3,631
Vehicle purchases (net outlay)	2,657	2,319	2,820	2,761	3,233	2,752	1,862	2,597	1,055
Cars and trucks, new	1,297	542	1,063	1,199	1,618	1,623	1,210	1,604	778
Cars and trucks, used	1,304	1,760	1,682	1,523	1,532	1,064	619	932	277
Other vehicles	55	17[c]	74	39	82	65[c]	32[c]	61[c]	[d]
Gasoline and motor oil	1,986	1,483	2,071	2,359	2,398	2,074	1,241	1,573	877
Other vehicle expenses	2,536	1,298	2,293	2,694	3,199	2,962	1,968	2,488	1,402
Vehicle finance charges	281	180	353	357	333	291	124	188	54
Maintenance and repairs	733	447	654	766	927	854	557	696	406
Vehicle insurance	1,075	465	837	1,055	1,406	1,307	972	1,214	712
Vehicle rental, leases, licenses, and other charges	447	206	450	516	534	510	314	390	230
Public transportation	479	234	487	549	579	535	338	376	297
Healthcare	3,126	676	1,805	2,520	3,173	3,895	4,846	4,906	4,779
Health insurance	1,785	381	1,083	1,436	1,688	2,017	3,027	3,042	3,011
Medical services	736	167	466	650	862	1,054	821	818	824
Drugs	486	97	195	335	485	679	828	865	787
Medical supplies	119	30	61	100	139	144	170	181	158
Entertainment	2,693	1,233	2,504	3,317	3,176	2,906	2,062	2,498	1,587
Fees and admissions	628	234	521	917	811	629	387	497	266
Audio and visual equipment and services	975	574	1,018	1,111	1,065	1,024	807	934	669
Pets, toys, hobbies, and playground equipment	690	295	546	816	855	777	580	775	367
Other entertainment supplies, equipment, and services	400	130	419	473	445	476	288	292	285
Personal care products and services	596	360	555	685	666	617	531	600	456
Reading	110	42	69	85	119	147	145	154	134
Education	1,068	1,910	808	935	2,055	1,003	162	181	141
Tobacco products and smoking supplies	380	330	368	417	513	410	207	275	133
Miscellaneous	816	243	631	967	1,051	952	663	820	491
Cash contributions	1,723	349	1,001	1,581	2,056	2,092	2,226	2,087	2,378
Personal insurance and pensions	5,471	1,988	5,303	7,122	7,654	6,793	1,856	2,669	964
Life and other personal insurance	309	31	156	270	427	446	320	397	234
Pensions and Social Security	5,162	1,957	5,147	6,851	7,226	6,347	1,537	2,272	730

now more likely to continue working, and working out, rather than retiring to the shuffleboard court or the rocking chair on the front porch. As a result, they are considered an important market for an expanding array of products, such as food, drinks, and anti-aging cosmetics, as well as products that are traditionally

TABLE 2.5

Average annual expenditures and characteristics, by age, 2009 [CONTINUED]

Item	All consumer units	Under 25 years	25–34 years	35–44 years	45–54 years	55–64 years	65 years and older	65–74 years	75 years and older
Sources of income and personal taxes:									
Money income before taxes	$62,857	$25,695	$58,946	$77,005	$80,976	$70,609	$39,862	$47,286	$31,715
Wages and salaries	50,339	22,749	54,461	69,677	72,345	53,711	12,699	18,760	6,048
Self-employment income	2,673	447	1,829	3,127	3,582	4,745	976	1,813	58
Social Security, private and government retirement	6,837	333	441	955	2,248	8,457	22,844	23,578	22,038
Interest, dividends, rental income, other property income	1,460	34	488	1,453	1,031	2,164	2,564	2,105	3,067
Unemployment and workers' compensation, veterans' benefits	432	230	478	498	614	540	119	180	51
Public assistance, supplemental security income, food stamps	435	416	434	487	459	540	280	345	209
Regular contributions for support	416	854	525	566	406	295	163	192	130
Other income	266	631	290	240	291	157	218	313	114
Personal taxes	2,104	173	1,707	2,105	3,515	3,023	807	1,140	443
Federal income taxes	1,404	25	1,063	1,306	2,510	2,090	490	761	194
2008 Tax stimulus (new UCC Q20082) (thru Q20091)	−1[c]	−1[c]	[d]	−2[c]	−2[c]	−1[c]	−1[c]	−1[c]	−1[c]
State and local income taxes	524	144	550	658	779	673	113	183	37
Other taxes	177	5	94	143	229	261	205	197	214
Income after taxes	60,753	25,522	57,239	74,900	77,460	67,586	39,054	46,147	31,272
Addenda:									
Net change in total assets and liabilities	−$5,416	$682	− $13,178	− $8,341	− $5,163	− $1,389	− $2,051	− $1,632	− $2,511
Net change in total assets	6,448	7,026	10,789	8,207	7,259	6,404	326	2,383	−1,932
Net change in total liabilities	11,864	6,343	23,968	16,548	12,423	7,793	2,377	4,016	579
Other financial information:									
Other money receipts	514	204	338	228	527	863	707	927	466
Mortgage principal paid on owned property	−2,211	−264	−1,454	−2,969	−3,220	−2,873	−1,165	−1,698	−579
Estimated market value of owned home	157,630	24,026	91,306	164,412	189,396	203,762	176,625	189,583	162,406
Estimated monthly rental value of owned home	856	158	570	914	1,019	1,056	923	983	856
Gifts of goods and services	1,067	386	641	797	1,653	1,582	839	989	676
Food	96	24	43	73	144	168	73	96	48
Alcoholic beverages	9	4[c]	7	12	6	11	9	13	5
Housing	202	77	131	155	271	300	191	157	229
Housekeeping supplies	31	15	19	27	29	56	29	24	35
Household textiles	9	6[c]	11	9	10	10	6	8	3
Appliances and miscellaneous housewares	15	4[c]	12	13	18	21	16	19	12
Major appliances	4	[b]	2[c]	3	6	7	5	7	3[c]
Small appliances and miscellaneous housewares	11	3[c]	10	10	12	15	10	11	9
Miscellaneous household equipment	41	17	25	34	51	60	45	56	33
Other housing	106	34	64	71	162	153	96	50	145
Apparel and services	237	134	243	227	295	284	177	204	147
Males, 2 and over	53	19	43	57	63	63	51	58	43
Females, 2 and over	86	49	65	82	129	93	72	74	71
Children under 2	48	45	74	46	44	61	22	32	11
Other apparel products and services	49	21	61	42	60	67	31	40	22
Jewelry and watches	14	10[c]	26	9	12	20	7	9	4
All other apparel products and services	35	10[c]	34	32	48	46	24	31	18[c]
Transportation	86	94	67	68	121	84	81	114	46
Healthcare	28	2[c]	5[c]	8	44	37	48	49[c]	48[c]
Entertainment	91	36	77	87	65	173	82	122	39
Toys, games, arts and crafts, and tricycles	34	29[c]	35	36	16	53	35	52	17[c]
Other entertainment	57	7	42	51	49	120	47	70	22
Personal care products and services	12	3	14	15	8	13	15	21	9
Reading	1	[d]	[b]	[b]	1	1	2	1	2
Education	229	[b]	23	83	624	387	59	48	70
All other gifts	76	11	31	69	74	125	102	165	33

[a]Value is less than or equal to 0.05.
[b]Value is less than or equal to 0.5.
[c]Data are likely to have large sampling errors.
[d]No data reported.

SOURCE: "Table 3. Age of Reference Person: Average Annual Expenditures and Characteristics, Consumer Expenditure Survey, 2009," in *Consumer Expenditures in 2009*, U.S. Department of Labor, U.S. Bureau of Labor Statistics, October 2010, http://www.bls.gov/cex/2009/Standard/age.pdf (accessed April 4, 2011)

marketed to older adults, such as health and life insurance plans and burial plots.

Baby Boomers: The Emerging "Silver" Market

The aging baby boomers (people born between 1946 and 1964) have been dubbed "zoomers" to reflect the generation's active lifestyle. Market researchers believe the sheer size of the boomer cohort and its history of self-indulgence, coupled with considerable purchasing power, ensure that this group will contain the most voracious older consumers ever.

The information in this section was drawn from the Boomer Marketing Report, a quarterly survey of 1,400 consumers by the Boomer Project/Survey Sampling International that aims to determine how this generation thinks, feels, and responds to marketing and advertising messages, and from 50 Things Every Marketer Needs to Know about Boomers over 50 (2006, http://www.boomer project.com/documents/white_papers/50_things.pdf). Included among the many insights that the Boomer Project research reveals are the following:

- Boomers at age 50 perceive themselves as 12 years younger, and they expect to live 35 more years. They consider themselves to be in early "middle age" and view 72 as the onset of old age.

- Boomers reject any and all age-related labels to describe themselves. They do not want to be called "seniors," "aged," or even "boomers," and they do not want to be compared to their parents' generation or any previous cohort of older adults.

- Boomers over the age of 50 do not want to reverse or stop the signs of aging, they simply want to postpone or slow the process. They are intent on seeking health rather than youth—feeling younger is as important as looking younger for boomers eager to age "on their own terms."

- Boomers want more time, which means that services that offer them free time to pursue work and leisure activities are likely to be in great demand. Examples of these include cleaning, home maintenance, and gardening services.

- Boomers are becoming less interested in material possessions and more interested in gaining a variety of experiences. Rather than embracing the premise that "he who has the most toys wins," boomers believe "he who chalks up the most experiences wins."

- Once dubbed the "me generation," boomers operate on the premise that they are entitled to special treatment, not because they have earned it by virtue of age, but simply because they deserve it. They want products and services that are relevant to them personally. They remain motivated to fulfill their own needs, whether these needs are for community, adventure, or a spiritual life.

- Boomers are life-long learners. Continuing education classes and opportunities to learn and enrich their lives through travel are important to this generation.

- Boomers are still interested in promoting social change. The generation known for protesting the Vietnam War (1954–1975) and questioning authority and traditional American social mores continues to support global and local humanitarian and environmental action.

- Boomers do not want to relocate to traditional retirement enclaves and communities; instead, they prefer to "age in place" in their present home or nearby. Having witnessed the institutionalization of their parents in nursing homes and in other assisted living facilities, boomers are intent on remaining in their home, and in the community, for as long as they can.

In "Baby Boomer Trends in Products and Services Expected to Reflect Preference for Style" (April 29, 2010, https://www.aarpglobalnetwork.org/), the AARP Global Network indicates that boomers are described as seeking instant gratification through purchasing and maintaining their preference for style and luxury as they age. They also do not want to be reminded of their advancing age. As a result, some manufacturers are redesigning their products. For example, traditional bifocal lenses were thick and had heavy, large-rimmed frames. In the 21st century bifocals are thinner, lighter, and more fashionable. Similarly, walkers are now available in metallic colors rather than in the traditional gunmetal gray.

The article "The New Target Demographic: Baby Boomers" (CBSNews.com, March 6, 2011) describes some of the ways that corporate America hopes baby boomers will spend some of their estimated $3.4 trillion in purchasing power. These include appliances that are easier to reach, adjustable beds, and technology such as home sensors and monitoring devices that detect falls and offer medication reminders to help older adults live more safely in their home.

SOCIAL SECURITY

We can never insure one hundred percent of the population against one hundred percent of the hazards and vicissitudes of life, but we have tried to frame a law which will give some measure of protection to the average citizen and to his family against the loss of a job and against poverty-ridden old age.

—President Franklin D. Roosevelt, on signing the Social Security Act, August 14, 1935

Social Security is a social insurance program that is funded through a dedicated payroll tax. It is also known as

Old-Age, Survivors, and Disability Insurance (OASDI), which describes its three major classes of beneficiaries.

During the Great Depression poverty among the older population escalated. In 1934 more than half of older adults lacked sufficient income. Even though 30 states had some form of an old-age pension program in place, by 1935 these programs were unable to meet the growing need. Just 3% of the older population received benefits under these state plans, and the average benefit amount was about 65 cents per day.

As advocated by President Franklin D. Roosevelt (1882–1945), social insurance would solve the problem of economic security for older adults by creating a work-related, contributory system in which workers would provide for their own future economic security through taxes paid while employed. By the time the Social Security Act was signed into law by President Roosevelt in August 1935, 34 nations were already operating some form of a social insurance program—government-sponsored efforts to provide for the economic well-being of a nation's citizens.

According to the SSA, in "Social Security Basic Facts" (May 17, 2011, http://www.ssa.gov/pressoffice/basicfact.htm), in 2011 more than nine out of 10 people aged 65 years and older received OASDI. Retired workers and their dependents accounted for more than two-thirds (69%) of total benefits paid, whereas survivors of deceased workers accounted for 12% of the total, and disabled workers and their dependents rounded out the total with 19% of benefits paid. An estimated 94% (157 million) of the U.S. workforce was covered by Social Security.

Even though Social Security was not initially intended as a full pension, 22% of married older adults and 43% of unmarried older adults relied almost exclusively (for 90% or more of their income) on the program in 2011. In "Guest Opinion: Social Security Lifts U.S. Seniors out of Poverty" (*Billings [MT] Gazette*, August 21, 2010), John Melcher observes that without Social Security "nearly one out of every two elderly people and 55 percent of all disabled people and their families would live in poverty." This capacity to lift older adults from poverty makes Social Security the country's most effective antipoverty program.

Benefits are funded through the Federal Insurance Contributions Act (FICA), which provides that a mandatory tax be withheld from workers' earnings and be matched by their employers. (Self-employed workers pay both the employer and employee shares of FICA taxes.) When covered workers retire (or are disabled), they draw benefits that are based on the amount they contributed to the fund. The amount of the benefit is directly related to the duration of employment and earnings—people who

have worked longer and earned higher wages receive larger benefits.

Workers can retire as early as age 62 and receive reduced Social Security benefits, or they can wait until full retirement age and receive full benefits. Until 2003 the full retirement age was 65, but beginning that year it began to increase gradually, such that for people born in 1960 or later, retirement age will be 67. A special credit is given to people who delay retirement beyond their full retirement age. This credit, which is a percentage added to the Social Security benefit, varies depending on the retiree's date of birth. Workers who reached full retirement age in 2008 or later can receive a credit of 8% per year.

Table 2.6 shows the relationship between earnings and Social Security benefits. It shows the average indexed monthly earnings (AIME; this is an amount that summarizes a worker's earnings) and the corresponding benefit amounts. Delaying retirement to age 70 yields the highest ration of retirement benefits to the AIME.

Benefits and Beneficiaries

The SSA indicates in "Social Security Basic Facts" that in 2011 the program paid benefits to 55 million people. The majority were older adults—37.9 million retired workers and their dependents, along with 6.4 million survivors of deceased workers, and 10 million disabled workers and their dependents. The Social Security and Medicare Boards of Trustees report in *Status of the Social Security and Medicare Programs: A Summary of the 2011 Annual Reports* (May 5, 2011, http://www.socialsecurity.gov/OACT/TRSUM/) that in 2010, 156 million people with earnings covered by Social Security paid payroll taxes. Social Security income in 2010 was an estimated $677.1 billion. Table 2.7 shows the number of beneficiaries of all the OASDI programs as well as the average monthly benefits that were paid in December 2009, the most recent month for which data were available as of June 2011.

Social Security Amendments of 1977

Ever since 1940, the year that Americans began receiving Social Security checks, monthly retirement benefits have steadily increased, but during the 1970s they soared. Legislation enacted in 1973 provided for automatic cost-of-living adjustments (COLAs) that were intended to prevent inflation from eroding Social Security benefits. The average benefit was indexed (annually adjusted) to keep pace with inflation as reflected by the CPI. COLAs were 9.9% in 1979 and peaked at 14.3% the following year. (See Table 2.8.) These increases threatened the continued financial viability of the entire system and prompted policy makers to reconsider the COLA formula.

TABLE 2.6

Benefit amount for worker with maximum-taxable earnings, 2011

Retirement in Jan.	Retirement at age 62[a]			Retirement at age 65[b]			Retirement at age 70[c]		
		Monthly benefits			Monthly benefits			Monthly benefits	
	AIME	At age 62	In 2011	AIME	At age 65	In 2011	AIME	At age 70	In 2011
1987	$2,205	$666	$1,320	$2,009	$789	$1,562	$1,725	$1,056	$2,092
1988	2,311	691	1,313	2,139	838	1,593	1,859	1,080	2,052
1989	2,490	739	1,350	2,287	899	1,643	2,000	1,063	1,943
1990	2,648	780	1,361	2,417	975	1,701	2,154	1,085	1,893
1991	2,792	815	1,350	2,531	1,022	1,693	2,332	1,163	1,927
1992	2,978	860	1,373	2,716	1,088	1,738	2,470	1,231	1,966
1993	3,154	899	1,395	2,878	1,128	1,750	2,605	1,289	1,998
1994	3,384	954	1,442	3,024	1,147	1,733	2,758	1,358	2,052
1995	3,493	972	1,429	3,219	1,199	1,762	2,896	1,474	2,167
1996	3,657	1,006	1,442	3,402	1,248	1,789	3,012	1,501	2,151
1997	3,877	1,056	1,471	3,634	1,326	1,847	3,189	1,609	2,242
1998	4,144	1,117	1,524	3,750	1,342	1,831	3,348	1,648	2,247
1999	4,463	1,191	1,604	3,926	1,373	1,848	3,496	1,684	2,268
2000	4,775	1,248	1,639	4,161	1,435	1,885	3,707	1,752	2,302
2001	5,126	1,314	1,668	4,440	1,538	1,952	3,912	1,879	2,385
2002	5,499	1,382	1,710	4,770	1,660	2,054	4,165	1,988	2,459
2003	5,729	1,412	1,722	5,099	1,721	2,100	4,321	2,045	2,496
2004	5,892	1,422	1,700	5,457	1,784	2,133	4,532	2,111	2,523
2005	6,137	1,452	1,690	5,827	1,874	2,181	4,786	2,252	2,621
2006	6,515	1,530	1,711	6,058	1,961	2,193	5,072	2,420	2,706
2007	6,852	1,598	1,729	6,229	1,998	2,163	5,406	2,672	2,892
2008	7,260	1,682	1,779	6,479	2,030	2,148	5,733	2,794	2,956
2009	7,685	1,769	1,769	6,861	2,172	2,172	6,090	3,054	3,054
2010	7,949	1,820	1,820	7,189	2,191	2,191	6,450	3,119	3,119
2011	7,928	1,803	1,803	7,579	2,249	2,249	6,683	3,193	3,193

AIME = Average Indexed Monthly Earnings.

[a]Retirement at age 62 is assumed here to be at exact age 62 and 1 month. Such early retirement results in a reduced monthly benefit.

[b]Retirement at age 65 is assumed to be at exact age 65 and 0 months. For retirement in 2003 and later, the monthly benefit is reduced for early retirement. (For people born before 1938, age 65 is the normal retirement age. Normal retirement age will gradually increase to age 67.)

[c]Retirement at age 70 maximizes the effect of delayed retirement credits.

Notes: Initial monthly benefits paid at ages 65 and 70 in 2000–2001 were slightly lower than the amounts shown above because such initial benefits were partially based on a cost-of-living adjustment (COLA) for December 1999 that was originally determined as 2.4 percent based on Consumer Price Indices published by the Bureau of Labor Statistics. Pursuant to Public Law 106-554, however, this COLA is effectively now 2.5 percent, and the above figures reflect the benefit change required by this legislation.

SOURCE: "Worker with Steady Earnings at the Maximum Level since Age 22," in *Workers with Maximum-Taxable Earnings*, U.S. Social Security Administration, Office of the Chief Actuary, October 29, 2010, http://www.socialsecurity.gov/OACT/COLA/examplemax.html (accessed April 7, 2011)

Some legislators felt that indexing vastly overcompensated for inflation, causing relative benefit levels to rise higher than at any previous time in the history of the program. In an attempt to prevent future Social Security benefits from rising to what many considered excessive levels, Congress passed the Social Security Amendments of 1977 to restructure the benefit plan and design more realistic formulas for benefits. Along with redefining COLAs, the 1977 amendments raised the payroll tax slightly, increased the wage base, and reduced benefits.

The 5.8% COLA increase in 2009 more than doubled from the previous year; however, there were no COLAs in 2010 and 2011. Table 2.8 shows how this COLA increase translated into SSI payments between 1975 and 2011.

The Earnings Test

Legislation enacted on January 1, 2000, changed the way in which the amount that beneficiaries could earn while also receiving retirement or survivors benefits was determined. The retirement earnings test applies only to people younger than normal retirement age, which ranges from age 65 to 67, depending on year of birth. Social Security withholds benefits if annual retirement earnings exceed a certain level, called a retirement earnings test exempt amount, for people who have not yet attained normal retirement age. These exempt amounts generally increase annually with increases in the national average wage index.

Table 2.9 shows the exempt amounts between 2000 and 2011. One dollar in Social Security benefits is withheld for every $2 of earnings more than the lower exempt amount. Similarly, $1 in benefits is withheld for every $3 of earnings more than the higher exempt amount.

SUPPLEMENTAL SECURITY INCOME

SSI is designed to provide monthly cash payments to those older, blind, and disabled people who have low incomes. Even though SSI is administered by the SSA, unlike Social Security benefits, SSI benefits are not based on prior work, and the funds come from general tax revenues rather than from Social Security taxes.

In 1972 Congress passed the legislation establishing SSI to replace several state-administered programs and to

TABLE 2.7

Number and average monthly benefit, by type of benefit and race, December 2009

Type of benefit	All races[a] Number	All races[a] Average monthly benefit (dollars)	White Number	White Average monthly benefit (dollars)	Black Number	Black Average monthly benefit (dollars)	Other[b] Number	Other[b] Average monthly benefit (dollars)
Total, OASDI	**52,522,819**	**1,064.40**	**43,547,872**	**1,103.10**	**5,722,458**	**905.30**	**2,864,708**	**798.70**
OASI	42,828,705	1,097.80	36,618,243	1,130.40	3,883,525	942.00	2,065,963	820.40
Retirement benefits	36,419,065	1,117.20	31,491,711	1,143.90	3,022,136	997.20	1,693,075	843.60
Retired workers	33,514,013	1,164.30	29,037,349	1,190.00	2,810,550	1,034.60	1,474,515	912.50
Spouses of retired workers	2,343,601	574.20	2,049,429	596.60	108,781	484.00	169,920	369.10
Children of retired workers	561,451	570.40	404,933	602.60	102,805	517.40	48,640	414.40
Survivor benefits	6,409,640	987.40	5,126,532	1,047.80	861,389	748.20	372,888	715.10
Children of deceased workers	1,921,148	747.40	1,270,359	805.50	426,761	624.50	199,069	630.30
Widowed mothers and fathers	159,870	841.60	111,746	897.30	22,495	714.50	22,295	682.00
Nondisabled widow(er)s	4,090,496	1,123.50	3,572,127	1,155.00	364,057	914.10	136,206	853.70
Disabled widow(er)s	236,480	682.70	171,519	708.60	47,902	605.20	14,669	619.90
Parents of deceased workers	1,646	987.80	781	1,031.00	174	976.40	649	942.20
DI	9,694,114	917.00	6,929,629	958.80	1,838,933	827.80	798,745	742.50
Disabled workers	7,788,013	1,064.30	5,658,054	1,099.00	1,437,673	979.60	589,232	916.00
Spouses of disabled workers	158,122	286.50	121,398	298.70	17,257	257.30	17,071	229.30
Children of disabled workers	1,747,979	317.90	1,150,177	338.70	384,003	285.00	192,442	256.60

OASDI = Old Age, Survivors, and Disability Insurance. OASI = Old Age and Survivors Insurance. DI = Disability Insurance.

Notes: Race and ethnic designations are collected from the form SS-5 (Application for a Social Security Card). For dependents and survivor beneficiaries, race is assumed to be the same as that shown on the SS-5 for the wage earner on whose earnings record the benefit is based.

Through 2008, beneficiaries whose record indicated more than one race were classified as "other." Beginning with 2009, these beneficiaries are classified as persons of unknown race.

[a]Includes 387,781 persons of unknown race.

[b]Includes Asians and Pacific Islanders, American Indians and Alaska Natives, and a subset of the total number of beneficiaries of Hispanic origin. The distribution of beneficiaries among those three groups is not available.

SOURCE: "Table 5.A1. Number and Average Monthly Benefit, by Type of Benefit and Race, December 2009," in *Annual Statistical Supplement, 2010*, U.S. Social Security Administration, February 2011, http://www.socialsecurity.gov/policy/docs/statcomps/supplement/2010/5a.pdf (accessed April 7, 2011)

provide a uniform federal benefit based on uniform eligibility standards. Even though SSI is a federal program, some states provide a supplement to the federal benefit.

In "SSI Federally Administered Payments" (March 2011, http://www.socialsecurity.gov/policy/docs/statcomps/ssi_monthly/2011-02/table02.pdf), the SSA reports that of the 7.7 million people receiving SSI benefits in February 2011, over 2 million were aged 65 years and older. (See Table 2.10.) Even though payments vary by age group, the average monthly benefit received by older adults in February 2011 was $402.80. (See Table 2.11.)

WHAT LIES AHEAD FOR SOCIAL SECURITY?

The Social Security program faces long-range financing challenges that, if unresolved, threaten its solvency (the ability to meet financial obligations on time) in the coming decades. Since the 1980s the program has been collecting more money than it has had to pay out and will continue to do so until 2015. The surplus is not, however, cash that is set aside. Rather, it is loaned to the U.S. Department of the Treasury, which places it in the general revenue pool and is spent as the government sees fit.

According to the SSA, in *The 2010 Annual Report of the Board of Trustees of the Federal Old-Age and Survivors Insurance and Federal Disability Insurance Trust Funds* (August 9, 2010, http://www.socialsecurity.gov/OACT/TR/2010/tr2010.pdf), without changes to the system, the amount of benefits owed will exceed taxes collected in 2015, and Social Security will have to tap into trust funds to pay benefits. The SSA estimates that the trust funds will be depleted in 2037, leaving Social Security unable to pay scheduled benefits in full to older adult retirees and their beneficiaries. The SSA urges immediate action, observing that "solvency of the combined OASDI Trust Funds for the next 75 years could be restored under the intermediate assumptions if increases were made equivalent to immediately and permanently increasing the Social Security payroll tax from its current level of 12.40 percent (for employees and employers combined) to 14.24 percent. Alternatively, changes could be made that are equivalent to reducing scheduled benefits by about 12.0 percent. Other ways of reducing the deficit include transfers of general revenue or some combination of approaches."

To a large extent, demographic changes precipitated this crisis. Social Security is a "pay-as-you-go" program, with the contributions of present workers paying the retirement benefits of those currently retired. The program is solvent (capable of meeting financial obligations) at this time because the number of employees contributing to the system is sufficient. The earliest wave of baby boomers is still in the workforce and at its peak earning years. The large cohort of boomers is funding the smaller cohort of retirees born during the low birthrate cycle of

TABLE 2.8

TABLE 2.9

Social Security Income federal payment amounts, 1975–2011

Year	COLA[a]	Eligible individual	Eligible couple
1975	8.0%	$157.70	$236.60
1976	6.4%	167.80	251.80
1977	5.9%	177.80	266.70
1978	6.5%	189.40	284.10
1979	9.9%	208.20	312.30
1980	14.3%	238.00	357.00
1981	11.2%	264.70	397.00
1982	7.4%	284.30	426.40
1983	7.0%[b]	304.30	456.40
1984	3.5%	314.00	472.00
1985	3.5%	325.00	488.00
1986	3.1%	336.00	504.00
1987	1.3%	340.00	510.00
1988	4.2%	354.00	532.00
1989	4.0%	368.00	553.00
1990	4.7%	386.00	579.00
1991	5.4%	407.00	610.00
1992	3.7%	422.00	633.00
1993	3.0%	434.00	652.00
1994	2.6%	446.00	669.00
1995	2.8%	458.00	687.00
1996	2.6%	470.00	705.00
1997	2.9%	484.00	726.00
1998	2.1%	494.00	741.00
1999	1.3%	500.00	751.00
2000	2.5%[c]	513.00	769.00
2001	3.5%	531.00	796.00
2002	2.6%	545.00	817.00
2003	1.4%	552.00	829.00
2004	2.1%	564.00	846.00
2005	2.7%	579.00	869.00
2006	4.1%	603.00	904.00
2007	3.3%	623.00	934.00
2008	2.3%	637.00	956.00
2009	5.8%	674.00	1,011.00
2010	0.0%	674.00	1,011.00
2011	0.0%	674.00	1,011.00

[a]COLA = Cost-of-living adjustment
[b]The increase effective for July 1983 was a legislated increase.
[c]Originally determined as 2.4 percent based on Consumer Price Indices published by the Bureau of Labor Statistics. Pursuant to Public Law 106-544; however, the COLA is effectively now 2.5 percent.

SOURCE: "SSI Monthly Payment Amounts, 1975–2011," in *SSI Federal Payment Amounts*, U.S. Social Security Administration, Office of the Chief Actuary, October 29, 2010, http://www.socialsecurity.gov/OACT/COLA/SSIamts.html (accessed April 7, 2011)

Annual retirement earnings test exempt amounts, 2000–11

Year	Lower amount[a]	Higher amount[b]
2000	$10,080	$17,000
2001	10,680	25,000
2002	11,280	30,000
2003	11,520	30,720
2004	11,640	31,080
2005	12,000	31,800
2006	12,480	33,240
2007	12,960	34,440
2008	13,560	36,120
2009	14,160	37,680
2010	14,160	37,680
2011	14,160	37,680

[a]Applies in years before the year of attaining normal retirement age (NRA).
[b]Applies in the year of attaining NRA, for months prior to such attainment.

SOURCE: "Annual Retirement Earnings Test Exempt Amounts," in *Exempt Amounts under the Earnings Test*, U.S. Social Security Administration, Office of the Chief Actuary, October 29, 2010, http://www.ssa.gov/OACT/COLA/rtea.html (accessed April 7, 2011)

- Increasing Social Security payroll taxes
- Investing trust funds in securities with potentially higher yields than the government bonds in which they are currently invested
- Increasing income taxes on Social Security benefits

    The ways to reduce expenditures include:

- Reducing initial benefits to retirees
- Raising the retirement age (already slated to rise from 65 to 67 by 2027)
- Lowering COLAs
- Limiting benefits based on beneficiaries' other income and assets

Ensuring the Long-Term Solvency of Social Security Is a Priority

Even though protecting Social Security is vitally important to the nation's retirees and aging baby boomers who will soon retire, some observers believe that actions to secure it may be deferred in favor of other economic priorities, including job creation and reducing the federal deficit. According to the SSA, in the press release "Social Security Board of Trustees: Long-Range Financing Outlook Remains Unchanged" (August 5, 2010, http://www.socialsecurity.gov/pressoffice/pr/trustee10-pr.htm), the SSA commissioner Michael J. Astrue (1956–) said, "The fact that the costs for the program will likely exceed tax revenue this year is not a cause for panic but it does send a strong message that it's time for us to make the tough choices that we know we need to make. I applaud President Obama for his creation of the Deficit Commission so we can start the national discussion needed to ensure that Social Security remains a foundation of economic security for our children and grandchildren."

the Great Depression. As a result, there are still fewer retirees depleting funds than there are workers contributing. The SSA notes that when monthly Social Security benefits began in 1940, a man aged 65 could expect to live an average of about 12.7 additional years; by 2015 a typical 65-year-old man is likely to live on average another 18.5 years. (See Table 2.12.)

Saving Social Security

There are three basic ways to resolve Social Security's financial problems: raise taxes, cut benefits, or make Social Security taxes earn more by investing the money. It is most likely that restoring Social Security's long-term financial balance will require a combination of increased revenues and reduced expenditures. The ways to increase revenues include:

TABLE 2.10

Social Security Income recipients by eligibility category and age, February 2010–February 2011

Month	Total	Eligibility category		Age		
		Aged	Blind and disabled	Under 18	18–64	65 or older
2010						
February	7,739,526	1,190,016	6,549,510	1,209,641	4,494,957	2,034,928
March	7,776,667	1,188,361	6,588,306	1,215,280	4,527,056	2,034,331
April	7,774,363	1,187,763	6,586,600	1,212,272	4,527,929	2,034,162
May	7,800,015	1,188,088	6,611,927	1,221,863	4,542,049	2,036,103
June	7,837,400	1,189,172	6,648,228	1,227,732	4,570,209	2,039,459
July	7,831,046	1,188,489	6,642,557	1,222,497	4,568,938	2,039,611
August	7,892,141	1,191,591	6,700,550	1,236,644	4,609,849	2,045,648
September	7,898,515	1,191,611	6,706,904	1,235,499	4,616,558	2,046,458
October	7,905,492	1,190,909	6,714,583	1,233,911	4,624,389	2,047,192
November	7,947,752	1,192,920	6,754,832	1,245,812	4,650,603	2,051,337
December	7,912,266	1,183,853	6,728,413	1,239,269	4,631,507	2,041,490
2011						
January	7,956,362	1,188,872	6,767,490	1,249,294	4,657,382	2,049,686
February	8,002,032	1,189,858	6,812,174	1,258,533	4,691,651	2,051,848

Note: Data are for the end of the specified month.

SOURCE: "Table 2. Recipients, by Eligibility Category and Age, February 2010–February 2011," in *SSI Monthly Statistics, February 2011*, U.S. Social Security Administration, Office of the Chief Actuary, March 2011, http://www.socialsecurity.gov/policy/docs/statcomps/ssi_monthly/2011-02/table02.pdf (accessed April 7, 2011)

HOW AMERICANS WOULD SAVE SOCIAL SECURITY. Americans are not completely confident that they will receive Social Security benefits when they retire. Table 2.13 shows that in 2010, 69% of people aged 55 years and older said they will receive Social Security benefits when they retire, whereas just 32% of those aged 35 to 54 years and 22% of people aged 18 to 34 years shared this optimism.

In *Americans Look to Wealthy to Help Save Social Security* (July 29, 2010, http://www.gallup.com/poll/141611/Americans-Look-Wealthy-Help-Save-Social-Security.aspx), Jeffrey M. Jones of the Gallup Organization indicates that of six potential approaches to address the challenge of funding Social Security in 2010, the majority of Americans favored measures that would only have an impact on the wealthy. About two-thirds (67%) of Americans said high-income workers should pay Social Security taxes on all of their wages and 63% favored limiting benefits for wealthy retirees. (See Table 2.14.) In contrast, 35% of Americans supported increasing the age of eligibility for full benefits and 34% supported increasing Social Security taxes for all workers.

TABLE 2.11

Average monthly SSI (Supplemental Security Income) payment, by eligibility category, age, and source of payment, February 2010–February 2011

[In dollars]

Month	Total	Eligibility category		Age		
		Aged	Blind and disabled	Under 18	18–64	65 or older
			All sources			
2010						
February	496.70	396.80	514.80	592.90	513.40	402.10
March	498.30	398.20	516.40	596.60	514.70	403.20
April	499.50	398.50	517.70	601.60	515.30	403.60
May	498.60	398.50	516.60	596.90	514.80	403.60
June	497.50	398.30	515.30	592.40	514.10	403.60
July	499.20	398.50	517.20	600.50	514.80	403.70
August	498.90	398.60	516.80	598.20	514.60	403.80
September	498.30	398.60	516.00	594.20	514.60	403.90
October	499.70	398.40	517.70	600.20	515.50	403.80
November	499.30	398.40	517.10	596.90	515.30	403.90
December	500.70	399.80	518.50	596.70	517.20	405.10
2011						
January	499.70	398.00	517.60	598.30	515.50	403.70
February	497.60	396.80	515.20	590.80	514.10	402.80
			Federal payments			
2010						
February	474.40	355.40	494.90	583.40	492.40	363.90
March	476.10	356.70	496.60	587.20	493.70	365.00
April	477.20	357.00	497.90	592.20	494.30	365.40
May	476.40	357.00	496.90	587.40	493.90	365.50
June	475.40	356.90	495.60	583.00	493.20	365.40
July	477.10	357.00	497.60	591.10	494.00	365.50
August	476.80	357.10	497.20	588.70	493.80	365.60
September	476.20	357.00	496.40	584.80	493.80	365.70
October	477.70	356.80	498.20	590.80	494.80	365.60
November	477.30	356.80	497.60	587.50	494.60	365.70
December	478.70	358.30	498.90	587.30	496.50	367.00
2011						
January	477.90	356.80	498.30	589.00	495.10	365.80
February	475.90	355.50	495.90	581.60	493.60	364.90
			State supplements			
2010						
February	124.60	134.60	121.20	51.10	130.90	136.00
March	124.70	134.70	121.30	51.10	130.90	136.10
April	124.70	134.70	121.30	51.10	130.90	136.10
May	124.50	134.70	121.20	51.00	130.80	136.10
June	124.40	134.70	121.00	50.90	130.60	136.00
July	124.40	134.70	121.00	51.00	130.60	136.00
August	124.30	134.70	120.90	50.90	130.50	136.00
September	124.30	134.70	120.90	50.80	130.40	136.10
October	124.30	134.80	120.90	50.80	130.40	136.10
November	124.20	134.70	120.70	50.70	130.30	136.00
December	124.30	134.90	120.80	50.80	130.40	136.20
2011						
January	124.70	134.30	121.60	50.90	131.40	135.90
February	124.50	134.20	121.40	50.80	131.10	135.80

Note: Data are for the end of the specified month and exclude retroactive payments.

SOURCE: "Table 7. Average Monthly Payment, by Eligibility Category, Age, and Source of Payment, February 2010–February 2011," in *SSI Monthly Statistics, March 2009*, U.S. Social Security Administration, Office of Policy, March 2011, http://www.socialsecurity.gov/policy/docs/statcomps/ssi_monthly/2011-02/table07.pdf (accessed April 7, 2011)

TABLE 2.12

Life expectancy at birth and at age 65, selected years 1940–2085

Calendar year	Intermediate				Low-cost				High-cost			
	At birth[a]		At age 65[b]		At birth[a]		At age 65[b]		At birth[a]		At age 65[b]	
	Male	Female	Male	Female	Male	Female	Male	Female	Male	Female	Male	Female
1940	70.1	76.1	12.7	14.7	69.8	75.8	12.7	14.7	70.4	76.6	12.7	14.7
1945	71.9	77.7	13.0	15.4	71.4	77.2	13.0	15.4	72.4	78.4	13.0	15.4
1950	73.1	79.0	13.1	16.2	72.5	78.2	13.1	16.2	73.9	79.9	13.1	16.2
1955	73.8	79.6	13.1	16.7	73.0	78.6	13.1	16.7	74.9	80.9	13.1	16.7
1960	74.6	80.1	13.2	17.4	73.5	78.9	13.2	17.4	76.0	81.6	13.2	17.4
1965	75.5	80.7	13.5	18.0	74.1	79.3	13.5	18.0	77.2	82.5	13.5	18.0
1970	76.6	81.5	13.8	18.5	75.0	79.8	13.8	18.5	78.7	83.7	13.8	18.5
1975	77.6	82.3	14.2	18.7	75.7	80.3	14.2	18.7	79.9	84.7	14.2	18.7
1980	78.5	83.0	14.7	18.8	76.3	80.8	14.7	18.8	81.2	85.6	14.7	18.8
1985	79.2	83.6	15.4	19.0	76.8	81.2	15.3	19.0	82.2	86.5	15.4	19.0
1990	79.9	84.1	15.9	19.2	77.2	81.5	15.9	19.2	83.1	87.3	16.0	19.3
1995	80.6	84.7	16.5	19.5	77.6	81.8	16.4	19.3	84.1	88.0	16.6	19.6
1996	80.7	84.8	16.7	19.5	77.7	81.9	16.6	19.4	84.3	88.2	16.8	19.7
1997	80.8	84.9	16.8	19.6	77.7	81.9	16.7	19.4	84.4	88.3	16.9	19.8
1998	80.9	85.0	16.9	19.6	77.8	82.0	16.8	19.4	84.6	88.4	17.1	19.9
1999	81.0	85.1	17.1	19.7	77.9	82.0	16.9	19.5	84.7	88.6	17.3	20.0
2000	81.1	85.2	17.2	19.8	77.9	82.1	17.0	19.5	84.9	88.7	17.4	20.1
2001	81.2	85.2	17.3	19.9	78.0	82.1	17.1	19.6	85.0	88.8	17.6	20.2
2002	81.3	85.3	17.4	19.9	78.0	82.1	17.1	19.6	85.2	88.9	17.7	20.3
2003	81.4	85.4	17.5	20.0	78.1	82.2	17.2	19.6	85.3	89.0	17.9	20.4
2004	81.5	85.5	17.6	20.1	78.1	82.2	17.3	19.7	85.5	89.2	18.0	20.6
2005	81.6	85.5	17.7	20.1	78.1	82.2	17.3	19.7	85.6	89.3	18.1	20.7
2006	81.7	85.6	17.8	20.2	78.2	82.3	17.4	19.7	85.8	89.4	18.3	20.8
2007	81.8	85.7	17.9	20.2	78.3	82.3	17.4	19.7	85.9	89.5	18.4	20.9
2008	81.9	85.8	18.0	20.3	78.3	82.4	17.5	19.8	86.1	89.7	18.6	21.0
2009	82.0	85.9	18.0	20.4	78.4	82.4	17.5	19.8	86.2	89.8	18.7	21.1
2010	82.1	86.0	18.1	20.4	78.4	82.5	17.5	19.8	86.4	89.9	18.9	21.2
2015	82.6	86.4	18.5	20.8	78.7	82.7	17.7	19.9	87.1	90.5	19.5	21.9
2020	83.0	86.8	18.8	21.1	78.9	82.9	17.8	20.1	87.7	91.1	20.2	22.5
2025	83.4	87.1	19.2	21.4	79.1	83.1	18.0	20.2	88.4	91.6	20.8	23.1
2030	83.8	87.5	19.5	21.7	79.4	83.3	18.1	20.3	89.0	92.1	21.4	23.7
2035	84.2	87.8	19.8	22.0	79.6	83.4	18.2	20.4	89.5	92.6	22.0	24.2
2040	84.6	88.1	20.1	22.3	79.8	83.6	18.4	20.6	90.1	93.0	22.5	24.8
2045	85.0	88.5	20.4	22.6	80.0	83.8	18.5	20.7	90.6	93.5	23.0	25.3
2050	85.3	88.8	20.7	22.9	80.2	84.0	18.6	20.8	91.1	93.9	23.5	25.7
2055	85.7	89.1	21.0	23.2	80.4	84.1	18.7	20.9	91.6	94.4	24.0	26.2
2060	86.0	89.3	21.2	23.5	80.6	84.3	18.9	21.0	92.1	94.8	24.5	26.6
2065	86.3	89.6	21.5	23.7	80.8	84.5	19.0	21.2	92.6	95.2	24.9	27.0
2070	86.7	89.9	21.8	24.0	81.0	84.6	19.1	21.3	93.0	95.6	25.3	27.4
2075	87.0	90.2	22.0	24.2	81.2	84.8	19.2	21.4	93.5	96.0	25.8	27.8
2080	87.3	90.4	22.3	24.5	81.4	84.9	19.3	21.5	93.9	96.4	26.2	28.2
2085	87.6	90.7	22.5	24.7	81.6	85.1	19.5	21.6	94.3	96.8	26.6	28.6

[a]Cohort life expectancy at birth for those born on January 1 of the calendar year is based on a combination of actual and estimated death rates for birth years 1940 through 2006. For birth years after 2006, these values are based solely on estimated death rates.
[b]Age 65 cohort life expectancy for those attaining age 65 on January 1 of calendar years 1940 though 2006 are either based on actual death rates or on a combination of actual and estimated death rates. After 2006 these values are based solely on estimated death rates.

SOURCE: "Table V.A4. Cohort Life Expectancy," in *The 2010 Annual Report of the Board of Trustees of the Federal Old-Age and Survivors Insurance and Federal Disability Insurance Trust Funds*, U.S. Social Security Administration, Office of the Chief Actuary, August 2010, http://www.socialsecurity.gov/OACT/TR/2010/tr2010.pdf (accessed April 7, 2011)

TABLE 2.13

Americans' expectations about whether they will receive Social Security benefits, by age group, 2010

DO YOU THINK THE SOCIAL SECURITY SYSTEM WILL BE ABLE TO PAY YOU A BENEFIT WHEN YOU RETIRE?

Asked of nonretirees, by age

	% yes	% no	% doesn't apply (vol.)	% no opinion
18 to 34	22	76	0	2
35 to 54	32	66	1	1
55+	69	26	4	2

(vol.) = Volunteered response

SOURCE: Frank Newport, "Do You Think the Social Security System Will Be Able to Pay You a Benefit When You Retire?" in *Six in 10 Workers Hold No Hope of Receiving Social Security*, The Gallup Organization, July 29, 2010, http://www.gallup.com/poll/141449/Six-Workers-Hold-No-Hope-Receiving-Social-Security.aspx (accessed April 7, 2011). Copyright © 2011 by The Gallup Organization. Reproduced by permission of The Gallup Organization.

TABLE 2.14

Public opinion on how to save Social Security, 2010

ASSUMING THERE WOULD BE NO CHANGE IN SOCIAL SECURITY BENEFITS FOR THOSE WHO ARE NOW AGE 55 OR OLDER, DO YOU THINK EACH OF THE FOLLOWING WOULD BE A GOOD IDEA OR A BAD IDEA TO ADDRESS CONCERNS WITH THE SOCIAL SECURITY SYSTEM?

	% Good idea	% Bad idea
Requiring higher-income workers to pay Social Security taxes on all of their wages	67	30
Limiting benefits for wealthy retirees	63	35
Further reducing the total amount of benefits a person would receive if they retired early	44	53
Reducing retirement benefits for people who are currently under age 55	39	57
Increasing the age at which people are eligible to receive full retirement benefits	35	63
Increasing Social Security taxes for all workers	34	64

SOURCE: Jeffrey M. Jones, "Assuming There Would Be No Change in Social Security Benefits for Those Who Are Now Age 55 or Older, Do You Think Each of the Following Would Be a Good Idea or a Bad Idea to Address Concerns with the Social Security System?" in *Americans Look to Wealthy to Help Save Social Security*, The Gallup Organization, July 29, 2010, http://www.gallup.com/poll/141611/Americans-Look-Wealthy-Help-Save-Social-Security.aspx (accessed April 7, 2011). Copyright © 2011 by The Gallup Organization. Reproduced by permission of The Gallup Organization.

CHAPTER 3

LIVING ARRANGEMENTS OF THE OLDER POPULATION

The vast majority of older Americans live independently in the community—they are not institutionalized in facilities such as nursing homes or retirement homes. According to the Administration on Aging, in *Justification of Estimates for Appropriations Committees: Fiscal Year 2011* (February 2010, http://www.aoa.gov/aoaroot/about/Budget/DOCS/AoA_CJ_FY_2011.pdf), approximately 1.7 million of the 39 million people aged 65 years and older in the United States lived in nursing homes in 2010. An additional 5% lived in some type of senior housing, which frequently offered supportive services for residents. Saadia Greenberg of the Administration on Aging notes in *A Profile of Older Americans: 2010* (2011, http://www.aoa.gov/aoaroot/aging_statistics/Profile/2010/docs/2010profile.pdf) that even though the overall numbers of older Americans living in nursing homes was small— nearly 1.6 million (4.1%) people who were 65 years and older in 2009—the percentage of older adults in nursing homes increased dramatically with advancing age, from 0.9% of 65- to 74-year-olds, to 3.5% of 75- to 84-year-olds, to 14.3% of those aged 85 years and older.

The living arrangements of older adults are important because they are closely associated with their health, well-being, and economic status. For example, older adults who live alone are more likely to live in poverty than those who live with their spouse or other family members. Older adults living alone may also be socially isolated, and their health may suffer because there are no family members or others nearby to serve as caregivers.

LIVING WITH A SPOUSE, OTHER RELATIVES, OR ALONE

Table 3.1 shows that 24.8 million out of 117.2 million (21.1%) households were headed by a person aged 65 years or older in 2009. It also shows a consistent increase in the number of households headed by people aged 75 years and older, from 8.4 million in 1990 to 12 million in 2009.

According to Greenberg, more than half (54.8%) of community-dwelling, civilian (noninstitutionalized— people who are not in the U.S. military, school, jail, or mental health facilities) older adults lived with their spouse in 2009. Significantly more older men than women—72% (11.4 million) of older men, compared to 42% (8.7 million) of older women—lived with their spouse. (See Figure 3.1.) This disparity occurs because women usually live longer than men, are generally younger than the men they marry, and are far less likely to remarry after the death of a spouse, largely because there are relatively few available older men. Among adults aged 75 years and older, less than one-third (28.2%) of women were living with their spouse in 2009.

In addition, the proportion of older adults living with their spouse decreased with age. U.S. Census Bureau data reveal that in 2009, 13.2 million (64.5%) adults aged 65 to 74 years lived with their spouse, compared to 7.5 million (43.4%) adults aged 75 years and older. (See Table 3.2.)

Greenberg reports that in 2009, 11.4 million (30.1%) community-dwelling older adults lived alone, including 8.3 million women and 3 million men. They represented 38.8% of older women and 18.7% of older men. The percentage of older adults who live alone rises with age. Half (49%) of women aged 75 years and older lived alone in 2009. Table 3.3 shows that the percentage of women aged 75 years and older living alone rose from 37% in 1970 to 54% in 1990 but decreased to 50.1% in 2008. During this same period the percentage of older men aged 75 years and older living alone remained relatively stable until 2005, and then dropped slightly to 21.5% in 2008.

Race and ethnicity play a role in the living arrangements of older adults. In 2009 older African-American and non-Hispanic white adults were more likely to live alone than older Hispanic and Asian-American adults— 1.2 million (36.5%) older African-American and 9.9 million (31%) older non-Hispanic white adults, compared to

TABLE 3.1

Households by age of householder and size of household, selected years 1990–2009

[In millions]

Age of householder and size of household	1990	2000	2005	2009 Total[a]	2009 White[b]	2009 Black[b]	2009 Asian[b]	2009 Hispanic[c]	2009 Non-Hispanic White[c]
Total	**93.3**	**104.7**	**113.3**	**117.2**	**95.3**	**14.6**	**4.6**	**13.4**	**82.9**
Age of householder:									
15 to 24 years old	5.1	5.9	6.7	6.4	4.9	1.0	0.3	1.2	3.9
25 to 29 years old	9.4	8.5	9.2	9.5	7.4	1.3	0.4	1.6	6.0
30 to 34 years old	11.0	10.1	10.1	9.8	7.6	1.4	0.6	1.7	6.0
35 to 44 years old	20.6	24.0	23.2	22.2	17.3	3.1	1.1	3.4	14.2
45 to 54 years old	14.5	20.9	23.4	24.6	20.0	3.1	1.0	2.5	17.6
55 to 64 years old	12.5	13.6	17.5	19.9	16.5	2.3	0.7	1.6	15.0
65 to 74 years old	11.7	11.3	11.5	12.8	10.9	1.3	0.4	0.9	10.1
75 years old and over	8.4	10.4	11.6	12.0	10.7	1.0	0.2	0.6	10.1
One person	23.0	26.7	30.1	31.7	25.5	4.6	0.9	2.2	23.4
Male	9.0	11.2	12.8	13.8	(NA)	(NA)	(NA)	(NA)	(NA)
Female	14.0	15.5	17.3	17.9	(NA)	(NA)	(NA)	(NA)	(NA)
Two persons	30.1	34.7	37.4	39.2	33.3	4.0	1.3	3.1	30.4
Three persons	16.1	17.2	18.3	18.6	14.6	2.5	1.0	2.6	12.2
Four persons	14.5	15.3	16.4	16.1	12.9	1.9	0.9	2.6	10.5
Five persons	6.2	7.0	7.2	7.1	5.9	1.0	0.3	1.7	4.3
Six persons	2.1	2.4	2.5	2.6	2.0	0.4	0.1	0.6	1.3
Seven persons or more	1.3	1.4	1.4	1.5	1.1	0.2	0.1	0.5	0.7

NA = Not available.

[a]Includes other races, not shown separately.

[b]Beginning with the 2003 Current Population Survey (CPS), respondents could choose more than one race. 2005 and 2009 data represent persons who selected this race group only and exclude persons reporting more than one race. The CPS in prior years only allowed respondents to report one race group.

[c]Hispanic persons may be any race.

SOURCE: "Table 62. Households by Age of Householder and Size of Household: 1990 to 2009," in *Statistical Abstract of the United States: 2011*, 130th ed., U.S. Census Bureau, http://www.census.gov/compendia/statab/2011/tables/11s0062.pdf (accessed April 8, 2011)

564,000 (20.8%) older Hispanic and 180,000 (13.9%) older Asian-American adults. (See Table 3.2.)

Among the racial and ethnic groups, in 2008 older Hispanic, African-American, and Asian-American women were the most likely to live with relatives other than a spouse (31%, 32%, and 32%, respectively). (See Figure 3.2.) The living arrangements of older men broke down somewhat differently along racial and ethnic lines than did those of older women. Older African-American men were nearly three times more likely to live alone than were older Asian-American men (30% versus 11%). Older Hispanic men were the most likely of any group of older men to live with relatives other than a spouse (15%) or to live with nonrelatives (5%).

Multigenerational Households

The Census Bureau reports in the press release "Grandparents Day 2010: Sept. 12" (July 12, 2010, http://www.census.gov/newsroom/releases/pdf/cb10ff-1_grandparent.pdf) that in 2010 approximately 2.6 million grandparents were responsible for most of the basic needs of their grandchildren. These grandparents represented 41% of all grandparents whose grandchildren lived with them. The 2008 American Community Survey finds that 6.4 million grandparents were living in the same household with their grandchildren under the age of 18 years and that

40.7% of these grandparents were responsible for their grandchildren. (See Table 3.4.) In "The Return of the Multi-generational Family Household" (March 18, 2010, http://pewsocialtrends.org/2010/03/18/the-return-of-the-multi-generational-family-household/), the Pew Research Center notes that the economic recession (which lasted from late 2007 to mid-2009), job losses, and foreclosures sparked a resurgence of multigenerational households in 2009. Pew finds that Hispanics (22%), African-Americans (23%), and Asian-Americans (25%) were more likely than whites (13%) to live in multigenerational households. Pew also explains that the large generation of baby boomers (people born between 1946 and 1964) offers older adults about 50% more adult children than either the previous or subsequent generation with whom they can live should the need arise. The baby-boom generation consists of approximately 75 million Americans and is the largest generation in U.S. history. By contrast, the preceding generation, dubbed the silent generation (1925–1945), and the subsequent generation, called Generation X (1965–1976), each number less than 50 million.

While much of the rise in multigenerational households may be attributable to the growing older population and economic considerations, some family members simply want to be closer to one another. The visibility of multigenerational families rose when 71-year-old Marian

FIGURE 3.1

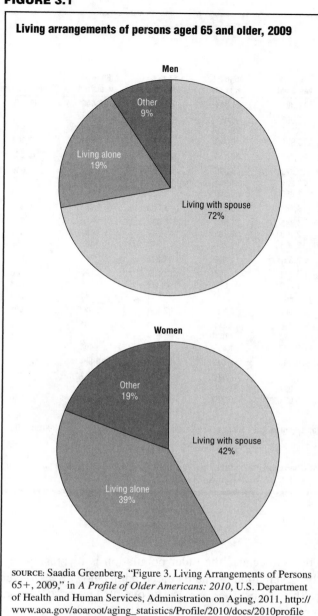

Living arrangements of persons aged 65 and older, 2009

Men

Other 9%
Living alone 19%
Living with spouse 72%

Women

Other 19%
Living with spouse 42%
Living alone 39%

SOURCE: Saadia Greenberg, "Figure 3. Living Arrangements of Persons 65+, 2009," in *A Profile of Older Americans: 2010*, U.S. Department of Health and Human Services, Administration on Aging, 2011, http://www.aoa.gov/aoaroot/aging_statistics/Profile/2010/docs/2010profile.pdf (accessed April 2, 2011)

Robinson (1937–) moved into the White House with her daughter, Michelle Obama (1964–), her granddaughters, Malia (1998–) and Sasha (2001–), and her son-in-law, President Barack Obama (1961–).

HOMELESSNESS

The U.S. Department of Housing and Urban Development's Office of Community Planning and Development notes in *The 2009 Annual Homeless Assessment Report to Congress* (June 2010, http://www.huduser.org/publications/pdf/5thHomelessAssessmentReport.pdf) that between 2007 and 2009 there was a slight increase in the percentage of homeless people over the age of 50 years. Table 3.5 shows that homeless individuals were much

more likely to be less than age 62 (age 62 is the federal housing program's beginning point for defining "elderly"). Older Americans may be less likely than younger Americans to be homeless because social programs such as Social Security, Supplemental Security Income (SSI), Medicare (a medical insurance program for older adults and people with disabilities), and senior housing act to prevent homelessness. Nonetheless, those older adults who become homeless spend longer periods in emergency shelters than younger homeless people. Table 3.6 shows that the percentage of adults aged 51 years and older who stayed more than 180 days in emergency shelters rose from 34.9% in 2007 to 40.5% in 2009.

Among the concerns about homelessness are the inherent health-related issues. The relationship between homelessness, health, and illness is complex. Some health problems precede homelessness and contribute to it, whereas others are consequences of homelessness; in addition, homelessness often complicates access and adherence to treatment. For example, mental illness or substance abuse (dependency on alcohol or drugs) may limit a person's ability to work, leading to poverty and homelessness. Without protection from the cold, rain, and snow, exposure to weather may result in illnesses such as bronchitis or pneumonia. Homelessness also increases exposure to crime and violence, which could lead to trauma and injuries.

There are many reasons that homeless people experience difficulties gaining access to health care services and receiving needed medical care. Lacking essentials such as transportation to medical facilities, money to pay for care, and knowledge about how to qualify for health insurance and where to obtain health care services makes seeking treatment complicated and frustrating. Psychological distress or mental illness may prevent homeless people from attempting to obtain needed care, and finding food and shelter may take precedence over seeking treatment. Even when the homeless do gain access to medical care, following a treatment plan, filling prescriptions, and scheduling follow-up appointments often present insurmountable challenges to those who do not have a telephone number, address, or safe place to store medications. Furthermore, because chronic (long-term) homelessness can cause or worsen a variety of health problems, homeless people may not live to old age with the same frequency as their age peers who are not homeless.

LONG-TERM CARE, SUPPORTIVE HOUSING, AND OTHER RESIDENTIAL ALTERNATIVES

Spouses and other relatives are still the major caretakers of older, dependent members of American society. However, the number of people aged 65 years and older living in long-term care facilities such as nursing homes

TABLE 3.2

Living arrangements by age and selected characteristics, 2009

[In thousands]

Living arrangement	Total	15 to 19 years old	20 to 24 years old	25 to 34 years old	35 to 44 years old	45 to 54 years old	55 to 64 years old	65 to 74 years old	75 years old and over
Total[a]	240,032	21,219	20,610	40,487	41,301	44,361	34,278	20,403	17,372
Alone	31,657	144	1,395	3,795	3,698	5,499	5,750	4,657	6,721
With spouse	121,689	153	2,851	19,189	26,672	28,766	23,349	13,162	7,547
With other persons	86,686	20,922	16,364	17,503	10,931	10,096	5,179	2,584	3,104
White[b]	194,288	16,218	16,053	31,684	32,755	36,154	28,721	17,419	15,283
Alone	25,462	98	1,069	2,825	2,673	4,320	4,591	3,839	6,046
With spouse	104,036	129	2,450	16,079	22,226	24,334	20,304	11,663	6,853
With other persons	64,791	15,994	12,534	12,780	7,856	7,500	3,826	1,917	2,384
Black[b]	28,906	3,349	2,971	5,375	5,168	5,284	3,530	1,854	1,375
Alone	4,645	29	224	652	745	913	904	642	535
With spouse	8,979	11	211	1,450	2,130	2,385	1,629	780	381
With other persons	15,282	3,309	2,536	3,273	2,293	1,986	997	432	459
Asian[b]	10,773	806	852	2,155	2,327	1,962	1,373	753	544
Alone	854	8	59	196	175	131	107	92	88
With spouse	6,353	7	108	1,169	1,730	1,529	1,042	516	253
With other persons	3,566	791	685	790	422	302	224	145	203
Hispanic origin[c]	33,440	3,878	3,610	8,126	7,028	5,121	2,961	1,627	1,090
Alone	2,195	24	120	348	359	411	369	301	263
With spouse	15,055	62	700	3,764	4,263	3,072	1,824	918	453
With other persons	16,190	3,792	2,790	4,014	2,406	1,638	768	408	374
Non-Hispanic white[b, c]	163,299	12,671	12,773	24,171	26,196	31,383	25,968	15,884	14,253
Alone	23,443	79	972	2,502	2,345	3,946	4,246	3,557	5,795
With spouse	89,879	73	1,794	12,524	18,227	21,460	18,595	10,788	6,418
With other persons	49,977	12,519	10,007	9,145	5,624	5,977	3,127	1,539	2,040

[a]Includes other races and non-Hispanic groups, not shown separately.
[b]Beginning 2005, data represent persons who selected this race group only and exclude persons reporting more than one race. The Current Population Survey (CPS) in 1990 and 2000 only allowed respondents to report one race group.
[c]Persons of Hispanic origin may be any race.

SOURCE: "Table 58. Living Arrangements of Persons 15 Years Old and over by Selected Characteristics: 2009," in *Statistical Abstract of the United States: 2011*, 130th ed., U.S. Census Bureau, http://www.census.gov/compendia/statab/2011/tables/11s0058.pdf (accessed April 8, 2011)

TABLE 3.3

Population aged 65 and over living alone, by age group and sex, selected years 1970–2008

Year	Men		Women	
	65–74	75 and over	65–74	75 and over
		Percent		
1970	11.3	19.1	31.7	37.0
1980	11.6	21.6	35.6	49.4
1990	13.0	20.9	33.2	54.0
2000	13.8	21.4	30.6	49.5
2003	15.6	22.9	29.6	49.8
2004	15.5	23.2	29.4	49.9
2005	16.1	23.2	28.9	47.8
2006	16.9	22.7	28.5	48.0
2007	16.7	22.0	28.0	48.8
2008	16.3	21.5	29.1	50.1

Reference population: These data refer to the civilian noninstitutionalized population.

SOURCE: "Table 5b. Population Age 65 and over Living Alone, by Age Group and Sex, Selected Years 1970–2008," in *Older Americans 2010: Key Indicators of Well-Being*, Federal Interagency Forum on Aging-Related Statistics, July 2010, http://www.agingstats.gov/agingstatsdotnet/Main_Site/Data/2010_Documents/Docs/OA_2010.pdf (accessed April 2, 2011)

is rising, because the older population is increasing rapidly. Even though many older adults now live longer, healthier lives, the increase in overall length of life has amplified the need for long-term care facilities and supportive housing.

Growth of the home health care industry during the early 1990s only slightly slowed the increase in the numbers of Americans entering nursing homes. Supportive housing (assisted living, congregate housing, and continuing care retirement communities) offers alternatives to nursing home care. The overarching goal of supportive housing is to enable older adults to receive needed assistance while retaining as much independence as possible.

There are three broad classes of supportive housing for older adults. The smallest and most affordable options usually house 10 or fewer older adults and are often in homes in residential neighborhoods. Residents share bathrooms, bedrooms, and living areas. These largely unregulated facilities are alternately known as board-and-care

FIGURE 3.2

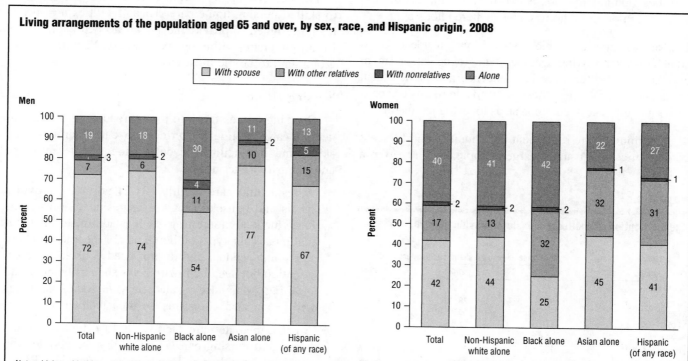

Living arrangements of the population aged 65 and over, by sex, race, and Hispanic origin, 2008

Notes: Living with other relatives indicates no spouse present. Living with nonrelatives indicates no spouse or other relatives present. The term "non-Hispanic white alone" is used to refer to people who reported being white and no other race and who are not Hispanic. The term "black alone" is used to refer to people who reported being black or African American and no other race, and the term "Asian alone" is used to refer to people who reported only Asian as their race. The use of single-race populations in this report does not imply that this is the preferred method of presenting or analyzing data. The U.S. Census Bureau uses a variety of approaches.
Reference population: These data do not include the noninstitutionalized group quarters population.

SOURCE: "Living Arrangements of the Population Age 65 and over, by Sex and Race and Hispanic Origin, Percent Distribution 2008," in *Older Americans 2010: Key Indicators of Well-Being*, Federal Interagency Forum on Aging-Related Statistics, July 2010, http://www.agingstats.gov/agingstatsdotnet/Main_Site/Data/2010_Documents/Docs/OA_2010.pdf (accessed April 2, 2011)

TABLE 3.4

Grandparents living with grandchildren, by race and sex, 2008

[In thousands]

Race, Hispanic origin, and sex	Grandparents living with own grandchildren, total	Grandparents responsible for grandchildren		
		Total	30 to 59 years old	60 years old and over
Grandparents living with own grandchildren under 18 years old (1,000)	6,432	2,618	1,754	864
Percent distribution				
Total	**100.0**	**100.0**	**100.0**	**100.0**
White alone	62.1	63.6	63.4	64.2
Black or African American alone	19.1	23.7	23.9	23.3
American Indian and Alaska Native alone	1.4	1.9	1.9	1.8
Asian alone	7.5	3.1	2.1	5.1
Native Hawaiian and other Pacific Islander alone	0.3	0.2	0.2	0.3
Some other race alone	7.9	5.6	6.5	3.8
Two or more races	1.7	1.8	2.0	1.5
Hispanic origin*	23.5	18.6	20.4	14.8
White alone, not Hispanic	47.5	51.6	50.5	54.0
Male	35.6	37.5	35.4	41.9
Female	64.4	62.5	64.6	58.1

*Persons of Hispanic origin may be any race.
Notes: Covers both grandparents living in own home with grandchildren present and grandparents living in grandchildren's home. The American Community Survey universe includes the household population and the population living in institutions, college dormitories, and other group quarters. Based on a sample and subject to sampling variability.

SOURCE: "Table 70. Grandparents Living with Grandchildren by Race and Sex, 2008," in *Statistical Abstract of the United States: 2011*, 130th ed., U.S. Census Bureau, http://www.census.gov/compendia/statab/2011/tables/11s0070.pdf (accessed April 8, 2011)

facilities, domiciliary care, personal care homes, adult foster care, senior group homes, and sheltered housing.

Residential care facilities, assisted living residences, and adult congregate living facilities tend to be larger, more expensive, and offer more independence and privacy than board-and-care facilities. Most offer private rooms or apartments as well as large common areas for activities and meals.

Continuing care retirement communities and life care communities are usually large complexes that offer a comprehensive range of services from independent living to skilled nursing home care. These facilities are specifically designed to provide nearly all needed care, except for hospital care, within one community. Facilities in this group tend to be the most costly.

Nursing Homes

Nursing homes fall into three broad categories: residential care facilities, intermediate care facilities, and skilled nursing facilities. Each provides a different range and intensity of services:

- A residential care facility (RCF) normally provides meals and housekeeping for its residents, plus some basic medical monitoring, such as administering medications. This type of home is for people who are fairly independent and do not need constant medical attention but need help with tasks such as laundry and cleaning. Many RCFs also provide social activities and recreational programs for their residents.

- An intermediate care facility (ICF) offers room and board and nursing care as necessary for people who can no longer live independently. Much like RCFs, ICFs provide exercise and social programs, and some even offer physical therapy and rehabilitation programs.

- A skilled nursing facility (SNF) provides around-the-clock nursing care, plus on-call physician coverage. SNFs are for patients who need intensive nursing care, as well as services such as occupational therapy, physical therapy, respiratory therapy, and rehabilitation.

TABLE 3.5

Age distribution of sheltered homeless individuals, 2007–09

Characteristic	Percentage of all sheltered homeless adults		
	2007	2008	2009
Age*			
18 to 30	26.2%	28.0%	28.7%
31 to 50	52.7%	50.9%	49.2%
51 to 61	17.4%	17.6%	18.5%
62 and older	3.8%	3.5%	3.6%
Veteran (adults)*	13.2%	11.6%	11.1%
Disabled (adults)*	37.1%	42.8%	37.8%

*Age is calculated based on a person's first time in shelter during the covered time period. A child is defined as a person age 17 or under, and an adult is defined as a person age 18 or older.

SOURCE: "Exhibit 4-6. Change in the Ages and Veteran and Disabled Status of Sheltered Homeless Adults, 2007–2009," in *The 2009 Annual Homeless Assessment Report to Congress*, U.S. Department of Housing and Urban Development, Office of Community Planning and Development, June 2010, http://www.huduser.org/publications/pdf/5thHomelessAssessmentReport.pdf (accessed April 8, 2011)

TABLE 3.6

Individuals who stayed in emergency shelters more than 180 days, by gender, race, and age group, 2007–09

Characteristics	Percentage of long-stayers 2007	Percentage of long-stayers 2008	Percentage of long-stayers 2009
Gender			
Male	73.5%	77.0%	72.1%
Female	26.5%	23.0%	27.9%
Race/ethnicity			
White, non-Hispanic/Latino	31.9%	34.8%	36.9%
White, Hispanic/Latino	11.0%	12.8%	8.1%
Black or African American	49.9%	45.4%	45.2%
Other racial groups	7.3%	7.1%	9.8%
Age[a]			
18 to 30	12.6%	16.7%	11.3%
31 to 50	50.3%	51.9%	47.0%
51 and older	34.9%	30.6%	40.5%
Veteran (adults only)[b]	—	15.4%	14.3%
Disabled (adults only)[b]	—	39.7%	34.6%

[a]Age categories do not sum to 100 percent because of the small numbers of people homeless alone who were under 18 years of age.
[b]Because of the very different rates of missing data between 2007 and 2008 for veteran and disability status, the comparison to 2007 is not shown for these characteristics.

SOURCE: "Exhibit 4-14. Individuals Who Stayed in Emergency Shelter More Than 180 Days, 2007–2009," in *The 2009 Annual Homeless Assessment Report to Congress*, U.S. Department of Housing and Urban Development, Office of Community Planning and Development, June 2010, http://www.huduser.org/publications/pdf/5thHomelessAssessmentReport.pdf (accessed April 8, 2011)

NURSING HOME RESIDENTS. The National Center for Health Statistics reports in *Health, United States, 2010* (February 2011, http://www.cdc.gov/nchs/data/hus/hus10.pdf) that there were 15,700 certified nursing homes in 2009. The center also notes that these facilities had an occupancy rate of 82.2% and housed over 1.4 million residents. (See Table 3.7.) The highest occupancy rates were in Minnesota (91.3%), Maine (91.2%), Rhode Island (91.2%), and North Dakota (91.1%). The lowest occupancy rates were in Oregon (62.6%), Oklahoma (65.6%), Utah (66.8%), and Missouri (67.9%).

TABLE 3.7

Residents and occupancy rates of nursing homes, by state, 1995–2009

[Data are based on a census of certified nursing facilities]

State	Residents				Occupancy rate*			
	1995	2000	2008	2009	1995	2000	2008	2009
United States	1,479,550	1,480,076	1,412,540	1,401,718	84.5	82.4	82.9	82.2
Alabama	21,691	23,089	23,205	23,186	92.9	91.4	86.5	86.3
Alaska	634	595	616	633	77.9	72.5	85.0	88.4
Arizona	12,382	13,253	12,201	11,908	76.6	75.9	76.1	74.1
Arkansas	20,823	19,317	17,753	17,801	69.5	75.1	72.5	72.9
California	109,805	106,460	103,487	102,747	78.3	80.8	84.4	84.4
Colorado	17,055	17,045	16,464	16,288	85.7	84.2	82.5	82.0
Connecticut	29,948	29,657	26,819	26,253	91.2	91.4	90.4	89.6
Delaware	3,819	3,900	3,999	4,256	80.6	79.5	82.1	85.9
District of Columbia	2,576	2,858	2,437	2,531	80.3	92.9	92.1	91.5
Florida	61,845	69,050	71,833	71,657	85.1	82.8	87.5	87.5
Georgia	35,933	36,559	35,276	34,899	94.3	91.8	88.7	87.3
Hawaii	2,413	3,558	3,840	3,841	96.0	88.8	90.2	90.6
Idaho	4,697	4,640	4,522	4,419	81.7	75.1	74.9	71.6
Illinois	83,696	83,604	76,282	75,673	81.1	75.5	74.9	74.1
Indiana	44,328	42,328	39,536	39,190	74.5	74.6	69.2	68.2
Iowa	27,506	29,204	26,292	25,814	68.8	78.9	78.1	77.5
Kansas	25,140	22,230	19,301	19,029	83.8	82.1	74.2	74.0
Kentucky	20,696	22,730	23,233	23,318	89.1	89.7	90.2	89.7
Louisiana	32,493	30,735	25,875	25,077	86.0	77.9	71.7	70.4
Maine	8,587	7,298	6,591	6,485	92.9	88.5	91.0	91.2
Maryland	24,716	25,629	25,243	25,025	87.0	81.4	86.4	86.0
Massachusetts	49,765	49,805	43,684	43,227	91.3	88.9	88.6	88.0
Michigan	43,271	42,615	40,224	40,306	87.5	84.1	85.0	85.3
Minnesota	41,163	38,813	31,056	30,073	93.8	92.1	91.0	91.3
Mississippi	15,247	15,815	16,246	16,294	94.9	92.7	88.6	88.3
Missouri	39,891	38,586	37,510	37,588	75.7	70.4	68.2	67.9
Montana	6,415	5,973	5,137	5,077	89.0	77.9	72.5	72.0
Nebraska	16,166	14,989	12,899	12,627	89.0	83.8	79.6	77.9
Nevada	3,645	3,657	4,724	4,699	91.2	65.9	83.2	82.2
New Hampshire	6,877	7,158	6,953	6,941	92.8	91.3	90.1	89.7
New Jersey	40,397	45,837	45,946	45,788	91.9	87.8	89.9	89.5
New Mexico	6,051	6,503	5,695	5,569	86.8	89.2	84.0	82.4
New York	103,409	112,957	110,940	109,867	96.0	93.7	92.2	90.2
North Carolina	35,511	36,658	38,025	37,587	92.7	88.6	86.9	85.2
North Dakota	6,868	6,343	5,847	5,777	96.4	91.2	91.4	91.1
Ohio	79,026	81,946	81,395	80,185	73.9	78.0	87.5	85.9
Oklahoma	26,377	23,833	19,518	19,209	77.8	70.3	65.5	65.6
Oregon	11,673	9,990	8,113	7,708	84.1	74.0	65.0	62.6
Pennsylvania	84,843	83,880	79,710	80,562	91.6	88.2	90.7	90.7
Rhode Island	8,823	9,041	7,955	8,040	91.8	88.0	89.7	91.2
South Carolina	14,568	15,739	17,004	17,148	87.3	86.9	90.5	89.9
South Dakot	7,926	7,059	6,528	6,476	95.5	90.0	99.0	93.9
Tennessee	33,929	34,714	32,288	31,876	91.5	89.9	87.4	85.7
Texas	89,354	85,275	90,385	90,534	72.6	68.2	71.3	70.2
Utah	5,832	5,703	5,456	5,358	82.1	74.5	68.5	66.8
Vermont	1,792	3,349	2,992	2,980	96.2	89.5	91.6	90.5
Virginia	28,119	27,091	28,279	28,392	93.5	88.5	88.6	88.8
Washington	24,954	21,158	18,760	18,188	87.7	81.7	84.1	82.5
West Virginia	10,216	10,334	9,710	9,613	93.7	90.5	89.1	88.7
Wisconsin	43,998	38,911	32,325	31,619	90.2	83.9	86.5	86.7
Wyoming	2,661	2,605	2,431	2,380	87.7	83.5	81.2	80.0

*Percentage of beds occupied (number of nursing home residents per 100 nursing home beds).

Note: Annual numbers of nursing homes, beds, and residents are based on a 15-month OSCAR (Online Survey Certification and Reporting Database) reporting cycle. Data for additional years are available.

SOURCE: Adapted from "Table 117. Nursing Homes, Beds, Residents, and Occupancy Rates, by State: United States, Selected Years 1995–2009," in *Health, United States 2010: With Special Feature on Death and Dying*, National Center for Health Statistics, 2011, http://www.cdc.gov/nchs/data/hus/hus10.pdf (accessed April 8, 2011). Non-government data from Cowles Research Group.

TABLE 3.8

Medicare-certified providers, selected years 1975–2008

[Data are compiled from various Centers for Medicare & Medicaid Services data systems]

Providers or suppliers	1975	1980	1985	1990	1996	1999	2003	2005	2007	2008
					Number of providers or suppliers					
Skilled nursing facilities	—	5,052	6,451	8,937	—	14,913	14,838	15,006	15,054	15,032
Home health agencies	2,242	2,924	5,679	5,730	8,437	7,857	6,928	8,090	9,024	9,407
Clinical Lab Improvement Act Facilities	—	—	—	—	159,907	171,018	176,947	196,296	206,065	210,872
End-stage renal disease facilities	—	999	1,393	1,937	2,876	3,787	4,309	4,755	5,095	5,317
Outpatient physical therapy	117	419	854	1,195	2,302	2,867	2,961	2,962	2,915	2,781
Portable X-ray	132	216	308	443	555	666	641	553	550	547
Rural health clinics	—	391	428	551	2,775	3,453	3,306	3,661	3,781	3,757
Comprehensive outpatient rehabilitation facilities	—	—	72	186	307	522	587	634	539	476
Ambulatory surgical centers	—	—	336	1,197	2,112	2,894	3,597	4,445	4,964	5,174
Hospices	—	—	164	825	1,927	2,326	2,323	2,872	3,255	3,346

—Data not available.

Notes: Data for 1975–1990 are as of July 1. Data for 1996–1999 and 2004–2008 are as of December 31. Data for 2001, 2002, and 2003 are as of December 2000, December 2001, and December 2002, respectively. Data for additional years are available.

SOURCE: "Table 119. Medicare-Certified Providers and Suppliers: United States, Selected Years 1975–2008," in *Health, United States 2010: With Special Feature on Death and Dying*, National Center for Health Statistics, 2011, http://www.cdc.gov/nchs/data/hus/hus10.pdf (accessed April 8, 2011)

The number of nursing homes has increased dramatically since 1980. Table 3.8 shows that the number of SNFs certified by Medicare grew from 5,052 in 1980 to 15,032 in 2008. In "Best Nursing Homes: Behind the Rankings" (*U.S. News & World Report*, February 7, 2011), Avery Comarow indicates that over 3.2 million Americans spent at least part of 2011 in a nursing home in the United States.

DIVERSIFICATION OF NURSING HOMES. To remain competitive with home health care and the increasing array of alternative living arrangements for older adults, many nursing homes have begun to offer alternative services and programs. The National Nursing Home Survey (http://www.cdc.gov/nchs/nnhs.htm), a continuing series of national sample surveys of nursing homes, their residents, and their staff, finds that in 2004 (the most recent survey as of June 2011) more than half of all nursing homes offered specialty units or programs such as hospice (end-of-life) care, pain management, and skin wound treatment programs. According to the Alzheimer's Association, in *2011 Alzheimer's Disease Fact and Figures* (2011, http://www.alz.org/downloads/Facts_Figures_2011.pdf), in 2010 about 5% of nursing home beds were in special units for people suffering from Alzheimer's disease or another dementia. (Alzheimer's disease is a progressive form of dementia that is characterized by impairment of memory and intellectual functions.)

Matt Sedensky observes in "For Nursing Homes, 'It's Diversify or Die'" (Associated Press, September 7, 2010) that many nursing homes are expanding their service offerings to include home-based services such as delivered meals, transportation, and assisted living to increase revenue. Elinor Ginzler, an expert in long-term care with the advocacy group AARP, asserts that "nursing homes are waking up more and more to the reality

that their old model of doing business is not going to hold up in the 21st century."

Collaborating with other providers of health care services or on their own, many nursing homes also offer services such as adult day care and visiting nurse services for people who still live at home. Other programs include respite plans that allow caregivers who need to travel for business or vacation to leave an older relative in the nursing home temporarily.

THE PIONEER NETWORK. In response to concerns about quality of life and quality of care issues in nursing homes, leaders in nursing home reform efforts from around the United States established the Pioneer Network in 2000 as a forum for the culture change movement. The culture change in this instance was a focus on person-directed values that affirm and support each person's individuality and abilities and that apply to elders and to those who work with them. The Pioneer Network explains in "Mission, Vision and Values" (2011, http://www.pioneernetwork.net/AboutUs/Values/) that it commits to the following values:

- Know each person

- Each person can and does make a difference

- Relationship is the fundamental building block of a transformed culture

- Respond to spirit, as well as mind and body

- Risk taking is a normal part of life

- Put person before task

- All elders are entitled to self-determination wherever they live

- Community is the antidote to institutionalization

- Do unto others as you would have them do unto you

- Promote the growth and development of all

- Shape and use the potential of the environment in all its aspects: physical, organizational, psycho/social/spiritual

- Practice self-examination, searching for new creativity and opportunities for doing better

- Recognize that culture change and transformation are not destinations but a journey, always a work in progress

INNOVATION AND CULTURE CHANGE IMPROVE THE QUALITY OF LIFE FOR RESIDENTS. Industry observers frequently decry the care that is provided in nursing homes. The media publicizes instances of elder abuse (neglect, exploitation, or mistreatment of older adults) and other quality of care issues. However, several organizations have actively sought to develop models of health service delivery that improve the clinical care and quality of life for nursing home residents.

The Innovations Exchange program (http://www.innovations.ahrq.gov/) by the Agency for Healthcare Research and Quality (AHRQ) offers profiles of nursing home innovations and assessments of the effectiveness of these innovations in terms of improving residents' quality of life and satisfaction. The program also examines nursing homes' ability to attract and retain staff and their financial performance. By sharing and publicizing these innovations, the AHRQ aims to improve the quality of nursing home care.

For example, in "Nursing Homes Create Home-Like, Resident-Focused Environment and Culture, Leading to Better Quality and Financial Performance, Higher Resident Satisfaction, and Lower Staff Turnover" (January 12, 2011, http://www.innovations.ahrq.gov/content.aspx?id=2621), the AHRQ describes the efforts of seven nursing homes in Texas to cultivate a culture change to help nursing homes "create a more homelike, resident-focused environment and culture that encourages spontaneity and close relationships between staff and residents and gives residents more choices and control over their lives."

Besides some physical modifications of the nursing homes to create more homelike dining rooms and bathrooms, the initiative created "neighborhoods" within the facility by naming specific hallways and groups of rooms. The nursing homes encouraged communal neighborhood activities, such as decorating the area or holding neighborhood celebrations of residents' birthdays. Nursing home staff, who were formerly rotated throughout the nursing home, were permanently assigned to a specific neighborhood so they could get to know the residents and develop ongoing relationships. Staff members were also given more scheduling flexibility, to better accommodate individual residents' preferences. At each nursing home a "quality

of life specialist" visited with residents daily to assess and improve their comfort and quality of life.

The AHRQ reports that this initiative resulted in improved quality of care as measured by key quality measures such as fewer reports of pain and fewer pressure ulcers (injuries to the skin and underlying tissue usually over a bony prominence that result from continuous pressure or friction in the area) as well as fewer formal complaints. Resident and family member satisfaction ratings rose from 59.5% in 2006 to 65% in 2007. Likewise, staff satisfaction increased between 2006 and 2007, from 58% to 75%. Staff retention also improved: the annual turnover rate of nursing assistants declined from 143% in 2005 to 96% in 2008.

The initiative also improved the nursing homes' financial performance. Between 2005 and 2007 the nursing homes' average census grew from 825 to 859, and this 10% increase meant the facilities were operating very close to their capacity. Higher census counts and reduced staff turnover also significantly improved the nursing homes' net revenues, which tripled during this period.

THE EDEN ALTERNATIVE. Developed in 1991 by William Thomas, the Eden Alternative is a movement that, like the Pioneer Network, seeks to transform nursing homes. The Eden Alternative strives to create nursing homes that are rich and vibrant human habitats where plants, children, and animals bring life-enriching energy to residents. The philosophy of the Eden Alternative is that providing a stimulant-rich environment will help minimize the hopelessness that is often felt by nursing home residents. Nursing homes based on this model are being opened across the country.

By providing gardenlike settings that are filled with plants and encouraging relationships with children and pets, the Eden Alternative hopes to improve the human spirit and dispel loneliness. The 10 principles (2011, http://www.edenalt.org/about/our-10-principles.html) of an Eden Alternative nursing home are:

1. The three plagues of loneliness, helplessness, and boredom account for the bulk of suffering among our Elders.

2. An Elder-centered community commits to creating a human habitat where life revolves around close and continuing contact with plants, animals, and children. It is these relationships that provide the young and old alike with a pathway to a life worth living.

3. Loving companionship is the antidote to loneliness. Elders deserve easy access to human and animal companionship.

4. An Elder-centered community creates opportunity to give as well as receive care. This is the antidote to helplessness.

5. An Elder-centered community imbues daily life with variety and spontaneity by creating an environment in which unexpected and unpredictable

interactions and happenings can take place. This is the antidote to boredom.

6. Meaningless activity corrodes the human spirit. The opportunity to do things that we find meaningful is essential to human health.

7. Medical treatment should be the servant of genuine human caring, never its master.

8. An Elder-centered community honors its Elders by de-emphasizing top-down bureaucratic authority, seeking instead to place the maximum possible decision-making authority into the hands of the Elders or into the hands of those closest to them.

9. Creating an Elder-centered community is a never-ending process. Human growth must never be separated from human life.

10. Wise leadership is the lifeblood of any struggle against the three plagues. For it, there can be no substitute.

Thomas's initiatives also include the Green House Project. This effort encompasses the design and construction of small group homes for older adults, built to a residential scale that situates necessary clinical care within a social model in which primacy is given to the older adults' quality of life. The goal of this social model is to provide frail older adults with an environment that promotes autonomy, dignity, privacy, and choice.

Green Houses are designed to feel more like homes than typical long-term care institutions and to blend easily into their community or surroundings. The first Green House in the nation opened in May 2003 in Tupelo, Mississippi, developed by United Methodist Senior Services of Mississippi. The Green House Project (http://www.the greenhouseproject.org/findhome) indicates that in 2011 more than 99 Green Houses were operating on 43 campuses in 27 states, with most featuring bright décor, gardens, pets, and on-site day care for children.

Assisted Living

Assisted living arose to bridge a gap in long-term care. It is intended to meet the needs of older adults who wish to live independently in the community but require some of the services (e.g., housekeeping, meals, transportation, and assistance with other activities of daily living) that are provided by a nursing home. (Activities of daily living are generally considered to include eating, bathing, dressing, getting to and using the bathroom, getting in or out of bed or a chair, and mobility.) Assisted living offers a flexible array of services that enable older adults to maintain as much independence as they can, for as long as possible.

Because assisted living refers to a concept and philosophy as opposed to a regulated provider of health services such as a hospital or SNF, there is no uniform description of the services an assisted living residence must offer, and as a result there is considerable variation among assisted living

facilities. These residences are regulated on a state level, and each state has its own definition of what constitutes an assisted living facility and its own set of rules that govern them. The AHRQ defines in "Assisted Living Defined" (January 14, 2011, http://www.ahrq.gov/RESEARCH/ ltcscan/ltc3.htm) the term *assisted living* as "a type of residential long-term care setting known by nearly 30 different names" that includes "24-hour service and oversight, services that meet scheduled and unscheduled needs, and care/services that promote independence, with an emphasis on dignity, autonomy, choice, privacy, and home-like environment."

In *Assisted Living Federation of America 2009: Core Principles* (April 2009, http://www.alfa.org/images/alfa/ PDFs/PublicPolicy/Core_Principles_2009.pdf), the Assisted Living Federation of America, the largest national association dedicated to operating assisted living communities for older adults, explains that "the goal of assisted living is to both provide resident-centered care, and provide that care in a residential setting. The philosophy provides residents freedom of choice, independence, and the opportunity to live, aging with dignity, privacy and respect. In contrast to other long term care options, Assisted Living embraces quality of life as well as quality of care, and supports the [residents'] decision to live and die in the place they call home."

Assisted living residences may be located on the grounds of retirement communities or in nursing homes, or they may be freestanding residential facilities. They vary in size and location as well as in services. Some are high-rise apartment complexes, whereas others are converted private homes. Most facilities contain between 25 and 120 units, which vary in size from one room to a full apartment.

The MetLife Mature Market Institute explains in *Market Survey of Long-Term Care Costs: The 2010 MetLife Market Survey of Nursing Home, Assisted Living, Adult Day Services, and Home Care Costs* (October 2010, http://www.metlife .com/assets/cao/mmi/publications/studies/2010/mmi-2010-market-survey-long-term-care-costs.pdf) that "nearly 1 million people live in approximately 39,500 assisted living residences in the U.S." A few key findings by the MetLife report include:

- More than two-thirds (68%) of assisted living facilities provided care for residents with Alzheimer's disease and other dementias in 2010.

- The average age of residents was 86.9 years old.

- The average length of stay was about 29.3 months.

Assisted living licensing regulations vary from state to state. Most states require staff certification and training and all assisted living facilities must comply with local building codes and fire safety regulations.

BOARD-AND-CARE FACILITIES. Board-and-care facilities were the earliest form of assisted living. In *Licensed Board and Care Homes: Preliminary Findings from the 1991 National Health Provider Inventory* (April 11, 1994, http://aspe.hhs.gov/daltcp/reports/licbchom.htm), Robert F. Clark et al. define the term *board-and-care homes* as "nonmedical community-based facilities that provide protective oversight and/or personal care in addition to meals and lodging to one or more residents with functional or cognitive limitations." Typically, board-and-care residents have their own bedrooms and bathrooms or share them with one other person, whereas other living areas are shared.

Even though many board-and-care facilities offer residents safe, homelike environments and attentive caregivers, there have been many well-publicized instances of fraud and abuse. Many observers attribute the variability in quality of these facilities to the fact that they are entirely unregulated in many states and as a result receive little oversight.

In an attempt to stem abuses, the federal government passed the Keys Amendment in 1978. Under the terms of this legislation, residents living in board-and-care facilities that fail to provide adequate care are subject to reduced SSI payments. This move was intended to penalize substandard board-and-care operators, but advocates for older adults contend that it actually penalizes the SSI recipients and that it has not reduced reports of abuse. With the 1992 reauthorization of the Older Americans Act of 1965, Congress provided for long-term care ombudsman programs that are designed to help prevent the abuse, exploitation, and neglect of residents in long-term care facilities such as board-and-care residences and nursing homes. Paid and volunteer ombudsmen monitor facilities and act as advocates for the residents.

COSTS OF ASSISTED LIVING. The cost of assisted living varies based on geography, unit size, and the services needed. According to the MetLife Mature Market Institute, in *Market Survey of Nursing Home*, the median (the middle value—half are higher and half are lower) monthly amount in 2010 was $3,048, up 11% from 2009. Most assisted living facilities charge monthly rates and some require long-term lease arrangements.

The MetLife Mature Market Institute report considers the cost for assisted living communities based on the number of services included in their base rates. Communities that included five or fewer services were "basic" and had an average monthly cost of $3,048, those providing six to nine services were "standard" and had an average monthly cost of $3,239, and those providing 10 or more services in their base rates were "inclusive" and had an average monthly cost of $3,477.

Residents or their families generally pay for assisted living using their own financial resources. Some health insurance programs or long-term care insurance policies reimburse for specific health-related care provided by assisted living facilities, and some state and local governments offer subsidies for rent or services for low-income older adults. Others may provide subsidies in the form of an additional payment for those who receive SSI or Medicaid (a federal and state health care program for people below the poverty level).

Continuing Care Retirement Communities

Continuing care retirement communities (CCRCs), also known as life care communities, offer a continuum of care (independent living, assisted living, and nursing home care) in a single facility or on common grounds. The goal of CCRCs is to enable residents to age in place (remaining in their own home rather than relocating to assisted living facilities or other supportive housing). When residents become ill or disabled, for example, they do not have to relocate to a nursing home, because health care services are available on the CCRC campus.

Like assisted living facilities, CCRCs vary in location, design, and amenities. They range from urban high rises to semirural campuses and from 100 to over 1,000 residents. Most include common dining rooms, activity and exercise areas, indoor and outdoor recreation areas, and swimming pools.

Typically, residents are required to pay an entrance fee and a fixed monthly fee in return for housing, meals, personal care, recreation, and nursing services. Many CCRCs offer other payment options, including both entrance fee and fee-for-service (paid for each visit, procedure, or treatment delivered) arrangements. In the past entrance fees were nonrefundable; however, by 2011 most newer CCRCs had instituted refundable or partially refundable entrance fees.

CCRCs may be operated by private, not-for-profit, and/or religious organizations. Entrance fees in these communities vary substantially, from $20,000 to $500,000, and monthly maintenance fees range from $600 to $2,000, depending on the size of the facility and the extent of services. With few exceptions, none of the costs of CCRCs are covered by government or private insurance. Paula Span reports in "C.C.R.C. Fees: Prepare to Be Bewildered" (*New York Times*, December 3, 2009) that in 2009 entrance fees ranged from a low of $43,000 for a studio in Missouri to a high of $496,000 for a three-bedroom villa in Oregon.

Cohousing and Shared Housing

Older adults may share living quarters to reduce expenses, share household and home maintenance responsibilities, and gain companionship. Many choose to share the same homes in which they raised their families, because these houses are often large enough to accommodate more than one or two people. Shared housing is often called cohousing, but the terms are not exactly the same.

Most shared housing consists of a single homeowner taking a roommate to share living space and expenses. Shared housing can also include households with three or more roommates and family-like cooperatives in which large groups of people live together. In contrast, cohousing usually refers to planned or intentional communities of private dwellings with shared common areas that include dining rooms, meeting rooms, recreation facilities, and lounges. Shared housing and cohousing are cost-effective alternatives for those who wish to remain in their own home and for older adults who cannot afford private assisted living or CCRCs.

The cohousing concept originated in Denmark during the 1960s and spread to the United States during the 1980s. According to the Cohousing Association of the United States (http://www.cohousing.org/directory), in 2011 there were 242 cohousing communities in various stages of development in 38 states. Cohousing participants are involved in planning the community and maintaining it, and most cohousing groups make their decisions by consensus.

Shared housing or intergenerational cohousing may also meet the needs of younger as well as older people. Along with the benefits of cost-sharing and companionship, home sharers and cohousing residents may exchange services—for example, help with household maintenance in exchange for babysitting.

Elder Cottage Housing Opportunity Units

Elder cottage housing opportunity (ECHO) units, or "granny flats," are small, freestanding, removable housing units that are located on the same lot as a single-family house. Another name used by local zoning authorities is accessory apartments or units. Accessory apartments are self-contained second living units built into or attached to an existing single-family dwelling. They are private, generally smaller than the primary unit, and usually contain one or two bedrooms, a bathroom, a sitting room, and a kitchen.

Generally, families construct ECHO units and accessory apartments for parents or grandparents so that the older adults can be nearby while maintaining their independence. Existing zoning laws and concerns about property values are obstacles to the construction of ECHO units, but as this alternative becomes more popular, local jurisdictions may be pressured to allow multifamily housing in neighborhoods that traditionally have had only single-family homes.

According to Tim Newcomb, in "Need Extra Income? Put a Cottage in Your Backyard" (*Time*, May 28, 2011), accessory dwelling units are appearing in communities across the country, most notably in Seattle, Washington; Portland, Oregon; Berkeley, California; Denver, Colorado; and Burlington, Vermont. Newcomb indicates that the units cost about $100 per square foot to construct and that they are generally between 400 and 800 square feet (37 and 74 square m) in size. Interest in the units comes from adult

children moving back onto family property, behind the family home; homeowners who choose to rent their home and relocate into a smaller dwelling adjacent to their home; and older adults who wish to live independently but close to family members or others whom they might rely on for assistance.

Retirement Communities

Developers such as the industry leader Del Webb (a division of Pulte Homes) have created and constructed communities and even entire small "cities" exclusively for older adults. Examples include the Sun City communities in Arizona, Florida, and Texas. The Arizona and Florida communities opened during the 1960s and the Texas community in 1996.

In 2011 Del Webb (http://www.delwebb.com/index .aspx) boasted over 50 communities in 20 states. Homes in most of these properties were available only to those families in which at least one member was 55 years or older, and no one under the age of 19 years was allowed to reside permanently. Sun City communities offer clubs, golf courses, social organizations, fitness clubs, organized travel, and recreational complexes. Medical facilities are located nearby.

Housing Slump Imperils Older Adults and Limits Their Mobility

Even though many older adults and baby boomers aspire to relocate to CCRCs or purchase new homes in active retirement communities, it is likely that only those with considerable financial resources will be able to do so. The decline in residential real estate prices, which began in 2006 and continued throughout 2011, made it difficult for older adults to sell their homes. Besides losing equity in their homes as prices declined, many older adults had also seen their retirement assets erode. Even though retirement accounts had generally rebounded by early 2011, the recession worried older adults, prompting many to forgo plans to relocate. As a result, plans to relocate were usually postponed.

According to Janna Herron and Derek Kravitz, in "Home Price Declines Deepen in Major US Markets" (Associated Press, March 29, 2011), in 2011 homes in many major markets across the United States declined to 10-year record lows. The median price of a home in the United States, which peaked above $230,000 in 2006, had fallen to $157,200 in April 2011. Declining home prices may pose the greatest threat to older adults with fixed incomes because they depend on their home equity to help finance their spending.

The National Association of Home Builders notes in the press release "55+ Housing Index Ends 2010 in Slump" (February 10, 2011, http://www.nahb.org/news _details.aspx?sectionID=1843&newsID=12148) that the market of buyers aged 55 years and older for single-family homes declined throughout 2010. Older adults who in the past might have purchased a new home in anticipation of retirement are no longer able to do so because their present homes have declined in value or remain unsold.

In "Housing Slump Changing Options for Older Americans" (Tribune Media Service, March 9, 2009), Mark Miller indicates that Larry Minnix, the chief executive officer of the American Association of Homes and Services for the Aging (now renamed LeadingAge), observes that because applications to CCRCs are declining, "some are suspending or postponing entry fees. Others are providing bridge loans or retaining real estate specialists to help people prepare and sell their homes. Everyone is trying to get creative in providing help."

OWNING AND RENTING A HOME

In the press release "Residential Vacancies and Homeownership in the Fourth Quarter 2010" (January 31, 2011, http://www.census.gov/hhes/www/housing/hvs/qtr410/files/q410press.pdf), the Census Bureau notes that the overall homeownership rate in the fourth quarter of 2010 was 66.5%, down slightly from the highest rate of 69.2% in the fourth quarter of 2004. In 2010, 81.6% of adults aged 65 to 69 years, 82.4% of those aged 70 to 74 years, and 78.9% of adults aged 75 years and older owned their own home. (See Table 3.9.)

Older householders are more likely to spend more than one-fourth of their income on housing costs than other age groups. Greenberg reports that in 2009, 48% of older adults devoted more than a quarter of their income to housing costs—42% of homeowners and 70% of renters. In 2009 the median value of homes owned by older adults was $150,000, but because the median purchase price of these homes was just $49,000, 65% of older homeowners had no mortgage debt—they owned their home free and clear.

Renters generally pay a higher percentage of their income for housing than do homeowners. Unlike most homeowners, who pay fixed monthly mortgage payments, renters often face annual rent increases. Many older adult renters living on fixed incomes are unprepared to pay these increases. Homeowners also benefit from their home equity and can borrow against it in times of financial need. In contrast, renters do not build equity and do not get a return on their investment. Also, mortgage payments are tax deductible, whereas rent payments are not.

The Subprime Mortgage and Loan Crisis Endangers Older Adults

Subprime mortgages and loans were designed to extend credit to high-risk borrowers—people with poor credit ratings. To compensate for these risks, subprime mortgages have higher interest rates—a subprime loan is always more expensive than a conventional loan made to a borrower with excellent credit. Many older adults were sold subprime loans when they applied for home equity

loans. Sharon Hermanson of the AARP Public Policy Institute reports in "The Subprime Market: Wealth Building or Wealth Stripping for Older Person" (June 2007, http://assets.aarp.org/rgcenter/consume/m_6_mortgage.pdf) that in 2007 one out of every five subprime mortgages ended in foreclosure and that borrowers aged 65 years and older were three times more likely to hold a subprime loan than borrowers under the age of 35 years.

STRATEGIC DEFAULTS. Faced with job losses, declining home values, or mounting medical bills, some older homeowners choose to walk away from their mortgages. Called strategic default, this practice, which was once considered as shameful as filing for bankruptcy, is no longer as stigmatized and is occurring more frequently among older adults. For example, the Nevada Association of Realtors finds in "The Face of Foreclosure: An Analysis of the Nevada Foreclosure Crisis" (January 2011, http://faceofforeclosure.com/NVAR-11-FOF-Report-vONLINE.pdf) that in 2011 a quarter of foreclosures in Nevada were strategic defaults and that 30% of older homeowners said they had entered into strategic default.

Reverse Mortgages

To supplement their retirement income or to pay for health care, many older Americans turn to reverse mortgages. Reverse mortgages allow older homeowners to convert some of their home equity into cash, making it possible for them to avoid selling their home.

With a traditional mortgage homeowners make monthly payments to the lender. In a reverse mortgage the lender pays the homeowner in monthly installments and in most cases no repayment is due until the homeowner dies, sells the house, or moves permanently. Reverse mortgages help homeowners who are house-rich (have considerable equity in their home) but cash-poor stay in their home and still meet their financial obligations.

Sale/Leaseback with Life Tenancy

Another option for older homeowners is a sale/leaseback in which the homeowner gives up ownership of a home and becomes a renter. The former homeowner frequently requests life tenancy—retaining the right to live in the house as a renter for the rest of his or her life. The buyer pays the former homeowner in monthly installments and is responsible for property taxes, insurance, maintenance, and repairs.

Renting Is Often Unaffordable

Megan DeCrappeo et al. of the National Low Income Housing Coalition document in *Out of Reach 2010: Renters in the Great Recession, the Crisis Continues* (June 2010, http://www.nlihc.org/oor/oor2010/oor2010pub.pdf) income and rental housing cost data for the 50 states, the District of Columbia, and Puerto Rico. For each area, the researchers calculate the income that is needed to be able to afford the

TABLE 3.9

Homeownership rates, by age of householder, 1982–2010

	1982	1983	1984	1985	1986	1987	1988	1989	1990	1991	1992	1993	1993¹r	1994	1995	1996
United States, total	64.8	64.6	64.5	63.9	63.8	64.0	63.8	63.9	63.9	64.1	64.1	64.5	64.0	64.0	64.7	65.4
Less than 25 years	19.3	18.8	17.9	17.2	17.2	16.0	15.8	16.6	15.7	15.3	14.9	15.0	14.8	14.9	15.9	18.0
25 to 29 years	38.6	38.3	38.6	37.7	36.7	36.4	35.9	35.3	35.2	33.8	33.6	34.0	33.6	34.1	34.4	34.7
30 to 34 years	57.1	55.4	54.8	54.0	53.6	53.5	53.2	53.2	51.8	51.2	50.5	51.0	50.8	50.6	53.1	53.0
35 to 39 years	67.6	66.5	66.1	65.4	64.8	64.1	63.6	63.4	63.0	62.2	61.4	62.1	61.8	61.2	62.1	62.1
40 to 44 years	73.0	72.8	72.3	71.4	70.5	70.8	70.7	70.2	69.8	69.5	69.1	69.0	68.6	68.2	68.6	69.0
45 to 49 years	76.0	75.3	74.6	74.3	74.1	74.6	74.4	74.1	73.9	73.7	74.2	73.9	73.7	73.8	73.7	74.4
50 to 54 years	78.8	78.8	78.4	77.5	78.1	77.8	77.1	77.2	76.8	76.1	76.2	77.1	77.2	76.8	77.0	77.2
55 to 59 years	80.0	80.1	80.1	79.2	80.0	80.0	79.3	79.1	78.8	79.5	79.3	78.8	78.9	78.4	78.8	79.4
60 to 64 years	80.1	79.8	79.9	79.9	79.8	80.4	79.8	80.1	79.8	80.5	81.2	80.9	80.9	80.1	80.3	80.7
65 to 69 years	77.9	78.7	79.3	79.5	79.4	79.5	80.0	80.0	80.0	81.4	80.8	80.6	80.7	80.6	81.0	82.4
70 to 74 years	75.2	75.4	75.5	76.8	77.2	77.7	77.7	77.8	78.4	78.8	79.0	79.9	79.9	80.1	80.9	81.4
75 years and over	71.0	71.9	71.5	69.8	70.0	70.8	70.8	71.2	72.3	73.1	73.3	73.3	73.4	73.5	74.6	75.3
Less than 35 years	41.2	40.7	40.5	39.9	39.6	39.5	39.3	39.1	38.5	37.8	37.6	37.9	37.3	37.3	38.6	39.1
35 to 44 years	70.0	69.3	68.9	68.1	67.3	67.2	66.9	66.6	66.3	65.8	65.1	65.4	65.1	64.5	65.2	65.5
45 to 54 years	77.4	77.0	76.5	75.9	76.0	76.1	75.6	75.5	75.2	74.8	75.1	75.4	75.3	75.2	75.2	75.6
55 to 64 years	80.0	79.9	80.0	79.5	79.9	80.2	79.5	79.6	79.3	80.0	80.2	79.8	79.9	79.3	79.5	80.0
65 years and over	74.4	75.0	75.1	74.8	75.0	75.5	75.6	75.8	76.3	77.2	77.1	77.3	77.3	77.4	78.1	78.9

	1997	1998	1999	2000	2001	2002	2002¹r	2003	2004	2005	2006	2007	2008	2009	2010
United States, total	65.7	66.3	66.8	67.4	67.8	67.9	67.9	68.3	69.0	68.9	68.8	68.1	67.8	67.4	66.9
Less than 25 years	17.7	18.2	19.9	21.7	22.5	23.0	22.9	22.8	25.2	25.7	24.8	24.8	23.6	23.3	22.8
25 to 29 years	35.0	36.2	36.5	38.1	38.9	39.0	38.8	39.8	40.2	40.9	41.8	40.6	40.0	37.7	36.8
30 to 34 years	52.6	53.6	53.8	54.6	54.8	55.0	54.9	56.5	57.4	56.8	55.9	54.4	53.5	52.5	51.6
35 to 39 years	62.6	63.7	64.4	65.0	65.5	65.2	65.2	65.1	66.2	66.6	66.4	65.0	64.6	63.4	61.9
40 to 44 years	69.7	70.0	69.9	70.6	70.8	71.7	71.7	71.3	71.9	71.7	71.2	70.4	69.4	68.7	67.9
45 to 49 years	74.2	73.9	74.5	74.7	75.4	74.9	74.8	75.4	76.3	75.0	74.9	74.0	73.6	72.3	72.0
50 to 54 years	77.7	77.8	77.8	78.5	78.2	77.8	77.9	77.9	78.2	78.3	77.7	76.9	76.4	76.5	75.0
55 to 59 years	79.7	79.8	80.7	80.4	81.0	80.8	80.8	80.9	81.2	80.6	80.4	79.9	79.4	78.6	77.7
60 to 64 years	80.5	82.1	81.3	80.3	81.8	81.5	81.6	81.9	82.4	81.9	81.5	81.5	80.9	80.6	80.4
65 to 69 years	81.9	81.9	82.9	83.0	82.4	82.8	82.9	82.5	83.2	82.8	82.4	81.7	81.6	82.0	81.6
70 to 74 years	82.0	82.2	82.8	82.6	82.5	82.5	82.5	82.0	83.4	82.9	83.0	82.4	81.7	81.9	82.4
75 years and over	75.8	76.2	77.1	77.7	78.1	78.4	78.4	78.7	78.8	78.4	79.1	78.7	78.6	78.9	78.9
Less than 35 years	38.7	39.3	39.7	40.8	41.2	41.3	41.3	42.2	43.1	43.0	42.6	41.7	41.0	39.7	39.1
35 to 44 years	66.1	66.9	67.2	67.9	68.2	68.6	68.8	68.3	69.2	69.3	68.9	67.8	67.0	66.2	65.0
45 to 54 years	75.8	75.7	76.0	76.5	76.7	76.3	76.3	76.6	77.2	76.6	76.2	75.4	75.0	74.4	73.5
55 to 64 years	80.1	80.9	81.0	80.3	81.3	81.1	81.1	81.4	81.7	81.2	80.9	80.6	80.1	79.5	79.0
65 years and over	79.1	79.3	80.1	80.4	80.3	80.5	80.6	80.5	81.1	80.6	80.9	80.4	80.1	80.5	80.5

SOURCE: Adapted from Robert R. Callis and Melissa Kresin, "Table 17. Homeownership Rates by Age of Householder and by Family Status: 1982 to 2010," in *Housing Vacancies and Homeownership (CPS/HVS)—Annual Statistics: 2010*, U.S. Department of Commerce, U.S. Census Bureau, Housing and Household Economic Statistics Division, 2011, http://www.census.gov/hhes/www/housing/hvs/annual10/ann10ind.html (accessed April 12, 2011)

fair market rent (FMR) of the housing. The researchers also calculate the number of full-time minimum-wage jobs that are necessary to afford the FMR, which highlights the hardships faced by many families of different sizes with varying numbers of wage earners.

DeCrappeo et al. observe that in 2009 an estimated 40% of foreclosures displaced renter households and that between 2007 and 2008 the number of renter households increased by 1.1 million, whereas the number of homeowners decreased. The national median housing wage, based on each county's housing wage for a two-bedroom unit at the FMR of $959, was $18.44 per hour in 2010. Because the median hourly wage and renters' average hourly wages are less than the national median housing wage, the researchers observe that even when workers are employed at prevailing wages, they will find it challenging to obtain affordable rental housing. In no state can an individual working a full-time minimum-wage job afford to rent a two-bedroom apartment. The maximum federal monthly SSI payment was just $674 for adults aged 65 years and older in 2010. Older adults relying solely on SSI payments (an estimated 56% of the 7.7 million SSI recipients depended on SSI alone in 2010) could not afford rental housing anywhere in the United States.

ADDITIONAL HOUSING CHALLENGES FOR OLDER ADULTS
Physical Hazards and Accommodations

Home characteristics that are considered desirable by younger householders may present challenges to older adults. For example, the staircase in a two-story house may become a formidable obstacle to an older adult suffering from arthritis, heart disease, or other disabling chronic conditions. Narrow halls and doorways cannot accommodate walkers and wheelchairs. High cabinets and shelves may be beyond the reach of an arthritis sufferer. Even though houses can be modified to meet the physical needs of older or disabled people, some older houses cannot be remodeled as easily, and retrofitting them may be quite costly. Owners of condominiums in Florida, whose young-old (aged 65 to 74 years) residents once prized second- and third-floor units for their breezes and golf course views, are now considering installing elevators for residents in their 80s and 90s who find climbing stairs much more difficult.

Older adults, as well as advocates on their behalf, express a strong preference for aging in place. Much research confirms that most people over the age of 55 years want to remain in familiar surroundings rather than move to alternative housing. To live more comfortably, those older adults who have the means can redesign and reequip their home to accommodate the physical changes that are associated with aging.

Simple adaptations include replacing doorknobs with levers that can be pushed downward with a fist or elbow, requiring no gripping or twisting; replacing light switches with flat "touch" switches; placing closet rods at adjustable heights; installing stoves with front- or side-mounted controls; and marking steps with bright colors. More complex renovations include replacing a bathroom with a wet room (a tiled space that is large enough to accommodate a wheelchair and that is equipped with a showerhead, a waterproof chair, and a sloping floor for a drain), placing electrical outlets higher than usual along walls, and widening passageways and doorways for walkers, wheelchairs, or scooters.

Anticipating the increase in the older population in the coming years, some real estate developers are manufacturing houses that are designed to meet the needs of older adults and prolong their ability to live independently. These houses feature accommodations such as nonskid flooring, walls strong enough to support the mounting of grab bars, outlets at convenient heights, levers instead of knobs on doors and plumbing fixtures, and doorways and hallways wide enough to allow wheelchair access.

More technologically advanced homes, called smart homes, feature an array of adaptive technologies, such as embedded computers, sensors that detect motion and falls, and automated blood pressure monitoring, that aim to help older adults remain in their homes and age in place. The AARP Global Network notes in "Smart Home Market to be Worth $13.4 billion by 2014" (February 23, 2011, https://www.aarpglobalnetwork.org/) that the smart home market will reach $13.4 billion by 2014.

PUBLIC HOUSING

Congress passed the U.S. Housing Act of 1937 to create low-income public housing, but according to the Milbank Memorial Fund and the Council of Large Public Housing Authorities, in *Public Housing and Supportive Services for the Frail Elderly: A Guide for Housing Authorities and Their Collaborators* (2006, http://www .milbank.org/reports/0609publichousing/0609publichousing .pdf), by 1952 only a small percentage of available housing was occupied by older adults. After 1956, when Congress authorized the development of dedicated public housing for the elderly and specifically made low-income older adults eligible for such housing, the situation began to improve. During the 1960s and 1970s many developments, specifically for low-income older adults, were constructed. Initially, these apartments were sufficient for most residents, but they were not designed to enable residents to age in place. They lacked the flexibility and the range of housing options necessary to meet the needs of frail older adults. The residents who entered public housing as young-old aged in place and are now the older-old (aged 75 years and older) and are in need of more supportive and health services than they were two decades ago.

Public housing itself has also aged—much of it is more than 30 years old. Many developments are badly rundown and in desperate need of renovation. Most are unequipped to offer the range of supportive services that are required by increasingly frail and dependent residents. Absent supportive services, the bleak alternative may be moving older people into costly, isolated institutions. Older adults may suffer unnecessary institutionalization, and nursing home care is far more costly than community-based services.

In December 2010 Section 202 Supportive Housing for the Elderly Act was passed. The National Low Income Housing Coalition explains in "Congress Passes Sections 811 and 202 Legislation, President Expected to Sign Bills into Law" (December 23, 2010, http://www.nlihc.org/detail/article.cfm?article_id=7567) that the act supports the development and maintenance of housing options for older adults with very low incomes. It encourages the enhancement of existing units and expanding access to assisted living facilities and programs that enable older adults to remain in the community. It also supports the Department of Housing and Urban Development's creation of an information clearing house of affordable housing projects for older adults.

Rebecca Kimitch describes in "El Monte Breaks Ground on Innovative Affordable Housing for Seniors" (*SGVtribune.com*, February 16, 2011) the construction of new senior apartments in Southern California that will help older adults age in place by bringing services such as meals on wheels, a wellness center, and a community garden to them. Slated for completion in mid-2012, the federally funded project consists of 68 one-bedroom rent-subsidized apartments and will also house a kitchen where residents can learn healthy cooking techniques.

CHAPTER 4
WORKING AND RETIREMENT: NEW OPTIONS FOR OLDER ADULTS

Americans head off to their jobs each day as much for daily meaning as for daily bread.

—Studs Terkel, *Working: People Talk about What They Do All Day and How They Feel about What They Do* (1974)

Historically, Americans aged 65 years and older have made substantial contributions to society. Examples of accomplished older adults include:

- Benjamin Franklin (1706–1790)—writer, scientist, inventor, and statesman—helped draft the Declaration of Independence at age 70.

- Thomas Alva Edison (1847–1931) worked on inventions, including the lightbulb, the microphone, and the phonograph, until his death at the age of 84.

- Rear Admiral Grace Murray Hopper (1906–1992), one of the early computer scientists and a coauthor of the computer language COBOL, maintained an active speaking and consulting schedule until her death at age 85.

- Margaret Mead (1901–1978), the noted anthropologist, returned to New Guinea when she was 72 and exhausted a much younger television film crew as they tried to keep up with her.

- Albert Einstein (1879–1955), who formulated the theory of relativity, was working on a unifying theory of the universe when he died at age 76.

- Georgia O'Keeffe (1887–1986) created masterful paintings when she was more than 80 years of age.

Older adults continue to play vital roles in industry, government, and the arts. Notable examples include:

- Former senator John Glenn (1921–), who piloted the first manned U.S. spacecraft to orbit the earth, returned to space at age 77 as a payload specialist.

- T. Boone Pickens (1928–) is a financier and chairman of BP Capital Management; in 2011 *Forbes* ranked him as the 328th richest person in the United States.

- U.S. senator John McCain (1936–; R-AZ) was 74 years old when he was elected in 2010 to a 13th term as senator. He was the Republican presidential candidate in the 2008 election.

- Madeleine Albright (1937–), U.S. secretary of state from 1997 to 2001, is the president of the Harry S. Truman Scholarship Foundation and the chairperson for the National Democratic Institute for International Affairs. She also serves as cochair for the Commission on Legal Empowerment of the Poor and for the Pew Global Attitudes Project.

- James E. Hansen (1941–) heads the National Aeronautics and Space Administration's Goddard Institute for Space Studies and is an adjunct professor in the Department of Earth and Environmental Sciences at Columbia University. He has increased public awareness of global warming and its effects on climate change.

- Robert Redford (1937–) is an Academy Award–winning actor, director, producer, businessman, environmentalist, philanthropist, and founder of the Sundance Film Festival.

- Nancy Pelosi (1940–; D-CA) served as the Speaker of the U.S. House of Representatives from January 2007 to January 2011. She was the first woman to hold that position.

DEFINING AND REDEFINING RETIREMENT

Retirement in the United States is usually defined by two actions: withdrawal from the paid labor force and receipt of income from pension plans, Social Security, or other retirement plans. There are, however, many people who may be viewed as being retired, even though they do not fulfill the criteria of the generally accepted definition of retirement. For example, workers who retire from the military or other federal employment, which provide pension benefits after 20 years of service, may choose to continue to work and remain in the labor force for years, collecting both a salary and a pension. Other workers retire from full-time employment but continue to work part time to supplement their pension, Social Security, or retirement benefits. As a result, not all workers collecting pensions are retired, and some workers collecting salaries are retired.

Besides expanding the definition of the term *retirement*, an increasing number of older Americans are not subscribing to the traditional timing and lifestyle of retirement. Retirement is no longer an event, it is a process, and work and retirement are no longer mutually exclusive. Even though many older adults still choose to retire from full-time employment at age 65, they remain active by exploring new careers, working part time, volunteering, and engaging in a variety of leisure activities. An increasing proportion of older adults work well beyond age 65, and some choose not to retire at all.

In 2011 prospective retirees included the baby boom generation (people born between 1946 and 1964). This generation faces unique difficulties when contemplating retirement—declining home values, high unemployment, low interest rates, and a depressed economy. In "Poll Reveals Baby Boomers' Retirement Fears" (Associated Press, April 5, 2011), Alan Fram reports that a March 2011 Associated Press–LifeGoesStrong.com poll found that only 11% of baby boomers said they will be able to live comfortably in retirement. Even though 55% of those surveyed said they are "somewhat certain" or "very certain" that they will be financially secure in retirement, 44% said they have no confidence that they will be able to stop working and live comfortably.

Fram notes that two-thirds of boomers viewed Social Security as a key component of their retirement income and the same proportion said they will continue to work after they retire (or reach retirement age). About one-third (35%) of those who plan to continue to work said they will do so "to make ends meet." Fewer plan to use their earnings to pay for "extras." One-quarter said they will never retire.

RECASTING WORK AND RETIREMENT

Throughout much of human history the average length of life was relatively short. According to Laura B. Shrestha of the Congressional Research Service, in *Life Expectancy in the United States* (August 16, 2006, http://aging.senate.gov/crs/aging1.pdf), in 1900 life expectancy was just 49.2 years. In a world where most people did not expect to live beyond age 50, it was essential that personal, educational, and professional milestones be attained by certain ages. Obtaining an education, job training, marriage, parenthood, and retirement not only were designated to particular periods of life but also were expected generally to occur only once in a lifetime.

This regimented pattern of life was maintained by tradition and, more recently, reinforced by laws and regulations. In the United States government regulations and institutional rules prescribed the ages at which education began, work-life ended, and pension and Social Security benefits commenced. This timetable was based on the assumptions that these activities were to be performed "on time" and in sequence and that most growth and development occurred during the first half of life, whereas the second half was, in general, characterized by decline and disinvestment.

Social and demographic trends (including increased longevity and improved health), technological advances, and economic realities have transformed the size and composition of the labor force as well as the nature of family and work. Examples of these changes include:

- Marriage and childbearing are often postponed in favor of pursuing education and careers. Advances in reproductive technology have enabled women to delay having children by 20 years. Table 4.1 shows that the rate of women aged 40 to 44 years giving birth rose from 9.8 births per 1,000 women in 2008 to 10.1 births per 1,000 women in 2009. The number of births to women aged 45 to 54 years rose from 7,650 in 2008 to 7,934 in 2009.

- Formal learning was once the exclusive province of the young; however, middle-aged and older adults are increasingly returning to school. According to the U.S. Census Bureau, in the press release "Back to School: 2010–2011" (June 15, 2010, http://www.census.gov/newsroom/releases/archives/facts_for_features_special _editions/cb10-ff14.html), 16% of all college students were aged 35 years and older in 2008 and 36% of these students attended school part time. Distance learning programs and classes offered online have created additional opportunities for older adults who wish to continue their education. Institutions that offer online education aimed at working adults anticipate increased growth in enrollment in response to persistent high unemployment rates.

- Career changes and retraining have become the norm rather than the exception. Americans once pursued a single career during their lifetime; many workers now change jobs and even careers several times. According to the American Council on Education (2011, http://www.acenet.edu), an increasing number of adults, from military veterans to people aged 50 years and older, are returning to work in second, third, or even fifth careers.

- Age-based mandatory retirement no longer exists in most private-sector industries. Historically, mandatory retirement ages were justified by the argument that some occupations were either too dangerous for older workers or required high levels of physical and mental acuity. Mandatory retirement is still compulsory

TABLE 4.1

Birth rates, by age of mother, 2008 and 2009

Age, race, and Hispanic origin of mother	2009		2008	
	Number	Rate	Number	Rate
All races and origins[a]				
Total[b]	4,131,019	66.7	4,247,694	68.6
10–14 years	5,030	0.5	5,764	0.6
15–19 years	409,840	39.1	434,758	41.5
15–17 years	124,256	20.1	135,664	21.7
18–19 years	285,584	66.2	299,094	70.6
20–24 years	1,006,055	96.3	1,052,184	103.0
25–29 years	1,166,904	110.5	1,195,774	115.1
30–34 years	955,300	97.7	956,716	99.3
35–39 years	474,143	46.6	488,875	46.9
40–44 years	105,813	10.1	105,973	9.8
45–54 years[c]	7,934	0.7	7,650	0.7

[a]Includes origin not stated.
[b]The total number includes births to women of all ages. The rate shown for all ages is the fertility rate, which is defined as the total number of births (regardless of the age of the mother) per 1,000 women aged 15–44 years.
[c]The birth rate for women aged 45–49 years is computed by relating the number of births to women aged 45 years and over to women aged 45–49 years, because most of the births in this group are to women aged 45–49.
Notes: Data for 2009 are based on a continuous file of records received from the states. Figures for 2009 are based on weighted data rounded to the nearest individual, so categories may not add to totals. Rates per 1,000 women in specified age and race and Hispanic origin group.

SOURCE: Adapted from Brady E. Hamilton, Joyce A. Martin, and Stephanie J. Ventura, "Table 2. Births and Birth Rates, by Age and Race and Hispanic Origin of Mother: United States, Final 2008 and Preliminary 2009," in "Births: Preliminary Data for 2009," *National Vital Statistics Reports*, vol. 59, no. 3, December 9, 2010, http://www.cdc.gov/nchs/data/nvsr/nvsr59/nvsr59_03.pdf (accessed April 12, 2011)

for federal law officers, correctional officers, firefighters, air traffic controllers, and commercial airline pilots. However, mandatory retirement ages have been faulted because they are arbitrary and are not based on actual physical evaluations of individual workers. As a result, some detractors view the practice of age-based mandatory retirement as a form of age discrimination.

Even though a conventional American life generally included education, work, and recreation/retirement, in this order, the current cohort (a group of individuals that shares a common characteristic such as birth years and is studied over time) of workers and retirees have the opportunity to blend, reorder, and repeat these activities as desired. Many gerontologists (professionals who study the social, psychological, and biological aspects of aging) and other aging researchers posit that there is a "third age"—a stage of working life when older workers can actively renegotiate their relationship with the labor force. Their choices, depending on life circumstances, may include remaining in the workforce, retiring, or returning to work for periods of part-time, full-time, or part-season employment. Not all workers and retirees will choose to stray from the conventional course, but increasingly they have the option to do so.

A CHANGING ECONOMY AND CHANGING ROLES
From Agricultural...

When the U.S. economy was predominantly agricultural, children were put to work as soon as they were able to contribute to the family upkeep. Similarly, workers who lived beyond age 65 did not retire; they worked as long as they were physically able. When older adults were no longer able to work, younger family members cared for them. Older people were valued and respected for their accumulated knowledge and experience and were integral members of the interconnected family and labor systems.

... to Industrial ...

The Industrial Revolution shifted workers from the farm to manufacturing jobs. The work was physically demanding, the hours long, and the tasks rigidly structured. Women labored in factories and at home caring for the family. Older people found themselves displaced—their skills and experience were not relevant to new technologies and they could not physically compete with the large number of young workers eager to exploit new economic opportunities.

As industrial workers matured, some were promoted to positions as supervisors and managers. For older workers who had been with the same company for many years, labor unions provided a measure of job security through the seniority system ("first hired, last fired"). However, in an increasingly youth-oriented society older workers were often rejected in favor of younger laborers. Frequent reports of age discrimination prompted Congress to pass the Age Discrimination in Employment Act (ADEA). Enacted in 1967 to protect workers aged 40 to 65 years, ADEA made it illegal for employers or unions to discharge, refuse to hire, or otherwise discriminate on the basis of age. Victims are eligible for lost wages—the amount is doubled in the most blatant cases—and workers wrongfully terminated may also seek reinstatement. The ADEA Amendments of 1978 made 70 the upper age limit and prohibited mandatory retirement for most workers in the private sector and in the federal government. In 1986 Congress again amended the act to eliminate the upper age limit.

... to Service and Information

The U.S. economy continued its dramatic shift away from smokestack industries such as mining and manufacturing to an economy in which service occupations and the production and dissemination of information predominate. As such, the demand for highly educated workers has grown, and the demand for workers who perform physical labor has slackened. Many information-age careers and service jobs, such as those in the fields of health, law, information technology, and communications, are ideally suited for older workers because they do not require physical labor, and employers benefit from the cumulative experience of older workers.

THE AGING LABOR FORCE

As the baby boom generation approaches retirement age, the proportion of the U.S. population aged 65 years and older will increase significantly between 2012 and 2035. However, the U.S. labor force is already undergoing a shift toward a greater number of older workers and a relative scarcity of new entrants.

Victor W. Marshall of the UNC Institute on Aging observes in *Health, Age, and Labor Force Disruption of Older Workers* (April 8, 2009, http://www.aging.unc.edu/infocenter/slides/MarshallV2009OlderWorkers.ppt) that the median (the middle value—half are higher and half are lower) age of the U.S. labor force is increasing from 35.4 years in 1986, to 40.8 years in 2006, to a projected 42.1 years in 2016.

Older Adults in the Labor Force

The U.S. Bureau of Labor Statistics (BLS; February 2011, http://www.bls.gov/cps/cpsaat3.pdf) reports that in 2010 older workers accounted for 17.4% of the entire U.S. labor force. In *Older Workers* (July 2008, http://www.bls.gov/spotlight/2008/older_workers/pdf/older_workers_bls_spotlight.pdf), the BLS notes that between 1948 and 2007 the labor force participation of men aged 65 years and older generally declined until the late 1990s, when rates leveled off or even rose slightly. The observed decline in older adults' participation in the labor force during the 1970s and into the 1980s has been attributed to widespread mandatory retirement practices in many industries that forced workers to retire at age 65. In addition, the eligibility age for Social Security benefits was reduced from 65 to 62 years of age during the 1960s, enabling workers to retire earlier. The relatively stable proportion of older workers in

the labor force since that time is in part because of the relaxation and elimination of mandatory retirement and the liberalization of the Social Security earnings test—the earnings limits that prompt a reduction of Social Security benefits. The labor force participation rate for older workers was at record lows during the 1980s and early 1990s but has been increasing since the late 1990s—a larger share of older workers are remaining in or returning to the labor force.

The BLS indicates that between 1977 and 2007 the employment of workers aged 65 years and older increased by 101%. The number of employed men over 65 increased by 75% and the number of employed women rose by 147%. Even though the overall percentage of workers aged 75 years and older was small, 0.8% in 2007, it increased a staggering 172% between 1977 and 2007. This increase in older workers may reflect several factors, including economic necessity, the fact that older adults are seeking to remain vital and active into their 70s, a desire for the challenge and social interactions that work offers, or some combination of these.

Unemployment Is High among Older Adults

The BLS reports in "Record Unemployment among Older Workers Does Not Keep Them out of the Job Market" (March 2010, http://www.bls.gov/opub/ils/pdf/opbils81.pdf) that the unemployment rate for workers aged 55 years and older has significantly increased since December 2007. In February 2010 a record-high 7.1% of older adults were unemployed. Even though there are fewer unemployed older adults than younger adults, older unemployed people are jobless longer than younger people—an average of 35.5 weeks, compared to 23.3 weeks for people aged 16 to 24 years and 30.3 weeks for those aged 25 to 54 years. (See Table 4.2.) Figure 4.1 shows the historic changes in unemployment rates among people aged 16 to 24 years, 25 to 54 years, and 55 years and older.

Despite high unemployment, older adults continue to participate in the labor force. Figure 4.2 shows that the labor force participation rate for older adults actually increased during much of the recession, and remained at about 40% in early 2010.

Older Women Opt to Work Rather Than Retire

Between 1963 and 2008 labor force participation rates generally rose among women aged 55 years and older, with the largest increase among female workers aged 55 to 61 years—from 44% in 1963 to 65% in 2008. (See Figure 4.3.) These increases reflect an overall increase of women in the labor force with each successive generation. During this same period the participation rate for women aged 62 to 64 years rose from 29% to 42%, and among women aged 65 to 69 years the rate increased from 17% to 26%. Even though the labor force participation of women aged 70 years and

TABLE 4.2

Unemployment statistics, by age group, February 2010

Characteristic	Total, 16 years and older	16 to 24 years	25 to 54 years	55 years and older
Total unemployed (in thousands)	**15,991**	**3,888**	**9,843**	**2,260**
Percentage unemployed 27 weeks or longer	39.3	28.5	41.3	49.1
Median number of weeks unemployed	19.6	14.4	20.6	26.7
Average number of weeks unemployed	29.3	23.3	30.3	35.5

SOURCE: "Table 1. Selected Labor Force Measures, by Age, February 2010, Not Seasonally Adjusted," in "Record Unemployment among Older Workers Does Not Keep Them out of the Job Market," *Issues in Labor Statistics*, Summary 10-04, March 2010, http://www.bls.gov/opub/ils/pdf/opbils81.pdf (accessed April 12, 2011)

FIGURE 4.1

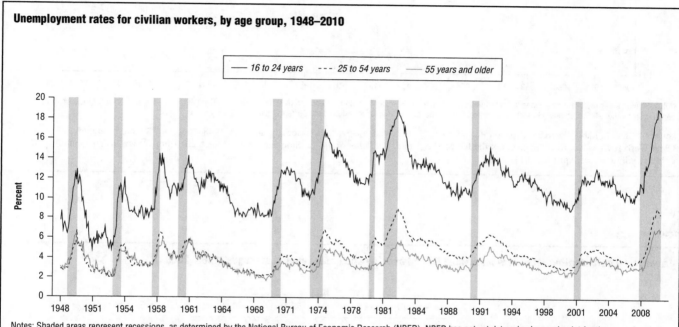

Unemployment rates for civilian workers, by age group, 1948–2010

Notes: Shaded areas represent recessions, as determined by the National Bureau of Economic Research (NBER). NBER has not yet determined an end point for the recession that began in December 2007. Beginning in 1994, data reflect the introduction of a major redesign of the Current Population Survey.

SOURCE: "Chart 1. Unemployment Rates for All Civilian Workers, by Age, Seasonally Adjusted, 1948–2010," in "Record Unemployment among Older Workers Does Not Keep Them out of the Job Market," *Issues in Labor Statistics*, Summary 10-04, March 2010, http://www.bls.gov/opub/ils/pdf/opbils81.pdf (accessed April 12, 2011)

older has remained essentially stable, in recent years participation among women in the other age groups has increased at a faster rate. These increases also serve to narrow the gap in labor force participation rates between men and women.

Most older women in the 21st century spent some time in the labor force when they were younger. However, the older the woman the less likely she is to have ever worked outside the home. In the United States the group of women in their late 50s and early 60s that was the first to work outside the home in large numbers is approaching retirement. Women in this cohort who are single, widowed, or divorced often continue to work to support themselves because they do not have sufficient Social Security credits to retire.

Married older women are increasingly choosing to keep working after their husband retires, breaking with the practice of joining their husband in retirement. In 1977 about one-third of employed women aged 65 years and older were married, but the BLS reports in *Older Worker* that by 2007 nearly half of employed women aged 65 years and older were married. Among the reasons cited for the growing proportion of older married women in the workforce are:

- Older women have careers they find personally satisfying as well as financially rewarding.

- They need to secure their retirement to prevent the poverty that has historically afflicted widows.

- Their income helps maintain the family standard of living and may be vital when their husband has been

FIGURE 4.2

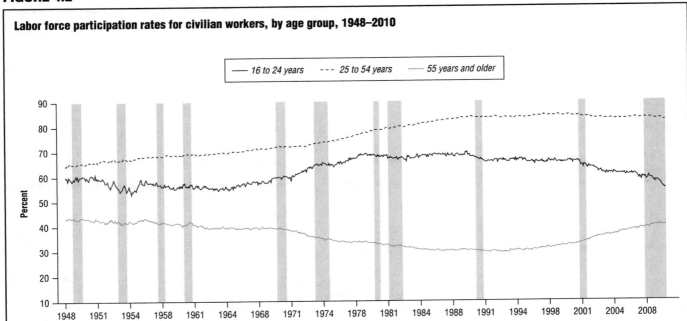

Labor force participation rates for civilian workers, by age group, 1948–2010

— 16 to 24 years   - - - 25 to 54 years   —— 55 years and older

Notes: Shaded areas represent recessions, as determined by the National Bureau of Economic Research (NBER). NBER has not yet determined an end point for the recession that began in December 2007. Beginning in 1994, data reflect the introduction of a major redesign of the Current Population Survey.

SOURCE: "Chart 2. Labor Force Participation Rates for All Civilian Workers, by Age, Seasonally Adjusted, 1948–2010," in "Record Unemployment among Older Workers Does Not Keep Them out of the Job Market," *Issues in Labor Statistics*, Summary 10-04, March 2010, http://www.bls.gov/opub/ils/pdf/opbils81.pdf (accessed April 12, 2011)

FIGURE 4.3

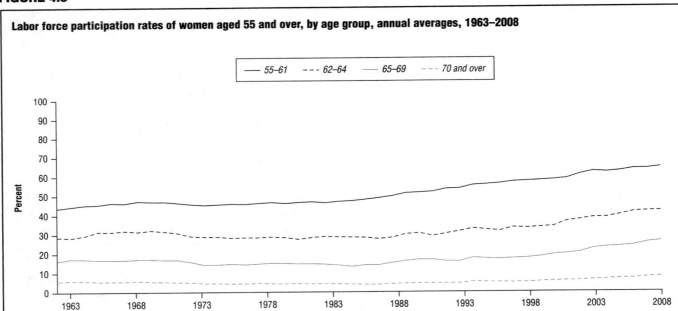

Labor force participation rates of women aged 55 and over, by age group, annual averages, 1963–2008

— 55–61   - - - 62–64   —— 65–69   - - - 70 and over

Notes: Data for 1994 and later years are not strictly comparable with data for 1993 and earlier years due to a redesign of the survey and methodology of the Current Population Survey. Beginning in 2000, data incorporate population controls from Census 2000.
Reference population: These data refer to the civilian noninstitutionalized population.

SOURCE: "Labor Force Participation Rates of Women Age 55 and over, by Age Group, Annual Averages, 1963–2008," in *Older Americans 2010: Key Indicators of Well-Being*, Federal Interagency Forum on Aging-Related Statistics, July 2010, http://www.agingstats.gov/agingstatsdotnet/Main_Site/Data/2010_Documents/Docs/OA_2010.pdf (accessed April 2, 2011)

pressured to retire by his employer or suffers failing health.

- They enjoy the social interactions at the workplace—women value relationships with coworkers more than men, and as a result women often find retirement more isolating.

The Aging Labor Force

In *Older Workers*, the BLS documents the extent to which the U.S. workforce has aged and projects an increasing proportion of older workers in the labor force. Between 2006 and 2016 the percentage of workers aged 55 to 64 years is expected to grow by 36.5%, and the percentages of workers aged 65 to 74 years and 75 years and older will each rise by more than 83%. (See Figure 4.4.) By 2016 workers aged 65 years and older will account for 6.1% of the total labor force.

Part-Time versus Full-Time Work

The BLS observes in *Older Workers* that the ratio of older workers choosing part-time or full-time work was relatively constant between 1977 and 1990, but between 1990 and 1995 the percentage of part-time workers rose with a corresponding decline in full-time employment. After 1995 the situation reversed, with full-time employment increasing dramatically. Between 1995 and 2007 the number of older full-time workers nearly doubled, whereas the number of part-timers increased by only 19%. By 2007, 56% of older workers were full time, up 12 percentage points from 1995, when 44% of older workers were full time.

Older workers may find increasing opportunities for flexible employment and alternative work arrangements, such as working as an independent contractor rather than as an employee or as an on-call worker rather than as a daily worker. For employers, hiring part-time older workers

is often an attractive alternative to hiring younger, full-time workers. Some employers value older workers' maturity, dependability, and experience. Others hire older workers to reduce payroll expenses. This reduction is achieved when part-time workers are hired as independent contractors and do not receive benefits, or when they are paid lower wages than full-time employees and not provided benefits.

Job Tenure

Older people tend to be stable employees who stay in the same job longer than younger people. Job tenure is measured as the median number of years that workers have been with their current employer. According to the BLS, in January 2010 workers aged 55 to 64 years had more than three times the median years of job tenure (10 years), compared to those aged 25 to 34 years (3.1 years). (See Table 4.3.)

DISPELLING MYTHS AND STEREOTYPES ABOUT OLDER WORKERS

Older workers are often stereotyped by the mistaken belief that performance declines with age. Performance studies, however, reveal that older workers perform intellectually as well as or better than workers 30 years younger by maintaining their problem solving, communication, and creative skills. In "Myths about Older Workers" (March 2009, http://jobsearchtoolkit.pbwiki.com/f/MythsAbout OlderWorkers.pdf), the North Carolina Collaboration on Lifelong Learning and Engagement asserts that older workers have high levels of productivity, in part because their maturity, stability, and better interpersonal skills enable them to make better use of their time.

Myth: Older Workers Have Overly Increased Absenteeism

Because aging is associated with declining health, older workers are often assumed to have markedly higher rates of illnesses and absences from work. Somewhat surprisingly, the chronic (long-term) health conditions that older adults may suffer tend to be manageable and do not affect attendance records. In fact, absence rates for older full-time wage and salary workers differ only slightly from those of younger workers. According to the BLS, in 2010 the absence rate for workers aged 55 years and older was 3.4%, compared to 3.1% for those aged 25 to 54 years. (See Table 4.4.)

Myth: It Costs More to Hire Older Workers

One widely accepted myth is that hiring and training older workers is not a sound investment because they will not remain on the job long. The BLS, however, indicates that in January 2010 workers aged 45 to 54 years had an average job tenure of 7.8 years, which was more than two times longer than the 3.1 years for workers aged 25 to 34 years. (See Table 4.3) Research conducted by the AARP repeatedly demonstrates that workers between the ages of

FIGURE 4.4

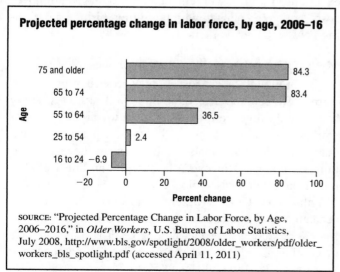

Projected percentage change in labor force, by age, 2006–16

SOURCE: "Projected Percentage Change in Labor Force, by Age, 2006–2016," in *Older Workers*, U.S. Bureau of Labor Statistics, July 2008, http://www.bls.gov/spotlight/2008/older_workers/pdf/older_workers_bls_spotlight.pdf (accessed April 11, 2011)

TABLE 4.3

Median years of tenure with current employer for employed workers, by age and sex, selected years 1996–2010

Age and sex	February 1996	February 1998	February 2000	January 2002	January 2004	January 2006	January 2008	January 2010
Total								
16 years and over	3.8	3.6	3.5	3.7	4.0	4.0	4.1	4.4
16 to 17 years	0.7	0.6	0.6	0.7	0.7	0.6	0.7	0.7
18 to 19 years	0.7	0.7	0.7	0.8	0.8	0.7	0.8	1.0
20 to 24 years	1.2	1.1	1.1	1.2	1.3	1.3	1.3	1.5
25 years and over	5.0	4.7	4.7	4.7	4.9	4.9	5.1	5.2
25 to 34 years	2.8	2.7	2.6	2.7	2.9	2.9	2.7	3.1
35 to 44 years	5.3	5.0	4.8	4.6	4.9	4.9	4.9	5.1
45 to 54 years	8.3	8.1	8.2	7.6	7.7	7.3	7.6	7.8
55 to 64 years	10.2	10.1	10.0	9.9	9.6	9.3	9.9	10.0
65 years and over	8.4	7.8	9.4	8.6	9.0	8.8	10.2	9.9
Men								
16 years and over	4.0	3.8	3.8	3.9	4.1	4.1	4.2	4.6
16 to 17 years	0.6	0.6	0.6	0.8	0.7	0.7	0.7	0.7
18 to 19 years	0.7	0.7	0.7	0.8	0.8	0.7	0.8	1.0
20 to 24 years	1.2	1.2	1.2	1.4	1.3	1.4	1.4	1.6
25 years and over	5.3	4.9	4.9	4.9	5.1	5.0	5.2	5.3
25 to 34 years	3.0	2.8	2.7	2.8	3.0	2.9	2.8	3.2
35 to 44 years	6.1	5.5	5.3	5.0	5.2	5.1	5.2	5.3
45 to 54 years	10.1	9.4	9.5	9.1	9.6	8.1	8.2	8.5
55 to 64 years	10.5	11.2	10.2	10.2	9.8	9.5	10.1	10.4
65 years and over	8.3	7.1	9.0	8.1	8.2	8.3	10.4	9.7
Women								
16 years and over	3.5	3.4	3.3	3.4	3.8	3.9	3.9	4.2
16 to 17 years	0.7	0.6	0.6	0.7	0.6	0.6	0.6	0.7
18 to 19 years	0.7	0.7	0.7	0.8	0.8	0.7	0.8	1.0
20 to 24 years	1.2	1.1	1.0	1.1	1.3	1.2	1.3	1.5
25 years and over	4.7	4.4	4.4	4.4	4.7	4.8	4.9	5.1
25 to 34 years	2.7	2.5	2.5	2.5	2.8	2.8	2.6	3.0
35 to 44 years	4.8	4.5	4.3	4.2	4.5	4.6	4.7	4.9
45 to 54 years	7.0	7.2	7.3	6.5	6.4	6.7	7.0	7.1
55 to 64 years	10.0	9.6	9.9	9.6	9.2	9.2	9.8	9.7
65 years and over	8.4	8.7	9.7	9.4	9.6	9.5	9.9	10.1

SOURCE: "Table 1. Median Years of Tenure with Current Employer for Employed Wage and Salary Workers by Age and Sex, Selected Years, 1996–2010," in *Employee Tenure in 2010*, U.S. Department of Labor, U.S. Bureau of Labor Statistics, September 2010, http://www.bls.gov/news.release/pdf/tenure.pdf (accessed April 12, 2011)

50 and 60 work for an average of 15 years. Furthermore, the Mature Workers Employment Alliance, an organization dedicated to assisting older workers in transitioning to new positions, asserts that the future work life of employees over the age of 50 generally exceeds the life of the technology for which they are trained.

In "Myths about Older Workers," the North Carolina Collaboration on Lifelong Learning and Engagement observes that older workers are less likely to change jobs frequently, which reduces the expenses that are associated with employee turnover. It also notes that some older workers may forgo benefits because they have insurance from previous employers or through Medicare.

The AARP observes that even though older workers' health, disability, and life insurance costs are higher than those of younger workers, they are offset by lower costs because of fewer dependents. Older workers have generally earned more vacation time and have higher pension costs, and they take fewer risks, which means they have lower accident rates. Workers over the age of 50 file fewer workers' compensation claims than younger workers—the largest numbers of claims are filed by workers between the ages of 30 and 34. Fringe benefit costs for workers of all ages are about the same overall. Finally, retaining experienced older workers actually reduces employer costs that are associated with recruiting, hiring, and training new, younger workers.

Myth: Older Workers Are Technophobes

Even though older workers may require more time to learn new technologies, their improved attitudes, study habits, and diligence often help them to surpass younger workers in training courses. There is a pervasive myth that older adults are unable to learn or use new information technology. However, the North Carolina Collaboration on Lifelong Learning and Engagement reports in "Myths about Older Workers" that during the 2006–07 academic year adults aged 50 years and older accounted for 7% of students enrolled in degree programs and 24% of continuing education programs. That same academic year over 125,000 adults aged 50 to 64 years and 30,000

TABLE 4.4

Absences from work, by age and sex, 2010

Age, sex, race, and Hispanic or Latino ethnicity	Full-time wage and salary workers (in thousands)[a]	2010					
		Absence rate[a]			Lost worktime rate[b]		
		Total	Illness or injury	Other reasons	Total	Illness or injury	Other reasons
Total, 16 years and over	**99,390**	**3.1**	**2.2**	**0.9**	**1.6**	**1.1**	**0.5**
16 to 19 years	1,017	3.5	2.6	0.9	1.1	0.7	0.4
20 to 24 years	7,518	3.0	2.1	0.9	1.3	0.8	0.5
25 years and over	90,855	3.1	2.2	0.9	1.6	1.1	0.5
25 to 54 years	73,026	3.1	2.1	1.0	1.6	1.0	0.5
55 years and over	17,830	3.4	2.8	0.6	1.8	1.6	0.3
Men, 16 years and over	**54,991**	**2.3**	**1.8**	**0.5**	**1.2**	**0.9**	**0.2**
16 to 19 years	606	2.8	2.2	0.6	1.1	0.8	0.3
20 to 24 years	4,125	2.0	1.5	0.5	0.7	0.6	0.2
25 years and over	50,260	2.3	1.8	0.5	1.2	1.0	0.2
25 to 54 years	40,763	2.2	1.6	0.5	1.1	0.9	0.2
55 years and over	9,497	2.9	2.4	0.5	1.6	1.4	0.2
Women, 16 years and over	**44,399**	**4.2**	**2.8**	**1.4**	**2.2**	**1.3**	**0.8**
16 to 19 years	411	4.5	3.2	1.3	1.2	0.6	0.5
20 to 24 years	3,393	4.3	2.9	1.4	2.1	1.2	0.9
25 years and over	40,596	4.2	2.8	1.4	2.2	1.4	0.8
25 to 54 years	32,263	4.2	2.7	1.5	2.2	1.3	1.0
55 years and over	8,333	4.0	3.3	0.8	2.1	1.7	0.3
White	80,517	3.1	2.2	0.9	1.6	1.1	0.5
Black or African American	11,656	3.5	2.6	0.9	1.9	1.4	0.5
Asian	4,962	2.4	1.6	0.8	1.2	0.7	0.5
Hispanic or Latino	14,816	3.0	2.1	0.9	1.4	0.9	0.5

[a]Absences are defined as instances when persons who usually work 35 or more hours a week worked less than 35 hours during the reference week for one of the following reasons: own illness, injury, or medical problems; child care problems; other family or personal obligations; civic or military duty; and maternity or paternity leave. Excluded are situations in which work was missed due to vacation or personal days, holiday, labor dispute, and other reasons. For multiple jobholders, absence data refer only to work missed at their main jobs. The absence rate is the ratio of workers with absences to total full-time wage and salary employment. All self-employed workers are excluded, both those with incorporated businesses as well as those with unincorporated businesses. The estimates of full-time wage and salary employment shown in this table do not match those in other tables because the estimates in this table are based on the full Current Population Survey (CPS) sample and those in the other tables are based on a quarter of the sample only.
[b]Hours absent as a percent of hours usually worked.
Notes: Since 2009, data reflect a modification in the estimation of the absence universe and are not strictly comparable with absence measures for prior years. The modification was made to enable users of the public-use microdata to reproduce the estimates of the absence universe and rates. Estimates for the above race groups (white, black or African American, and Asian) do not sum to totals because data are not presented for all races. Persons whose ethnicity is identified as Hispanic or Latino may be of any race. Updated population controls are introduced annually with the release of January data.

SOURCE: "46. Absences from Work of Employed Full-time Wage and Salary Workers by Age, Sex, Race, and Hispanic or Latino Ethnicity," in *Labor Force Statistics from the Current Population Survey*, U.S. Department of Labor, U.S. Bureau of Labor Statistics, 2011, http://www.bls.gov/cps/cpsaat46.pdf (accessed April 12, 2011)

adults aged 65 years and older were attending community college and close to 5,000 adults aged 65 years and older were enrolled in a computer course.

Myth: Older Workers Are Not Innovators

The stereotype of older workers as being slow to learn new skills, unwilling to take risks, and unable to adapt to change is fading as older entrepreneurs and innovators gain recognition. Stefan Theil reports in "The Golden Age of Innovation" (*Newsweek*, August 27, 2010) that rather than a young college graduate, the average founder of a high-tech start-up company is about 40 years old. Furthermore, older entrepreneurs tend to be more successful than younger ones—their experience, extensive networks of business contacts and associates, and interpersonal skills serve them well. In fact, Theil notes that "the highest rate of entrepreneurship in America has shifted to the 55-to-64 age group, with people older than 55 almost twice as likely to found successful companies than those between 20 and 34." Older entrepreneurs tend to be less visible than their younger counterparts. They are more likely to sell products

and services to other companies rather than to consumers and they work in biotechnology, energy, or information technology hardware.

Theil offers examples from *Forbes*'s Fast Tech 500, the fastest-growing technology companies. First Solar, a manufacturer of solar panels and solar energy systems, was founded by a 68-year-old. The founders of Riverbed Technology, which increases the speed of data transfers over wide area networks, were ages 51 and 33. The founders of Compellent Technologies, which provides computer facilities management, were 45, 55, and 58.

AGE DISCRIMINATION

But more and more, America will come to believe that there is no fixed age for retirement, that work is important to people and organizations, and that age itself should not disqualify anyone from being hired or discourage anyone from seeking work.

—William Novelli, "Seizing the Human Capital in Older Workers" (November 10, 2004)

Even though the 1967 ADEA and its amendments were enacted to ban discrimination against workers based on their age, the act was also intended to promote the employment of older workers based on their abilities. Besides making it illegal for employers to discriminate based on age in hiring, discharging, and compensating employees, the act also prohibited companies from coercing older workers into accepting incentives to early retirement. In 1990 ADEA was strengthened with the passing of the Older Workers Benefit Protection Act. Besides prohibiting discrimination in employee benefits based on age, it provides that an employee's waiver of the right to sue for age discrimination, a clause sometimes included in severance packages, is invalid unless it is "voluntary and knowing."

However, age bias and discrimination persist, even though age discrimination in the workplace is against the law. More than 15,000 claims of age discrimination are filed with the Equal Employment Opportunity Commission (EEOC) every year. Most cases involve older workers who believe they were terminated unfairly, but a number of the cases involve workers who feel they have met age discrimination in hiring practices.

The number of claims received by the EEOC rose from 19,921 in fiscal year (FY) 2002 to 23,264 in FY 2010. (See Table 4.5.) The EEOC resolved all of these charges in FY 2010; however, agency data reveal that most claimants do not win. Of the claims that were resolved in FY 2010, the EEOC found "reasonable cause" that age discrimination may have occurred in just 753 cases and found "no reasonable cause" in 16,308 cases.

Pressure to Retire

There are many forms of subtle discrimination against older workers as well as ways that employers can directly or indirectly exert pressure on older employees to resign or retire. This form of discrimination is "under the radar" and in many instances violates the spirit, if not the letter, of ADEA.

From an employer's standpoint, age discrimination is simply the consequence of efforts to reduce payroll expenses. Employment decisions are not only based on how much an employee contributes to the company but also on the salary and benefits the company must provide the employee, relative to the cost of other employees. Because salary tends to increase with longevity on the job, older workers usually receive higher wages than younger ones. Thus, if two employees are equally productive and the older one has a higher salary, a company has an economic incentive to lay off the older worker or strongly encourage early retirement.

For many workers, early retirement is untenable. Early retirement benefits are almost always less than regular retirement benefits and may be insufficient to allow a retiree to live comfortably without working. Finding a new job is more challenging for older workers, particularly during periods of high unemployment, and they are frequently unemployed for longer periods than are younger job seekers. Furthermore, workers who refuse to accept early retirement may find themselves without jobs at all, perhaps with no pension and no severance pay.

Some labor economists contend that early retirements, whether voluntary or coerced, deprive the nation of skilled workers needed for robust growth and divest the government of the revenue that these workers would have contributed in payroll taxes.

Filing ADEA Claims: Suing the Company

Older workers often have experience and qualifications which are too often overlooked in favor of younger employees who may not be as qualified. The law requires that employers assess employees equally and base their decisions on set criteria, irrespective of age.

—Lucy Orta, quoted by Steve Green in "Black Gaming Settles Age Discrimination Lawsuit" (*Las Vegas Sun*, December 21, 2010)

The costs involved in filing an age discrimination suit are high. Besides the financial outlay for legal representation, workers who sue their employers may be stigmatized and face further discrimination—future employers' reluctance to hire a worker who has filed a discrimination suit against a former employer. Workers caught in this scenario can suffer emotional and financial damage that may adversely affect them for the rest of their life. Nonetheless, many workers do choose to sue their employers.

U.S. Supreme Court Decisions Augment ADEA

In response to the recession (which lasted from late 2007 to mid-2009) and the continuing economic uncertainty in 2010 and 2011, many companies instituted layoffs and reductions in force in an effort to reduce costs and remain viable. Because reductions in force aim to reduce payroll, some target higher-paid workers, who are often also older adults with longer tenures. ADEA is violated if an employment policy that seems neutral, such as the criteria for workers to be laid off, actually exerts a statistically significant adverse or "disparate impact" when applied to workers aged 40 years and older versus younger workers.

The 2005 U.S. Supreme Court decision in *Smith v. City of Jackson* (544 U.S. 228), that workers aged 40 years and older may prove discrimination under ADEA using a disparate impact theory, strengthened protections for older workers. The court stated that plaintiffs in age discrimination lawsuits do not have to prove that employers intended to discriminate, only that layoffs had a "disparate impact" on older workers. This ruling is significant because claimants are not required to show that an employer deliberately targeted a single employee or group of employees. Instead, claimants can prevail if they

TABLE 4.5

Age Discrimination in Employment Act (ADEA) charges, fiscal years 1997–2010

	Fiscal year 1997	Fiscal year 1998	Fiscal year 1999	Fiscal year 2000	Fiscal year 2001	Fiscal year 2002	Fiscal year 2003	Fiscal year 2004	Fiscal year 2005	Fiscal year 2006	Fiscal year 2007	Fiscal year 2008	Fiscal year 2009	Fiscal year 2010
Receipts	15,785	15,191	14,141	16,008	17,405	19,921	19,124	17,837	16,585	16,548	19,103	24,582	22,778	23,264
Resolutions	18,279	15,995	15,448	14,672	15,155	18,673	17,352	15,792	14,076	14,146	16,134	21,415	20,529	24,800
Resolutions by type														
Settlements	642	755	816	1,156	1,006	1,222	1,285	1,377	1,326	1,417	1,795	1,974	1,935	2,250
	3.5%	4.7%	5.3%	7.9%	6.6%	6.5%	7.4%	8.7%	9.4%	10.0%	11.1%	9.2%	9.4%	9.1%
Withdrawals w/benefits	762	580	578	560	551	671	710	787	764	767	958	1,252	1,161	1,322
	4.2%	3.6%	3.7%	3.8%	3.6%	3.6%	4.1%	5.0%	5.4%	5.4%	5.9%	5.8%	5.7%	5.3%
Administrative closures	4,986	4,175	3,601	3,232	3,963	6,254	2,824	3,550	2,537	2,639	2,754	6,387	4,031	4,167
	27.3%	26.1%	23.3%	22.0%	26.1%	33.5%	16.3%	22.5%	18.0%	18.7%	17.1%	29.8%	19.6%	16.8%
No reasonable cause	11,163	9,863	9,172	8,517	8,388	9,725	11,976	9,563	8,866	8,746	10,002	11,124	12,788	16,308
	61.1%	61.7%	59.4%	58.0%	55.3%	52.1%	69.0%	60.6%	63.0%	61.8%	62.0%	51.9%	62.3%	65.8%
Reasonable cause	726	622	1,281	1,207	1,247	801	557	515	583	612	625	678	614	753
	4.0%	3.9%	8.3%	8.2%	8.2%	4.3%	3.2%	3.3%	4.1%	4.3%	3.9%	3.2%	3.0%	3.0%
Successful conciliations	74	119	184	241	409	208	166	139	169	177	186	220	202	252
	0.4%	0.7%	1.2%	1.6%	2.7%	1.1%	1.0%	0.9%	1.2%	1.3%	1.2%	1.0%	1.0%	1.0%
Unsuccessful conciliations	652	503	1,097	966	838	593	391	376	414	435	439	458	412	501
	3.6%	3.1%	7.1%	6.6%	5.5%	3.2%	2.3%	2.4%	2.9%	3.1%	2.7%	2.1%	2.0%	2.0%
Merit resolutions	2,130	1,957	2,675	2,923	2,804	2,694	2,552	2,679	2,673	2,796	3,378	3,904	3,710	4,325
	11.7%	12.2%	17.3%	19.9%	18.5%	14.4%	14.7%	17.0%	19.0%	19.8%	20.9%	18.2%	18.1%	17.4%
Monetary benefits (millions)*	$44.3	$34.7	$38.6	$45.2	$53.7	$55.7	$48.9	$69.0	$77.7	$51.5	$66.8	$82.8	$72.1	$93.6

*Does not include monetary benefits obtained through litigation.

Note: The total of individual percentages may not always sum to 100% due to rounding.

SOURCE: "Age Discrimination in Employment Act FY 1997–FY 2010," U.S. Equal Opportunity Commission, 2011, http://www.eeoc.gov/eeoc/statistics/enforcement/adea.cfm (accessed April 11, 2011)

are able to demonstrate that an employer used a neutral business practice—with no intent to discriminate—that had an adverse impact on people aged 40 years and older.

In 2008 the Supreme Court ruled in *Meacham et al. v. Knolls Atomic Power Laboratory* (553 U.S. ___) that an employer defending against a disparate impact age bias claim, and not the employee making the charge, bears the burden of proving that the adverse action—in this case a reduction in workforce plan—was based on a reasonable factor other than age. The disparate impact theory is based on the principle that a policy that appears neutral may still have an adverse impact on a protected class, in this case, older workers.

The Supreme Court ruling in *Gross v. FBL Financial Services, Inc.* (No. 08-441 [2009]) essentially reversed its earlier position, making it more difficult for older workers to prevail in age discrimination suits. The ruling eliminated the requirement that employers prove they had a legitimate reason other than age for laying off older workers. Instead, the burden of proof now falls to the older worker, who must prove that age was the key factor. The ruling reversed a jury verdict in favor of an insurance adjuster in Iowa who filed a claim because his company demoted him and gave his job to a younger worker. According to David G. Savage, in "Supreme Court Makes Age Bias Suits Harder to Win" (*Los Angeles Times*, June 19, 2009), the high court opined that "the judge had erred by allowing the plaintiff to win without proving he had been demoted because of his age." In "Reductions in Force: The Supreme Court Escalates the Legal Risks" (July 2008, http://www.lorman.com/newsletters/article.php?article_id=1028&newsletter_id=223&category_id=8&topic=LIT), Frank C. Morris Jr. of Epstein Becker & Green P.C. states that "precisely at a time when the economy may force employers to make more [reductions in force] decisions, the Supreme Court has made defending such decisions decidedly harder for employers."

RECENT AGE DISCRIMINATION CASES AND COURT DECISIONS. The article "3M Settles Age-Discrimination Suit for up to $12M" (CBS Minnesota, March 19, 2011) reports that in March 2011, 3M Co. settled an age discrimination suit filed in 2004 that charged the company with downgrading older workers' performance reviews and favoring younger workers for training and advancement. Even though a company spokesperson said the proposed settlement, which applied to about 7,000 current and former employees, was not "an admission of liability," 3M could pay as much as $12 million to the plaintiffs in this case.

In December 2010 Black Gaming LLC, which operates a resort and casino in Las Vegas, Nevada, settled an age discrimination suit brought by two sales managers, ages 55 and 67 at the time the suit was filed in 2007, who were terminated and replaced with younger workers. In "Black Gaming Settles Age Discrimination Lawsuit" (*Las Vegas Sun*, December 21, 2010), Steve Green reports that in addition to paying each of the wrongfully terminated workers $30,000, Black Gaming agreed to:

- Designate an EEO compliance officer
- Develop procedures to address complaints of discrimination, harassment and retaliation
- Provide annual training for its supervisory and human resources staff on age discrimination
- Provide similar training for all new hires
- Hold supervisory and human resources staff accountable for compliance with equal employment policies via their performance evaluations

Richard Sandomir reports in "Sportscasting Fixture Files Age-Discrimination Lawsuit" (*New York Times*, October 13, 2010) that in October 2010, 69-year-old sportscaster Sal Marchiano filed an age discrimination suit against WPIX-TV/Channel 11, claiming that he was terminated from his position because of his age. Marchiano asserted that he was given no reason for his termination but later discovered that the reason was his age. The suit seeks his reinstatement as well as damages, in an amount to be determined when the case goes to trial.

BABY BOOMERS AND RETIREES WANT TO DO GOOD WORK

Baby Boomers Will Transform Retirement

Unexpectedly large numbers of boomers are looking for purpose-driven jobs that provide them with both means and meaning.

—Marc Freedman, quoted in "Groundbreaking New Survey Asks American Workers, Ages 44–70, about Longer Working Lives" (June 18, 2008)

In *Americans Seek Meaningful Work in the Second Half of Life: MetLife Foundation/Civic Ventures Encore Career Survey* (June 2008 http://www.encore.org/files/Encore_Survey.pdf), the MetLife Foundation and Civic Ventures indicate that between 5.3 million and 8.4 million Americans aged 44 to 70 years are launching "encore careers"—work that combines generating income and helping others. The following are some of the key findings and trends that were uncovered by the survey:

- A majority of Americans aged 44 to 70 years want to use their skills and experience to help others.
- Older adults want to do well by doing good—they will seek opportunities in social services, health care, and education that will enable them to generate income and improve the lives of others.
- Among those already in encore careers, 84% report a high level of satisfaction with their work and 94% say they are making a difference.
- The coming generation of older adults may not pursue volunteer opportunities as vigorously as past generations.

They are motivated to assume positions of leadership and equate paid work with being taken seriously.

- Nearly six out of 10 (59%) older adults with encore careers work full time, 73% say they have the flexibility to work when they want to and take time off when needed, and 76% are receiving the compensation (salary and benefits) they need.

- Even older adults who are already retired may return to work in an encore career. Many are willing to retrain and learn new skills to engage in meaningful work.

- Sixty percent of older adults already in encore careers are aged 51 to 62 years and 52% have professional or managerial backgrounds.

- Older adults are interested in achieving a satisfying work-life balance, and they have soundly rejected the notion that the years after age 50 represent a period of decline and disengagement.

- The commitment to service of the current group of older adults is attributable not only to their idealism but also to their historic effort to find meaning and identity in work and the desire to work with others who share common goals.

- Older adults are concerned that the opportunities they seek may not be readily available. There is guidance to help workers plan their financial futures, but there is no comparable "road map" to help them navigate second careers. Older adults are lacking the preparation to obtain jobs in nonprofit service organizations; likewise, this sector is similarly unprepared to accommodate the boomers who are poised to enter it.

- Members of the baby boom generation are experienced at overcoming obstacles and breaking down barriers. As veterans of antiwar protests of the 1960s and the women's movement of the 1970s, boomers are used to speaking up and creating change. If the force of a social movement is required to create career opportunities for older adults, then these seasoned agitators may well be the ones to accomplish this objective.

The survey concludes that the option of pursuing an encore career is considered desirable by a large number of older adults. The MetLife Foundation and Civic Ventures researchers assert that "the millions now in encore careers constitute a new social phenomenon with promise for individuals and society. The tens of millions interested in joining them could add up to one of the most unexpected and significant consequences of an aging America."

Volunteerism in Retirement

Volunteerism among older adults is a relatively new phenomenon. Historically, older adults were seen as the segment of society most in need of care and support. As medical technology enables people to live longer, healthier lives, and as stereotypes about aging shatter, the older population is being recognized as a valuable resource for volunteer organizations.

Every day millions of older Americans perform volunteer work in their communities. Often having more free time as well as the wisdom and experience derived from years of living, they make ideal volunteers. Older adult volunteers are highly educated and skilled and can offer volunteer organizations many of the professional services they would otherwise have to purchase, such as legal, accounting, public relations, information systems support, and human resource management. Perhaps more important, they have empathy and compassion because they have encountered many of the same problems that are faced by those they seek to help.

According to the BLS, in *Volunteering in the United States—2010* (January 26, 2011, http://www.bls.gov/news.release/pdf/volun.pdf), volunteer rates in September 2010 were the lowest for people aged 65 years and older (23.6% of the population) and for those aged 16 to 24 years (21.9%). (See Table 4.6.) Volunteers aged 65 years and older did, however, devote the most time—a median of 96 hours during the year—to volunteer activities. (See Table 4.7.) Older volunteers were more likely to work for religious organizations than younger volunteers. The BLS notes that 44.6% of volunteers aged 65 years and older volunteered primarily for religious organizations, compared to 28.2% of volunteers aged 16 to 24 years. (See Table 4.8.)

NATIONAL SERVICE ORGANIZATIONS. Efforts to establish a national senior service during the administration of President John F. Kennedy (1917–1963) are described by Peter Shapiro in *A History of National Service in America* (1994). In 1963 Kennedy proposed the National Service Corps (NSC) "to provide opportunities for service for those aged persons who can assume active roles in community volunteer efforts." When the NSC was proposed, a scant 11% of the older population was involved in any kind of volunteerism. The plan to engage older adults in full-time, intensive service, with a minimum one-year commitment, to combat urban and rural poverty was viewed as revolutionary. Even though the NSC proposal was championed by the Kennedy administration and widely supported in the public and private sectors, it was defeated in Congress, where reactionary lawmakers linked it to efforts aimed at promoting racial integration in the South.

Despite the defeat of the NSC, the idea of harnessing the volunteer power of older adults caught on. The Economic Opportunity Act of 1964 gave rise to the Volunteers in Service to America (VISTA) and eventually led to the launch of service programs involving low-income older adults, such as the Foster Grandparent, Senior Companion, and Senior Community Service Employment Programs. The Foster Grandparent Program matched

TABLE 4.6

Volunteers by age groups and other selected characteristics, September 2006–September 2010

[Numbers in thousands]

Characteristic	September 2006 Number	September 2006 Percent of population	September 2007 Number	September 2007 Percent of population	September 2008 Number	September 2008 Percent of population	September 2009 Number	September 2009 Percent of population	September 2010 Number	September 2010 Percent of population
Sex										
Total, both sexes	**61,199**	**26.7**	**60,838**	**26.2**	**61,803**	**26.4**	**63,361**	**26.8**	**62,790**	**26.3**
Men	25,546	23.0	25,724	22.9	26,268	23.2	26,655	23.3	26,787	23.2
Women	35,653	30.1	35,114	29.3	35,535	29.4	36,706	30.1	36,004	29.3
Age										
Total, 16 years and over	**61,199**	**26.7**	**60,838**	**26.2**	**61,803**	**26.4**	**63,361**	**26.8**	**62,790**	**26.3**
16 to 24 years	8,044	21.7	7,798	20.8	8,239	21.9	8,290	22.0	8,297	21.9
25 to 34 years	9,096	23.1	9,019	22.6	9,154	22.8	9,511	23.5	9,140	22.3
35 to 44 years	13,308	31.2	12,902	30.5	13,016	31.3	12,835	31.5	12,904	32.2
45 to 54 years	13,415	31.2	13,136	30.1	13,189	29.9	13,703	30.8	13,435	30.3
55 to 64 years	8,819	27.9	9,316	28.4	9,456	28.1	9,894	28.3	9,830	27.2
65 years and over	8,518	23.8	8,667	23.8	8,749	23.5	9,129	23.9	9,184	23.6
Race and Hispanic or Latino ethnicity										
White	52,850	28.3	52,586	27.9	53,078	27.9	54,078	28.3	53,556	27.8
Black or African American	5,211	19.2	5,010	18.2	5,325	19.1	5,712	20.2	5,580	19.4
Asian	1,881	18.5	1,887	17.7	2,022	18.7	2,060	19.0	2,207	19.6
Hispanic or Latino ethnicity	4,212	13.9	4,279	13.5	4,662	14.4	4,873	14.7	4,982	14.7
Educational attainment[a]										
Less than a high school diploma	2,615	9.3	2,394	9.0	2,427	9.4	2,242	8.6	2,231	8.8
High school graduates, no college[b]	11,537	19.2	11,379	18.6	10,998	19.1	11,408	18.8	10,887	17.9
Some college or associate degree	15,196	30.9	15,468	30.7	15,519	30.0	15,931	30.5	15,505	29.2
Bachelor's degree and higher[c]	23,808	43.3	23,799	41.8	24,620	42.2	25,490	42.8	25,870	42.3
Employment status										
Civilian labor force	43,579	28.5	43,405	28.1	44,313	28.5	44,833	29.0	44,522	28.7
Employed	41,861	28.7	41,708	28.3	42,131	28.9	41,372	29.7	40,980	29.2
Full time[d]	32,951	27.3	32,714	26.9	33,344	27.8	32,085	28.7	31,625	28.2
Part time[e]	8,910	35.5	8,994	35.4	8,788	34.2	9,287	33.7	9,355	33.2
Unemployed	1,718	23.8	1,697	23.2	2,181	22.3	3,462	22.9	3,542	23.8
Not in the labor force	17,621	23.1	17,433	22.3	17,491	22.2	18,528	22.6	18,268	22.0

[a]Data refer to persons 25 years and over.
[b]Includes persons with a high school diploma or equivalent.
[c]Includes persons with bachelor's, master's, professional, and doctoral degrees.
[d]Usually work 35 hours or more a week at all jobs.
[e]Usually work less than 35 hours a week at all jobs.
Notes: Estimates for the above race groups (white, black or African American, and Asian) do not sum to totals because data are not presented for all races. Persons whose ethnicity is identified as Hispanic or Latino may be of any race. Updated population controls are introduced annually with the release of January data. Data on volunteers relate to persons who performed unpaid volunteer activities for an organization at any point in the year ending in September.

SOURCE: "Table A. Volunteers by Selected Characteristics, September 2006 through September 2010," in *Volunteering in the United States, 2010*, U.S. Department of Labor, U.S. Bureau of Labor Statistics, January 26, 2011, http://www.bls.gov/news.release/pdf/volun.pdf (accessed April 14, 2011)

1,000 older adults aged 60 years and older with 2,500 children living in orphanages and other institutions. The older adults would spend four hours a day, five days a week, feeding, cuddling, rocking, and exercising disabled children.

The success of the Foster Grandparent Program exceeded all expectations. In 1971 the program was incorporated into the newly created ACTION agency, along with the Peace Corps, VISTA, the Service Corps of Retired Executives (SCORE), and the Active Corps of Executives. Foster Grandparents has since become part of the Senior Corps, a network of programs that tap the experience, skills, and talents of older adults to meet community challenges. Through its three programs—Foster Grandparents, Senior Companions, and Retired and Senior Volunteer Program— nearly half a million Americans aged 55 years and older

assisted local nonprofits, public agencies, and faith-based organizations in 2010. In "Fact Sheet" (February 2011, http://www.seniorcorps.gov/pdf/factsheet_seniorcorps.pdf), the Senior Corps notes that its volunteers worked with 315,374 children in 2010.

Another successful national volunteer program involving older adults is SCORE, the first initiative to use retired business executives as counselors and consultants to small businesses. Established by the Small Business Administration (SBA) in 1964, the program works with recipients of SBA loans and other entrepreneurs, assisting them to draft business plans, evaluate profitability, and develop marketing and sales strategies. One objective of the program is to reduce default rates on these loans. SCORE mentors business owners and provides one-on-one counseling, consultation via e-mail, and training sessions on topics that range

TABLE 4.7

Volunteers by annual hours volunteered and other selected characteristics, September 2010

Characteristics in September 2010	Total volunteers (thousands)	Percent distribution of total annual hours spent volunteering at all organizations							Median annual hours[a]
		Total	1 to 14 hour(s)	15 to 49 hours	50 to 99 hours	100 to 499 hours	500 hours and over	Not reporting annual hours	
Sex									
Total, both sexes	62,790	100.0	20.5	24.7	15.6	28.1	5.7	5.4	52
Men	26,787	100.0	20.3	24.9	15.9	28.0	5.6	5.3	52
Women	36,004	100.0	20.6	24.6	15.3	28.2	5.7	5.5	52
Age									
Total, 16 years and over	62,790	100.0	20.5	24.7	15.6	28.1	5.7	5.4	52
16 to 24 years	8,297	100.0	24.3	27.0	15.3	23.6	3.6	6.2	40
16 to 19 years	4,403	100.0	23.7	28.0	18.0	21.9	2.0	6.4	40
20 to 24 years	3,894	100.0	25.1	25.8	12.2	25.4	5.4	6.1	40
25 years and over	54,493	100.0	19.9	24.4	15.6	28.8	6.0	5.3	52
25 to 34 years	9,140	100.0	26.0	27.0	14.6	22.8	3.9	5.7	40
35 to 44 years	12,904	100.0	23.1	26.0	15.6	26.5	4.9	3.9	48
45 to 54 years	13,435	100.0	19.6	25.2	16.2	28.5	5.5	5.0	52
55 to 64 years	9,830	100.0	17.0	23.3	16.1	30.8	6.5	6.2	60
65 years and over	9,184	100.0	13.0	19.4	15.3	36.4	9.5	6.3	96
Race and Hispanic or Latino ethnicity									
White	53,556	100.0	20.4	24.7	15.8	28.3	5.7	5.1	52
Black or African American	5,580	100.0	19.2	24.2	14.6	28.8	5.6	7.6	52
Asian	2,207	100.0	23.0	25.5	14.1	24.6	5.2	7.6	48
Hispanic or Latino ethnicity	4,982	100.0	22.0	24.2	14.3	28.3	6.8	4.4	52
Educational attainment[b]									
Less than a high school diploma	2,231	100.0	20.5	24.9	15.6	27.7	5.7	5.6	52
High school graduates, no college[c]	10,887	100.0	21.6	23.5	15.2	27.8	6.1	5.8	52
Some college or associate degree	15,505	100.0	21.3	24.2	14.4	28.3	6.9	5.0	52
Bachelor's degree and higher[d]	25,870	100.0	18.3	24.8	16.5	29.7	5.4	5.3	56
Marital status									
Single, never married	14,145	100.0	24.5	26.6	15.2	23.0	4.0	6.6	40
Married, spouse present	38,765	100.0	19.0	24.3	15.8	30.0	6.0	4.8	56
Other marital status[e]	9,880	100.0	20.5	23.5	15.2	28.0	6.7	6.0	52
Presence of own children under 18 years[f]									
Men									
No own children under 18 years old	17,662	100.0	20.0	24.6	15.4	28.1	6.0	6.0	52
With own children under 18 years old	9,124	100.0	21.0	25.4	16.8	28.0	4.8	3.9	52
Women									
No own children under 18 years old	22,467	100.0	19.1	24.0	15.3	29.0	6.2	6.3	52
With own children under 18 years old	13,536	100.0	23.2	25.6	15.4	26.8	4.8	4.2	48
Employment status									
Civilian labor force	44,522	100.0	22.2	26.2	15.8	26.1	4.7	5.1	48
Employed	40,980	100.0	22.2	25.9	16.0	26.1	4.5	5.2	48
Full time[g]	31,625	100.0	22.7	26.2	15.9	25.7	4.3	5.3	48
Part time[h]	9,355	100.0	20.7	25.2	16.3	27.4	5.5	4.9	52
Unemployed	3,542	100.0	21.6	29.3	13.8	25.4	6.3	3.6	47
Not in the labor force	18,268	100.0	16.5	21.1	15.0	33.2	8.0	6.3	72

[a]For those reporting annual hours.
[b]Data refer to persons 25 years and over.
[c]Includes persons with a high school diploma or equivalent.
[d]Includes persons with bachelor's, professional, and doctoral degrees.
[e]Includes divorced, separated, and widowed persons.
[f]Own children include sons, daughters, stepchildren, and adopted children. Not included are nieces, nephews, grandchildren, and other related and unrelated children.
[g]Usually work 35 hours or more a week at all jobs.
[h]Usually work less than 35 hours a week at all jobs.
Notes: Data on volunteers relate to persons who performed unpaid volunteer activities for an organization at any point from September 1, 2009, through the survey period in September 2010. Estimates for the above race groups (white, black or African American, and Asian) do not sum to totals because data are not presented for all races. Persons whose ethnicity is identified as Hispanic or Latino may be of any race.

SOURCE: "Table 2. Volunteers by Annual Hours of Volunteer Activities and Selected Characteristics, September 2010," in *Volunteering in the United States, 2010*, U.S. Department of Labor, U.S. Bureau of Labor Statistics, January 26, 2011, http://www.bls.gov/news.release/pdf/volun.pdf (accessed April 14, 2011)

from pricing strategies to marketing. In 2010 SCORE (http://www.score.org/ourimpact) helped to launch 58,637 businesses, created 71,449 jobs, and saved an additional 17,629 jobs. SCORE volunteers contributed 1,251,331 hours of time to mentor and train 590,550 small business owners in 2010.

TABLE 4.8

Volunteers by type of organization and other selected characteristics, September 2010

			Percent distribution of volunteers by type of main organization[a]									
Characteristics in September 2010	Total volunteers (thousands)	Total	Civic, political, professional, or international	Educa-tional or youth service	Environ-mental or animal care	Hospital or other health	Public safety	Religious	Social or community service	Sport, hobby, cultural, or arts	Other	Not deter-mined
Sex												
Total, both sexes	**62,790**	**100.0**	**5.3**	**26.5**	**2.4**	**7.9**	**1.3**	**33.8**	**13.6**	**3.3**	**3.7**	**2.2**
Men	26,787	100.0	6.4	25.4	2.4	6.5	2.2	32.9	14.2	3.9	4.0	2.1
Women	36,004	100.0	4.5	27.2	2.5	9.0	0.6	34.5	13.1	2.8	3.5	2.2
Age												
Total, 16 years and over	**62,790**	**100.0**	**5.3**	**26.5**	**2.4**	**7.9**	**1.3**	**33.8**	**13.6**	**3.3**	**3.7**	**2.2**
16 to 24 years	8,297	100.0	4.2	30.3	3.3	9.0	1.8	28.2	13.5	3.4	3.5	2.9
16 to 19 years	4,403	100.0	3.3	33.6	2.0	8.0	1.4	30.0	12.6	3.2	2.6	3.2
20 to 24 years	3,894	100.0	5.4	26.5	4.7	10.0	2.2	26.2	14.5	3.6	4.4	2.6
25 years and over	54,493	100.0	5.5	25.9	2.3	7.8	1.2	34.7	13.6	3.3	3.8	2.0
25 to 34 years	9,140	100.0	4.6	31.4	2.7	9.4	1.5	28.0	13.6	3.0	3.5	2.4
35 to 44 years	12,904	100.0	4.2	40.3	1.9	6.4	1.0	27.4	11.9	2.7	2.5	1.6
45 to 54 years	13,435	100.0	5.0	27.8	2.3	6.7	1.2	35.6	11.9	3.4	3.8	2.1
55 to 64 years	9,830	100.0	6.9	15.3	2.7	7.9	1.5	40.0	15.1	3.5	4.8	2.3
65 years and over	9,184	100.0	7.2	8.6	2.0	9.4	0.9	44.6	16.8	4.0	4.6	2.0
Race and Hispanic or Latino ethnicity												
White	53,556	100.0	5.5	26.8	2.7	8.1	1.4	32.6	13.6	3.5	3.8	2.1
Black or African American	5,580	100.0	4.6	23.0	0.5	5.9	0.3	45.4	13.7	1.6	2.8	2.2
Asian	2,207	100.0	2.3	27.0	1.3	8.3	0.3	38.9	10.9	3.3	4.1	3.6
Hispanic or Latino ethnicity	4,982	100.0	3.1	35.7	1.4	5.3	1.2	35.9	10.9	2.2	2.7	1.7
Educational attainment[b]												
Less than a high school diploma	2,231	100.0	3.3	23.9	0.4	4.7	1.0	49.7	11.1	1.2	3.6	1.2
High school graduates, no college[c]	10,887	100.0	5.1	23.7	1.5	8.1	1.8	39.0	12.9	2.5	3.8	1.6
Some college or associate degree	15,505	100.0	5.5	25.2	2.4	8.4	1.7	34.3	13.2	3.1	4.2	1.9
Bachelor's degree and higher[d]	25,870	100.0	5.7	27.3	2.7	7.6	0.7	31.9	14.3	3.9	3.5	2.4
Marital status												
Single, never married	14,145	100.0	5.7	28.4	3.5	9.4	1.4	25.1	15.2	4.1	4.2	3.1
Married, spouse present	38,765	100.0	5.0	27.5	1.9	6.8	1.3	37.5	12.2	3.0	3.1	1.8
Other marital status[e]	9,880	100.0	5.9	19.8	3.1	10.2	1.0	32.2	16.7	3.3	5.3	2.4
Presence of own children under 18 years[f]												
Men												
No own children under 18 years old	17,662	100.0	7.8	18.1	2.9	7.6	2.4	33.5	16.3	4.1	5.0	2.4
With own children under 18 years old	9,124	100.0	3.5	39.6	1.3	4.5	1.8	31.9	10.1	3.6	2.2	1.5
Women												
No own children under 18 years old	22,467	100.0	5.6	16.7	3.2	10.7	0.8	37.1	15.8	3.5	4.0	2.7
With own children under 18 years old	13,536	100.0	2.7	44.8	1.3	6.1	0.2	30.3	8.7	1.8	2.6	1.3
Employment status												
Civilian labor force	44,522	100.0	5.3	28.3	2.5	7.9	1.4	32.1	13.2	3.4	3.7	2.2
Employed	40,980	100.0	5.3	28.0	2.5	7.9	1.4	32.2	13.3	3.5	3.6	2.3
Full time[g]	31,625	100.0	5.8	27.9	2.5	7.9	1.6	31.4	13.6	3.5	3.6	2.3
Part time[h]	9,355	100.0	3.8	28.5	2.4	7.9	0.9	34.9	12.2	3.5	3.8	2.1
Unemployed	3,542	100.0	5.0	31.5	3.0	8.6	1.6	30.2	12.4	2.1	4.3	1.2
Not in the labor force	18,268	100.0	5.3	21.9	2.3	8.0	0.9	38.2	14.4	3.1	3.8	2.1

[a]Main organization is defined as the organization for which the volunteer worked the most hours during the year.
[b]Data refer to persons 25 years and over.
[c]Includes persons with a high school diploma or equivalent.
[d]Includes persons with bachelor's, professional, and doctoral degrees.
[e]Includes divorced, separated, and widowed persons.
[f]Own children include sons, daughters, stepchildren, and adopted children. Not included are nieces, nephews, grandchildren, and other related and unrelated children.
[g]Usually work 35 hours or more a week at all jobs.
[h]Usually work less than 35 hours a week at all jobs.
Notes: Data on volunteers relate to persons who performed unpaid volunteer activities for an organization at any point from September 1, 2009, through the survey period in September 2010. Estimates for the above race groups (white, black or African American, and Asian) do not sum to totals because data are not presented for all races. Persons whose ethnicity is identified as Hispanic or Latino may be of any race.

SOURCE: "Table 4. Volunteers by Type of Main Organization for Which Volunteer Activities Were Performed and Selected Characteristics, September 2010," in *Volunteering in the United States, 2010*, U.S. Department of Labor, U.S. Bureau of Labor Statistics, January 26, 2011, http://www.bls.gov/news.release/pdf/volun.pdf (accessed April 14, 2011).

CHAPTER 5
EDUCATION, VOTING, AND POLITICAL BEHAVIOR

EDUCATIONAL ATTAINMENT OF OLDER AMERICANS

Educational attainment influences employment and socioeconomic status, which in turn affect the quality of life of older adults. Higher levels of education are often associated with greater earning capacity, higher standards of living, and better overall health status.

As of 2008, 77% of the older population had earned a high school diploma and 21% had obtained an undergraduate college degree. (See Figure 5.1.) These figures are in contrast to those from 1965, when just 24% of older adults had earned a high school diploma and only 5% had graduated from college.

Even though educational attainment has increased among older adults, significant differences remain between racial and ethnic groups. Among adults aged 65 years and older in 2008, 82% of non-Hispanic whites and 74% of Asian-Americans had graduated from high school, compared to 60% of African-Americans and 46% of Hispanics. (See Figure 5.2.) Older Asian-Americans were the most likely to have graduated from college (32%), followed by older non-Hispanic whites (22%); just 12% of African-Americans and 9% of Hispanics aged 65 years and older had earned bachelor's degrees.

Lifelong Learning

Live as if you were to die tomorrow. Learn as if you were to live forever.

—Mohandas Gandhi

Campuses are graying as a growing number of older people head back to school. Older adults, both working and retired, are major participants in programs once called adult education (college courses that do not lead to a formal degree). Older adults are also increasingly attending two- and four-year colleges to pursue undergraduate and graduate degrees, as well as taking personal enrichment classes and courses that are sponsored by community senior centers

and parks and recreation facilities. For example, in "2011 Community College Fast Facts" (2011, http://www.aacc.nche.edu/AboutCC/Documents/FactSheet2011.pdf), the American Association of Community Colleges, an advocacy organization for the nation's community (two-year) colleges, indicates that as of 2008, 15% of community college students were aged 40 years and older.

In 2009, 10% of students in all undergraduate programs were aged 40 years and older. (See Table 5.1.) Over 529,000 students aged 40 years and older attended full time, and an additional 1.2 million were part-time students. About 1.7 million of these older students were pursuing undergraduate degrees and nearly 559,000 were studying to obtain graduate degrees.

The ETS Policy Information Center notes in "Adult Education in America" (*Policy Notes*, vol. 16, no. 1, winter 2008) that in 2007 more than 2.7 million people participated in adult education programs. Older adults have the time and resources to seek learning for personal and social reasons. Some universities allow older people to audit courses (take classes without receiving credit toward a degree) for reduced or waived tuition and fees.

Older adults' motivations for returning to school have changed over time. Even though they once may have taken courses primarily for pleasure, older students in the 21st century are likely to return to school for work-related adult education. They are learning new skills, retraining for new careers, or enhancing their existing skills to remain competitive in their fields. Homemakers displaced by divorce or widowhood are often seeking education and training to enable them to reenter the workforce.

ELDERHOSTELS MEET OLDER ADULTS' NEEDS FOR EDUCATION AND ADVENTURE. Founded in 1975, Elderhostel (2011, http://www.elderhostel.org/) is a nonprofit organization that offers learning adventures for people aged 55 years and older. In *2010 Annual Report* (2011,

FIGURE 5.1

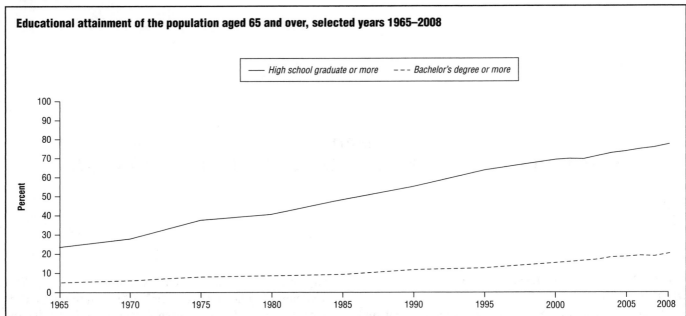

Educational attainment of the population aged 65 and over, selected years 1965–2008

——— High school graduate or more   - - - Bachelor's degree or more

Notes: A single question which asks for the highest grade or degree completed is now used to determine educational attainment. Prior to 1995, educational attainment was measured using data on years of school completed.
Reference population: These data refer to the civilian noninstitutionalized population.

SOURCE: "Educational Attainment of the Population Age 65 and over, Selected Years, 1965–2008," in *Older Americans 2010: Key Indicators of Well-Being*, Federal Interagency Forum on Aging-Related Statistics, July 2010, http://www.agingstats.gov/agingstatsdotnet/Main_Site/Data/2010_Documents/Docs/OA_2010.pdf (accessed April 2, 2011)

FIGURE 5.2

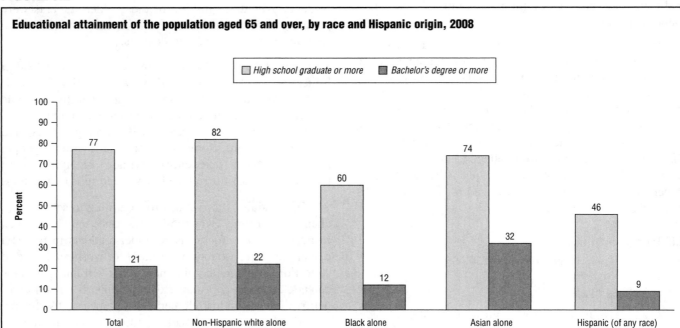

Educational attainment of the population aged 65 and over, by race and Hispanic origin, 2008

▢ High school graduate or more   ▪ Bachelor's degree or more

Note: The term "non-Hispanic white alone" is used to refer to people who reported being white and no other race and who are not Hispanic. The term "black alone" is used to refer to people who reported being black or African American and no other race, and the term "Asian alone" is used to refer to people who reported only Asian as their race. The use of single-race populations in this report does not imply that this is the preferred method of presenting or analyzing data. The U.S. Census Bureau uses a variety of approaches.
Reference population: These data refer to the civilian noninstitutionalized population.

SOURCE: "Educational Attainment of the Population Age 65 and over, by Race and Hispanic Origin, 2008," in *Older Americans 2010: Key Indicators of Well-Being*, Federal Interagency Forum on Aging-Related Statistics, July 2010, http://www.agingstats.gov/agingstatsdotnet/Main_Site/Data/2010_Documents/Docs/OA_2010.pdf (accessed April 2, 2011)

TABLE 5.1

Enrollment in degree-granting institutions by sex, age, and attendance status, Fall 2007 and 2009

Age of student and attendance status	Fall 2007 All levels			Fall 2009 All levels			Fall 2009 Undergraduate			Fall 2009 Postbaccalaureate		
	Total	Males	Females	Total	Males	Females	Total	Males	Females	Total	Males	Females
1	2	3	4	5	6	7	8	9	10	11	12	13
All students	**18,248,128**	**7,815,914**	**10,432,214**	**20,427,711**	**8,769,504**	**11,658,207**	**17,565,320**	**7,595,481**	**9,969,839**	**2,862,391**	**1,174,023**	**1,688,368**
Under 18	668,426	277,582	390,844	757,239	314,150	443,089	756,952	314,045	442,907	287	105	182
18 and 19	3,963,371	1,794,001	2,169,370	4,300,248	1,946,838	2,353,410	4,298,311	1,946,160	2,352,151	1,937	678	1,259
20 and 21	3,642,872	1,647,492	1,995,380	4,003,222	1,814,622	2,188,600	3,971,829	1,802,523	2,169,306	31,393	12,099	19,294
22 to 24	3,009,713	1,381,504	1,628,209	3,315,227	1,520,388	1,794,839	2,725,760	1,282,572	1,443,188	589,467	237,816	351,651
25 to 29	2,550,482	1,091,510	1,458,972	2,961,851	1,277,580	1,684,271	2,044,157	881,057	1,163,100	917,694	396,523	521,171
30 to 34	1,365,912	551,208	814,704	1,635,355	663,459	971,896	1,177,534	457,992	719,542	457,821	205,467	252,354
35 to 39	980,818	368,814	612,004	1,128,666	426,387	702,279	841,719	305,628	536,091	286,947	120,759	166,188
40 to 49	1,266,171	423,603	842,568	1,449,671	498,553	951,118	1,097,374	371,599	725,775	352,297	126,954	225,343
50 to 64	627,603	208,067	419,536	734,572	247,034	487,538	536,289	184,110	352,179	198,283	62,924	135,359
65 and over	77,379	31,040	46,339	69,844	29,251	40,593	61,650	25,505	36,145	8,194	3,746	4,448
Age unknown	95,381	41,093	54,288	71,816	31,242	40,574	53,745	24,290	29,455	18,071	6,952	11,119
Full-time	**11,269,892**	**5,029,444**	**6,240,448**	**12,722,782**	**5,670,644**	**7,052,138**	**11,143,499**	**4,976,727**	**6,166,772**	**1,579,283**	**693,917**	**885,366**
Under 18	171,784	69,033	102,751	177,445	71,603	105,842	177,332	71,566	105,766	113	37	76
18 and 19	3,383,318	1,522,297	1,861,021	3,640,621	1,636,522	2,004,099	3,638,867	1,635,905	2,002,962	1,754	617	1,137
20 and 21	2,964,697	1,346,897	1,617,800	3,249,604	1,477,485	1,772,119	3,221,556	1,466,453	1,755,103	28,048	11,032	17,016
22 to 24	1,986,776	949,700	1,037,076	2,198,573	1,047,143	1,151,430	1,737,688	855,243	882,445	460,885	191,900	268,985
25 to 29	1,284,698	584,798	699,900	1,540,444	705,203	835,241	980,396	444,069	536,327	560,048	261,134	298,914
30 to 34	565,710	235,321	330,389	725,901	304,439	421,462	505,141	197,344	307,797	220,760	107,095	113,665
35 to 39	347,864	130,397	217,467	447,946	169,775	278,171	332,217	118,170	214,047	115,729	51,605	64,124
40 to 49	380,043	125,982	254,061	501,869	173,301	328,568	379,205	126,766	252,439	122,664	46,535	76,129
50 to 64	145,757	47,812	97,945	207,365	70,665	136,700	145,838	50,045	95,793	61,527	20,620	40,907
65 and over	4,868	2,260	2,608	6,642	2,871	3,771	4,378	1,853	2,525	2,264	1,018	1,246
Age unknown	34,377	14,947	19,430	26,372	11,637	14,735	20,881	9,313	11,568	5,491	2,324	3,167
Part-time	**6,978,236**	**2,786,470**	**4,191,766**	**7,704,929**	**3,098,860**	**4,606,069**	**6,421,821**	**2,618,754**	**3,803,067**	**1,283,108**	**480,106**	**803,002**
Under 18	496,642	208,549	288,093	579,794	242,547	337,247	579,620	242,479	337,141	174	68	106
18 and 19	580,053	271,704	308,349	659,627	310,316	349,311	659,444	310,255	349,189	183	61	122
20 and 21	678,175	300,595	377,580	753,618	337,137	416,481	750,273	336,070	414,203	3,345	1,067	2,278
22 to 24	1,022,937	431,804	591,133	1,116,654	473,245	643,409	988,072	427,329	560,743	128,582	45,916	82,666
25 to 29	1,265,784	506,712	759,072	1,421,407	572,377	849,030	1,063,761	436,988	626,773	357,646	135,389	222,257
30 to 34	800,202	315,887	484,315	909,454	359,020	550,434	672,393	260,648	411,745	237,061	98,372	138,689
35 to 39	632,954	238,417	394,537	680,720	256,612	424,108	509,502	187,458	322,044	171,218	69,154	102,064
40 to 49	886,128	297,621	588,507	947,802	325,252	622,550	718,169	244,833	473,336	229,633	80,419	149,214
50 to 64	481,846	160,255	321,591	527,207	176,369	350,838	390,451	134,065	256,386	136,756	42,304	94,452
65 and over	72,511	28,780	43,731	63,202	26,380	36,822	57,272	23,652	33,620	5,930	2,728	3,202
Age unknown	61,004	26,146	34,858	45,444	19,605	25,839	32,864	14,977	17,887	12,580	4,628	7,952

TABLE 5.1

Enrollment in degree-granting institutions by sex, age, and attendance status, Fall 2007 and 2009 [CONTINUED]

Age of student and attendance status	Fall 2007 All levels			Fall 2009 All levels			Fall 2009 Undergraduate			Fall 2009 Postbaccalaureate		
	Total	Males	Females	Total	Males	Females	Total	Males	Females	Total	Males	Females
1	2	3	4	5	6	7	8	9	10	11	12	13
				Percentage distribution								
All students	100.0	100.0	100.0	100.0	100.0	100.0	100.0	100.0	100.0	100.0	100.0	100.0
Under 18	3.7	3.6	3.7	3.7	3.6	3.8	4.3	4.1	4.4	#	#	#
18 and 19	21.7	23.0	20.8	21.1	22.2	20.2	24.5	25.6	23.6	0.1	0.1	0.1
20 and 21	20.0	21.1	19.1	19.6	20.7	18.8	22.6	23.7	21.8	1.1	1.0	1.1
22 to 24	16.5	17.7	15.6	16.2	17.3	15.4	15.5	16.9	14.5	20.6	20.3	20.8
25 to 29	14.0	14.0	14.0	14.5	14.6	14.4	11.6	11.6	11.7	32.1	33.8	30.9
30 to 34	7.5	7.1	7.8	8.0	7.6	8.3	6.7	6.0	7.2	16.0	17.5	14.9
35 to 39	5.4	4.7	5.9	5.5	4.9	6.0	4.8	4.0	5.4	10.0	10.3	9.8
40 to 49	6.9	5.4	8.1	7.1	5.7	8.2	6.2	4.9	7.3	12.3	10.8	13.3
50 to 64	3.4	2.7	4.0	3.6	2.8	4.2	3.1	2.4	3.5	6.9	5.4	8.0
65 and over	0.4	0.4	0.4	0.3	0.3	0.3	0.4	0.3	0.4	0.3	0.3	0.3
Age unknown	0.5	0.5	0.5	0.4	0.4	0.3	0.3	0.3	0.3	0.6	0.6	0.7
Full-time	100.0	100.0	100.0	100.0	100.0	100.0	100.0	100.0	100.0	100.0	100.0	100.0
Under 18	1.5	1.4	1.6	1.4	1.3	1.5	1.6	1.4	1.7	#	#	#
18 and 19	30.0	30.3	29.8	28.6	28.9	28.4	32.7	32.9	32.5	0.1	0.1	0.1
20 and 21	26.3	26.8	25.9	25.5	26.1	25.1	28.9	29.5	28.5	1.8	1.6	1.9
22 to 24	17.6	18.9	16.6	17.3	18.5	16.3	15.6	17.2	14.3	29.2	27.7	30.4
25 to 29	11.4	11.6	11.2	12.1	12.4	11.8	8.8	8.9	8.7	35.5	37.6	33.8
30 to 34	5.0	4.7	5.3	5.7	5.4	6.0	4.5	4.0	5.0	14.0	15.4	12.8
35 to 39	3.1	2.6	3.5	3.5	3.0	3.9	3.0	2.4	3.5	7.3	7.4	7.2
40 to 49	3.4	2.5	4.1	3.9	3.1	4.7	3.4	2.5	4.1	7.8	6.7	8.6
50 to 64	1.3	1.0	1.6	1.6	1.2	1.9	1.3	1.0	1.6	3.9	3.0	4.6
65 and over	#	#	#	0.1	0.1	0.1	#	#	#	0.1	0.1	0.1
Age unknown	0.3	0.3	0.3	0.2	0.2	0.2	0.2	0.2	0.2	0.3	0.3	0.4
Part-time	100.0	100.0	100.0	100.0	100.0	100.0	100.0	100.0	100.0	100.0	100.0	100.0
Under 18	7.1	7.5	6.9	7.5	7.8	7.3	9.0	9.3	8.9	#	#	#
18 and 19	8.3	9.8	7.4	8.6	10.0	7.6	10.3	11.8	9.2	#	#	#
20 and 21	9.7	10.8	9.0	9.8	10.9	9.0	11.7	12.8	10.9	0.3	0.2	0.3
22 to 24	14.7	15.5	14.1	14.5	15.3	14.0	15.4	16.3	14.7	10.0	9.6	10.3
25 to 29	18.1	18.2	18.1	18.4	18.5	18.4	16.6	16.7	16.5	27.9	28.2	27.7
30 to 34	11.5	11.3	11.6	11.8	11.6	12.0	10.5	10.0	10.8	18.5	20.5	17.3
35 to 39	9.1	8.6	9.4	8.8	8.3	9.2	7.9	7.2	8.5	13.3	14.4	12.7
40 to 49	12.7	10.7	14.0	12.3	10.5	13.5	11.2	9.3	12.4	17.9	16.8	18.6
50 to 64	6.9	5.8	7.7	6.8	5.7	7.6	6.1	5.1	6.7	10.7	8.8	11.8
65 and over	1.0	1.0	1.0	0.8	0.9	0.8	0.9	0.9	0.9	0.5	0.6	0.4
Age unknown	0.9	0.9	0.8	0.6	0.6	0.6	0.5	0.6	0.5	1.0	1.0	1.0

Rounds to zero.

Note: Degree-granting institutions grant associate's or higher degrees and participate in Title IV federal financial aid programs. Detail may not sum to totals because of rounding.

SOURCE: Thomas D. Snyder and Sally A. Dillow, "Table 200. Total Fall Enrollment in Degree-Granting Institutions, by Level of Enrollment, Sex, Age, and Attendance Status of Student: 2007 and 2009," in *Digest of Education Statistics: 2010*, National Center for Education Statistics, April 2011, http://nces.ed.gov/programs/digest/d10/tables/dt10_200.asp?referrer=list (accessed April 14, 2011)

http://www.roadscholar.org/support/EH_AnnualReport_Feb11_NoDonors.pdf), Elderhostel states that it provided educational opportunities to 97,700 older adults in 2010. Approximately 4,300 Elderhostel programs per year are conducted in the United States and around the world. In 2010 the programs began to operate under a new name: Road Scholar. The Road Scholar programs are diverse and range from three- to five-day classes, field trips, and cultural excursions. Traditional programs provide older adults with opportunities to study diverse cultures, explore ancient histories, study literature and art, and learn about modern peoples and issues. Some participants attend programs that are held on local college and university campuses, whereas others embark on more extensive programs that involve transcontinental travel.

Adventure programs feature outdoor sports such as walking, hiking, camping, kayaking, and biking. The programs combine adventure and learning. For example, a bicycle tour of the Netherlands also includes instruction about the country's history, art, and people. Shipboard programs explore history, art, ecology, and culture while aboard a floating classroom.

Service-learning programs involve both education and hands-on work to serve the needs of a community. Older adults conduct wildlife or marine research, tutor school children, or build affordable housing. The organization also offers a series of intergenerational programs in which older adults and their grandchildren explore subjects that appeal to both young and old, including dinosaurs, hot-air ballooning, and space travel.

Elderhostel notes that of those who participated in the Road Scholar programs in 2010:

- 90% of participants learned something new

- 85% met interesting fellow participants

- 45% were revitalized by their program experience

- 25% stepped outside their comfort zone

- 20% had their perspective on the world changed

- 15% fulfilled a lifelong dream

OLDER ADULTS ARE ONLINE. Rapid technological change has intensified the need for computer and information management skills and ongoing training of the workforce. The growing importance of knowledge- and information-based jobs has created a workforce that is rapidly becoming accustomed to continuous education, training, and retraining throughout one's work life.

Computer technology, especially use of the Internet, has also gained importance in Americans' lives outside of work, facilitating communication via e-mail and enabling interactions and transactions that once required travel now to occur in their home. Examples include online banking and shopping, e-mail communication with physicians and other health care providers, and participation in online support groups.

In *Generations 2010* (December 16, 2010, http://www.pewinternet.org/~/media//Files/Reports/2010/PIP_Generations_and_Tech10_final.pdf), Kathryn Zickuhr of the Pew Research Center reports high Internet use by older adults—in 2010, 81% of adults aged 46 to 55 years, 76% of adults aged 56 to 64 years, 58% of adults aged 65 to 73 years, and 30% of adults aged 74 years and older were online.

Zickuhr notes that 66% of American adults had a broadband Internet connection at home in 2010. The percentage of adults with broadband service decreased with advancing age: 68% of adults aged 46 to 55 years, 61% of adults aged 56 to 64 years, 44% of adults aged 65 to 73 years, and 20% of adults aged 74 years and older. The same pattern persisted for wireless Internet access: 55% of adults aged 46 to 55 years, 46% of adults aged 56 to 64 years, 33% of adults aged 65 to 73 years, and 9% of adults aged 74 years and older.

Older adults use the Internet to conduct research, send e-mail, and purchase products, whereas more younger adults use it for socializing and entertainment. According to Zickuhr, of older adults who went online in 2010, the vast majority sent and received e-mail: 91% of adults aged 46 to 55 years, 93% of adults aged 56 to 64 years, 90% of adults aged 65 to 73 years, and 88% of adults aged 74 years and older. Similar proportions used search engines. From half to nearly three-quarters of older adults visited government websites and about 40% sought financial information online. Zickuhr indicates that 50% of adults aged 46 to 55 years and 43% of adults aged 56 to 64 years used social networking sites in 2010. Among older adults aged 65 to 73 years the percentage fell to 34% and just 16% of adults aged 74 years and older used social networking sites.

In 2010 older Internet users were less likely than younger Internet users to play games and watch videos online, send instant messages, download music, read or create blogs, or visit virtual worlds. There was much less variation by age for other online activities. Older and younger users were about the same in terms of looking for health information, researching and rating products, obtaining news, donating to charity, and making travel reservations.

OLDER ADULTS JOIN SOCIAL NETWORKS. Zickuhr finds that even though young people were still much more likely than older adult Internet users to participate in social networking sites in 2010, use by older adults had risen sharply since 2008. Use of social networking sites by adults aged 46 to 55 years rose by 30 percentage points, from 20% in December 2008 to 50% in May 2010. During this same period there was also an increase among adults aged 56 to 64 years, from 9% in December 2008 to 43% in May 2010. The sharpest increase was among the oldest generation of Internet users—among adults aged 74 years and older social networking use soared from 4% in December 2008 to 16% in May 2010.

Older adults worldwide are flocking to social networking sites. The article "More Silver Surfers Are Using Social Networking Sites" (Techsling.com, November 10, 2010) reports that in the United Kingdom nearly half of women aged 55 years and older visit social networking sites and about one-third of adults aged 55 years and older watch videos on websites such as YouTube. In June 2011 Facebook (http://www.facebook.com/press/info.php?statistics) had over 500 million users worldwide and was rapidly growing among adults aged 55 years and older. Jean Koppen of the AARP reports in *Social Media and Technology Use among Adults 50+* (June 2010, http://www.aact.org/resources/socmedia.pdf) that in 2010, 27% of adults aged 50 years and older engaged in social networking, and among adults aged 50 years and older who used social networking sites, 62% were connected to their children, 36% were connected to grandchildren, and 73% were connected to relatives other than children and grandchildren.

THEY ALSO TEXT, BLOG, AND TWEET. Even though there are few reliable statistics about the numbers of older adults who use personal digital assistants (small mobile hand-held devices that provide computing and information storage and retrieval capabilities) and smartphones (mobile phones that offer advanced capabilities, often with the functionality of a personal computer), and who create and maintain blogs, send text messages, or "tweet" (post or enter a status update on Twitter, a blogging service that limits entries to 140 characters), the ranks of older bloggers and Twitterers are growing.

Koppen reports that in 2010, 9% of adults aged 50 years and older accessed the Internet using a mobile phone, smartphone (iPhone or Blackberry), or iPad. Of Internet users aged 50 years and older, just 3% said they use Twitter and 73% said they do not use social media websites at all.

Zickuhr finds that in 2010, 11% each of adults aged 46 to 55 years and 56 to 64 years wrote blogs. In "SMS Becoming Prevalent among Older Generations: Study" (January 13, 2010, http://www.mobilemarketer.com/cms/news/research/5077.html), Chris Harnick reports that 60% of adults aged 45 years and older send text messages.

OLDER ADULTS PLAY VIDEO GAMES. Video games are also popular among older adults. For some, the console game versions of their once-favorite sports help them to stay "in the game," even when an injury, disability, or illness prevents them from actually participating in tennis, bowling, or golf. Others feel that playing video games helps them to exercise their brains, eye-hand coordination, and reflexes. Still others simply find video games as diverting and entertaining as do younger players.

According to John Gaudiosi, in "GDC 2011: Game Developers Focus on New Baby Boomer Casual Gamers" (GamerLive.TV, March 3, 2011), almost half (46%) of all social gamers are aged 50 years and older and 20% are over the age of 60 years. Gaudiosi asserts that baby boomers (people born between 1946 and 1964) are a rapidly growing group of users and opines that older adults "enjoy playing multi-player games in real-time with new online friends— it's the hip new way to socialize, especially since daily face-to-face human interaction may be limited due to mobility and health problems."

In "Can Training in a Real-Time Strategy Video Game Attenuate Cognitive Decline in Older Adults?" (*Psychology and Aging*, vol. 23, no. 4, December 2008), Chandramallika Basak et al. find that older adults can improve a number of cognitive functions by playing *Rise of Nations*, a strategic video game that focuses on nation-building and territorial expansion. The researchers trained older adults in the real-time strategy video game for 23.5 hours in an attempt to improve their cognitive functions. A battery of cognitive tasks was used to assess the older adults before, during, and after video-game training. The older adults trained to play the game improved significantly more than the control participants, who had not received the training, in functions such as task switching, working memory, visual short-term memory, and reasoning.

Anita Hamilton reports in "Can Gaming Slow Mental Decline in the Elderly?" (*Time*, July 11, 2009) that in 2009 the psychologists Anne McLaughlin and Jason Allaire of North Carolina State University began a four-year study to determine whether playing video games can help preserve older adults' memories and problem-solving skills and protect against cognitive declines that are associated with aging. The study is following 270 older adults who play the Wii game *Boom Blox*, which entails demolishing targets using a variety of weapons, such as slingshots and cannonballs, and requires a range of cognitive skills including memory, reasoning, and problem-solving.

THE POLITICS OF OLDER ADULTS

Older adults are vitally interested in politics and government, and they are especially interested in the issues that directly influence their lives, including eligibility for and reform to Social Security as well as benefits and coverage by Medicare. Historically, they are more likely to vote than adults in other age groups, and because many have retired from the workforce they have time to advocate for the policies and candidates they favor.

Half of Older Voters Favor Obama in the 2012 Presidential Election

The Gallup Organization conducted a poll in February 2011 and found that adults aged 65 years and older were about as likely to support President Barack Obama

(1961–) as a Republican candidate (43% versus 45%) for the 2012 presidential election. (See Table 5.2.) These findings were consistent with the president's approval ratings. A May 2010 Gallup poll found lower approval rates among older adults. Less than half (48%) of adults aged 50 to 64 years and 43% of those aged 65 years and older gave President Obama a favorable job approval rating. (See Table 5.3.)

Percentage supporting re-election of President Obama, by age group, February 2011

Based on registered voters

	Obama	Republican candidate	Other/ not sure
	%	%	%
Men	42	45	13
Women	47	44	9
White	39	51	11
Nonwhite	63	26	10
18 to 34	51	44	5
35 to 54	43	44	13
55 and older	43	45	12
Republican	7	88	5
Independent	41	41	18
Democrat	84	10	6

SOURCE: Lydia Saad, "President Obama Generic Re-Elect—by Major Subgroups," in *Nameless Republican Ties Obama in 2012 Election Preferences*, The Gallup Organization, February 16, 2011, http://www .gallup.com/poll/146138/Nameless-Republican-Ties-Obama-2012-Election-Preferences.aspx (accessed April 18, 2011). Copyright © 2011 by The Gallup Organization. Reproduced by permission of The Gallup Organization.

Job approval ratings of President Obama, by age group, May 2010

	Approval
Party	
Democrat	82%
Independent	47%
Republican	14%
Democrat-Republican gap	68 pct. pts.
Race	
White	43%
Black	89%
Black-white gap	46 pct. pts.
Age	
18 to 29 years	58%
30 to 49 years	50%
50 to 64 years	48%
65 years and older	43%
Young-old gap	15 pct. pts.

May 3–9, 2010, Gallup daily tracking.

SOURCE: Jeffrey M. Jones, "Job Approval Ratings of Barack Obama, by Selected Subgroup," in *Obama Approval Continues to Show Party, Age, Race Gaps*, The Gallup Organization, May 11, 2010, http://www.gallup.com/poll/ 127481/Obama-Approval-Continues-Show-Party-Age-Race-Gaps.aspx (accessed April 18, 2011). Copyright © 2011 by The Gallup Organization. Reproduced by permission of The Gallup Organization.

OLDER ADULTS' RATINGS OF PAST PRESIDENTS. In February 2009 the Gallup Organization asked adults to choose the "greatest" president from among presidents historically regarded as the most revered by Americans: George Washington (1732–1799), Abraham Lincoln (1809–1865), Franklin D. Roosevelt (1882–1945), John F. Kennedy (1917–1963), and Ronald Reagan (1911–2004). (See Figure 5.3.) Roosevelt received the highest percentage of adults aged 65 years and older, presumably because they are old enough to remember him and continue to benefit from the Social Security Act he signed in 1935. In contrast, younger people were more likely to name Lincoln as the greatest president—22% of adults aged 18 to 34 years choose him, compared to 23% of adults aged 35 to 64 years and 20% of adults aged 65 years and older.

Older Americans Express Increased Confidence in the Economy

In 2011 younger Americans were more optimistic about the U.S. economy than were older Americans. The Gallup Organization found that in January 2011, 52% of Americans aged 18 to 29 years said the economy is "getting better," compared to just 37% of adults aged 50 to 64 years and 35% of adults aged 65 years and older. (See Table 5.4.) Nonetheless, the greatest increase in confidence in the economy between 2010 and 2011 was among older adults. The percentage of adults aged 65 years and older who said the economy is improving rose by five percentage points in one year.

"GRAY POWER": A POLITICAL BLOC

AARP's mission is to enhance the quality of life for all as we age, leading positive social change and delivering value to members through information, advocacy and service. We believe strongly in the principles of collective purpose, collective voice, and collective purchasing power, and these principles guide all organization efforts. AARP works tirelessly to fulfill its vision: a society in which everyone ages with dignity and purpose, and in which AARP helps people fulfill their goals and dreams. AARP speaks with one voice—united by a common motto: "To serve, not be served."

—AARP, "About AARP" (2011)

Adults aged 55 to 74 years vote more than any other age group, and it is inevitable that the increasing number of Americans in this cohort will wield an enormous political impact. With nearly 40 million members, the AARP (2011, http://www.aarp.org/about-aarp/policies/) exercises considerable influence when lobbying and educating political leaders about the issues that concern older Americans.

As part of its mission, the AARP advocates on behalf of older adults. The AARP is known as a powerful advocate on a range of legislative, consumer, and legal issues. To this end, the organization monitors issues that are pertinent to the lives of older Americans, assesses public opinion on such issues, and keeps policy makers

FIGURE 5.3

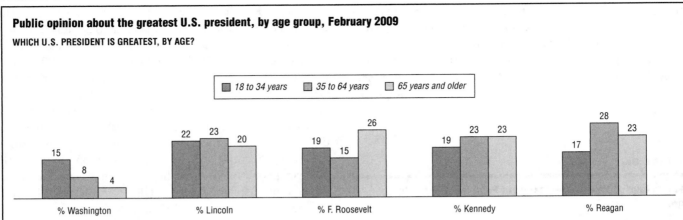

Public opinion about the greatest U.S. president, by age group, February 2009

WHICH U.S. PRESIDENT IS GREATEST, BY AGE?

■ 18 to 34 years ■ 35 to 64 years □ 65 years and older

SOURCE: Lydia Saad, "Which U.S. President Is Greatest, by Age?" in *Best President? Lincoln on Par with Reagan, Kennedy*, The Gallup Organization, February 11, 2009, http://www.gallup.com/poll/114292/Best-President-Lincoln-Par-Reagan-Kennedy.aspx (accessed April 18, 2011). Copyright © 2011 by The Gallup Organization. Reproduced by permission of The Gallup Organization.

TABLE 5.4

Public opinion about the U.S. economy, 2010 and 2011

Percentage of Americans saying the economy is "getting better," January 2010 and January 2011

Monthly averages

	Getting better, January 2010	Getting better, January 2011	Change, 2010 to 2011
	%	%	Pct. pts.
All	38	41	3
Men	39	43	4
Women	37	39	2
18 to 29 years	52	52	0
30 to 40 years	38	42	4
50 to 64 years	36	37	1
65 years and older	30	35	5
East	40	42	2
Midwest	39	42	3
South	36	39	3
West	41	42	1
Upper income	43	50	7
Middle and lower income	39	40	1
Democrat	54	55	1
Independent	34	38	4
Republican	26	30	4

SOURCE: Dennis Jacobe, "Percentage of Americans Saying the Economy is 'Getting Better' by Demographics, January 2010 and January 2011," in *Economic Optimism in U.S. Ties Three-Year High*, The Gallup Organization, February 8, 2011, http://www.gallup.com/poll/145997/Economic-Optimism-Ties-Three-Year- High.aspx, (accessed April 18, 2011). Copyright © 2011 by The Gallup Organization. Reproduced by permission of The Gallup Organization.

apprised of these opinions. Advocacy efforts also include becoming involved in litigation when the decision could have a significant effect on the lives of older Americans. In cases regarding age discrimination, pensions, health care, economic security, and consumer issues, AARP lawyers will file amicus briefs (legal documents filed by individuals or groups that are not actual parties to a lawsuit but that are interested in influencing the outcome of the lawsuit) and support third-party lawsuits to promote the interests of older people.

Historically, the AARP has issued policy statements about topics such as age discrimination, quality of care in nursing facilities, Social Security, Medicare and other health coverage, paying for prescription drugs and long-term care, nontraditional living arrangements, and pension plan reforms. It also offers pertinent information for older adults on topics such as health, travel, employment, technology, volunteer and learning opportunities, and member discounts and benefits.

The AARP regularly responds to political and policy issues of concern to its constituency. For example, AARP notes in "Tell Congress: Keep Your Promises" (2011, http://action.aarp.org/site/PageServer?pagename=Advocacy _Home) that in 2011 it advocated to protect Social Security from budget cuts and reductions in benefits to "ensure that Washington doesn't unfairly target cuts in benefits that today's older Americans have earned over a lifetime of hard work."

Silver-Haired Legislatures

The health of a democratic society may be measured by the quality of functions performed by private citizens.

—Alexis de Tocqueville

As of 2011, 31 states had "silver-haired legislatures" (activists aged 60 years and older who propose and track legislation affecting older adults). Members of these legislatures are elected by their peers and try to influence bills pertaining to medical care, pension plan reform, consumer protection, and age discrimination, often by educating the real legislators and policy makers about the issues. Their ranks include former teachers, judges, doctors, business owners, and even retired legislators.

CHAPTER 6
ON THE ROAD: OLDER ADULT DRIVERS

Older adults who maintain active lifestyles and are mobile are healthier and live longer than their transportation-disadvantaged counterparts.... Public transit may provide older adults with greater mobility options, but it is generally underutilized, even if it is available.

—Rhianna JoIris Babka, Jill F. Cooper, and David R. Ragland, *Evaluation of Urban Travel Training for Older Adults* (November 15, 2008)

Readily available transportation is a vital factor in the quality of life of older adults. Transportation is essential for accessing health care, establishing and maintaining social and family relationships, obtaining food and other necessities, and preserving independence and self-esteem.

The ability to drive often determines whether an older adult is able to live independently. Driving is the primary mode of transportation in the United States, and personal vehicles remain the transportation mode of choice for almost all Americans, including older people. Surveys conducted by the AARP repeatedly confirm that people over the age of 65 years make nearly all their trips in private vehicles, either as drivers or passengers. Even in urban areas where public transit is readily available, private vehicles are still used by most older people, with nondrivers relying heavily on family members or friends for transport. According to Liberty Mutual, in "On the Road: Transportation Alternatives" (2011, http://www.libertymutualsolutions.com/ArticleDetails .aspx?id=59), older adult nondrivers rely on alternative forms of transportation, such as rides from family or friends, public transportation, walking, or rides in senior vans or taxicabs.

The National Highway Traffic Safety Administration (NHTSA) states in *Enhancing the Effectiveness of Safety Warning Systems for Older Drivers: Project Report* (December 2010, http://www.nhtsa.gov/DOT/NHTSA/NVS/Crash% 20Avoidance/Technical%20Publications/2010/811417.pdf) that people aged 65 years and older are the fastest-growing segment of the driving population. In "Older Adult Drivers: Get the Facts" (March 14, 2011, http://www.cdc.gov/ Motorvehiclesafety/Older_Adult_Drivers/adult-drivers _factsheet.html), the Centers for Disease Control and Prevention reports that the number of older drivers increased by 23% between 1999 and 2009, when 33 million adults aged 65 years and older were licensed drivers.

Federal Highway Administration data reveal that in 2009 the percentage of older drivers was comparable for men and women aged 65 to 74 years, but for people aged 75 years and older slightly more women than men were licensed drivers. (See Table 6.1.) Donald H. Camph notes in *A New Vision of America's Highways: Long-Distance Travel, Recreation, Tourism, and Rural Travel* (March 2007, http:// www.transportationvision.org/docs/vision_HighwayTravel .pdf) that as the huge cohort (a group of individuals that shares a common characteristic such as birth years and is studied over time) of baby boomers (people born between 1946 and 1964) joins the ranks of older adults, the number of drivers aged 65 years and older will continue to grow, exceeding 40 million by 2020.

Camph observes, however, that even though many older adults drive and many more are expected to in the future, driving is not a viable alternative for a significant number of older people. Many older adults choose to stop or limit their driving for health or safety reasons. Others do not have access to a vehicle. Camph also asserts that "more than 50 percent of nondrivers age 65 and older—or 3.6 million Americans—stay home on any given day at least partially because they lack transportation options."

Limited income also restricts many older adults' use of automobiles. According to the U.S. Bureau of Labor Statistics, car ownership costs are the second-largest household expense in the United States, and the average household spends nearly as much to own and operate a car as it does on food and health care combined. Table 6.2 shows that the average costs associated with car ownership rose from $7,417 in 2000 to $8,604 in 2008, largely in response to increased spending on gas and motor oil. The cost of owning

TABLE 6.1

Licensed drivers, by sex and percentage in each age group and relation to population, 2009

	Male drivers			Female drivers			Total drivers		
Age	Number	Percent of total drivers	Drivers as percent of age group*	Number	Percent of total drivers	Drivers as percent of age group*	Number	Percent of total drivers	Drivers as percent of age group*
Under 16	205,819	0.2	9.7	203,707	0.2	10.1	409,526	0.2	9.9
16	661,542	0.6	30.5	653,647	0.6	31.8	1,315,189	0.6	31.1
17	1,074,210	1.0	48.7	1,038,004	1.0	49.4	2,112,214	1.0	49.0
18	1,454,714	1.4	64.6	1,371,428	1.3	64.2	2,826,142	1.3	64.4
19	1,682,410	1.6	73.0	1,586,960	1.5	72.9	3,269,370	1.6	72.9
(19 and under)	5,078,695	4.9	46.0	4,853,746	4.6	46.3	9,932,441	4.7	46.1
20	1,725,164	1.7	77.3	1,664,945	1.6	79.0	3,390,109	1.6	78.1
21	1,737,152	1.7	78.7	1,701,252	1.6	81.7	3,438,404	1.6	80.1
22	1,748,368	1.7	79.6	1,721,289	1.6	83.2	3,469,657	1.7	81.3
23	1,783,529	1.7	80.3	1,755,998	1.7	84.2	3,539,527	1.7	82.2
24	1,809,248	1.7	80.9	1,664,945	1.6	79.3	3,474,193	1.7	80.1
(20–24)	8,803,461	8.4	79.4	8,508,429	8.1	81.5	17,311,890	8.3	80.4
25–29	9,220,823	8.8	83.0	9,259,978	8.8	87.7	18,480,801	8.8	85.3
30–34	8,920,803	8.6	88.3	8,925,213	8.5	91.3	17,846,016	8.5	89.7
35–39	9,425,284	9.0	91.0	9,366,230	8.9	92.0	18,791,514	9.0	91.5
40–44	9,729,068	9.3	92.6	9,637,551	9.1	91.9	19,366,619	9.2	92.3
45–49	10,577,280	10.1	93.6	10,611,435	10.1	92.0	21,188,715	10.1	92.8
50–54	10,176,767	9.8	95.3	10,300,410	9.8	92.9	20,477,177	9.8	94.1
55–59	8,924,975	8.6	97.0	9,081,971	8.6	93.0	18,006,946	8.6	94.9
60–64	7,512,657	7.2	99.2	7,637,238	7.2	92.7	15,149,895	7.2	95.8
65–69	5,469,758	5.2	99.2	5,617,954	5.3	89.6	11,087,712	5.3	94.1
70–74	3,938,666	3.8	96.5	4,098,377	3.9	83.2	8,037,043	3.8	89.2
75–79	2,943,028	2.8	93.5	3,172,884	3.0	76.0	6,115,912	2.9	83.5
80–84	2,060,345	2.0	89.6	2,354,148	2.2	66.8	4,414,493	2.1	75.8
85 and over	1,480,203	1.4	83.0	1,799,469	1.7	46.8	3,279,672	1.6	58.2
Total	**104,261,813**	**100.0**	**87.0**	**105,356,573**	**100.0**	**84.1**	**209,618,386**	**100.0**	**85.5**

*These percentages are computed using population estimates of the Bureau of the Census. Under-16 age group is compared to 14 and 15-year-old population estimates; the other age brackets coincide with those from the Bureau of the Census.

SOURCE: "Distribution of Licensed Drivers—2009 by Sex and Percentage in Each Age Group and Relation to Population," in *Highway Statistics 2009*, U.S. Department of Transportation, Federal Highway Administration, December 2010, http://www.fhwa.dot.gov/policyinformation/statistics/2009/pdf/dl20.pdf (accessed April 18, 2011)

and operating an automobile, especially during periods of rising fuel prices, may be prohibitive for older adults living on fixed incomes. As a result, an ever-increasing proportion of the older population depends on alternative forms of transport in those areas where such transport is available; however, some older adults remain isolated and immobilized by the absence of accessible, affordable transportation in their communities.

According to the U.S. Government Accountability Office (GAO), in *Transportation-Disadvantaged Seniors: Efforts to Enhance Senior Mobility Could Benefit from Additional Guidance and Information* (August 2004, http://www.gao.gov/new.items/d04971.pdf), in 2004 adults aged 75 years and older who lived in small towns (45%) and rural areas (23%) were much less likely than residents of cities (84%) and suburbs (69%) to have access to public transportation. Rhianna JoIris Babka, Jill F. Cooper, and David R. Ragland observe in *Evaluation of Urban Travel Training for Older Adults* (November 15, 2008, http://www.tsc.berkeley.edu/news/TSCtrb2009/TrainingRhiannaJill09-2843.pdf) that even when public transportation is available, it is underutilized, at least in part because many older adults are unfamiliar with public transit and how to use it.

TRANSPORTATION INITIATIVES ADDRESS NEEDS OF OLDER ADULTS

Because ensuring access to transportation is key to older adults' independence and quality of life, several federal agencies and initiatives aim to address this need. The Federal Interagency Coordinating Council on Access and Mobility sponsors United We Ride, an interagency national initiative that supports states and their localities to develop coordinated human service delivery systems. The National Center on Senior Transportation (NCST) aims to assist older adults to remain active vital members of their communities by offering a range of transportation options and alternatives. The NCST-sponsored Senior Transportation program is a collaborative effort that coordinates a range of research and services intended to develop new transportation solutions, especially for rural areas. The program also champions the creative use of technology to connect with volunteers, older drivers, and older adults in need of transportation services. The NCST is overseen by the Easter Seals Inc. and receives funding via the U.S. Department of Transportation's Federal Transit Administration.

In "Tips & Facts" (2011, http://seniortransportation.easterseals.com/site/PageServer?pagename=NCST2_older_tips), the NCST reports that:

TABLE 6.2

Average annual expenditures of all consumer units, by selected types of expenditures, selected years 1990–2008

[In thousands]

Type of expenditure	1990	1995	2000	2004	2005	2006	2007	2008
Number of consumer units (1,000)	96,968	103,123	109,367	116,282	117,356	118,843	120,171	120,770
Expenditures, total* (dol.)	28,381	32,264	38,045	43,395	46,409	48,398	49,638	50,486
Food	4,296	4,505	5,158	5,781	5,931	6,111	6,133	6,443
Food at home*	2,485	2,803	3,021	3,347	3,297	3,417	3,465	3,744
Meats, poultry,fish, and eggs	668	752	795	880	764	797	777	846
Dairy products	295	297	325	371	378	368	387	430
Fruits and vegetables	408	457	521	561	552	592	600	657
Other food at home	746	856	927	1,075	1,158	1,212	1,241	1,305
Food away from home	1,811	1,702	2,137	2,434	2,634	2,694	2,668	2,698
Alcoholic beverages	293	277	372	459	426	497	457	444
Housing*	8,703	10,458	12,319	13,918	15,167	16,366	16,920	17,109
Shelter	4,836	5,928	7,114	7,998	8,805	9,673	10,023	10,183
Utilities, fuels, and public services	1,890	2,191	2,489	2,927	3,183	3,397	3,477	3,649
Apparel and services	1,618	1,704	1,856	1,816	1,886	1,874	1,881	1,801
Transportation*	5,120	6,014	7,417	7,801	8,344	8,508	8,758	8,604
Vehicle purchases	2,129	2,638	3,418	3,397	3,544	3,421	3,244	2,755
Gasoline and motor oil	1,047	1,006	1,291	1,598	2,013	2,227	2,384	2,715
Other vehicle expenses	1,642	2,015	2,281	2,365	2,339	2,355	2,592	2,621
Health care	1,480	1,732	2,066	2,574	2,664	2,766	2,853	2,976
Entertainment	1,422	1,612	1,863	2,218	2,388	2,376	2,698	2,835
Reading	153	162	146	130	126	117	118	116
Tobacco products, smoking supplies	274	269	319	288	319	327	323	317
Personal insurance and pensions	2,592	2,964	3,365	4,823	5,204	5,270	5,336	5,605
Life and other personal insurance	345	373	399	390	381	322	309	317
Pensions and Social Security	2,248	2,591	2,966	4,433	4,823	4,948	5,027	5,288

*Includes expenditures not shown separately.

Notes: Based on Consumer Expenditure Survey. Data are averages for the noninstitutional population. Expenditures reported here are out-of-pocket. Consumer units include families, single persons living alone or sharing a household with others but who are financially independent, or two or more persons living together who share expenses.

SOURCE: "Table 683. Average Annual Expenditures of All Consumer Units by Selected Major Types of Expenditure: 1990–2008," in *Statistical Abstract of the United States: 2011*, 130th ed., U.S. Census Bureau, 2011, http://www.census.gov/compendia/statab/2011/tables/11s0683.pdf (accessed April 18, 2011)

- In 2006 Americans took 10.1 billion trips on public transportation.

- Most (83%) older Americans say "public transit provides easy access to the things that they need in everyday life" and 80% believe public transportation is safer than driving alone, especially at night.

- Public transportation ridership increased by 30% between 1995 and 2006, growing at more than twice the rate of the U.S. population (12%) and higher than the 24% growth in highway use during the same period.

Department of Transportation's Initiatives

In his March 2009 statement to the U.S. House of Representatives' Committee on Appropriations Subcommittee on Transportation, Housing and Urban Development, and Related Agencies, Ray H. LaHood (1945–; http://testimony.ost.dot.gov/test/pasttest/09test/lahood9.htm), the U.S. secretary of transportation, outlined President Barack Obama's (1961–) national priorities for transportation. As part of a Department of Transportation initiative to foster livable communities and transit-oriented development, LaHood promised to "build on innovative ways of doing business that promote mobility and enhance the unique characteristics of our neighborhoods, communities and regions" and to "plan for the unique transportation needs of individual communities; and better accommodate the needs of our aging population."

In March 2011 LaHood (http://fastlane.dot.gov/2011/03/aarp-a-great-partner-in-safety-livability.html) addressed the AARP Driver Safety Program National Leadership Conference and described joint initiatives that are being undertaken by the Department of Transportation and AARP, such as efforts to improve roadway design and ways to "increase pedestrian and public transportation options."

MOTOR VEHICLE ACCIDENTS

The Insurance Institute for Highway Safety (IIHS), a nonprofit, scientific, and educational organization that is dedicated to reducing the losses from motor vehicle accidents, reports that, apart from the youngest drivers, older drivers have the highest rates of fatal crashes per mile driven. Even though older drivers tend to limit their number of miles driven as they age and they drive at the safest times (in daylight and avoiding rush-hour traffic) their rate of accidents per mile is extremely high. In "Fatality Facts 2009: Older People" (December 10, 2010, http://www.iihs.org/research/fatality_facts_2009/olderpeople.html), the IIHS observes that among drivers involved in fatal crashes in 2009, the proportion in multiple-vehicle

FIGURE 6.1

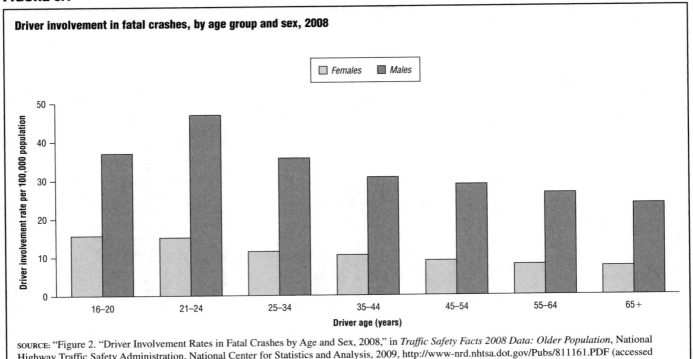

Driver involvement in fatal crashes, by age group and sex, 2008

SOURCE: "Figure 2. "Driver Involvement Rates in Fatal Crashes by Age and Sex, 2008," in *Traffic Safety Facts 2008 Data: Older Population*, National Highway Traffic Safety Administration, National Center for Statistics and Analysis, 2009, http://www-nrd.nhtsa.dot.gov/Pubs/811161.PDF (accessed April 18, 2011)

crashes at intersections increased with driver age, starting at ages 70 to 74. Nearly half (42%) of the fatal motor vehicle accidents among drivers aged 80 years and older were multiple-vehicle crashes, compared to about 20% for drivers younger than age 50. The oldest and youngest drivers have the highest fatality rates on a per-mile-driven basis, but a key difference between the two age groups is that older drivers involved in crashes are less likely than younger drivers to hurt others—older drivers pose more of a danger to themselves. Drivers under the age of 30 are responsible for far more of the injuries and deaths of others than are older adult drivers. Figure 6.1 shows that the rate of driver involvement in fatal crashes in 2008 was much higher in the younger age groups than among the older age groups.

Table 6.3 shows that in 2007 the death rate (the number of deaths per 100,000 people) for motor vehicle–related injuries for adults aged 65 years and older was 18.6%, compared to 14.2% for adults aged 45 to 64 years. The higher fatality rates of adults aged 75 to 84 years and 85 years and older who were involved in crashes—21.8% and 23.2%, respectively—are attributable to older adults' fragility as opposed to the likelihood of being involved in an accident. Older people are more susceptible to injury, especially chest injuries, and are more likely to die as a result of those injuries. However, the IIHS indicates that relatively few deaths (less than 1%) of adults aged 70 years and older are attributable to motor vehicle accidents.

The IIHS reports that in 2009, 80% of motor vehicle crash fatalities among people aged 70 years and older involved occupants in passenger vehicles and 14% were pedestrians. The death rate per 100,000 people for pedestrians aged 70 years and older in 2009 was higher than for pedestrians in all younger age groups.

In 2009, 80% of fatal crashes involving drivers aged 80 years and older were multiple-vehicle accidents. Of those, over four out of 10 (42%) occurred at intersections. The IIHS observes that drivers over the age of 65 are more likely than younger drivers to have accidents when making left turns and attributes this to the fact that older drivers take longer to make turns, increasing the risk of a crash.

Older adults also suffer nonfatal injuries as drivers or passengers in motor vehicle crashes. In 2009 the National Center for Injury Prevention and Control recorded 237,518 nonfatal injuries in adults aged 65 to 85 years. (See Table 6.4; this figure shows the 174,999 injuries to occupants of vehicles and the 62,519 injuries attributable to other transport.) Motor vehicle accidents (called unintentional MV-occupant) were the fourth-leading cause of nonfatal injuries among adults aged 65 to 85 years in the United States in 2009.

The data about older drivers are not all bad. According to the Centers for Disease Control and Prevention, in "Older Adult Drivers: Fact Sheet" (April 19, 2011, http://www.cdc.gov/Motorvehiclesafety/Older_Adult_Drivers/index.html), older adults wear seatbelts more often than

TABLE 6.3

Death rates for motor vehicle-related injuries, by selected characteristics, selected years 1950–2007

[Data are based on death certificates]

Sex, race, Hispanic origin, and age	1950[a,b]	1960[a,b]	1970[b]	1980[b]	1990[b]	2000[c]	2006[c]	2007[c]
All persons				Deaths per 100,000 resident population				
All ages, age-adjusted[d]	24.6	23.1	27.6	22.3	18.5	15.4	15.0	14.4
All ages, crude	23.1	21.3	26.9	23.5	18.8	15.4	15.1	14.6
Under 1 year	8.4	8.1	9.8	7.0	4.9	4.4	3.4	2.9
1–14 years	9.8	8.6	10.5	8.2	6.0	4.3	3.4	3.2
1–4 years	11.5	10.0	11.5	9.2	6.3	4.2	3.6	3.3
5–14 years	8.8	7.9	10.2	7.9	5.9	4.3	3.3	3.2
15–24 years	34.4	38.0	47.2	44.8	34.1	26.9	26.0	24.9
15–19 years	29.6	33.9	43.6	43.0	33.1	26.0	23.2	22.0
20–24 years	38.8	42.9	51.3	46.6	35.0	28.0	28.8	27.8
25–34 years	24.6	24.3	30.9	29.1	23.6	17.3	18.2	17.5
35–44 years	20.3	19.3	24.9	20.9	16.9	15.3	15.3	14.8
45–64 years	25.2	23.0	26.5	18.0	15.7	14.3	14.9	14.2
45–54 years	22.2	21.4	25.5	18.6	15.6	14.2	15.3	14.9
55–64 years	29.0	25.1	27.9	17.4	15.9	14.4	14.3	13.3
65 years and over	43.1	34.7	36.2	22.5	23.1	21.4	19.0	18.6
65–74 years	39.1	31.4	32.8	19.2	18.6	16.5	15.4	15.2
75–84 years	52.7	41.8	43.5	28.1	29.1	25.7	22.3	21.8
85 years and over	45.1	37.9	34.2	27.6	29.1	25.7	22.3	21.8
Male								
All ages, age-adjusted[d]	38.5	35.4	41.5	33.6	26.5	21.7	21.4	20.9
All ages, crude	35.4	31.8	39.7	35.3	26.7	21.3	21.4	20.9
Under 1 year	9.1	8.6	9.3	7.3	5.0	4.6	3.3	2.6
1–14 years	12.3	10.7	13.0	10.0	7.0	4.9	3.7	3.7
1–4 years	13.0	11.5	12.9	10.2	6.9	4.7	3.8	3.7
5–14 years	11.9	10.4	13.1	9.9	7.0	5.0	3.7	3.7
15–24 years	56.7	61.2	73.2	68.4	49.5	37.4	36.6	35.1
15–19 years	46.3	51.7	64.1	62.6	45.5	33.9	30.2	28.5
20–24 years	66.7	73.2	84.4	74.3	53.3	41.2	42.9	41.7
25–34 years	40.8	40.1	49.4	46.3	35.7	25.5	27.4	26.2
35–44 years	32.5	29.9	37.7	31.7	24.7	22.0	21.8	21.7
45–64 years	37.7	33.3	38.9	26.5	21.9	20.2	21.7	21.0
45–54 years	33.6	31.6	37.2	27.6	22.0	20.4	22.6	22.2
55–64 years	43.1	35.6	40.9	25.4	21.7	19.8	20.5	19.4
65 years and over	66.6	52.1	54.4	33.9	32.1	29.5	26.5	27.1
65–74 years	59.1	45.8	47.3	27.3	24.2	21.7	21.1	21.6
75–84 years	85.0	66.0	68.2	44.3	41.2	35.6	30.8	31.9
85 years and over	78.1	62.7	63.1	56.1	64.5	57.5	41.0	39.8
Female								
All ages, age-adjusted[d]	11.5	11.7	14.9	11.8	11.0	9.5	8.8	8.2
All ages, crude	10.9	11.0	14.7	12.3	11.3	9.7	9.0	8.4
Under 1 year	7.6	7.5	10.4	6.7	4.9	4.2	3.5	3.2
1–14 years	7.2	6.3	7.9	6.3	4.9	3.7	3.1	2.8
1–4 years	10.0	8.4	10.0	8.1	5.6	3.8	3.4	3.0
5–14 years	5.7	5.4	7.2	5.7	4.7	3.6	2.9	2.7
15–24 years	12.6	15.1	21.6	20.8	17.9	15.9	14.7	14.1
15–19 years	12.9	16.0	22.7	22.8	20.0	17.5	15.7	15.2
20–24 years	12.2	14.0	20.4	18.9	16.0	14.2	13.7	12.9
25–34 years	9.3	9.2	13.0	12.2	11.5	8.8	8.7	8.4
35–44 years	8.5	9.1	12.9	10.4	9.2	8.8	8.8	7.7
45–64 years	12.6	13.1	15.3	10.3	10.1	8.7	8.3	7.7
45–54 years	10.9	11.6	14.5	10.2	9.6	8.2	8.2	7.8
55–64 years	14.9	15.2	16.2	10.5	10.8	9.5	8.5	7.6
65 years and over	21.9	20.3	23.1	15.0	17.2	15.8	13.5	12.5
65–74 years	20.6	19.0	21.6	13.0	14.1	12.3	10.6	9.7
75–84 years	25.2	23.0	27.2	18.5	21.9	19.2	16.5	14.9
85 years and over	22.1	22.0	18.0	15.2	18.3	19.3	15.2	15.2

any other age group except infants and preschool children, they take fewer risks than younger drivers by limiting their driving during bad weather and at night, and they are less likely to drink and drive than other adult drivers. Table 6.5 reveals that of adult drivers who were involved in fatal crashes in 2008, older drivers and older pedestrians were the least likely to have elevated blood alcohol concentration.

AGE-RELATED CHANGES MAY IMPAIR OLDER DRIVERS' SKILLS

Most older adults retain their driving skills, but some age-related changes in vision, hearing, cognitive functions (attention, memory, and reaction times), reflexes, and flexibility of the head and neck may impair the skills that are critical for safe driving. For example, reaction time becomes slower and more variable with advancing

TABLE 6.3

Death rates for motor vehicle-related injuries, by selected characteristics, selected years 1950–2007 [CONTINUED]

[Data are based on death certificates]

Sex, race, Hispanic origin, and age	1950[a, b]	1960[a, b]	1970[b]	1980[b]	1990[b]	2000[c]	2006[c]	2007[c]
White male[e]				Deaths per 100,000 resident population				
All ages, age-adjusted[d]	37.9	34.8	40.4	33.8	26.3	21.8	21.8	21.3
All ages, crude	35.1	31.5	39.1	35.9	26.7	21.6	22.0	21.5
Under 1 year	9.1	8.8	9.1	7.0	4.8	4.2	3.2	2.7
1–14 years	12.4	10.6	12.5	9.8	6.6	4.8	3.5	3.7
15–24 years	58.3	62.7	75.2	73.8	52.5	39.6	39.2	37.4
25–34 years	39.1	38.6	47.0	46.6	35.4	25.1	27.6	26.5
35–44 years	30.9	28.4	35.2	30.7	23.7	21.8	22.2	21.8
45–64 years	36.2	31.7	36.5	25.2	20.6	19.7	21.6	21.1
65 years and over	67.1	52.1	54.2	32.7	31.4	29.4	26.8	27.2

[a]Includes deaths of persons who were not residents of the 50 states and the District of Columbia (D.C.).
[b]Underlying cause of death was coded according to the 6th Revision of the International Classification of Diseases (ICD) in 1950, 7th Revision in 1960, 8th Revision in 1970, and 9th Revision in 1980–1998.
[c]Starting with 1999 data, cause of death is coded according to ICD-10.
[d]Age-adjusted rates are calculated using the year 2000 standard population. Prior to 2003, age-adjusted rates were calculated using standard million proportions based on rounded population numbers. Starting with 2003 data, unrounded population numbers are used to calculate age-adjusted rates.
[e]The race groups, white, black, Asian or Pacific Islander, and American Indian or Alaska Native, include persons of Hispanic and non-Hispanic origin. Persons of Hispanic origin may be of any race. Death rates for the American Indian or Alaska Native and Asian or Pacific Islander populations are known to be underestimated.
Notes: Starting with *Health, United States, 2003*, rates for 1991–1999 were revised using intercensal population estimates based on the 2000 census. Rates for 2000 were revised based on 2000 census counts. Rates for 2001 and later years were computed using 2000-based postcensal estimates. Age groups were selected to minimize the presentation of unstable age-specific death rates based on small numbers of deaths and for consistency among comparison groups. Starting with 2003 data, some states allowed the reporting of more than one race on the death certificate. The multiple-race data for these states were bridged to the single-race categories of the 1977 Office of Management and Budget standards for comparability with other states. Data for additional years are available.

SOURCE: Adapted from "Table 37. Death Rates for Motor Vehicle-Related Injuries, by Sex, Race, Hispanic Origin, and Age: United States, Selected Years 1950–2007," in *Health, United States, 2010. With Special Feature on Death and Dying*, National Center for Health Statistics, 2011, http://www.cdc.gov/nchs/data/hus/hus10.pdf#037 (accessed April 18, 2011)

TABLE 6.4

Ten leading causes of nonfatal injuries, ages 65–85, 2009

Rank	Age groups 65–85	
1	Unintentional fall	2,202,024
2	Unintentional struck by/against	242,014
3	Unintentional overexertion	180,152
4	Unintentional MV-occupant	174,999
5	Unintentional cut/pierce	127,735
6	Unintentional other bite/sting	86,559
7	Unintentional poisoning	65,707
8	Unintentional other transport	62,519
9	Unintentional unknown/unspecified	59,185
10	Unintentional other specified	48,972

SOURCE: "10 Leading Causes of Nonfatal Injury, United States 2009, All Races, Both Sexes, Disposition: All Cases," National Center for Injury Prevention and Control, 2010, http://webappa.cdc.gov/sasweb/ncipc/nfirates2001.html (accessed April 18, 2011)

age, and arthritis (inflammation that causes pain and loss of movement of the joints) in the neck or shoulder may limit sufferers' ability to turn their neck well enough to merge into traffic, see when backing up, and navigate intersections where the angle of intersecting roads is less than perpendicular.

Changes such as reduced muscle mass and the resultant reduction in strength, as well as decreases in the efficiency of the circulatory, cardiac, and respiratory systems are strictly related to aging. Others are attributable to the fact that certain diseases, such as arthritis and glaucoma (a disease in which fluid pressure inside the eyes slowly rises, leading to vision loss or blindness), tend to strike at later ages. The functional losses that are associated with these chronic (long-term) conditions are usually gradual, and many afflicted older drivers are able to adapt to them. Most older adults do not experience declines until very old age, and most learn to adjust to the limitations imposed by age-related changes. Still, a substantial proportion of older adults do stop driving in response to age-related changes. In "Realizing Dignified Transportation for Seniors" (April 14, 2009, http://media.itnamerica.org/press/ITNAmerica/__www.philanthropystories.org_30Grantsin30Days_RealizingDi.pdf), Philanthropy New York, a community of philanthropic foundations that provides more than $4 billion to thousands of nonprofit organizations around the world, reports that each year more than 1 million older adults stop driving because of declines in their fitness level, vision, and ability to think clearly.

The *Physician's Guide to Assessing and Counseling Older Drivers* (February 2010, http://www.ama-assn.org/resources/doc/public-health/older-drivers-guide.pdf), which was copublished by the American Medical Association (AMA) and the NHTSA, details medical conditions and their potential effect on driving and highlights treatment methods and counseling measures that can minimize these effects. In

TABLE 6.5

Drivers and pedestrians involved in fatal accidents, by age group and blood alcohol concentration, 2008

Age group (years)	Drivers involved in fatal crashes			Pedestrian fatalities		
		BAC = 0.08+			BAC = 0.08+	
	Total	Number	Percent of total	Total	Number	Percent of total
<16	213	21	10	316	14	4
16–20	5,729	996	17	286	85	30
21–34	15,057	4,826	32	852	427	50
35–54	17,075	3,945	23	1,542	751	49
55–64	5,695	708	12	547	191	35
65+	5,569	304	5	803	66	8
Total	50,186[a]	10,946	22	4,378[b]	1,551	35

BAC = blood alcohol concentration
[a]Includes 848 drivers of unknown age.
[b]Includes 32 pedestrian fatalities of unknown age.

SOURCE: "Table 1. Age and Alcohol, 2008," in *Traffic Safety Facts 2008 Data: Older Population*, National Highway Traffic Safety Administration, National Center for Statistics and Analysis, 2009, http://www-nrd.nhtsa.dot.gov/Pubs/811161.PDF (accessed April 18, 2011)

the preface the AMA and the NHTSA identify motor vehicle injuries as the leading cause of injury-related deaths among 65- to 75-year-olds and the second-leading cause of deaths among 75- to 84-year-olds. The AMA and the NHTSA posit that significant growth in the older population and an increase in miles driven by older adults could act to triple the number of traffic fatalities in the coming years. Believing that the medical community can help stem this increase, the AMA and the NHTSA call on physicians to help their patients maintain or even improve their driving skills by periodically assessing them for disease- and medication-related conditions that might impair their capacity to function as safe drivers.

Acute and Chronic Medical Problems

According to the AMA and the NHTSA, in *Physician's Guide to Assessing and Counseling Older Drivers*, patients discharged from the hospital following treatment for serious illnesses may be temporarily, or even permanently, unable to drive safely. Examples of acute (short-term) medical problems that can impair driving performance include:

- Acute myocardial infarction (heart attack)

- Stroke (sudden death of a portion of the brain cells due to a lack of blood flow and oxygen) and other traumatic brain injury

- Syncope (fainting) and vertigo (dizziness)

- Seizures (sudden attacks or convulsions characterized by generalized muscle spasms and loss of consciousness)

- Surgery

- Delirium (altered mental state characterized by wild, irregular, and incoherent thoughts and actions) from any cause

The AMA and the NHTSA note that a variety of chronic medical conditions can also compromise driving function, including:

- Visual disorders such as cataracts, diabetic retinopathy (damage to the blood vessels that supply the retina that can result in blindness), macular degeneration (a degenerative condition that can cause blurred vision), glaucoma, retinitis pigmentosa (an inherited condition that causes night blindness and tunnel vision), and low visual acuity (the inability to distinguish fine details) even after correction with lenses. Along with visual acuity, other visual functions decline with advancing age. For example, sensitivity to glare increases and may be exacerbated by cataracts. Because driving is largely a visual task, impaired vision can significantly compromise the ability to read signs, see lane lines, and identify pedestrians in the dark or during inclement weather.

- Cardiovascular disorders such as angina (chest pain from a blockage in a coronary artery that prevents oxygen-rich blood from reaching part of the heart) or syncope pose dangers to drivers because acute pain or even transient loss of consciousness increases the risk of accidents.

- Neurologic diseases such as seizures, dementia (loss of intellectual functioning accompanied by memory loss and personality changes), multiple sclerosis (a progressive nerve disease that can result in the loss of the ability to walk or speak), Parkinson's disease (a degenerative disease that causes tremors and slowed movement and speech), peripheral neuropathy (numbness or tingling in the hands and/or feet), and residual deficits (losses or disability) resulting from stroke all may impair the driver's ability to operate a vehicle and/or exercise sufficient caution when driving.

- Psychiatric diseases, especially those mental disorders in which patients suffer hallucinations, severe anxiety, and irrational thoughts and are unable to distinguish between reality and imagination, can affect judgment and impair the driver's ability to operate a vehicle.

- Metabolic diseases, such as diabetes mellitus (a condition in which there is increased sugar in the blood and urine because the body is unable to use sugar to produce energy) and hypothyroidism (decreased production of the thyroid hormone by the thyroid gland), can act to impair judgment and response time.

- Musculoskeletal disabilities, such as arthritis and injuries, can impair response time.

The AMA and the NHTSA note that driving requires a range of sophisticated cognitive skills, which is why some cognitive changes can compromise driving ability. It is not unusual for memory, attention, processing speed, and executive skills (the capacity for logical analysis) to decline with advancing age. Weakening memory may make it difficult for some older drivers to process information from traffic signs and to navigate correctly. As multiple demands are made on older drivers' attention, the AMA and the NHTSA state that "drivers must possess selective attention—the ability to prioritize stimuli and focus on only the most important—in order to attend to urgent stimuli (such as traffic signs) while not being distracted by irrelevant ones (such as roadside ads)." Selective attention problems challenge older drivers to distinguish the most critical information when they are faced with many signs and signals. Drivers have to divide their attention to concentrate "on the multiple stimuli involved in most driving tasks." Processing speed affects perception-reaction time and is critical in situations where drivers must immediately choose between actions such as accelerating, braking, or steering. Executive skills enable drivers to make correct decisions after evaluating the stimuli that are related to driving, such as to stop at a red light or stop at a crosswalk when a pedestrian is crossing the street.

Medications

The AMA and the NHTSA indicate in *Physician's Guide to Assessing and Counseling Older Drivers* that many commonly used prescription and over-the-counter (nonprescription) medications can impair driving performance. In general, drugs with strong central nervous system effects, such as antidepressants, antihistamines, muscle relaxants, narcotic analgesics (painkillers), anticonvulsants (used to prevent seizures), and stimulants, have the potential to adversely affect the ability to operate a motor vehicle. The extent to which driving skills are compromised varies from person to person and between different medications that are used for the same purpose. The effects of prescription and over-the-counter medications may be intensified in combination with other drugs or alcohol.

The AMA and the NHTSA note that driving performance can be affected by medication side effects, such as "drowsiness, dizziness, blurred vision, unsteadiness, fainting, [and] slowed reaction time." Generally, these side effects are dose-dependent and lessen over time, but older adults are often more sensitive to the effects of medications and may take longer to metabolize them, prolonging their effects. Medications such as prescription sleep aids "that cause drowsiness, euphoria, and/or anterograde amnesia may also diminish insight, and the patient may experience impairment without being aware of it."

Some Fears about Older Drivers Are Unwarranted

As the ranks of older adults swell, many states and organizations—the AMA and the NHTSA are chief among these groups—are taking action to ensure driver safety. Concern about older driver safety has intensified in recent years in response to a spate of media reports describing serious crashes involving older drivers. However, some of this concern may be unwarranted. In *Declines in Fatal Crashes of Older Drivers: Changes in Crash Risk and Survivability* (June 2010, http://www.iihs.org/research/topics/pdf/r1140.pdf), Ivan Cheung and Anne T. McCartt of the IIHS observe that "older driver fatal crash involvement rates per licensed driver declined substantially in the United States during 1997–2006 and declined much faster than the rate for middle-age drivers." Figure 6.2 shows declining fatality rates among older adults by age group between 1998 and 2008. Cheung and McCartt conducted an analysis of crash data in 13 states to determine whether this decline was attributable to the reduced likelihood of crashing or the improved survival of crash victims. They find that the reduction in deaths is the result of both fewer crashes and improved survival of accident victims.

These findings contradict earlier research, which predicted that older drivers would make up a substantially larger proportion of drivers in fatal crashes. The precise reasons for the fatality declines have not yet been pinpointed, but Cheung and McCartt suggest that older adults increasingly self-limit driving as they age and develop physical and cognitive impairments. For example, adults aged 80 years and older were more than twice as likely as those aged 65 to 69 years to avoid night driving and driving in ice or snow and to make fewer trips and travel shorter distances. According to Tara Parker-Pope, in "Declining Car Risk for Older Drivers" (*New York Times*, January 12, 2009), research suggests that older drivers are in better overall health than their counterparts were during the late 1990s, so they are less likely to make a driving mistake that can lead to an accident.

Ensuring the Safety of Older Drivers

In *Physician's Guide to Assessing and Counseling Older Drivers*, the AMA and the NHTSA advocate coordinated efforts among the medical and research communities, policy

FIGURE 6.2

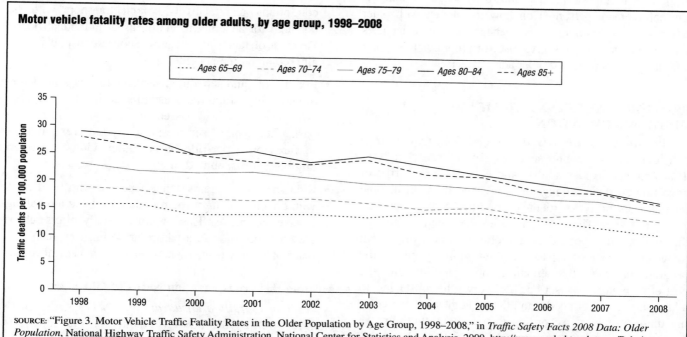

Motor vehicle fatality rates among older adults, by age group, 1998–2008

······ Ages 65–69   - - - Ages 70–74   —— Ages 75–79   —— Ages 80–84   - - - Ages 85+

SOURCE: "Figure 3. Motor Vehicle Traffic Fatality Rates in the Older Population by Age Group, 1998–2008," in *Traffic Safety Facts 2008 Data: Older Population*, National Highway Traffic Safety Administration, National Center for Statistics and Analysis, 2009, http://www-nrd.nhtsa.dot.gov/Pubs/811161.PDF (accessed April 18, 2011)

makers, community planners, the automobile industry, and government agencies to achieve the common goal of safe transportation for the older population. The AMA and the NHTSA call for refined diagnostic tools to assist physicians in assessing patients' crash risk, improved access to driver assessment and rehabilitation, safer roads and vehicles, and better alternatives to driving for older adults.

Some auto insurance companies reduce payments for older adults who successfully complete driving classes such as the AARP Driver Safety Program. In "AARP Driver Safety Program History and Facts" (January 1, 2010, http://www.aarp.org/home-garden/transportation/info-05-2010/dsp_article_program_history_and_facts.html), the AARP notes that since 2006 it has offered an online classroom refresher course that provides guidance in assessing physical abilities and making adjustments accordingly. By 2010, 36 states and the District of Columbia granted insurance discounts to drivers who have taken the course. The American Automobile Association offers a similar program called Safe Driving for Mature Operators that strives to improve the skills of older drivers. These courses address the aging process and help drivers adjust to age-related changes that can affect driving. Both organizations also provide resources that help older drivers and their families determine whether they can safely continue driving.

As of June 2011, there were no upper age limits for driving. The National Institute on Aging observes that because people age at different rates, it is not possible to choose a specific age at which to suspend driving. Setting an age limit would leave some drivers on the road too long, whereas others would be forced to stop driving prematurely. Heredity, general health, lifestyle, and surroundings all influence how people age.

Many states are acting to reduce risks for older drivers by improving roadways to make driving less hazardous. According to the GAO, in *Older Driver Safety: Knowledge Sharing Should Help States Prepare for Increase in Older Driver Population* (April 2007, http://www.gao.gov/new.items/d07413.pdf), several states have adopted Federal Highway Administration practices to help older drivers including:

• Wider highway lanes

• Intersections that give drivers a longer view of oncoming traffic and allow more time for left turns

• Road signs with larger, more visible letters and numbers

• Advance street name signs before intersections

In December 2010 the Department of Transportation released *Older Driver Program: Five-Year Strategic Plan, 2012–2017* (http://www.nhtsa.gov/staticfiles/nti/pdf/811432.pdf) to assist the states to prepare for the more than 40 million drivers aged 65 years and older who will take to the roads in the coming decade. The plan calls for enhanced communication and education about older drivers and the development and promotion of older driver licensing policies, such as policies that restrict, rather than rescind, older drivers' licenses. It suggests development of screening programs for Department of Motor Vehicles personnel for use in the license renewal process and for enhanced training of law enforcement personnel on how to interact with older drivers. It also encourages partnerships between agencies and between public- and private-sector programs to support safe driving practices and older adult drivers.

PROVIDING ALTERNATIVE MEANS OF TRANSPORTATION

In *Transportation-Disadvantaged Seniors*, the GAO considers issues and services for "transportation-disadvantaged" older adults—those who cannot drive or have limited their driving, or those who have an income restraint, disability, or medical condition that limits their ability to travel. The GAO identifies the federal programs that address this population's mobility issues, the extent to which these programs meet their mobility needs, the program practices that enhance their mobility and the cost-effectiveness of service delivery, the obstacles to addressing mobility needs, and the strategies for overcoming these obstacles. According to the GAO, there are 15 federal programs that are designed to meet the transportation needs of older adults. For example, the U.S. Department of Health and Human Services funds both Community Services Block Grant Programs, which provide taxicab vouchers and bus tokens that enable low-income older adults to take general trips, and Social Services Block Grants, which provide assistance for transport to and from medical or social service appointments.

The GAO points out that besides the programs that are intended to provide assistance specifically to older people, there are other programs that are designed to aid transportation-disadvantaged segments of the population, including older adults. For example, the Americans with Disabilities Act (ADA) of 1990 required that changes to public transportation be made to provide better accessibility for people with disabilities; about half of ADA-eligible riders are aged 65 years and older. Also, the Transportation Equity Act for the 21st Century, enacted in 1998, authorized funds for several programs, including a formula grant that supported states' efforts to meet the special transportation needs of older adults and people with disabilities.

Types of Transportation for Nondrivers

Transportation for older adults can include door-to-door services such as taxis or van services, public buses that travel along fixed routes, or ride sharing in carpools. According to the Administration on Aging (AoA), in *Because We Care: A Guide for People Who Care* (2009, http://www.uwex.edu/CES/flp/families/documents/Because WeCare.pdf), there are three general classes of alternative transportation for older adults:

- Demand response generally requires advance reservations and provides door-to-door service from one specific location to another. Such systems offer older adults comfortable and relatively flexible transport, with the potential for adapting to the needs of individual riders. Payment of fares for demand-response transport is usually required on a per-ride basis.

- Fixed route and scheduled services follow a predetermined route, stopping at established locations at specific times to allow passengers to board and disembark. This type of service typically requires payment of fares on a per-ride basis. Older adults are often eligible for discounted rates.

- Ride sharing programs connect people who need rides with drivers who have room in their cars and are willing to take passengers. This system generally offers scheduled transportation to a particular destination, such as a place of employment, a senior center, or a medical center.

Meeting the Transportation Needs of Older Adults

In *Transportation-Disadvantaged Seniors*, the GAO cites research by the Beverly Foundation that identifies five attributes that are necessary for alternative transportation services for older adults:

- Availability—older adults can travel to desired locations at the times they want to go.

- Accessibility—vehicles can be accessed by those with disabilities; services can be door-to-door or door-through-door as necessary; stops are pedestrian-friendly. Door-through-door transport offers personal, hands-on assistance for older adults who may have difficulties exiting their homes, disembarking from vehicles, and/or opening doors. It is also called assisted transportation, supported (or supportive) transportation, and escorted transportation.

- Acceptability—transport is safe, clean, and easy to use.

- Affordability—financial assistance is available if necessary.

- Adaptability—multiple trips and special equipment can be accommodated.

The GAO highlights specific unmet needs: "Seniors who rely on alternative transportation have difficulty making trips for which the automobile is better suited, such as trips that involve carrying packages;...life-enhancing needs are less likely to be met than life-sustaining needs; and...mobility needs are less likely to be met in nonurban communities (especially rural communities) than in urban communities." However, the GAO notes that there are limited data available to quantify or assess the extent of the needs that go unmet. It also identifies obstacles to addressing transportation-disadvantaged older adults' mobility needs, potential strategies that federal and other government entities might take to better meet these needs, and trade-offs that are associated with implementing each strategy. For example, the GAO finds that older drivers are not encouraged to investigate or plan for a time when they will be unable to drive. One way to address this obstacle might be to institute educational programs that would ease older adults' transition from driver to nondriver. This strategy does, however, have the potential to increase demand for alternative transportation services and the costs that are associated with their provision.

To increase and improve alternative transportation services, the GAO suggests enlisting the aid of volunteer drivers, sponsoring demonstration programs, identifying best practices, increasing cooperation among federal programs, and establishing a central clearinghouse of information that could be accessed by stakeholders in the various programs. It recommends that the AoA improve the value and consistency of information pertaining to older adults' transportation needs that is received from area agencies on aging, including providing guidance for those agencies on assessing mobility needs. The AoA is also called on to keep older adults and their caregivers better informed of alternative transportation programs and to ensure that the best methods and practices are shared among transportation and social service providers to enhance the older population's mobility.

CHAPTER 7
THE HEALTH AND MEDICAL PROBLEMS OF OLDER ADULTS

Among the fears many people have about aging is coping with losses—not only declining mental and physical abilities but also the prospect of failing health, chronic (long-term) illness, and disability. Even though aging is associated with physiological changes, the rate and extent of these changes varies widely. One person may be limited by arthritis at age 65, whereas another is vigorous and active at age 90.

Despite the increasing proportion of active healthy older adults, it is true that the incidence (the rate of new cases of a disorder over a specified period) and prevalence (the total number of cases of a disorder in a given population at a specific time) of selected diseases as well as the utilization of health care services increase with advancing age. For example, the incidence of diabetes, heart disease, breast cancer, Parkinson's disease, and Alzheimer's disease (a progressive disease that is characterized by memory loss, impaired thinking, and declining ability to function) increases with age. In contrast, the incidence of other diseases, such as human immunodeficiency virus (HIV) infection, multiple sclerosis, and schizophrenia, decreases with age.

This chapter considers the epidemiology of aging—the distribution and determinants of health and illness in the population of older adults. It describes trends in aging and the health of aging Americans; distinctions among healthy aging, disease, and disability; health promotion and prevention as applied to older people; and selected diseases and conditions that are common in old age.

GENERAL HEALTH OF OLDER AMERICANS

The proportion of adults rating their health as fair or poor increases with advancing age. In 2009, 19.1% of adults aged 55 to 64 years, 19.9% of adults aged 65 to 74 years, and 28.9% of adults aged 75 years and older considered themselves to be in fair or poor health, compared to just 6.3% of adults aged 18 to 44 years. (See Table 7.1.)

The Federal Interagency Forum on Aging-Related Statistics indicates in *Older Americans 2010: Key Indicators of Well-Being* (July 2010, http://www.agingstats .gov/agingstatsdotnet/Main_Site/Data/2010_Documents/ Docs/OA_2010.pdf) that between 2006 and 2008, 80% of non-Hispanic whites aged 65 to 74 years said their health was good or better than good, compared to just 68% of non-Hispanic whites aged 85 years and older. (See Figure 7.1.) Older people of other races and ethnic categories followed this same pattern. Across all older age groups, non-Hispanic white respondents were more likely to report good health than non-Hispanic African-American and Hispanic respondents.

The Federal Interagency Forum on Aging-Related Statistics notes that most older people have at least one chronic condition and many have several. Among the most frequently occurring conditions of older adults in 2007–08 were hypertension (53% of men and 58% of women), arthritic symptoms (42% of men and 55% of women), all types of heart disease (38% of men and 27% of women), and cancer (24% of men and 21% of women). (See Figure 7.2.)

Figure 7.3 shows that rates of chronic conditions that limited one to two activities of daily living (ADLs) among Americans aged 65 years and older decreased from 20% in 1992 to 18% in 2007 and that the percentage reporting difficulty with five to six activities decreased by half, from 4% to 2% during the same period. The National Center for Health Statistics reports in *Health, United States, 2009* (January 2010, http://www.cdc.gov/nchs/data/hus/hus09.pdf) that among adults aged 55 to 64 years, the conditions most likely to limit activity in 2006–07 were arthritis or other musculoskeletal problems, heart or other circulatory disorders, diabetes, mental illness, lung diseases, and fractures or joint injury. Among older people aged 65 years and older, arthritis and heart disease continued to limit activity the most; however, among adults aged 75 years and older, problems with vision, hearing, and senility also contributed to limiting activity.

TABLE 7.1

Percentage of adults who reported their health as fair or poor, by selected characteristics, selected years 1991–2009

[Data are based on household interviews of a sample of the civilian noninstitutionalized population]

Characteristic	1991[a]	1995[a]	1997	2000	2005	2007	2008	2009
				Percent of persons with fair or poor health				
All ages, age-adjusted[b, c]	10.4	10.6	9.2	9.0	9.2	9.5	9.5	9.4
All ages, crude[c]	10.0	10.1	8.9	8.9	9.3	9.8	9.9	9.9
Age								
Under 18 years	2.6	2.6	2.1	1.7	1.8	1.7	1.8	1.8
Under 6 years	2.7	2.7	1.9	1.5	1.6	1.5	1.2	1.3
6–17 years	2.6	2.5	2.1	1.8	1.9	1.7	2.1	2.0
18–44 years	6.1	6.6	5.3	5.1	5.5	5.9	6.3	6.3
18–24 years	4.8	4.5	3.4	3.3	3.3	3.3	4.0	3.6
25–44 years	6.4	7.2	5.9	5.7	6.3	6.8	7.2	7.2
45–54 years	13.4	13.4	11.7	11.9	11.6	13.3	12.9	13.1
55–64 years	20.7	21.4	18.2	17.9	18.3	17.9	18.8	19.1
65 years and over	29.0	28.3	26.7	26.9	26.6	26.8	24.9	24.0
65–74 years	26.0	25.6	23.1	22.5	23.4	23.4	21.8	19.9
75 years and over	33.6	32.2	31.5	32.1	30.2	30.7	28.4	28.9
Sex[b]								
Male	10.0	10.1	8.8	8.8	8.8	9.1	9.1	9.1
Female	10.8	11.1	9.7	9.3	9.5	9.9	9.8	9.7
Race[b, d]								
White only	9.6	9.7	8.3	8.2	8.6	8.8	8.9	8.7
Black or African American only	16.8	17.2	15.8	14.6	14.3	14.2	14.6	14.2
American Indian or Alaska Native only	18.3	18.7	17.3	17.2	13.2	17.1	14.5	16.3
Asian only	7.8	9.3	7.8	7.4	6.8	7.1	6.7	8.4
Native Hawaiian or other Pacific Islander only	—	—	—	*	*	*	*	*
2 or more races	—	—	—	16.2	14.5	16.8	12.9	15.3
Black or African American; White	—	—	—	14.5*	8.3	16.6*	20.2	18.0
American Indian or Alaska Native; White	—	—	—	18.7	17.2	19.2	14.6	15.2
Hispanic origin and race[b, d]								
Hispanic or Latino	15.6	15.1	13.0	12.8	13.3	13.0	12.8	13.3
Mexican	17.0	16.7	13.1	12.8	14.3	13.2	13.4	13.7
Not Hispanic or Latino	10.0	10.1	8.9	8.7	8.7	9.1	9.1	8.9
White only	9.1	9.1	8.0	7.9	8.0	8.3	8.4	8.0
Black or African American only	16.8	17.3	15.8	14.6	14.4	14.1	14.6	14.2
Percent of poverty level[b, e]								
Below 100%	22.8	23.7	20.8	19.6	20.4	21.0	21.8	21.8
100%–199%	14.7	15.5	13.9	14.1	14.4	15.3	15.4	14.9
200%–399%	7.9	7.9	8.2	8.4	8.3	9.0	8.7	8.6
400% or more	4.9	4.7	4.1	4.5	4.7	4.7	4.4	4.3
Hispanic origin and race and percent of poverty level[b, d, e]								
Hispanic or Latino:								
Below 100%	23.6	22.7	19.9	18.7	20.2	21.0	21.0	22.1
100%–199%	18.0	16.9	13.5	15.3	15.3	15.1	14.6	16.2
200%–399%	10.3	10.1	10.0	10.3	10.3	10.5	10.7	9.7
400% or more	6.6	4.0	5.7	5.5	7.6	7.2	5.6	5.6
Not Hispanic or Latino:								
White only:								
Below 100%	21.9	22.8	19.7	18.8	20.1	20.9	22.1	20.5
100%–199%	14.0	14.8	13.3	13.4	13.8	15.2	15.7	14.6
200%–399%	7.5	7.3	7.7	7.9	7.9	8.4	8.3	8.1
400% or more	4.7	4.6	3.9	4.2	4.3	4.3	4.1	4.0
Black or African American only:								
Below 100%	25.8	27.7	25.3	23.8	23.3	22.6	25.1	25.2
100%–199%	17.0	19.3	19.2	18.2	17.6	17.7	18.1	16.6
200%–399%	12.0	11.4	12.2	11.7	11.2	11.3	11.2	11.0
400% or more	5.9	6.5	6.1	7.3	7.1	7.2	6.9	5.9

Instrumental activities of daily living (IADLs) and measures of physical, cognitive, and social functioning are ways to assess disability and often determine whether older adults can live independently in the community. IADLs include activities such as light housework, meal preparation, doing the laundry, grocery shopping, getting around outside the home, managing money, taking medications as prescribed, and using the telephone. Noninstitutionalized individuals (people who are not in the U.S. military, school, jail, or mental health facilities) are considered chronically disabled if they cannot perform one or more IADL for 90 days or longer. Measures of physical functioning, such as the ability to stoop or kneel, lift heavy objects, walk a few blocks, or reach above the

TABLE 7.1

Percentage of adults who reported their health as fair or poor, by selected characteristics, selected years 1991–2009 [CONTINUED]

[Data are based on household interviews of a sample of the civilian noninstitutionalized population]

Characteristic	1991[a]	1995[a]	1997	2000	2005	2007	2008	2009
Disability measure among adults 18 years and over[b, f]			Percent of persons with fair or poor health					
Any basic actions difficulty or complex activity limitation	—	—	27.0	27.6	28.5	31.2	28.5	30.3
Any basic actions difficulty	—	—	27.3	27.7	29.1	31.6	28.7	30.9
Any complex activity limitation	—	—	42.9	45.6	46.3	50.8	47.9	48.8
No disability	—	—	3.4	3.8	3.6	4.0	4.2	3.6
Geographic region[b]								
Northeast	8.3	9.1	8.0	7.6	7.5	8.4	8.0	8.4
Midwest	9.1	9.7	8.1	8.0	8.3	8.6	8.8	8.6
South	13.1	12.3	10.8	10.7	11.0	11.0	11.0	10.9
West	9.7	10.1	8.8	8.8	8.6	9.0	9.0	8.8
Location of residence[b, g]								
Within MSA	9.9	10.1	8.7	8.5	8.7	9.0	9.1	9.1
Outside MSA	11.9	12.6	11.1	11.1	11.2	12.0	11.7	11.2

—Data not available.

*Estimates are considered unreliable.

[a]Data prior to 1997 are not strictly comparable with data for later years due to the 1997 questionnaire redesign.

[b]Estimates are age-adjusted to the year 2000 standard population using six age groups: under 18 years, 18–44 years, 45–54 years, 55–64 years, 65–74 years, and 75 years and over. The disability measure is age-adjusted using the five adult age groups.

[c]Includes all other races not shown separately and unknown disability status.

[d]The race groups white, black, American Indian or Alaska Native, Asian, Native Hawaiian or Other Pacific Islander, and 2 or more races include persons of Hispanic and non-Hispanic origin. Persons of Hispanic origin may be of any race. Starting with 1999 data, race-specific estimates are tabulated according to the 1997 Revisions to the Standards for the Classification of Federal Data on Race and Ethnicity and are not strictly comparable with estimates for earlier years. The five single-race categories plus multiple-race categories shown in the table conform to the 1997 Standards. Starting with 1999 data, race-specific estimates are for persons who reported only one racial group; the category 2 or more races includes persons who reported more than one racial group. Prior to 1999, data were tabulated according to the 1977 Standards with four racial groups and the Asian only category included Native Hawaiian or Other Pacific Islander. Estimates for single-race categories prior to 1999 included persons who reported one race or, if they reported more than one race, identified one race as best representing their race. Starting with 2003 data, race responses of other race and unspecified multiple race were treated as missing, and then race was imputed if these were the only race responses. Almost all persons with a race response of other race were of Hispanic origin.

[e]Percent of poverty level is based on family income and family size and composition using U.S. Census Bureau poverty thresholds. Missing family income data were imputed for starting in 1991.

[f]Any basic actions difficulty or complex activity limitation is defined as having one or more of the following limitations or difficulties: movement difficulty, emotional difficulty, sensory (seeing or hearing) difficulty, cognitive difficulty, self-care (ADL or IADL) limitation, social limitation, or work limitation. Starting with 2007 data, the hearing question, a component of the basic actions difficulty measure, was revised. Consequently, data prior to 2007 are not comparable with data for 2007 and beyond.

[g]MSA is metropolitan statistical area. Starting with 2006 data, MSA status is determined using 2000 census data and the 2000 standards for defining MSAs.

Note: Data for additional years are available.

SOURCE: "Table 50. Respondent-Assessed Health Status, by Selected Characteristics: United States, Selected Years 1991–2009," in *Health, United States 2010: With Special Feature on Death and Dying*, National Center for Health Statistics, 2011, http://www.cdc.gov/nchs/data/hus/hus10.pdf (accessed April 8, 2011)

head, are also used to monitor progressive disability. In 2007, 42% of adults aged 65 years and older reported a functional limitation and 25% said they had trouble with at least one ADL. (See Figure 7.3.) Older women reported more difficulties with physical functioning than older men in 2007—32% of women were unable to perform at least one physical function task, compared to 19% of men. (See Figure 7.4.)

Hospital Utilization and Physician Visits

Adults aged 65 years and older have the highest rates of inpatient hospitalization and the longest average lengths of stay (ALOS). In 2007 people aged 65 years and older had 3,395.1 hospital discharges per 10,000 population—nearly three times the number of discharges of adults aged 45 to 64 years. (See Table 7.2.) The highest number of discharges and the longest ALOS were among adults aged 75 years and older, 4,392.4 and 5.7 days, respectively.

The ALOS for adults aged 65 years and older was 5.6 days in 2007, compared to 5.1 days for people aged 45 to 64

years. (See Table 7.2.) The ALOS among all age groups had declined since 1980, from a high of 7.5 days to 4.8 days in 2007. Among patients aged 75 years and older, the ALOS decreased by half, from 11.4 days in 1980 to 5.7 days in 2007.

Shorter stays are in part because of the federal government's introduction of diagnosis-related groups (DRG) during the mid-1980s. (DRGs are categories of illnesses that prescribe, and allow for, a set duration of treatment.) DRG-based reimbursement encourages hospitals to discharge patients as quickly as possible by compensating hospitals for a predetermined number of days per diagnosis, regardless of the actual length of stay. Shorter lengths of stay are also attributable to the increasing use of outpatient settings as opposed to hospital admission for an expanding range of procedures such as hernia repairs, gallbladder removal, and cataract surgery.

The growing older population also uses more physician services. Visit rates increase with age among adults

FIGURE 7.1

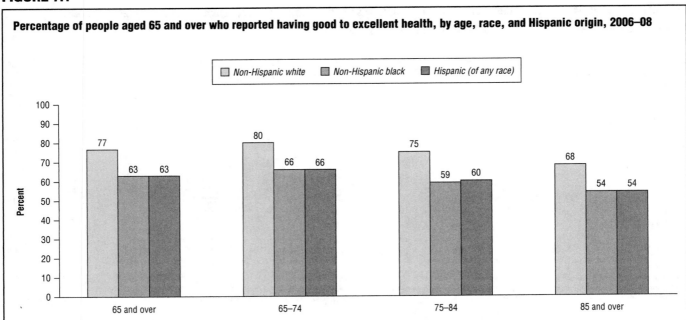

Percentage of people aged 65 and over who reported having good to excellent health, by age, race, and Hispanic origin, 2006–08

Note: Data are based on a 3-year average from 2006–2008.
Reference population: These data refer to the civilian noninstitutionalized population.

SOURCE: "Respondent-Reported Good to Excellent Health among the Population 65 and over, by Age Group, Race, and Hispanic Origin, 2006–2008," in *Older Americans 2010: Key Indicators of Well-Being*, Federal Interagency Forum on Aging-Related Statistics, July 2010, http://www.agingstats.gov/agingstatsdotnet/Main_Site/Data/2010_Documents/Docs/OA_2010.pdf (accessed April 2, 2011)

FIGURE 7.2

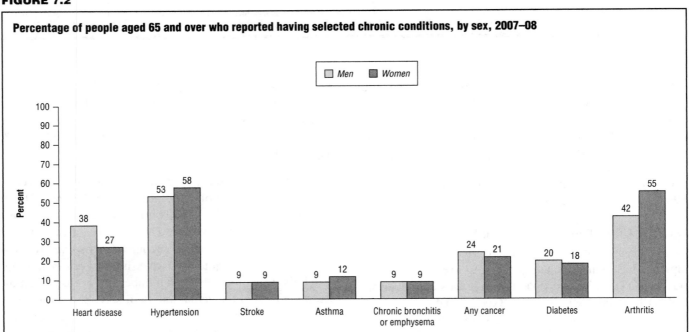

Percentage of people aged 65 and over who reported having selected chronic conditions, by sex, 2007–08

Note: Data are based on a 2-year average from 2007–2008.
Reference population: These data refer to the civilian noninstitutionalized population.

SOURCE: "Chronic Health Conditions among the Population Age 65 and over, by Sex, 2007–2008," in *Older Americans 2010: Key Indicators of Well-Being*, Federal Interagency Forum on Aging-Related Statistics, July 2010, http://www.agingstats.gov/agingstatsdotnet/Main_Site/Data/2010_Documents/Docs/OA_2010.pdf (accessed April 2, 2011)

FIGURE 7.3

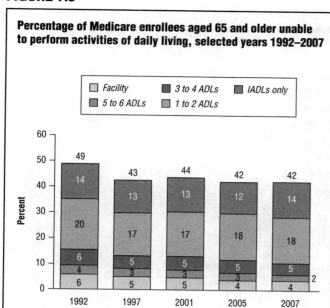

Percentage of Medicare enrollees aged 65 and older unable to perform activities of daily living, selected years 1992–2007

IADLs = Instrumental activities of daily living
ADLs = Activities of daily living
Note: A residence is considered a long-term care facility if it is certified by Medicare or Medicaid; has 3 or more beds and is licensed as a nursing home or other long-term care facility and provides at least one personal care service; or provides 24-hour, 7-day-a-week supervision by a caregiver. ADL limitations refer to difficulty performing (or inability to perform for a health reason) one or more of the following tasks: bathing, dressing, eating, getting in/out of chairs, walking, or using the toilet. IADL limitations refer to difficulty performing (or inability to perform for a health reason) one or more of the following tasks: using the telephone, light housework, heavy housework, meal preparation, shopping, or managing money. Rates are age adjusted using the 2000 standard population. Data for 1992, 2001, and 2007 do not sum to the totals because of rounding.
Reference population: These data refer to Medicare enrollees.

SOURCE: "Percentage of Medicare Enrollees Age 65 and over Who Have Limitations in Activities of Daily Living (ADLs) or Instrumental Activities of Daily Living (IADLs), or Who Are in a Facility, Selected Years 1992–2007," in *Older Americans 2010: Key Indicators of Well-Being*, Federal Interagency Forum on Aging-Related Statistics, July 2010, http://www.agingstats.gov/agingstatsdotnet/Main_Site/Data/2010_Documents/Docs/OA_2010.pdf (accessed April 2, 2011).

aged 65 years and older and were nearly one and a half times as high as visit rates for children under the age of 18 years in 2008. (See Table 7.3.) Even though women generally make more visits than men, the gender gap practically disappears among older adults. Older adults also make more visits to primary care physicians (general and family practitioners and specialists in internal medicine) and to physician specialists. (See Table 7.4.)

CHRONIC DISEASES AND CONDITIONS

Chronic diseases are prolonged illnesses such as arthritis, asthma, heart disease, diabetes, and cancer that do not resolve spontaneously and are rarely cured. According to the Centers for Disease Control and Prevention (CDC), in "Chronic Diseases and Health Promotion" (July 7, 2010, http://www.cdc.gov/chronicdisease/overview/index.htm), chronic illnesses account for 70% of all deaths in the United States annually. In 2007 five of the seven leading

causes of death among older adults were chronic diseases: heart disease, malignant neoplasms (cancer), cerebrovascular diseases (stroke), chronic lower respiratory diseases, and diabetes mellitus (a condition in which there is increased sugar in the blood and urine because the body is unable to use sugar to produce energy). (See Table 7.5.) Even though other chronic conditions such as arthritis, asthma, and chronic bronchitis are not immediately life threatening, they compromise the quality of life of affected individuals and place an enormous financial burden on individuals, families, and the U.S. health care system.

The prevalence of some chronic conditions such as hypertension and diabetes is increasing in the general population and among older adults. In 2007–08 more than half (55.7%) of people aged 65 years and older had hypertension and 18.6% suffered from diabetes. (See Table 7.6.) Between 1997–98 and 2007–08 the rate of diabetes increased dramatically, from 13% to 18.6%. (See Table 7.7.) The rate of hypertension also witnessed an increase during this same period, from 46.5% to 55.7%. The increase in these conditions is largely attributable to increasing rates of obesity, which is implicated in the development of these and many other chronic conditions.

Arthritis

The word *arthritis* literally means "joint inflammation," and it is applied to dozens of related diseases known as rheumatic diseases. When a joint (the point where two bones meet) becomes inflamed, swelling, redness, pain, and loss of motion occur. In the most serious forms of the disease, the loss of motion can be physically disabling.

More than 100 types of arthritis have been identified, but four major types affect large numbers of older Americans:

- Osteoarthritis—the most common type, generally affects people as they grow older. Sometimes called degenerative arthritis, it causes the breakdown of bones and cartilage (connective tissue that attaches to bones) and pain and stiffness in the fingers, knees, feet, hips, and back. In "Epidemiology of Osteoarthritis" (*Rheumatic Disease Clinics of North America*, vol. 34, no. 3, August 2008), Yuqing Zhang and Joanne M. Jordan report that approximately 27 million Americans are affected by osteoarthritis. Approximately 37% of participants aged 60 years and older in the National Health and Nutrition Survey had x-ray evidence of arthritis of the knee.

- Fibromyalgia—affects the muscles and connective tissues and causes widespread pain, as well as fatigue, sleep problems, and stiffness. Fibromyalgia also causes "tender points" that are more sensitive to pain than other areas of the body. In "Fibromyalgia Fact Sheet" (November 19, 2010, http://www.fmaware.org/PageServerc145.html?

FIGURE 7.4

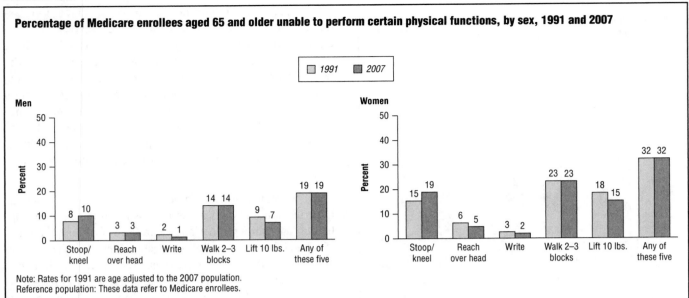

Percentage of Medicare enrollees aged 65 and older unable to perform certain physical functions, by sex, 1991 and 2007

Note: Rates for 1991 are age adjusted to the 2007 population.
Reference population: These data refer to Medicare enrollees.

SOURCE: "Percentage of Medicare Enrollees Age 65 and over Who Are Unable to Perform Certain Physical Functions, by Sex, 1991 and 2007," in *Older Americans 2010: Key Indicators of Well-Being*, Federal Interagency Forum on Aging-Related Statistics, July 2010, http://www.agingstats.gov/agingstatsdotnet/Main_Site/Data/2010_Documents/Docs/OA_2010.pdf (accessed April 2, 2011)

pagename=fibromyalgia_fmFactSheet), the National Fibromyalgia Association estimates that 10 million Americans suffer from this condition.

- Rheumatoid arthritis—an inflammatory form of arthritis caused by a flaw in the body's immune system. The result is inflammation and swelling in the joint lining, followed by damage to bone and cartilage in the hands, wrists, feet, knees, ankles, shoulders, or elbows. The Arthritis Foundation indicates in "What Is Rheumatoid Arthritis?" (2011, http://www.arthritistoday.org/conditions/rheumatoid-arthritis/all-about-ra/what-is-ra.php) that rheumatoid arthritis affects approximately 1.3 million Americans.

- Gout—inflammation of a joint caused by an accumulation of a natural substance, uric acid, in the joint, usually the big toe, knee, or wrist. The uric acid forms crystals in the affected joint, causing severe pain and swelling. This form affects more men than women, claiming about a million sufferers.

PREVALENCE. Arthritis is a common problem. In "Quick Stats on Arthritis" (October 20, 2010, http://www.cdc.gov/arthritis/resources/quickstats.htm), the CDC reports that 50 million Americans had been diagnosed with arthritis in 2010 and nearly 21 million had activity limitations that were attributable to the disease. The CDC predicts in "NHIS Arthritis Surveillance" (October 20, 2010, http://www.cdc.gov/arthritis/data_statistics/national_nhis.htm#disability) that the total number of people suffering from arthritis will increase to 67 million by 2030. (See Figure 7.5.)

Arthritis is the leading cause of disability in the United States. Rheumatic and musculoskeletal disorders are the most frequently reported cause of impairment in the adult population, the leading cause of limitation of mobility, and the second-leading cause of activity restriction.

Osteoporosis

Osteoporosis is a skeletal disorder that is characterized by compromised bone strength, which predisposes affected individuals to increased risk of fracture. The National Osteoporosis Foundation (NOF; 2011, http://www.nof.org/node/40) defines osteoporosis as "a disease characterized by low bone mass and structural deterioration of bone tissue, leading to bone fragility and an increased susceptibility to fractures, especially of the hip, spine and wrist, although any bone can be affected." Even though some bone loss occurs naturally with advancing age, the stooped posture (kyphosis) and loss of height (greater than 1 to 2 inches [2.5 to 5.1 cm]) that are experienced by many older adults result from vertebral fractures caused by osteoporosis.

According to the NOF, 10 million Americans have osteoporosis and another 34 million are considered at risk of developing the condition. The NOF describes osteoporosis as "a major public health threat for an estimated 44 million Americans, or 55 percent of the people 50 years of age and older." Like other chronic conditions that disproportionately affect older adults, the prevalence of bone disease and fractures is projected to increase markedly as the population ages.

TABLE 7.2

Hospital discharges, days of care, and average length of stay, by selected characteristics, selected years 1980–2007

[Data are based on a sample of hospital records]

Characteristic	1980[a]	1985[a]	1990	1995	2000	2005	2006	2007
	Discharges per 10,000 population								
Total, age-adjusted[b]	1,744.5	1,522.3	1,252.4	1,180.2	1,132.8	1,162.4	1,153.1	1,124.0
Total, crude	1,676.8	1,484.1	1,222.7	1,157.4	1,128.3	1,174.4	1,168.7	1,143.9
Age								
Under 18 years	756.5	614.0	463.5	423.7	402.6	411.0	393.9	376.7
Under 1 year	2,317.6	2,137.9	1,915.3	1,977.6	2,027.6	1,949.3	1,818.4	1,639.3
1–4 years	864.6	650.2	466.9	457.1	458.0	429.7	418.8	389.9
5–17 years	609.3	477.4	334.1	290.2	268.6	286.5	276.0	271.5
18–44 years	1,578.8	1,301.2	1,026.6	914.3	849.4	898.0	906.7	888.8
18–24 years	1,570.3	1,297.8	1,065.3	928.9	854.1	862.4	870.4	846.1
25–44 years	1,582.8	1,302.5	1,013.8	909.9	847.9	910.3	919.3	903.8
25–34 years	1,682.9	1,416.9	1,140.3	1,015.0	942.5	1,007.8	1,011.2	1,003.5
35–44 years	1,438.3	1,153.1	868.8	808.0	764.8	821.5	834.6	810.4
45–64 years	1,947.6	1,707.8	1,354.5	1,185.4	1,114.2	1,147.0	1,161.2	1,143.9
45–54 years	1,750.2	1,470.7	1,123.9	984.7	920.8	964.3	970.5	959.3
55–64 years	2,153.6	1,948.0	1,632.6	1,483.4	1,415.0	1,402.4	1,422.1	1,391.2
65 years and over	3,836.9	3,698.0	3,341.2	3,477.4	3,533.6	3,595.6	3,507.9	3,395.1
65–74 years	3,158.4	2,972.6	2,616.3	2,600.0	2,546.0	2,628.9	2,533.6	2,439.9
75 years and over	4,893.0	4,756.1	4,340.3	4,590.7	4,619.6	4,588.4	4,512.6	4,392.4
75–84 years	4,638.6	4,464.2	3,957.0	4,155.7	4,124.4	4,131.7	4,025.9	3,983.3
85 years and over	5,764.6	5,728.9	5,606.3	5,925.1	6,050.9	5,758.1	5,711.4	5,358.9
Sex[b]								
Male	1,543.9	1,382.5	1,130.0	1,048.5	990.8	1,013.0	1,000.5	973.8
Female	1,951.9	1,675.6	1,389.5	1,317.3	1,277.3	1,319.6	1,312.3	1,280.6
Sex and age								
Male, all ages	1,390.4	1,240.2	1,002.2	941.7	910.6	959.0	954.9	936.7
Under 18 years	762.6	626.4	463.1	431.3	408.6	412.2	401.5	385.6
18–44 years	950.9	776.9	579.2	507.2	450.0	471.1	476.8	460.8
45–64 years	1,953.1	1,775.6	1,402.7	1,212.0	1,127.4	1,148.8	1,175.7	1,156.6
65–74 years	3,474.1	3,255.2	2,877.6	2,762.2	2,649.1	2,742.6	2,584.3	2,559.3
75–84 years	5,093.5	5,031.8	4,417.3	4,361.1	4,294.1	4,388.1	4,220.3	4,162.6
85 years and over	6,372.3	6,406.9	6,420.9	6,387.9	6,166.6	5,984.1	5,983.5	5,440.6
Female, all ages	1,944.0	1,712.2	1,431.7	1,362.9	1,336.6	1,382.2	1,375.3	1,344.0
Under 18 years	750.2	601.0	464.1	415.7	396.2	409.8	385.9	367.3
18–44 years	2,180.2	1,808.3	1,468.0	1,318.0	1,248.1	1,330.9	1,343.5	1,324.5
45–64 years	1,942.5	1,645.9	1,309.7	1,160.5	1,101.7	1,145.3	1,147.3	1,131.7
65–74 years	2,916.6	2,754.8	2,411.2	2,469.4	2,461.0	2,533.1	2,490.7	2,338.4
75–84 years	4,370.4	4,130.4	3,678.9	4,024.1	4,013.5	3,957.7	3,893.0	3,859.8
85 years and over	5,500.3	5,458.0	5,289.6	5,743.7	6,003.3	5,654.4	5,584.1	5,320.0
Geographic region[b]								
Northeast	1,622.9	1,428.7	1,332.2	1,335.3	1,274.8	1,245.9	1,261.4	1,274.6
Midwest	1,925.2	1,584.7	1,287.5	1,132.8	1,109.2	1,174.9	1,168.0	1,125.5
South	1,814.1	1,569.4	1,325.0	1,252.4	1,209.2	1,202.5	1,198.8	1,139.9
West	1,519.7	1,469.6	1,006.6	967.4	894.0	1,005.9	964.1	966.0
	Days of care per 10,000 population								
Total, age-adjusted[b]	13,027.0	10,017.9	8,189.3	6,386.2	5,576.8	5,541.7	5,474.7	5,404.1
Total, crude	12,166.8	9,576.6	7,840.5	6,201.7	5,546.5	5,620.9	5,577.8	5,539.4
Age								
Under 18 years	3,415.1	2,812.3	2,263.1	1,846.7	1,789.7	1,918.3	1,857.6	1,785.0
Under 1 year	13,213.9	14,141.2	11,484.7	10,834.5	11,524.0	12,131.6	11,624.2	8,466.7
1–4 years	3,333.5	2,280.4	1,700.1	1,525.6	1,482.2	1,355.3	1,405.4	1,280.3
5–17 years	2,698.5	2,049.8	1,633.2	1,240.3	1,172.1	1,300.9	1,239.1	1,406.4
18–44 years	8,323.6	6,294.7	4,676.7	3,517.2	3,093.8	3,305.0	3,360.6	3,258.0
18–24 years	7,174.6	5,287.2	4,015.9	2,987.4	2,679.5	2,819.9	2,889.4	2,738.7
25–44 years	8,861.4	6,685.2	4,895.5	3,676.4	3,225.5	3,472.8	3,524.5	3,439.7
25–34 years	8,497.5	6,688.9	4,939.7	3,536.1	3,161.7	3,434.3	3,462.2	3,423.1
35–44 years	9,386.6	6,680.4	4,844.8	3,812.3	3,281.5	3,507.9	3,581.9	3,455.2
45–64 years	15,969.5	12,015.9	9,139.3	6,574.5	5,515.4	5,717.3	5,793.0	5,868.2
45–54 years	13,167.2	9,692.8	6,996.6	5,162.0	4,374.2	4,711.2	4,667.4	4,745.9
55–64 years	18,895.4	14,369.5	11,722.6	8,671.6	7,290.8	7,124.0	7,333.6	7,371.8
65 years and over	40,983.5	32,279.7	28,956.1	23,736.5	21,118.9	19,882.8	19,197.5	18,951.7
65–74 years	31,470.3	24,373.3	20,878.2	16,847.0	14,389.7	13,985.3	13,170.2	13,274.8
75 years and over	55,788.2	43,812.7	40,090.8	32,478.1	28,518.6	25,939.4	25,413.1	24,878.5
75–84 years	51,836.2	40,521.6	35,995.1	28,947.5	25,397.8	23,155.3	22,671.7	22,658.1
85 years and over	69,332.0	54,782.4	53,616.9	43,305.9	37,537.8	33,071.5	32,165.5	30,124.5

TABLE 7.2

Hospital discharges, days of care, and average length of stay, by selected characteristics, selected years 1980–2007 [CONTINUED]

[Data are based on a sample of hospital records]

Characteristic	1980[a]	1985[a]	1990	1995	2000	2005	2006	2007
Sex[b]				Days of care per 10,000 population				
Male	12,475.8	9,792.1	8,057.8	6,239.0	5,358.8	5,301.3	5,208.8	5,157.4
Female	13,662.9	10,340.4	8,404.5	6,548.8	5,809.7	5,828.7	5,764.2	5,685.1
Sex and age								
Male, all ages	10,674.1	8,518.8	6,943.0	5,507.5	4,860.8	4,979.7	4,947.3	4,937.6
Under 18 years	3,473.1	2,942.7	2,335.7	1,998.0	1,955.7	2,006.2	1,968.0	1,858.1
18–44 years	6,102.4	4,746.6	3,517.4	2,729.7	2,175.0	2,282.7	2,375.6	2,241.8
45–64 years	15,894.9	12,290.1	9,434.2	6,822.7	5,704.4	5,773.5	6,004.3	6,103.5
65–74 years	33,697.6	26,220.5	22,515.5	17,697.4	14,897.4	14,502.6	13,262.1	13,666.7
75–84 years	54,723.3	44,087.4	38,257.8	29,642.6	26,616.7	25,106.9	23,972.7	23,894.6
85 years and over	77,013.1	58,609.5	60,347.3	45,263.6	37,765.3	35,179.0	32,604.0	31,480.6
Female, all ages	13,560.1	10,566.3	8,691.1	6,863.4	6,202.7	6,239.5	6,186.8	6,121.1
Under 18 years	3,354.5	2,675.5	2,186.8	1,687.9	1,615.1	1,826.1	1,741.8	1,708.3
18–44 years	10,450.7	7,792.0	5,820.3	4,297.9	4,010.8	4,341.8	4,361.5	4,292.3
45–64 years	16,037.1	11,765.5	8,865.1	6,341.7	5,336.4	5,663.9	5,592.2	5,644.3
65–74 years	29,764.7	22,949.2	19,592.7	16,162.0	13,971.3	13,549.0	13,092.4	12,942.1
75–84 years	50,133.3	38,424.7	34,628.3	28,502.5	24,601.0	21,830.1	21,782.1	21,806.2
85 years and over	65,990.5	53,253.6	51,000.5	42,538.6	37,444.4	32,103.5	31,960.3	29,479.5
Geographic region[b]								
Northeast	14,024.4	11,143.1	10,266.8	8,389.7	7,185.9	6,636.5	6,608.5	7,284.4
Midwest	14,871.9	10,803.6	8,306.5	5,908.8	5,005.3	4,954.3	4,893.5	4,775.3
South	12,713.5	9,642.6	8,204.1	6,659.9	5,925.1	5,830.4	5,844.8	5,555.7
West	9,635.2	8,300.7	5,755.1	4,510.6	4,082.0	4,690.3	4,451.6	4,184.5
				Average length of stay in days				
Total, age-adjusted[b]	7.5	6.6	6.5	5.4	4.9	4.8	4.7	4.8
Total, crude	7.3	6.5	6.4	5.4	4.9	4.8	4.8	4.8
Age								
Under 18 years	4.5	4.6	4.9	4.4	4.4	4.7	4.7	4.7
Under 1 year	5.7	6.6	6.0	5.5	5.7	6.2	6.4	5.2
1–4 years	3.9	3.5	3.6	3.3	3.2	3.2	3.4	3.3
5–17 years	4.4	4.3	4.9	4.3	4.4	4.5	4.5	5.2
18–44 years	5.3	4.8	4.6	3.8	3.6	3.7	3.7	3.7
18–24 years	4.6	4.1	3.8	3.2	3.1	3.3	3.3	3.2
25–44 years	5.6	5.1	4.8	4.0	3.8	3.8	3.8	3.8
25–34 years	5.0	4.7	4.3	3.5	3.4	3.4	3.4	3.4
35–44 years	6.5	5.8	5.6	4.7	4.3	4.3	4.3	4.3
45–64 years	8.2	7.0	6.7	5.5	5.0	5.0	5.0	5.1
45–54 years	7.5	6.6	6.2	5.2	4.8	4.9	4.8	4.9
55–64 years	8.8	7.4	7.2	5.8	5.2	5.1	5.2	5.3
65 years and over	10.7	8.7	8.7	6.8	6.0	5.5	5.5	5.6
65–74 years	10.0	8.2	8.0	6.5	5.7	5.3	5.2	5.4
75 years and over	11.4	9.2	9.2	7.1	6.2	5.7	5.6	5.7
75–84 years	11.2	9.1	9.1	7.0	6.2	5.6	5.6	5.7
85 years and over	12.0	9.6	9.6	7.3	6.2	5.7	5.6	5.6
Sex[b]								
Male	8.1	7.1	7.1	6.0	5.4	5.2	5.2	5.3
Female	7.0	6.2	6.0	5.0	4.5	4.4	4.4	4.4
Sex and age								
Male, all ages	7.7	6.9	6.9	5.8	5.3	5.2	5.2	5.3
Under 18 years	4.6	4.7	5.0	4.6	4.8	4.9	4.9	4.8
18–44 years	6.4	6.1	6.1	5.4	4.8	4.8	5.0	4.9
45–64 years	8.1	6.9	6.7	5.6	5.1	5.0	5.1	5.3
65–74 years	9.7	8.1	7.8	6.4	5.6	5.3	5.1	5.3
75–84 years	10.7	8.8	8.7	6.8	6.2	5.7	5.7	5.7
85 years and over	12.1	9.1	9.4	7.1	6.1	5.9	5.4	5.8
Female, all ages	7.0	6.2	6.1	5.0	4.6	4.5	4.5	4.6
Under 18 years	4.5	4.5	4.7	4.1	4.1	4.5	4.5	4.7
18–44 years	4.8	4.3	4.0	3.3	3.2	3.3	3.2	3.2
45–64 years	8.3	7.1	6.8	5.5	4.8	4.9	4.9	5.0
65–74 years	10.2	8.3	8.1	6.5	5.7	5.3	5.3	5.5
75–84 years	11.5	9.3	9.4	7.1	6.1	5.5	5.6	5.6
85 years and over	12.0	9.8	9.6	7.4	6.2	5.7	5.7	5.5

The NOF reports that one out of two women and one out of four men over the age of 50 will have an osteoporosis-related fracture in their remaining lifetime. The aging of the population and the historic lack of focus on bone health may together cause the number of fractures due to osteoporosis in the United States to exceed 3 million by 2025.

TABLE 7.2

Hospital discharges, days of care, and average length of stay, by selected characteristics, selected years 1980–2007 [CONTINUED]

[Data are based on a sample of hospital records]

Characteristic	1980[a]	1985[a]	1990	1995	2000	2005	2006	2007
Geographic region[b]				**Average length of stay in days**				
Northeast	8.6	7.8	7.7	6.3	5.6	5.3	5.2	5.7
Midwest	7.7	6.8	6.5	5.2	4.5	4.2	4.2	4.2
South	7.0	6.1	6.2	5.3	4.9	4.8	4.9	4.9
West	6.3	5.6	5.7	4.7	4.6	4.7	4.6	4.3

[a]Comparisons of data from 1980–1985 with data from subsequent years should be made with caution because estimates of change may reflect improvements in the survey design rather than true changes in hospital use.

[b]Estimates are age-adjusted to the year 2000 standard population using six age groups: under 18 years, 18–44 years, 45–54 years, 55–64 years, 65–74 years, and 75 years and over.

Notes: Excludes newborn infants. Rates are based on the civilian population as of July 1. Starting with *Health, United States, 2003*, rates for 2000 and beyond are based on the 2000 census. Rates for 1990–1999 use population estimates based on the 1990 census adjusted for net underenumeration using the 1990 National Population Adjustment Matrix from the U.S. Census Bureau. Rates for 1990–1999 are not strictly comparable with rates for 2000 and beyond because population estimates for 1990–1999 have not been revised to reflect the 2000 census. Data for additional years are available.

SOURCE: "Table 99. Discharges, Days of Care, and Average Length of Stay in Nonfederal Short-Stay Hospitals, by Selected Characteristics: United States, Selected Years 1980–2007," in *Health, United States 2010: With Special Feature on Death and Dying*, National Center for Health Statistics, 2011, http://www.cdc.gov/nchs/data/hus/hus10.pdf (accessed April 8, 2011)

One of the goals of the treatment of osteoporosis is to maintain bone health by preventing bone loss and by building new bone. Another goal is to minimize the risk and impact of falls, because they can cause fractures. Figure 7.6 shows the pyramid of prevention and treatment of osteoporosis. At its base is nutrition (with adequate intake of calcium, vitamin D, and other minerals), physical exercise, and preventive measures to reduce the risk of falls. The second layer of the pyramid involves identifying and treating diseases that can cause osteoporosis, such as thyroid disease. The peak of the pyramid involves drug therapy for osteoporosis. There are two primary types of drugs used to treat osteoporosis. Antiresorptive agents act to reduce bone loss, and anabolic agents are drugs that build bone. Antiresorptive therapies include use of bisphosphonates, estrogen, selective estrogen receptor modulators, and calcitonin. They reduce bone loss, stabilize the architecture of the bone, and decrease bone turnover (the continuous process of remodeling in which bone is lost through resorption and new bone is formed).

Diabetes

Diabetes is a disease that affects the body's use of food, causing blood glucose (sugar levels in the blood) to become too high. People with diabetes can convert food to glucose, but there is a problem with insulin. In one type of diabetes (insulin-dependent diabetes, or type 1), the pancreas does not manufacture enough insulin, and in another type (noninsulin-dependent, or type 2), the body has insulin but cannot use the insulin effectively (this latter condition is called insulin resistance). When insulin is either absent or ineffective, glucose cannot get into the cells to be used for energy. Instead, the unused glucose builds up in the bloodstream and circulates through the kidneys. If the blood-glucose level rises high enough,

the excess glucose "spills" over into the urine, causing frequent urination. This leads to an increased feeling of thirst as the body tries to compensate for the fluid that is lost through urination.

Type 2 diabetes is most often seen in adults and is the most common type of diabetes in the United States. In type 2 diabetes the pancreas produces insulin, but it is not used effectively and the body resists responding to it. Heredity is a predisposing factor in the genesis of diabetes, but because the pancreas continues to produce insulin in people suffering from type 2 diabetes, the disease is considered more of a problem of insulin resistance, in which the body is not using the hormone efficiently.

Because diabetes deprives cells of the glucose needed to function properly, several complications can develop to further threaten the lives of diabetics. The healing process of the body is slowed and there is an increased risk of infection. Complications of diabetes include higher risk and rates of heart disease; circulatory problems, especially in the legs, which are sometimes severe enough to require surgery or even amputation; diabetic retinopathy, a condition that can cause blindness; kidney disease that may require dialysis; and dental problems. Close attention to preventive health care, such as regular eye, dental, and foot examinations and control of blood sugar levels, have been shown to prevent or delay some of the consequences of diabetes.

The relatively recent rise in type 2 diabetes in the United States is in part attributed to rising obesity among adults. Between 1997 and 2010 the percent of adults diagnosed with diabetes increased from 5% to about 9%. (See Figure 7.7.) Of all adult age groups, the highest rate of diagnosed diabetes was among adults aged 65 years and older. (See Figure 7.8.) However, these rates

TABLE 7.3

Visits to physician offices, hospital outpatient departments, and emergency departments, by selected characteristics, 1995–2008

[Data are based on reporting by a sample of office-based physicians, hospital outpatient departments, and hospital emergency departments]

Age, sex, and race	All places[a]				Physician offices			
	1995	2000	2007	2008	1995	2000	2007	2008
	Number of visits in thousands							
Total	860,859	1,014,848	1,200,017	1,189,619	697,082	823,542	994,321	955,969
Under 18 years	194,644	212,165	240,813	225,531	150,351	163,459	194,959	171,744
18–44 years	285,184	315,774	335,440	328,438	219,065	243,011	257,257	243,979
45–64 years	188,320	255,894	334,088	341,595	159,531	216,783	283,890	284,110
45–54 years	104,891	142,233	170,514	169,674	88,266	119,474	141,478	137,776
55–64 years	83,429	113,661	163,574	171,921	71,264	97,309	142,412	146,335
65 years and over	192,712	231,014	289,675	294,054	168,135	200,289	258,214	256,135
65–74 years	102,605	116,505	142,528	144,878	90,544	102,447	127,805	127,125
75 years and over	90,106	114,510	147,147	149,177	77,591	97,842	130,409	129,010
	Number of visits per 100 persons							
Total, age-adjusted[b]	334	374	402	393	271	304	332	315
Total, crude	329	370	405	398	266	300	336	320
Under 18 years	275	293	327	306	213	226	264	233
18–44 years	264	291	304	298	203	224	233	221
45–64 years	364	422	439	441	309	358	373	367
45–54 years	339	385	392	386	286	323	325	313
55–64 years	401	481	503	513	343	412	438	437
65 years and over	612	706	799	790	534	612	712	688
65–74 years	560	656	746	729	494	577	669	639
75 years and over	683	766	859	860	588	654	761	743
Sex and age								
Male, age-adjusted[b]	290	325	351	334	232	261	290	265
Male, crude	277	314	345	330	220	251	285	262
Under 18 years	273	302	331	307	209	231	268	233
18–44 years	190	203	205	188	139	148	151	131
45–54 years	275	316	321	319	229	260	262	255
55–64 years	351	428	452	441	300	367	396	373
65–74 years	508	614	732	687	445	539	661	604
75 years and over	711	771	888	886	616	670	801	768
Female, age-adjusted[b]	377	420	452	451	309	345	374	363
Female, crude	378	424	462	464	310	348	384	376
Under 18 years	277	285	321	304	217	221	261	232
18–44 years	336	377	402	407	265	298	315	311
45–54 years	400	451	460	450	339	384	386	369
55–64 years	446	529	550	580	382	453	477	496
65–74 years	603	692	758	765	534	609	676	669
75 years and over	666	763	840	843	571	645	735	728
Race and age[c]								
White, age-adjusted[b]	339	380	398	395	282	315	335	324
White, crude	338	381	407	406	281	316	345	336
Under 18 years	295	306	330	312	237	243	273	246
18–44 years	267	301	298	299	211	239	235	230
45–54 years	334	386	381	387	286	330	324	325
55–64 years	397	480	498	512	345	416	442	446
65–74 years	557	641	735	729	496	568	666	648
75 years and over	689	764	856	855	598	658	765	743

may significantly underestimate the true prevalence of diabetes in the United States in view of National Health and Nutrition Survey findings, which show that sizable numbers of adults have undiagnosed diabetes.

Prostate Problems

Prostate problems typically occur after age 50. There are three common prostate disorders: prostatitis (inflammation of the prostate gland), benign prostatic hyperplasia (BPH; noncancerous enlargement of the prostate), and prostate cancer. Prostatitis causes painful or difficult urination and frequently occurs in younger men. BPH can also create problems with urination, but it is most common in older men. According to the National Kidney and Urological Diseases Information Clearinghouse, in *Prostate Enlargement: Benign Prostatic Hyperplasia* (June 2006, http://kidney.niddk.nih.gov/kudiseases/pubs/prostateenlargement/), 50% of men in their 60s and 90% of men in their 80s and 90s suffer from BPH.

Prostate cancer is the second-most common cause of cancer death after lung cancer in American men and the sixth-leading cause of death of men overall. The

TABLE 7.3

Visits to physician offices, hospital outpatient departments, and emergency departments, by selected characteristics, 1995–2008 [CONTINUED]

[Data are based on reporting by a sample of office-based physicians, hospital outpatient departments, and hospital emergency departments]

Age, sex, and race	All places[a]				Physician offices			
	1995	2000	2007	2008	1995	2000	2007	2008
				Number of visits per 100 persons				
Black or African American, age-adjusted	309	353	475	443	204	239	339	296
Black or African American, crude	281	324	450	421	178	214	317	276
Under 18 years	193	264	351	335	100	167	247	208
18–44 years	260	257	380	343	158	149	241	201
45–54 years	387	383	490	445	281	269	341	289
55–64 years	414	495	592	589	294	373	444	422
65–74 years	553	656	900	809	429	512	748	636
75 years and over	534	745	966	942	395	568	769	762

[a]All places includes visits to physician offices and hospital outpatient and emergency departments.
[b]Estimates are age-adjusted to the year 2000 standard population using six age groups: under 18 years, 18–44 years, 45–54 years, 55–64 years, 65–74 years, and 75 years and over.
[c]Estimates by racial group should be used with caution because information on race was collected from medical records. In 2008, race data were missing and imputed for 30% of ambulatory care visits, including 33% of visits to physician offices, 21% of visits to hospital outpatient departments, and 16% of visits to hospital emergency departments. Information on the race imputation process used in each data year is available in the public use file documentaiton. Starting with 1999 data, the instruction for the race item on the Patient Record Form was changed so that more than one race could be recorded. In previous years only one race could be checked. Estimates for race in this table are for visits where only one race was recorded. Because of the small number of responses with more than one racial group checked, estimates for visits with multiple races checked are unreliable and are not presented. Notes: Rates for 1995–2000 were computed using 1990-based postcensal estimates of the civilian noninstitutionalized population as of July 1, adjusted for net underenumeration using the 1990 National Population Adjustment Matrix from the U.S. Census Bureau. Starting with 2001 data, rates were computed using 2000-based postcensal estimates of the civilian noninstitutionalized population as of July 1. The difference between rates for 2000 computed using 1990-based postcensal estimates and 2000 census counts is minimal. Rates will be overestimated to the extent that visits by institutionalized persons are counted in the numerator (for example, hospital emergency department visits by nursing home residents) and institutionalized persons are omitted from the denominator (the civilian noninstitutionalized population). Starting with *Health, United States, 2005*, data for physician offices for 2001 and beyond use a revised weighting scheme. Data for additional years are available.

SOURCE: Adapted from "Table 91. Visits to Physician Offices, Hospital Outpatient Departments, and Hospital Emergency Departments, by Selected Characteristics: United States, Selected Years 1995–2008," in *Health, United States 2010: With Special Feature on Death and Dying*, National Center for Health Statistics, 2011, http://www.cdc.gov/nchs/data/hus/hus10.pdf (accessed April 8, 2011)

American Cancer Society reports in *Cancer Facts and Figures, 2010* (2010, http://www.cancer.org/acs/groups/content/@epidemiologysurveilance/documents/document/acspc-026238.pdf) that an estimated 217,730 men were diagnosed with prostate cancer in 2010 and 32,050 died from it. When it is diagnosed and treated early, prostate cancer is generally not life threatening, because it progresses slowly and remains localized for a long time. As a result, many men who are diagnosed late in life do not die from this disease.

Urinary Incontinence

Urinary incontinence is the uncontrollable loss of urine that is so severe that it has social or hygienic consequences. In *Urological Diseases in America* (2007, http://kidney.niddk.nih.gov/statistics/uda/Urologic_Diseases_in_America.pdf), the National Institutes of Health reports that between 15% and 50% of women of all ages suffer from incontinence ranging from mild leakage to uncontrollable wetting and that the rate tends to increase with advancing age. The problem is more common in women than men, although it affects men of all ages, including 17% of men over the age of 60. Urinary incontinence can lead to many complications. For example, if left untreated it increases the risk of developing serious bladder and kidney infections, skin rashes, and pressure sores and of falls that result from rushing to use the toilet.

Age-related changes affect the ability to control urination. The maximum capacity of urine that the bladder can hold diminishes, as does the ability to postpone urination when a person feels the urge to urinate. As a person ages, the rate of urine flow out of the bladder and through the urethra slows, and the volume of urine remaining in the bladder after urination is finished increases. In women the urethra shortens and its lining becomes thinner as the level of estrogen declines during menopause, decreasing the ability of the urinary sphincter to close tightly. Among older men, the prostate gland enlarges, sometimes blocking the flow of urine through the urethra. Age-related changes increase the risk for incontinence, but it typically occurs as a symptom of an illness or other medical disorder.

Even though urinary incontinence is common, highly treatable, and frequently curable, it is underdiagnosed and often untreated because sufferers do not seek treatment. Many older adults are fearful, embarrassed, or incorrectly assume that incontinence is a normal consequence of growing old. The disorder exacts a serious emotional toll—sufferers are often homebound, isolated, or depressed and are more likely to report their health as fair to poor than their peers. In addition, urinary incontinence is often a reason for institutionalization, because many of those afflicted have some activity limitations and because incontinence is difficult for caregivers to manage.

TABLE 7.4

Visits to primary care physicians, by age, sex, and race, selected years 1980–2008

[Data are based on reporting by a sample of office-based physicians]

	Type of primary care generalist physician[a]											
Age, sex, and race	All primary care generalists				General and family practice				Internal medicine			
	1980	1990	2000	2008	1980	1990	2000	2008	1980	1990	2000	2008
	Percent of all physician office visits											
Total	**66.2**	**63.6**	**58.9**	**59.6**	**33.5**	**29.9**	**24.1**	**23.2**	**12.1**	**13.8**	**15.3**	**16.0**
Under 18 years	77.8	79.5	79.7	84.9	26.1	26.5	19.9	16.9	2.0	2.9	*	*
18–44 years	65.3	65.2	62.1	67.9	34.3	31.9	28.2	29.4	8.6	11.8	12.7	13.4
45–64 years	60.2	55.5	51.2	51.5	36.3	32.1	26.4	26.0	19.5	18.6	20.1	20.5
45–54 years	60.2	55.6	52.3	53.5	37.4	32.0	27.8	28.4	17.1	17.1	18.7	19.0
55–64 years	60.2	55.5	49.9	49.7	35.4	32.1	24.7	23.9	21.8	20.0	21.7	21.9
65 years and over	61.6	52.6	46.5	43.9	37.5	28.1	20.2	18.5	22.7	23.3	24.5	23.6
65–74 years	61.2	52.7	46.6	44.1	37.4	28.1	19.7	20.3	22.1	23.0	24.5	21.9
75 years and over	62.3	52.4	46.4	43.6	37.6	28.0	20.8	16.8	23.5	23.7	24.5	25.3
Sex and age												
Male												
Under 18 years	77.3	78.1	77.7	84.2	25.6	24.1	18.3	16.4	2.0	3.0	*	*
18–44 years	50.8	51.8	51.5	57.9	38.0	35.9	34.2	37.1	11.5	15.0	14.4	19.3
45–64 years	55.6	50.6	49.4	46.6	34.4	31.0	28.7	27.4	20.5	19.2	19.8	19.2
65 years and over	58.2	51.2	43.1	39.5	35.6	27.7	19.3	18.2	22.3	23.3	23.8	21.3
Female												
Under 18 years	78.5	81.1	82.0	85.5	26.6	29.1	21.7	17.4	2.0	2.8	*	*
18–44 years	72.1	71.3	67.2	72.1	32.5	30.0	25.3	26.1	7.3	10.3	11.9	10.9
45–64 years	63.4	58.8	52.5	54.9	37.7	32.8	24.9	25.1	18.9	18.2	20.2	21.3
65 years and over	63.9	53.5	48.9	47.0	38.7	28.3	20.9	18.7	22.9	23.3	25.0	25.3
Race and age[b]												
White												
Under 18 years	77.6	79.2	78.5	84.0	26.4	27.1	21.2	17.9	2.0	2.3	*	*
18–44 years	64.8	64.4	61.4	66.6	34.5	31.9	29.2	30.7	8.6	10.6	11.0	12.8
45–64 years	59.6	54.2	49.3	51.9	36.0	31.5	27.3	26.8	19.2	17.6	17.1	20.1
65 years and over	61.4	51.9	45.1	43.5	36.6	27.5	20.3	18.9	23.3	23.1	23.0	23.0
Black or African American												
Under 18 years	79.9	85.5	87.3	90.0	23.7	20.2	*	14.3*	2.2*	9.8	*	*
18–44 years	68.5	68.3	65.0	74.9	31.7	31.9	22.0	25.9	9.0	18.1	20.9	15.9*
45–64 years	66.1	61.6	61.7	51.0	38.6	31.2	23.3	20.3	22.6	26.9	35.9	25.9
65 years and over	64.6	58.6	52.8	52.9	49.0	28.9	18.5*	18.1	14.2	28.7	33.4	31.7

*Estimates are considered unreliable.
[a]Type of physician is based on physician's self-designated primary area of practice. Primary care generalist physicians are defined as practitioners in the fields of general and family practice, general internal medicine, general obstetrics and gynecology, and general pediatrics and exclude primary care specialists. Primary care generalists in general and family practice exclude primary care specialities, such as sports medicine and geriatrics. Primary care internal medicine physicians exclude internal medicine specialists, such as allergists, cardiologists, and endocrinologists. Primary care obstetrics and gynecology physicians exclude obstetrics and gynecology specialities, such as gynecological oncology, maternal and fetal medicine, obstetrics and gynecology critical care medicine, and reproductive endocrinology. Primary care pediatricians exclude pediatric specialists, such as adolescent medicine specialists, neonatologists, pediatric allergists, and pediatric cardiologists.
[b]Estimates by racial group should be used with caution because information on race was collected from medical records. In 2008, race data were missing and imputed for 33% of visits to physician offices. Information on the race imputation process used in each data year is available in the public use file documentaiton. Starting with 1999 data, the instruction for the race item on the Patient Record Form was changed so that more than one race could be recorded. In previous years only one racial category could be checked. Estimates for racial groups presented in this table are for visits where only one race was recorded. Because of the small number of responses with more than one racial group checked, estimates for visits with multiple races checked are unreliable and are not presented.
Notes: This table presents data on visits to physician offices and excludes visits to other sites, such as hospital outpatient and emergency departments. In 1980, the survey excluded Alaska and Hawaii. Data for all other years include all 50 states and the District of Columbia. Visits with specialty of physician unknown are excluded. Starting with *Health, United States, 2005*, data for 2001 and later years for physician offices use a revised weighting scheme. Data for additional years are available.

SOURCE: Adapted from "Table 92. Visits to Primary Care Generalist and Specialist Physicians, by Selected Characteristics and Type of Physician: United States, Selected Years 1980–2008," in *Health, United States 2010: With Special Feature on Death and Dying*, National Center for Health Statistics, 2011, http://www.cdc.gov/nchs/data/hus/hus10.pdf (accessed April 8, 2011)

Malnutrition

The older population is especially vulnerable to nutrition-related health problems. As people age, their energy needs decline, and it is vital for them to consume nutrient-dense foods in a lower calorie diet. According to the National Resource Center on Nutrition, Physical Activity, and Aging, in "Malnutrition and Older Americans" (2011, http://nutritionandaging.fiu.edu/aging_network/malfact2.asp),

35% to 50% of older adults in long-term care facilities and up to 65% of older adults in hospitals are at risk for malnutrition. Concerning homebound older adults, an estimated 1 million are also at risk for malnutrition.

Older adults' nutrition may be affected by many factors, including loneliness, depression, a cognitive disorder, a poor appetite, or a lack of transportation. Poor nutrition may arise in response to a major life change such as the

TABLE 7.5

Leading causes of death and numbers of deaths, by age, 1980 and 2007

[Data are based on death certificates]

Age and rank order	1980 Cause of death	Deaths	2007 Cause of death	Deaths
25–44 years				
Rank	All causes	108,658	All causes	122,178
1	Unintentional injuries	26,722	Unintentional injuries	31,908
2	Malignant neoplasms	17,551	Malignant neoplasms	16,751
3	Diseases of heart	14,513	Diseases of heart	15,062
4	Homicide	10,983	Suicide	12,000
5	Suicide	9,855	Homicide	7,810
6	Chronic liver disease and cirrhosis	4,782	Human immunodeficiency virus (HIV) disease	4,663
7	Cerebrovascular diseases	3,154	Chronic liver disease and cirrhosis	2,954
8	Diabetes mellitus	1,472	Cerebrovascular diseases	2,638
9	Pneumonia and influenza	1,467	Diabetes mellitus	2,594
10	Congenital anomalies	817	Septicemia	1,207
45–64 years				
Rank	All causes	425,338	All causes	471,796
1	Diseases of heart	148,322	Malignant neoplasms	153,338
2	Malignant neoplasms	135,675	Diseases of heart	102,961
3	Cerebrovascular diseases	19,909	Unintentional injuries	32,508
4	Unintentional injuries	18,140	Diabetes mellitus	17,057
5	Chronic liver disease and cirrhosis	16,089	Chronic lower respiratory diseases	16,930
6	Chronic obstructive pulmonary diseases	11,514	Cerebrovascular diseases	16,885
7	Diabetes mellitus	7,977	Chronic liver disease and cirrhosis	16,216
8	Suicide	7,079	Suicide	12,847
9	Pneumonia and influenza	5,804	Nephritis, nephrotic syndrome and nephrosis	6,673
10	Homicide	4,019	Septicemia	6,662
65 years and over				
Rank	All causes	1,341,848	All causes	1,755,567
1	Diseases of heart	595,406	Diseases of heart	496,095
2	Malignant neoplasms	258,389	Malignant neoplasms	389,730
3	Cerebrovascular diseases	146,417	Cerebrovascular diseases	115,961
4	Pneumonia and influenza	45,512	Chronic lower respiratory diseases	109,562
5	Chronic obstructive pulmonary diseases	43,587	Alzheimer's disease	73,797
6	Atherosclerosis	28,081	Diabetes mellitus	51,528
7	Diabetes mellitus	25,216	Influenza and pneumonia	45,941
8	Unintentional injuries	24,844	Nephritis, nephrotic syndrome and nephrosis	38,484
9	Nephritis, nephrotic syndrome, and nephrosis	12,968	Unintentional injuries	38,292
10	Chronic liver disease and cirrhosis	9,519	Septicemia	26,362

Notes: For cause of death codes based on the International Classification of Diseases, 9th Revision (ICD-9) in 1980 and ICD-10 in 2007.

SOURCE: Adapted from "Table 27. Leading Causes of Death and Numbers of Deaths, by Age: United States, 1980 and 2007," in *Health, United States 2010: With Special Feature on Death and Dying*, National Center for Health Statistics, 2011, http://www.cdc.gov/nchs/data/hus/hus10.pdf (accessed April 8, 2011)

TABLE 7.6

Percentage of people aged 65 and over who reported having selected chronic conditions, by sex, 2007–08

	Heart disease	Hypertension	Stroke	Asthma	Chronic bronchitis or emphysema	Any cancer	Diabetes	Arthritis
				Percent				
Total	**31.9**	**55.7**	**8.8**	**10.4**	**9.0**	**22.5**	**18.6**	**49.5**
Men	38.2	53.1	8.7	8.9	8.6	23.9	19.5	42.2
Women	27.1	57.6	8.9	11.5	9.2	21.4	17.9	54.9
Non-Hispanic white	33.7	54.3	8.7	10.2	9.7	24.8	16.4	50.6
Non-Hispanic black	27.2	71.1	10.8	11.3	5.9	13.3	29.7	52.2
Hispanic	23.8	53.1	7.7	10.9	6.2	12.4	27.3	42.1

Notes: Data are based on a 2-year average from 2007–2008.
Reference population: These data refer to the civilian noninstitutionalized population.

SOURCE: "Table 16a. Percentage of People Age 65 and over Who Reported Having Selected Chronic Health Conditions, by Sex, 2007–2008," in *Older Americans 2010: Key Indicators of Well-Being*, Federal Interagency Forum on Aging-Related Statistics, July 2010, http://www.agingstats.gov/agingstatsdotnet/Main_Site/Data/2010_Documents/Docs/OA_2010.pdf (accessed April 2, 2011)

TABLE 7.7

Percentage of people aged 65 and over who reported having selected chronic conditions, selected years 1997–2008

	Heart disease	Hypertension	Stroke	Emphysema	Asthma	Chronic bronchitis	Any cancer	Diabetes	Arthritis
					Percent				
1997–1998	32.3	46.5	8.2	5.2	7.7	6.4	18.7	13.0	na
1999–2000	29.8	47.4	8.2	5.2	7.4	6.2	19.9	13.7	na
2001–2002	31.5	50.2	8.9	5.0	8.3	6.1	20.8	15.4	na
2003–2004	31.8	51.9	9.3	5.2	8.9	6.0	20.7	16.9	50.0
2005–2006	30.9	53.3	9.3	5.7	10.6	6.1	21.1	18.0	49.5
2007–2008	31.9	55.7	8.8	5.1	10.4	5.4	22.5	18.6	49.5

na = Comparable data for arthritis not available prior to 2003–2004.
Notes: Data are based on 2-year averages.
Reference population: These data refer to the civilian noninstitutionalized population.

SOURCE: "Table 16b. Percentage of People Age 65 and over Who Reported Having Selected Chronic Health Conditions, 1997–2008," in *Older Americans 2010: Key Indicators of Well-Being*, Federal Interagency Forum on Aging-Related Statistics, July 2010, http://www.agingstats.gov/agingstatsdotnet/Main_Site/Data/2010_Documents/Docs/OA_2010.pdf (accessed April 2, 2011)

FIGURE 7.5

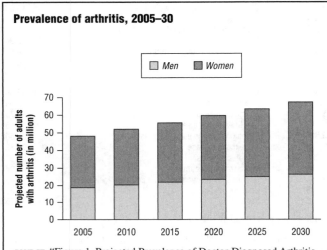

Prevalence of arthritis, 2005–30

SOURCE: "Figure 1. Projected Prevalence of Doctor-Diagnosed Arthritis among U.S. Adults Ages 18+ Years, 2005–2030," in *NHIS Arthritis Surveillance*, Centers for Disease Control and Prevention, National Center for Chronic Disease Prevention and Health Promotion, October 20, 2010, http://www.cdc.gov/arthritis/data_statistics/national_nhis.htm#disability (Accessed April 19, 2011)

death of a spouse. An older adult may forgo meal preparation when there is no longer someone else to cook for or eat with; and a bereaved or frail older adult may not have the stamina or motivation to shop or cook. Malnutrition may also be the result of poverty. When faced with fixed incomes and competing needs, older adults may be forced to choose between buying food or the prescription medications they need.

Hearing Loss

There are many causes of hearing loss, the most common being age-related changes in the ear's mechanism. Hearing loss is a common problem among older adults

and can seriously compromise quality of life. People suffering from hearing loss may withdraw from social contact and are sometimes misdiagnosed as cognitively impaired or mentally ill. In 2008, 42% of older men and 30% of older women reported having trouble hearing. (See Figure 7.9.)

Brandon Isaacson of the Southwestern Medical Center in Dallas, Texas, notes in "Hearing Loss" (*Medical Clinics of North America*, vol. 94, no. 5, September 2010) that nearly 10% of adults suffer from hearing loss and that the incidence markedly increases with advancing age. The most common cause of hearing loss is age-related degeneration of the inner ear, which affects about 50% of adults aged 75 years and older. Age-related hearing loss typically affects the higher frequencies first, and then over time it begins to involve the middle and lower frequencies. Men are more frequently affected than women and certain chronic conditions, such as high blood pressure and vascular disease, increase the risk of developing this form of hearing loss.

In "Hearing Loss Prevalence and Risk Factors among Older Adults in the United States" (*Journals of Gerontology, Series A: Biological Sciences and Medical Sciences*, vol. 66A, no. 5, May 2011), Frank R. Lin et al. analyze the relationship between hearing loss and cognitive and functional decline (diminished abilities to think, reason, and perform the activities of daily living). The researchers find that hearing loss is associated with an increased risk of cognitive decline in older adults. Lin et al. report in "Hearing Loss and Incident Dementia" (*Archives of Neurology*, vol. 68, no. 2, February 2011) on a relationship between hearing loss and Alzheimer's disease. The researchers determine that mild hearing loss is associated with a slight increase in the risk of Alzheimer's, but that the worse the hearing loss, the greater the risk for Alzheimer's. It is not yet known whether hearing loss is a marker or an early indicator of Alzheimer's disease, or whether correcting hearing loss might serve to prevent the onset of Alzheimer's.

FIGURE 7.6

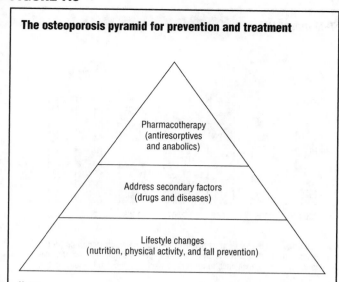

The osteoporosis pyramid for prevention and treatment

Pharmacotherapy
(antiresorptives
and anabolics)

Address secondary factors
(drugs and diseases)

Lifestyle changes
(nutrition, physical activity, and fall prevention)

Note:

The base of the pyramid: The first step in the prevention and treatment of osteoporosis and the prevention of fractures is to build a foundation of nutrition and lifestyle measures that maximize bone health. The diet should not only be adequate in calcium and vitamin D, but should have a healthy balance of other nutrients. A weight-bearing exercise program should be developed. Cigarette smoking and excessive alcohol use must be avoided. In the older individual, at high risk for fractures, the changes in lifestyle would include a plan not only to maximize physical activity, but also to minimize the risk of falls. The use of hip protectors can be considered in some high-risk patients. Diseases that increase the risk of falls by causing visual impairment, postural hypotension (a drop in blood pressure on standing, which leads to dizziness), or poor balance should be treated. Drugs that cause bone loss or increase the risk of falls should be avoided or given at the lowest effective dose.

The second level of the pyramid: The next step is to identify and treat diseases that produce secondary osteoporosis or aggravate primary osteoporosis. These measures are the foundation upon which specific pharmacotherapy is built and should never be forgotten.

The third level of the pyramid: If there is sufficiently high risk of fracture to warrant pharmacotherapy, the patient is usually started on antiresorptives. Anabolic agents are used in individuals in whom antiresorptive therapy is not adequate to prevent bone loss or fractures.

SOURCE: "Figure 9-1. The Osteoporosis Pyramid for Prevention and Treatment," in *Bone Health and Osteoporosis: A Report of the Surgeon General*, U.S. Department of Health and Human Services, Public Health Service, Office of the Surgeon General, October 14, 2004, http://www.surgeongeneral.gov/library/bonehealth/chapter_9 .html#APyramidApproach (accessed April 19, 2011)

Older adults are often reluctant to admit to hearing problems, and sometimes hearing loss is so gradual that even the afflicted person may not be aware of it for some time. For those who seek treatment, there is an expanding array of devices and services to mitigate the effects of hearing loss. Hearing-impaired people may benefit from high-tech hearing aids, amplifiers for doorbells and telephones, infrared amplifiers, and even companion dogs that are trained to respond to sounds for their owner.

Vision Changes

Almost no one escapes age-related changes in vision. Over time it becomes increasingly difficult to read small print or thread a needle at the usual distance. For many older adults, night vision declines. This is often caused by a condition called presbyopia (tired eyes) and is a common occurrence. People who were previously nearsighted may actually realize some improvement in eyesight as they become slightly farsighted. In 2008, 15% of men and 19% of women aged 65 years and older reported vision problems. (See Figure 7.9.)

Major Eye Diseases

Cataracts, glaucoma, age-related macular degeneration, and diabetic retinopathy are the leading causes of vision impairment and blindness in older adults. Cataracts are the leading cause of blindness in the world. Glaucoma is a chronic disease that often requires life-long treatment to control. Age-related macular degeneration is the most common cause of blindness and vision impairment in Americans aged 60 years and older. Diabetic retinopathy is a common complication of diabetes and is considered a leading cause of blindness in the industrialized world.

CATARACTS. A cataract is an opacity, or clouding, of the naturally clear lens of the eye. The prevalence of cataracts increases dramatically with age and most develop slowly over time as they progressively cause cloudy vision and eventually almost complete blindness. Once a clouded lens develops, surgery to remove the affected lens and replace it with an artificial lens is the recommended treatment. Research to Prevent Blindness (RPB) reports in "Cataract" (March 11, 2011, http://www.rpbusa.org/rpb/ eye_info/cataract/) that cataracts affect more than half of Americans aged 65 years and older.

GLAUCOMA. Glaucoma is a disease that causes gradual damage to the optic nerve, which carries visual information from the eye to the brain. The loss of vision is not experienced until a significant amount of nerve damage has occurred. Because the onset is gradual and insidious (subtle), as many as half of all people with glaucoma are unaware of having the disease. The RPB reports in "Glaucoma" (April 1, 2009, http://www.rpbusa.org/rpb/ eye_info/glaucoma/) that glaucoma affects approximately 2.2 million Americans and that an additional 2 million people may be affected but are unaware that they have the disease.

Routine glaucoma testing is especially important for older people. There is no cure for glaucoma and no way to restore lost vision; however, medication can generally manage the condition. At later stages, laser therapy and surgery are effective in preventing further damage.

AGE-RELATED MACULAR DEGENERATION. Age-related macular degeneration (AMD) is a condition in which the macula, a specialized part of the retina that is responsible for sharp central and reading vision, is damaged. Symptoms include blurred vision, a dark spot in the center of the vision field, and vertical line distortion. Prevent Blindness America indicates in "Vision Problems in the U.S."

FIGURE 7.7

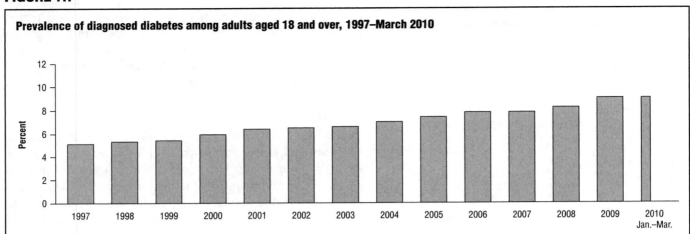

Prevalence of diagnosed diabetes among adults aged 18 and over, 1997–March 2010

Notes: Prevalence of diagnosed diabetes is based on self-report of ever having been diagnosed with diabetes by a doctor or other health professional. Persons reporting "borderline" diabetes status and women reporting diabetes only during pregnancy were not coded as having diabetes in the analyses. The analyses excluded persons with unknown diabetes status (about 0.1% of respondents each year). Beginning with the 2003 data, the National Health Interview Survey transitioned to weights derived from the 2000 census. In this early release, estimates for 2000–2002 were recalculated using weights derived from the 2000 census.

SOURCE: P.M. Barnes et al., "Figure 14.1. Prevalence of Diagnosed Diabetes among Adults Aged 18 Years and over: United States, 1997–March 2010," in *Early Release of Selected Estimates Based on Data from the January–March 2010 National Health Interview Survey*, Centers for Disease Control and Prevention, National Center for Health Statistics, September 2010, http://www.cdc.gov/nchs/data/nhis/earlyrelease/201009_14.pdf (accessed April 19, 2011)

FIGURE 7.8

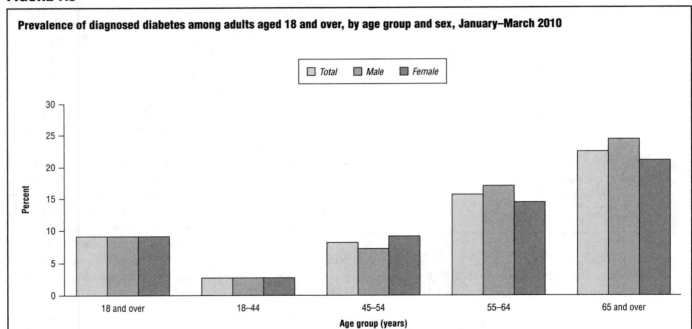

Prevalence of diagnosed diabetes among adults aged 18 and over, by age group and sex, January–March 2010

Notes: Prevalence of diagnosed diabetes is based on self-report of ever having been diagnosed with diabetes by a doctor or other health professional. Persons reporting "borderline" diabetes status and women reporting diabetes only during pregnancy were not coded as having diabetes in the analyses. The analyses excluded 5 persons (0.1%) with unknown diabetes status.

SOURCE: P.M. Barnes et al., "Figure 14.2. Prevalence of Diagnosed Diabetes among Adults Aged 18 Years and over, by Age Group and Sex: United States, 1997–March 2010," in *Early Release of Selected Estimates Based on Data from the January–March 2010 National Health Interview Survey*, Centers for Disease Control and Prevention, National Center for Health Statistics, September 2010, http://www.cdc.gov/nchs/data/nhis/earlyrelease/201009_14.pdf (accessed April 19, 2011)

(2008, http://www.preventblindness.org/vpus/) that over 2 million adults aged 50 years and older have the advanced form of the condition.

In "Forecasting Age-Related Macular Degeneration through the Year 2050: The Potential Impact of New Treatments" (*Archives of Ophthalmology*, vol. 127, no. 4, April

FIGURE 7.9

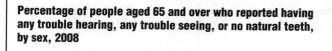

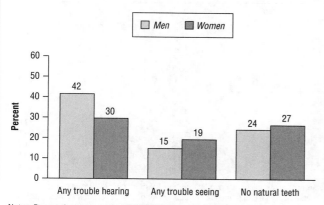

Percentage of people aged 65 and over who reported having any trouble hearing, any trouble seeing, or no natural teeth, by sex, 2008

Notes: Respondents were asked "WITHOUT the use of hearing aids or other listening devices, is your hearing excellent, good, a little trouble hearing, moderate trouble, a lot of trouble, or are you deaf?" For the purposes of this indicator, the category "Any trouble hearing" includes: "a little trouble hearing, moderate trouble, a lot of trouble, and deaf." This question differs slightly from the question used to calculate the estimates shown in previous editions of *Older Americans*. Regarding their vision, respondents were asked "Do you have any trouble seeing, even when wearing glasses or contact lenses?" and the category "Any trouble seeing" includes those who in a subsequent question report themselves as blind. Lastly, respondents were asked in one question, "Have you lost all of your upper and lower natural (permanent) teeth?"
Reference population: These data refer to the civilian noninstitutionalized population.

SOURCE: "Limitations in Hearing and Vision, and No Natural Teeth, among the Population 65 and over, by Sex, 2008," in *Older Americans 2010: Key Indicators of Well-Being*, Federal Interagency Forum on Aging-Related Statistics, July 2010, http://www.agingstats.gov/agingstatsdotnet/Main_Site/Data/2010_Documents/Docs/OA_2010.pdf (accessed April 2, 2011)

2009), David B. Rein et al. predict that the prevalence of early AMD will increase substantially, from 9.1 million in 2010 to 17.8 million in 2050. The researchers forecast significant increases in early and advanced AMD that will result in visual impairment in the coming decades, with nearly all these increases attributable to the aging of the U.S. population. However, Rein et al. observe that medical therapies, such as adequate intake of zinc, vitamins A and C, and beta carotene, can reduce the effects of vision loss and blindness that are attributable to AMD by as much as 35% in 2050.

DIABETIC RETINOPATHY. Diabetic retinopathy occurs when the small blood vessels in the retina do not perform properly. Blood vessels can become blocked, break down, leak fluid that distorts vision, and sometimes release blood into the center of the eye, causing blindness. Laser treatment, called photocoagulation, can help reduce the risk of loss of vision in advanced cases of diabetic retinopathy. The disorder is a leading cause of blindness, but is less common among older adults than other types of visual impairment. Prevent Blindness America indicates in

"Vision Problems in the U.S." that diabetic retinopathy affects 4.5 million Americans aged 40 years and older. The prevalence of diabetic retinopathy increases with age, reflecting the higher rates of diabetes in older people.

Oral Health Problems

According to the CDC, in "Oral Health—Preventing Cavities, Gum Disease, Tooth Loss, and Oral Cancers: At a Glance 2010" (February 19, 2010, http://www.cdc.gov/chronicdisease/resources/publications/AAG/doh.htm), one-fourth of adults aged 65 years and older have lost all their teeth. Figure 7.9 shows that in 2008, 24% of men and 27% of women aged 65 years and older had no natural teeth. For people aged 85 years and older in 2008, 33.9% had none of their teeth. (See Table 7.8.) Older adults living in poverty were much more likely to have lost their teeth than those living above poverty, 41.8% and 23.4%, respectively.

In "Tooth Loss and Periodontal Disease Predict Poor Cognitive Function in Older Men" (*Journal of the American Geriatric Society*, vol. 58, no. 4, April 2010), Elizabeth Krall Kaye et al. look at the relationship between periodontal disease, which affects the gums and bone supporting the teeth, and tooth loss and cognitive decline. The researchers find that among older men (the study did not consider women), cognitive decline increased as more teeth were lost due to periodontal disease and caries (tooth decay).

Parkinson's Disease

According to the Parkinson's Disease Foundation, in "Statistics on Parkinson's" (2011, www.pdf.org/en/parkinson_statistics), Parkinson's disease (PD) describes a condition marked by a characteristic set of symptoms that affects about 1 million people in the United States. An estimated 60,000 people in the United States are diagnosed with PD each year and thousands of others have the disease but are not diagnosed. The incidence of PD increases with advancing age—just 4% of cases are diagnosed in people under the age of 50 years. In "Movement Disorders" (*Medical Clinics of North America*, vol. 93, no. 2, March 2009), Meghan K. Harris et al. observe that the prevalence of PD is 1% to 2% in the population aged 65 years and older and up to 4% in individuals older than 85. PD usually begins during the 70s, but up to 10% of those affected are aged 50 years and younger.

PD is caused by the death of about half a million brain cells in the basal ganglia. These cells secrete dopamine, a neurotransmitter (chemical messenger), whose function is to allow nerve impulses to move smoothly from one nerve cell to another. These nerve cells, in turn, transmit messages to the muscles of the body to begin movement. When the normal supply of dopamine is reduced, the messages are not correctly sent, and the symptoms—mild tremor (shaking), change in walking, or a decreased arm swing—of PD begin to appear.

TABLE 7.8

Percentage of people aged 65 and over who reported having any trouble hearing, any trouble seeing, or no natural teeth, by selected characteristics, 2008

Sex	Age and poverty status	Any trouble hearing	Any trouble seeing	No natural teeth
		Percent		
Both sexes	65 and over	34.8	17.5	25.6
	65–74	27.8	14.3	20.4
	75–84	36.6	18.6	30.7
	85 and over	60.1	28.4	33.9
	Below poverty	28.2	23.8	41.8
	Above poverty	35.5	17.0	23.4
Men	65 and over	41.5	14.9	24.3
	65–74	36.0	11.3	19.2
	75–84	43.7	17.2	30.7
	85 and over	66.7	28.5	33.0
Women	65 and over	29.6	19.4	26.6
	65–74	20.7	16.9	21.4
	75–84	31.7	19.5	30.8
	85 and over	56.6	28.4	34.4

Notes: Respondents were asked "WITHOUT the use of hearing aids or other listening devices, is your hearing excellent, good, a little trouble hearing, moderate trouble, a lot of trouble, or are you deaf?" For the purposes of this indicator, the category "Any trouble hearing" includes: "a little trouble hearing, moderate trouble, a lot of trouble, and deaf." This question differs slightly from the question used to calculate the estimates shown in previous editions of *Older Americans*. Regarding their vision, respondents were asked "Do you have any trouble seeing, even when wearing glasses or contact lenses?" and the category "Any trouble seeing" includes those who in a subsequent question report themselves as blind. Lastly, respondents were asked in one question, "Have you lost all of your upper and lower natural (permanent) teeth?"
Reference population: These data refer to the civilian noninstitutionalized population.

SOURCE: "Table 17a. Percentage of People Age 65 and over Who Reported Having Any Trouble Hearing, Trouble Seeing, or No Natural Teeth, by Selected Characteristics, 2008," in *Older Americans 2010: Key Indicators of Well-Being*, Federal Interagency Forum on Aging-Related Statistics, July 2010, http://www.agingstats.gov/agingstatsdotnet/Main_Site/Data/2010_Documents/Docs/OA_2010.pdf (accessed April 2, 2011)

The four early warning signs of PD are tremors, muscle stiffness, unusual slowness (bradykinesia), and a stooped posture. Medications can control initial symptoms, but over time they become less effective. As the disease worsens, patients develop more severe tremors, causing them to fall or jerk uncontrollably. (The jerky body movements PD patients experience are known as dyskinesias.) At other times, rigidity sets in, rendering them unable to move. About one-third of patients also develop dementia (loss of intellectual functioning accompanied by memory loss and personality changes).

TREATMENT OF PARKINSON'S DISEASE. Management of PD is individualized and includes not only drug therapy but also daily exercise. Exercise can often lessen the rigidity of muscles, prevent weakness, and improve the ability to walk.

The main goal of drug treatment is to restore the chemical balance between dopamine and another neurotransmitter, acetylcholine. Most patients are given levodopa (L-dopa), a compound that the body converts into dopamine. Treatment with L-dopa does not, however, slow the progressive course of the disease or even delay the changes in the brain PD produces, and it may produce some unpleasant side effects such as dyskinesias.

INFECTIOUS DISEASES

Infectious (contagious) diseases are caused by microorganisms (viruses, bacteria, parasites, or fungi) that are transmitted from one person to another through casual contact, such as with the transmittal of influenza, through bodily fluids, such as with the transmittal of HIV, or from contaminated food, air, or water supplies. The CDC reports that in 2007 influenza and pneumonia remained among the top 10 causes of death for older adults, responsible for 45,941 deaths of people aged 65 years and older. (See Table 7.5.) Influenza-related deaths can result from pneumonia as well as from exacerbation of chronic diseases.

Influenza

Influenza (flu) is a contagious respiratory disease caused by a virus. The virus is expelled by an infected individual in droplets into the air and may be inhaled by anyone nearby. It can also be transmitted by direct hand contact. The flu primarily affects the lungs, but the whole body experiences symptoms. Influenza is an acute (short-term) illness that is characterized by fever, chills, weakness, loss of appetite, and aching muscles in the head, back, arms, and legs. Influenza infection may also produce a sore throat, a dry cough, nausea, and burning eyes. The accompanying fever rises quickly—sometimes reaching 104 degrees Fahrenheit (40 degrees Celsius)—but usually subsides after two or three days. Influenza leaves the patient exhausted.

For healthy individuals, the flu is typically a moderately severe illness, with most adults back to work or school within a week. For the very old and older people who are not in good general health, however, the flu can

FIGURE 7.10

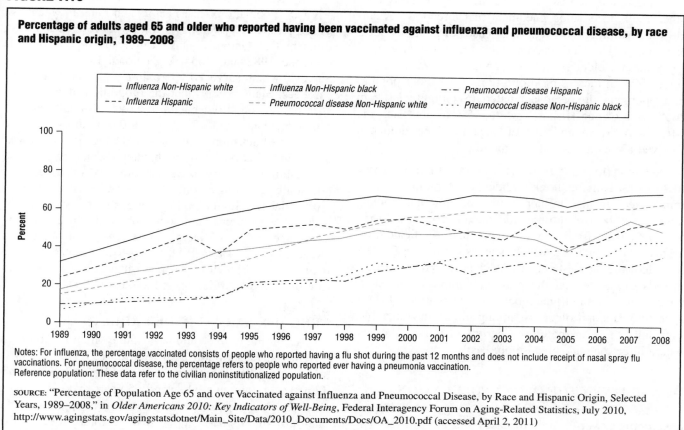

Percentage of adults aged 65 and older who reported having been vaccinated against influenza and pneumococcal disease, by race and Hispanic origin, 1989–2008

Notes: For influenza, the percentage vaccinated consists of people who reported having a flu shot during the past 12 months and does not include receipt of nasal spray flu vaccinations. For pneumococcal disease, the percentage refers to people who reported ever having a pneumonia vaccination.
Reference population: These data refer to the civilian noninstitutionalized population.

SOURCE: "Percentage of Population Age 65 and over Vaccinated against Influenza and Pneumococcal Disease, by Race and Hispanic Origin, Selected Years, 1989–2008," in *Older Americans 2010: Key Indicators of Well-Being*, Federal Interagency Forum on Aging-Related Statistics, July 2010, http://www.agingstats.gov/agingstatsdotnet/Main_Site/Data/2010_Documents/Docs/OA_2010.pdf (accessed April 2, 2011)

be severe and even fatal. Complications such as secondary bacterial infections may develop, taking advantage of the body's weakened condition and lowered resistance. The most common bacterial complication is pneumonia, affecting the lungs, but sinuses, bronchi (larger air passages of the lungs), and inner ears can also become secondarily infected with bacteria. Less common but serious complications include viral pneumonia, encephalitis (inflammation of the brain), acute renal (kidney) failure, and nervous system disorders. These complications can be fatal.

Influenza can be prevented by inoculation with a current influenza vaccine, which is formulated annually to contain the influenza viruses expected to cause the flu the upcoming year. Immunization produces antibodies to the influenza viruses, which become most effective after one or two months. The CDC advises that older adults get flu shots early in the fall, because peak flu activity usually occurs around the beginning of the new calendar year. In 2008, 70% of non-Hispanic white, 55% of Hispanic, and 50% of non-Hispanic African-American older adults reported receiving influenza shots within the past 12 months. (See Figure 7.10.) In "Questions & Answers: Seasonal Flu Shot" (February 8, 2011, http://www.cdc.gov/flu/about/qa/flushot.htm), the CDC reports that in February 2010 vaccine experts voted that everyone six months and older

should get a flu vaccine each year starting with the 2010–11 flu season. The CDC also observes that immunization reduces hospitalization by 30% to 70% among noninstitutionalized older adults. Among nursing home residents, the flu shot reduces the risk of hospitalization by 50% to 60% and the risk of death by 80%.

Pneumonia

Pneumonia is a serious lung infection. Symptoms of pneumonia are fever, chills, cough, shortness of breath, chest pain, and increased sputum production. Pneumonia may be caused by viruses, bacteria, or fungi; however, the pneumococcus bacterium is the most important cause of serious pneumonia.

In older adults pneumococcal pneumonia is a common cause of hospitalization and death. Joseph P. Lynch and George G. Zhanel indicate in "Streptococcus pneumoniae: Epidemiology, Risk Factors, and Strategies for Prevention" (*Seminars in Respiratory and Critical Care Medicine*, vol. 30, no. 2, April 2009) that there are 45 to 90 cases per 100,000 population per year in adults aged 65 years and older. About one-quarter of adults aged 65 years and older who contract pneumococcal pneumonia develop bacteremia (bacteria in the blood), and as many as 30% of older adults who develop bacteremia die.

Older adults are two to three times more likely than other adults to develop pneumococcal infections. A single vaccination can prevent most cases of pneumococcal pneumonia. The CDC recommends that all people aged 65 years and older receive the pneumonia vaccine, and since 1998 an increasing proportion of the older population reports having been vaccinated. (See Figure 7.10.) In 2008, 64% of non-Hispanic white, 45% of non-Hispanic African-American, and 35% of Hispanic older adults had received a pneumococcal vaccination.

MANDATORY IMMUNIZATION FOR NURSING HOME RESIDENTS. Nursing home residents are required to be immunized against influenza and pneumonia; nursing homes that fail to enforce this requirement risk losing reimbursement from the Medicare and Medicaid programs. The regulation, which was issued by the Centers for Medicare and Medicaid Services in August 2005, intends to ensure that the most vulnerable older adults receive their flu and pneumococcal vaccinations. People aged 65 years and older are among the most vulnerable, especially those in the close quarters of nursing homes, where infection can spread more easily.

DISABILITY IN THE OLDER POPULATION

Americans are not only living longer but also are developing fewer chronic diseases and disabilities. The current cohort (a group of individuals that shares a common characteristic such as birth years and is studied over time) of older Americans are defying the stereotype that aging is synonymous with increasing disability and dependence.

In "Recent Declines in Chronic Disability in the Elderly U.S. Population: Risk Factors and Future Dynamics" (*Annual Review of Public Health*, vol. 29, April 2008), Kenneth G. Manton of Duke University reports on data from the 1982 and 2004–05 National Long-Term Care Surveys, which surveyed approximately 20,000 Medicare enrollees. Manton notes that the proportion of Americans aged 65 years and older with a chronic disability significantly declined about 2.2% per year during this period due to improved nutrition, sanitation, and education. However, he cautions that obesity may threaten the downward trend in disability. Obesity increases the risk of developing potentially disabling chronic diseases such as heart disease, type 2 diabetes, high blood pressure, stroke, osteoarthritis, respiratory problems, and some forms of cancer. Among adults aged 65 to 74 years, the percentage of obese men increased from 24% in 1988–94 to 40% in 2007–08. (See Figure 7.11.) Likewise, the percentage of obese women rose from 27% to 35% during the same period.

DRUG USE AMONG OLDER ADULTS

According to the National Institute on Drug Abuse, in "Trends in Prescription Drug Abuse" (2011, http://www.nida.nih.gov/ResearchReports/Prescription/prescription5.html), even though adults aged 65 years and older make up 13% of the population, they account for approximately one-third of all medications that are prescribed in the United States. Dima M. Qato et al. find in "Use of Prescription and Over-the-Counter Medications and Dietary Supplements among Older Adults in the United States" (*Journal of the American Medical Association*, vol. 300, no. 24, December 24, 2008) that 29% of older adults use at

FIGURE 7.11

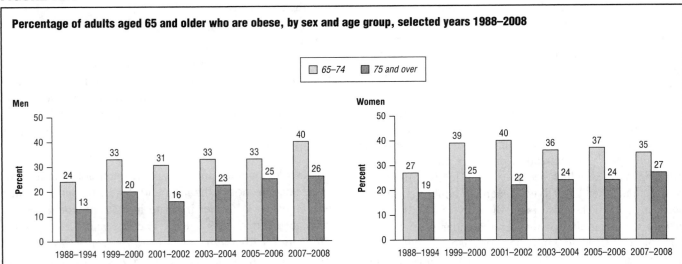

Percentage of adults aged 65 and older who are obese, by sex and age group, selected years 1988–2008

Notes: Data are based on measured height and weight. Height was measured without shoes. Obese is defined by a Body Mass Index (BMI) of 30 kilograms/meter^2 or greater. Reference population: These data refer to the civilian noninstitutionalized population.

SOURCE: "Percentage of People Age 65 and over Who Are Obese, by Sex and Age Group, Selected Years, 1988–2008," in *Older Americans 2010: Key Indicators of Well-Being*, Federal Interagency Forum on Aging-Related Statistics, July 2010, http://www.agingstats.gov/agingstatsdotnet/Main_Site/Data/2010_Documents/Docs/OA_2010.pdf (accessed April 2, 2011)

FIGURE 7.12

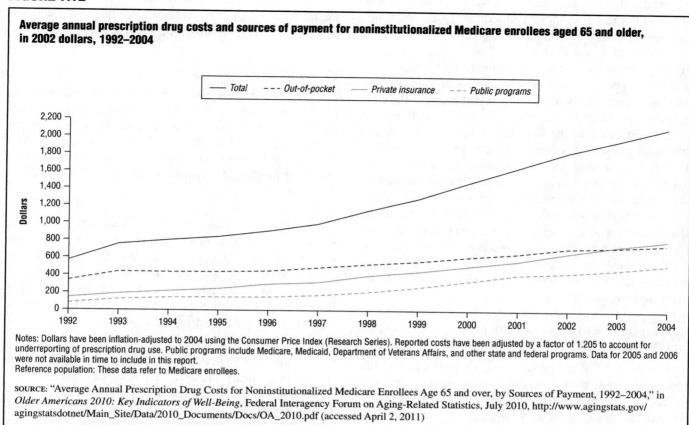

Average annual prescription drug costs and sources of payment for noninstitutionalized Medicare enrollees aged 65 and older, in 2002 dollars, 1992–2004

Notes: Dollars have been inflation-adjusted to 2004 using the Consumer Price Index (Research Series). Reported costs have been adjusted by a factor of 1.205 to account for underreporting of prescription drug use. Public programs include Medicare, Medicaid, Department of Veterans Affairs, and other state and federal programs. Data for 2005 and 2006 were not available in time to include in this report.
Reference population: These data refer to Medicare enrollees.

SOURCE: "Average Annual Prescription Drug Costs for Noninstitutionalized Medicare Enrollees Age 65 and over, by Sources of Payment, 1992–2004," in *Older Americans 2010: Key Indicators of Well-Being*, Federal Interagency Forum on Aging-Related Statistics, July 2010, http://www.agingstats.gov/agingstatsdotnet/Main_Site/Data/2010_Documents/Docs/OA_2010.pdf (accessed April 2, 2011)

least five prescription drugs and about 70% of older adults who take prescription medications also use over-the-counter (nonprescription) drugs, dietary supplements, or both. The researchers explain that "several factors have likely contributed to this increase in the rate of [the use of five or more medications] among older adults over the last decade. These include intensification of therapy for common chronic medical conditions (eg, diabetes, cardiovascular disease), increased access to medications because of policy changes (eg, Medicare Part D and assistance programs), and growth of the generic drug market." Qato et al. conclude that older adults are not only the largest per capita consumers of prescription medications but also are at high risk for adverse medication-related interactions.

Prescription drug costs have skyrocketed since the early 1990s. In 2004 the average cost per person was $2,107. (See Figure 7.12.) Out-of-pocket costs for prescription drugs have increased, creating serious financial hardships for many older adults. The American Federation of State, County, and Municipal Employees (AFSCME) indicates in *Hard to Swallow: Older Americans and the High Cost of Prescription Drugs* (December 15, 2010, http://www.afscme.org/news-publications/publications/for-leaders/labor-links/health-care/pdf/Hard_to_Swallow.pdf) that Americans aged 65 years and older account for 34% of all prescriptions dispensed and 42% of every dollar spent on prescription medications. The AFSCME also

notes that between 1992 and 2010 the average older adult's prescription drug cost increased by 72%, from $28.50 to $72.94.

Historically, Medicare did not cover most outpatient prescription drugs; however, beginning in January 2006 it started covering prescription drugs. It pays for brand-name and generic drugs and offers a choice of prescription drug plans to Medicare beneficiaries. The cost, or monthly premium, for Medicare prescription drug coverage varies depending on the plan—whether the plan has a deductible and the amount of coinsurance or co-payment for each prescription.

Older Adults Respond Differently to Drugs

Many factors influence the efficacy (the ability of an intervention to produce the intended diagnostic or therapeutic effect in optimal circumstances), safety, and success of drug therapy with older patients. These factors include the effects of aging on pharmacokinetics—the absorption, distribution, metabolism, and excretion of drugs. Of the four, absorption is the least affected by aging. In older people, absorption is generally complete, just slower. The distribution of most medications is related to body weight and composition changes that occur with aging such as decreased lean muscle mass, increased fat mass, and decreased total body water.

Health professionals who care for older adults know that drug dosages must often be modified based on changing organ function and estimates of lean body mass. They coined the adage "start low and go slow" to guide prescribing drugs for older adults. For example, some initial doses of drugs should be lower because older adults have decreased total body water, which might increase the concentration of the drug. Fat-soluble drugs may also have to be administered in lower doses because they may accumulate in fatty tissues, resulting in longer durations of action. The mechanism used to clear a drug via metabolism in the liver or clearance (excretion) through the kidneys changes with aging and is affected by interactions with other medications. Pharmacodynamics (tissue sensitivity to drugs) also changes with advancing age. Among older adults, the complete elimination of a drug from body tissues, including the brain, can take weeks longer than it might in younger people because of a combination of pharmacokinetic and pharmacodynamic effects.

Adherence, Drug-Drug Interactions, and Polypharmacy

Adherence (taking prescription medications regularly and correctly) is a challenge for older people who may suffer from memory loss, impaired vision, or arthritis. Abigail Flinders et al. note in "Prescribing for Older People" (*Nursing Older People*, vol. 21, no. 2, March 2009) that about half of older adults fail to take their medications at the right times and in the right amounts. Strategies to improve adherence include weekly pill boxes, calendars, and easy-to-open bottles with large-print labels.

Qato et al. indicate that drug-drug interactions are more frequent among older adults because they are more likely than people of other ages to be taking multiple medications. Dangerous drug-drug interactions may occur when two or more drugs act together to either intensify or diminish one another's potency and effectiveness or when in combination they produce adverse side effects. For example, a person who takes heparin, a blood-thinning medication, should not take aspirin, which also acts to thin the blood. Similarly, antacids can interfere with the absorption of certain drugs that are used to treat Parkinson's disease, hypertension, and heart disease.

Polypharmacy is the use of many medications at the same time. It also refers to prescribing more medication than is needed or a medication regimen that includes at least one unnecessary medication. The major risk associated with polypharmacy is the potential for adverse drug reactions and interactions. Drug-induced adverse events may masquerade as other illnesses or precipitate confusion, falls, and incontinence, potentially prompting the physician to prescribe yet another drug. This "prescribing cascade" is easily prevented. It requires that physicians ensure that all medications prescribed are appropriate, safe, effective, and taken correctly. It may also be prevented by older adults' maintenance of accurate and complete records of all their prescription and over-the-counter drug use.

LEADING CAUSES OF DEATH

The top three leading causes of death among adults aged 65 years and older—heart disease, malignant neoplasms, and cerebrovascular diseases—were unchanged between 1980 and 2007. (See Table 7.5.) In 2007 Alzheimer's disease held fifth place on the list of leading causes of death and was responsible for 73,797 deaths.

Heart Disease

Even though deaths from heart disease have declined, it still kills more Americans than any other single disease. According to the American Heart Association, in "Understand Your Risk of Heart Attack" (2011, http://www.heart.org/HEARTORG/Conditions/HeartAttack/UnderstandYourRiskofHeartAttack/Understand-Your-Risk-of-Heart-Attack_UCM_002040_Article.jsp), 82% of people who die of heart disease are aged 65 years and older.

Several factors account for the decreasing numbers of deaths from heart disease, including better control of hypertension and cholesterol levels and changes in exercise and nutrition. The increasing ranks of trained mobile emergency personnel (paramedics) and the widespread use of cardiopulmonary resuscitation and immediate treatment have also increased the likelihood of surviving an initial heart attack.

The growing use of statin drugs (drugs that reduce blood cholesterol levels) to reduce the risk of heart disease as well as procedures such as cardiac catheterization, coronary bypass surgery, pacemakers, angioplasty (a procedure to open narrowed or blocked blood vessels of the heart), and stenting (using wire scaffolds that hold arteries open) have improved the quality, and in some instances extended the lives, of people with heart disease.

However, the Mayo Clinic explains in "Statins: Are These Cholesterol-Lowering Drugs Right for You?" (February 11, 2010, http://www.mayoclinic.com/health/statins/CL00010) that statin use may produce side effects such as joint and muscle pain, nausea, diarrhea, and constipation. Even though these common side effects often subside with continued use of the drugs, less frequent but serious side effects such as liver and kidney damage and severe muscle pain may occur with statin treatment.

Cancer

Cancer is the second-leading cause of death among older adults. (See Table 7.5.) The American Cancer Society indicates in *Cancer Facts and Figures, 2010* that about 78% of all cancers are diagnosed after age 55. The likelihood of dying of cancer increases every decade after the age of 30. In 2007 among adults aged 65 to 74 years, there

TABLE 7.9

Death rates for malignant neoplasms, selected characteristics, selected years 1950–2007

[Data are based on death certificates]

Sex, race, Hispanic origin, and age	1950[a, b]	1960[a, b]	1970[b]	1980[b]	1990[b]	2000[c]	2006[c]	2007[c]
All persons			Deaths per 100,000 resident population					
All ages, age-adjusted[d]	193.9	193.9	198.6	207.9	216.0	199.6	180.7	178.4
All ages, crude	139.8	149.2	162.8	183.9	203.2	196.5	187.0	186.6
Under 1 year	8.7	7.2	4.7	3.2	2.3	2.4	1.8	1.7
1–4 years	11.7	10.9	7.5	4.5	3.5	2.7	2.3	2.2
5–14 years	6.7	6.8	6.0	4.3	3.1	2.5	2.2	2.4
15–24 years	8.6	8.3	8.3	6.3	4.9	4.4	3.9	3.9
25–34 years	20.0	19.5	16.5	13.7	12.6	9.8	9.0	8.5
35–44 years	62.7	59.7	59.5	48.6	43.3	36.6	31.9	30.8
45–54 years	175.1	177.0	182.5	180.0	158.9	127.5	116.3	114.3
55–64 years	390.7	396.8	423.0	436.1	449.6	366.7	321.2	315.4
65–74 years	698.8	713.9	754.2	817.9	872.3	816.3	727.2	715.5
75–84 years	1,153.3	1,127.4	1,169.2	1,232.3	1,348.5	1,335.6	1,263.8	1,256.3
85 years and over	1,451.0	1,450.0	1,320.7	1,594.6	1,752.9	1,819.4	1,606.1	1,590.2
Male								
All ages, age-adjusted[d]	208.1	225.1	247.6	271.2	280.4	248.9	220.1	217.5
All ages, crude	142.9	162.5	182.1	205.3	221.3	207.2	196.6	197.0
Under 1 year	9.7	7.7	4.4	3.7	2.4	2.6	1.8	1.8
1–4 years	12.5	12.4	8.3	5.2	3.7	3.0	2.5	2.3
5–14 years	7.4	7.6	6.7	4.9	3.5	2.7	2.5	2.4
15–24 years	9.7	10.2	10.4	7.8	5.7	5.1	4.6	4.5
25–34 years	17.7	18.8	16.3	13.4	12.6	9.2	8.6	8.2
35–44 years	45.6	48.9	53.0	44.0	38.5	32.7	27.4	26.4
45–54 years	156.2	170.8	183.5	188.7	162.5	130.9	119.0	117.5
55–64 years	413.1	459.9	511.8	520.8	532.9	415.8	363.6	358.5
65–74 years	791.5	890.5	1,006.8	1,093.2	1,122.2	1,001.9	870.4	854.3
75–84 years	1,332.6	1,389.4	1,588.3	1,790.5	1,914.4	1,760.6	1,631.3	1,617.4
85 years and over	1,668.3	1,741.2	1,720.8	2,369.5	2,739.9	2,710.7	2,248.7	2,249.2
Female								
All ages, age-adjusted[d]	182.3	168.7	163.2	166.7	175.7	167.6	153.6	151.3
All ages, crude	136.8	136.4	144.4	163.6	186.0	186.2	177.6	176.5
Under 1 year	7.6	6.8	5.0	2.7	2.2	2.3	1.8	1.6
1–4 years	10.8	9.3	6.7	3.7	3.2	2.5	2.1	2.2
5–14 years	6.0	6.0	5.2	3.6	2.8	2.2	2.0	2.3
15–24 years	7.6	6.5	6.2	4.8	4.1	3.6	3.1	3.2
25–34 years	22.2	20.1	16.7	14.0	12.6	10.4	9.5	8.9
35–44 years	79.3	70.0	65.6	53.1	48.1	40.4	36.4	35.2
45–54 years	194.0	183.0	181.5	171.8	155.5	124.2	113.7	111.3
55–64 years	368.2	337.7	343.2	361.7	375.2	321.3	281.8	275.2
65–74 years	612.3	560.2	557.9	607.1	677.4	663.6	605.9	597.6
75–84 years	1,000.7	924.1	891.9	903.1	1,010.3	1,058.5	1,012.5	1,007.4
85 years and over	1,299.7	1,263.9	1,096.7	1,255.7	1,372.1	1,456.4	1,305.5	1,276.7
White male[e]								
All ages, age-adjusted[d]	210.0	224.7	244.8	265.1	272.2	243.9	217.9	215.1
All ages, crude	147.2	166.1	185.1	208.7	227.7	218.1	208.7	208.8
25–34 years	17.7	18.8	16.2	13.6	12.3	9.2	8.6	8.1
35–44 years	44.5	46.3	50.1	41.1	35.8	30.9	26.7	25.9
45–54 years	150.8	164.1	172.0	175.4	149.9	123.5	113.6	112.0
55–64 years	409.4	450.9	498.1	497.4	508.2	401.9	352.9	346.7
65–74 years	798.7	887.3	997.0	1,070.7	1,090.7	984.3	862.0	845.4
75–84 years	1,367.6	1,413.7	1,592.7	1,779.7	1,883.2	1,736.0	1,631.3	1,617.4
85 years and over	1,732.7	1,791.4	1,772.2	2,375.6	2,715.1	2,693.7	2,258.3	2,253.2

were 715.5 deaths per 100,000 people; for adults aged 75 to 84 years, this rate was 1,256.3 deaths per 100,000 people; and for adults aged 85 years and older, it was 1,590.2 deaths per 100,000 people. (See Table 7.9.)

Success in treating certain cancers, such as Hodgkin's disease and some forms of leukemia, has been offset by the rise in rates of other cancers, such as breast and lung cancers. Table 7.5 shows that the number of cancer deaths among adults aged 65 years and older rose sharply from 258,389 in 1980 to 389,730 in 2007. Progress in treating cancer has largely been related to screenings, early diagnoses, and new drug therapies.

Stroke

Stroke (cerebrovascular disease or "brain attack") is the third-leading cause of death and is the principal cause of disability among older adults. (See Table 7.5.) In "Stroke Risk Factors" (2011, http://www.heart.org/STROKEORG/

TABLE 7.9

Death rates for malignant neoplasms, selected characteristics, selected years 1950–2007 [CONTINUED]

[Data are based on death certificates]

Sex, race, Hispanic origin, and age	1950[a, b]	1960[a, b]	1970[b]	1980[b]	1990[b]	2000[c]	2006[c]	2007[c]
Black or African American male[e]				Deaths per 100,000 resident population				
All ages, age-adjusted[d]	178.9	227.6	291.9	353.4	397.9	340.3	284.9	282.3
All ages, crude	106.6	136.7	171.6	205.5	221.9	188.5	172.3	172.9
25–34 years	18.0	18.4	18.8	14.1	15.7	10.1	10.0	9.5
35–44 years	55.7	72.9	81.3	73.8	64.3	48.4	36.5	34.0
45–54 years	211.7	244.7	311.2	333.0	302.6	214.2	182.2	178.0
55–64 years	490.8	579.7	689.2	812.5	859.2	626.4	542.9	544.1
65–74 years	636.5	938.5	1,168.9	1,417.2	1,613.9	1,363.8	1,156.5	1,139.5
75–84 years[f]	853.5	1,053.3	1,624.8	2,029.6	2,478.3	2,351.8	1,979.1	1,936.9
85 years and over	—	1,155.2	1,387.0	2,393.9	3,238.3	3,264.8	2,543.3	2,637.1

— Data not available.

[a]Includes deaths of persons who were not residents of the 50 states and the District of Columbia (D.C.).

[b]Underlying cause of death was coded according to the 6th Revision of the International Classification of Diseases (ICD) in 1950, 7th Revision in 1960, 8th Revision in 1970, and 9th Revision in 1980–1998.

[c]Starting with 1999 data, cause of death is coded according to ICD-10.

[d]Age-adjusted rates are calculated using the year 2000 standard population. Prior to 2003, age-adjusted rates were calculated using standard million proportions based on rounded population numbers. Starting with 2003 data, unrounded population numbers are used to calculate age-adjusted rates.

[e]The race groups, white, black, Asian or Pacific Islander, and American Indian or Alaska Native, include persons of Hispanic and non-Hispanic origin. Persons of Hispanic origin may be of any race. Death rates for the American Indian or Alaska Native and Asian or Pacific Islander populations are known to be underestimated.

[f]In 1950, rate is for the age group 75 years and over.

Notes: Starting with *Health, United States, 2003*, rates for 1991–1999 were revised using intercensal population estimates based on the 2000 census. Rates for 2000 were revised based on 2000 census counts. Rates for 2001 and later years were computed using 2000-based postcensal estimates. Age groups were selected to minimize the presentation of unstable age-specific death rates based on small numbers of deaths and for consistency among comparison groups. Starting with 2003 data, some states allowed the reporting of more than one race on the death certificate. The multiple-race data for these states were bridged to the single-race categories of the 1977 Office of Management and Budget standards for comparability with other states. Data for additional years are available.

SOURCE: Adapted from "Table 32. Death Rates for Malignant Neoplasms, by Sex, Race, Hispanic Origin, and Age: United States, Selected Years 1950–2007," in *Health, United States 2010: With Special Feature on Death and Dying*, National Center for Health Statistics, 2011, http://www.cdc.gov/nchs/data/hus/hus10.pdf (accessed April 8, 2011)

AboutStroke/UnderstandingRisk/Understanding-Risk_UCM _308539_SubHomePage.jsp), the American Heart Association reports that "the chance of having a stroke approximately doubles for each decade of life after age 55."

According to the National Center for Health Statistics, in *Health, United States, 2010* (February 2011, http://www .cdc.gov/nchs/data/hus/hus10.pdf), in 1980 strokes killed 146,417 people aged 65 years and older. In 2007, among people aged 65 years and older, 115,961 deaths were attributable to stroke. The death rate for people aged 65 to 74 years declined as well, from 219 per 100,000 population in 1980 to 93 per 100,000 population in 2007. (See Table 7.10.) There was a comparable decline for people aged 75 to 84 years. There were 322.3 deaths per 100,000 population for this age group in 2007, down from 786.9 deaths per 100,000 population in 1980. The improvement was even greater for people aged 85 years and older. There were 1,015.5 deaths per 100,000 population for this age group in 2007, less than half the rate of 2,283.7 per 100,000 population in 1980.

HEALTHY AGING

According to the CDC, ample research demonstrates that healthy lifestyles have a greater effect than genetic factors in helping older people prevent the deterioration that is traditionally associated with aging. People who are physically active, eat a healthy diet, do not use tobacco, and practice other healthy behaviors reduce their risk for chronic diseases, have half the rate of disability of those who do not, and can delay disability by as many as 10 years.

Among the recommended health practices for older adults is participating in screening programs and early detection practices such as screenings for hypertension, cancer, diabetes, and depression. Screening detects diseases early in their course, when they are most treatable; however, many older adults do not obtain the recommended screenings. For example, even though immunizations reduce the risk for hospitalization and death from influenza and pneumonia, the Federal Interagency Forum on Aging-Related Statistics notes in *Older Americans 2010* that in 2008, 33% of older adults had not received flu shots and 40% of older adults had not been vaccinated against pneumonia.

Because falls are the most common cause of injuries and injury deaths in older adults, injury prevention is a vitally important way to prevent disability. The CDC reports in "Falls among Older Adults: An Overview" (December 8, 2010, http://www.cdc.gov/HomeandRe creationalSafety/Falls/adultfalls.html) that over one-third of adults aged 65 years and older fall each year, and of those who fall, 20% to 30% suffer injuries that impair

TABLE 7.10

Death rates for cerebrovascular disease, selected characteristics, selected years 1950–2007

[Data are based on death certificates]

Sex, race, Hispanic origin, and age	1950[a, b]	1960[a, b]	1970[b]	1980[b]	1990[b]	2000[c]	2006[c]	2007[c]
All persons				Deaths per 100,000 resident population				
All ages, age-adjusted[d]	180.7	177.9	147.7	96.2	65.3	60.9	43.6	42.2
All ages, crude	104.0	108.0	101.9	75.0	57.8	59.6	45.8	45.1
Under 1 year	5.1	4.1	5.0	4.4	3.8	3.3	3.4	3.1
1–4 years	0.9	0.8	1.0	0.5	0.3	0.3	0.3	0.3
5–14 years	0.5	0.7	0.7	0.3	0.2	0.2	0.2	0.2
15–24 years	1.6	1.8	1.6	1.0	0.6	0.5	0.5	0.5
25–34 years	4.2	4.7	4.5	2.6	2.2	1.5	1.3	1.2
35–44 years	18.7	14.7	15.6	8.5	6.4	5.8	5.1	4.9
45–54 years	70.4	49.2	41.6	25.2	18.7	16.0	14.7	14.6
55–64 years	194.2	147.3	115.8	65.1	47.9	41.0	33.3	32.1
65–74 years	554.7	469.2	384.1	219.0	144.2	128.6	96.3	93.0
75–84 years	1,499.6	1,491.3	1,254.2	786.9	498.0	461.3	335.1	322.3
85 years and over	2,990.1	3,680.5	3,014.3	2,283.7	1,628.9	1,589.2	1,039.6	1,015.5
Male								
All ages, age-adjusted[d]	186.4	186.1	157.4	102.2	68.5	62.4	43.9	42.5
All ages, crude	102.5	104.5	94.5	63.4	46.7	46.9	37.0	36.4
Under 1 year	6.4	5.0	5.8	5.0	4.4	3.8	3.9	3.5
1–4 years	1.1	0.9	1.2	0.4	0.3	*	0.3	0.2
5–14 years	0.5	0.7	0.8	0.3	0.2	0.2	0.3	0.2
15–24 years	1.8	1.9	1.8	1.1	0.7	0.5	0.5	0.5
25–34 years	4.2	4.5	4.4	2.6	2.1	1.5	1.4	1.2
35–44 years	17.5	14.6	15.7	8.7	6.8	5.8	5.3	5.3
45–54 years	67.9	52.2	44.4	27.2	20.5	17.5	16.4	16.2
55–64 years	205.2	163.8	138.7	74.6	54.3	47.2	38.7	38.0
65–74 years	589.6	530.7	449.5	258.6	166.6	145.0	108.0	105.2
75–84 years	1,543.6	1,555.9	1,361.6	866.3	551.1	490.8	345.5	333.2
85 years and over	3,048.6	3,643.1	2,895.2	2,193.6	1,528.5	1,484.3	932.4	895.7
Female								
All ages, age-adjusted[d]	175.8	170.7	140.0	91.7	62.6	59.1	42.6	41.3
All ages, crude	105.6	111.4	109.0	85.9	68.4	71.8	54.4	53.5
Under 1 year	3.7	3.2	4.0	3.8	3.1	2.7	2.9	2.6
1–4 years	0.7	0.7	0.7	0.5	0.3	0.4	0.4	0.4
5–14 years	0.4	0.6	0.6	0.3	0.2	0.2	0.2	0.2
15–24 years	1.5	1.6	1.4	0.8	0.6	0.5	0.5	0.4
25–34 years	4.3	4.9	4.7	2.6	2.2	1.5	1.2	1.3
35–44 years	19.9	14.8	15.6	8.4	6.1	5.7	4.8	4.6
45–54 years	72.9	46.3	39.0	23.3	17.0	14.5	13.0	12.9
55–64 years	183.1	131.8	95.3	56.8	42.2	35.3	28.2	26.6
65–74 years	522.1	415.7	333.3	188.7	126.7	115.1	86.5	82.7
75–84 years	1,462.2	1,441.1	1,183.1	740.1	466.2	442.1	328.0	314.9
85 years and over	2,949.4	3,704.4	3,081.0	2,323.1	1,667.6	1,632.0	1,089.8	1,072.4
White male[e]								
All ages, age-adjusted[d]	182.1	181.6	153.7	98.7	65.5	59.8	41.7	40.2
All ages, crude	100.5	102.7	93.5	63.1	46.9	48.4	37.7	37.0
45–54 years	53.7	40.9	35.6	21.7	15.4	13.6	12.8	13.0
55–64 years	182.2	139.0	119.9	64.0	45.7	39.7	31.5	31.4
65–74 years	569.7	501.0	420.0	239.8	152.9	133.8	97.1	94.3
75–84 years	1,556.3	1,564.8	1,361.6	852.7	539.2	480.0	338.5	323.1
85 years and over	3,127.1	3,734.8	3,018.1	2,230.8	1,545.4	1,490.7	941.3	905.0

mobility and independence. Removing tripping hazards in the home, such as rugs, and installing grab bars in bathrooms are simple measures that can greatly reduce older Americans' risk for falls and fractures.

The current cohort of older adults is better equipped to prevent the illness, disability, and death associated with many chronic diseases than any previous generation. They are less likely to smoke, drink, or experience detrimental stress than younger people, and older adults have better eating habits than their younger counterparts. For example, the percentage of men aged 65 years and older who smoke cigarettes declined from 29% in 1965 to 11% in 2008. (See Figure 7.13.) In contrast, the percentage of women the same age who smoke remained relatively constant during this period, decreasing slightly from 10% to 8%.

Older adults are, however, less likely to exercise than younger adults. In 2008, only 22% of adults aged 65 years and older said they regularly engaged in leisure-time physical activity, and the percent participating

TABLE 7.10

Death rates for cerebrovascular disease, selected characteristics, selected years 1950–2007 [CONTINUED]

[Data are based on death certificates]

Sex, race, Hispanic origin, and age	1950[a, b]	1960[a, b]	1970[b]	1980[b]	1990[b]	2000[c]	2006[c]	2007[c]
Black or African American male[e]				Deaths per 100,000 resident population				
All ages, age-adjusted[d]	228.8	238.5	206.4	142.0	102.2	89.6	67.1	67.1
All ages, crude	122.0	122.9	108.8	73.0	53.0	46.1	39.3	39.5
45–54 years	211.9	166.1	136.1	82.1	68.4	49.5	43.5	41.0
55–64 years	522.8	439.9	343.4	189.7	141.7	115.4	105.9	99.8
65–74 years	783.6	899.2	780.1	472.3	326.9	268.5	218.7	223.3
75–84 years[f]	1,504.9	1,475.2	1,445.7	1,066.3	721.5	659.2	471.1	491.9
85 years and over	—	2,700.0	1,963.1	1,873.2	1,421.5	1,458.8	882.0	866.9

*Rates based on fewer than 20 deaths are considered unreliable and are not shown.
—Data not available.
[a]Includes deaths of persons who were not residents of the 50 states and the District of Columbia (D.C.).
[b]Underlying cause of death was coded according to the 6th revision of the International Classification of Diseases (ICD) in 1950, 7th Revision in 1960, 8th Revision in 1970, and 9th Revision in 1980–1998.
[c]Starting with 1999 data, cause of death is coded according to ICD-10.
[d]Age-adjusted rates are calculated using the year 2000 standard population. Prior to 2003, age-adjusted rates were calculated using standard million proportions based on rounded population numbers. Starting with 2003 data, unrounded population numbers are used to calculate age-adjusted rates.
[e]The race groups, white, black, Asian or Pacific Islander, and American Indian or Alaska Native, include persons of Hispanic and non-Hispanic origin. Persons of Hispanic origin may be of any race. Death rates for the American Indian or Alaska Native and Asian or Pacific Islander populations are known to be underestimated.
[f]In 1950, rate is for the age group 75 years and over.
Notes: Starting with *Health, United States, 2003*, rates for 1991–1999 were revised using intercensal population estimates based on the 2000 census. Rates for 2000 were revised based on 2000 census counts. Rates for 2001 and later years were computed using 2000-based postcensal estimates. For the period 1980–1998, cerebrovascular diseases was coded using ICD-9 codes that are most nearly comparable with cerebrovascular diseases codes in the 113 cause list for ICD-10. Age groups were selected to minimize the presentation of unstable age-specific death rates based on small numbers of deaths and for consistency among comparison groups. Starting with 2003 data, some states allowed the reporting of more than one race on the death certificate. The multiple-race data for these states were bridged to the single-race categories of the 1977 Office of Management and Budget standards for comparability with other states. Data for additional years are available.

SOURCE: Adapted from "Table 31. Death Rates for Cerebrovascular Diseases, by Sex, Race, Hispanic Origin, and Age: United States, Selected Years 1950–2007," in *Health, United States 2010: With Special Feature on Death and Dying*, National Center for Health Statistics, 2011, http://www.cdc.gov/nchs/data/hus/hus10.pdf (accessed April 8, 2011)

FIGURE 7.13

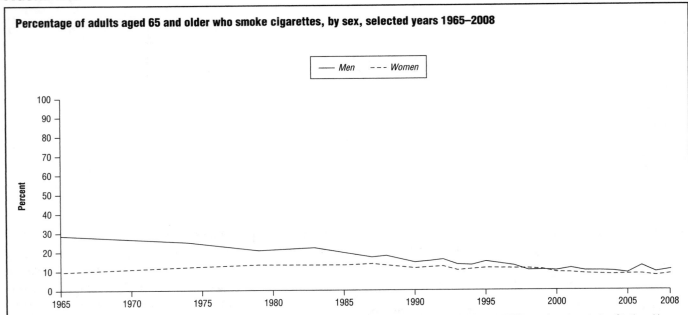

Percentage of adults aged 65 and older who smoke cigarettes, by sex, selected years 1965–2008

Notes: Data starting in 1997 are not strictly comparable with data for earlier years due to the 1997 National Health Interview Survey (NHIS) questionnaire redesign. Starting with 1993 data, current cigarette smokers were defined as ever smoking 100 cigarettes in their lifetime and smoking now on every day or some days.
Reference population: These data refer to the civilian noninstitutionalized population.

SOURCE: "Percentage of People Age 65 and over Who Are Current Cigarette Smokers, by Sex, Selected Years, 1965–2008," in *Older Americans 2010: Key Indicators of Well-Being*, Federal Interagency Forum on Aging-Related Statistics, July 2010, http://www.agingstats.gov/agingstatsdotnet/Main_Site/Data/2010_Documents/Docs/OA_2010.pdf (accessed April 2, 2011)

FIGURE 7.14

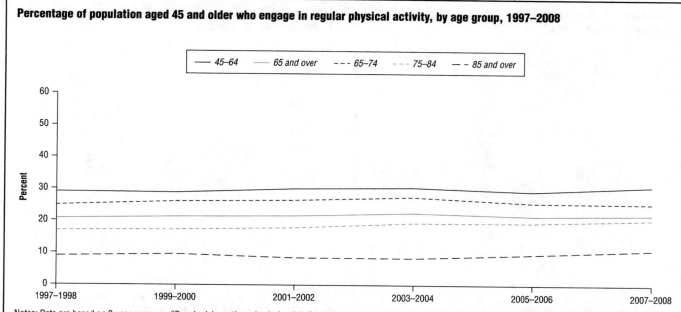

Percentage of population aged 45 and older who engage in regular physical activity, by age group, 1997–2008

Notes: Data are based on 2-year averages. "Regular leisure time physical activity" is defined as "engaging in light-moderate leisure time physical activity for greater than or equal to 30 minutes at a frequency greater than or equal to five times per week, or engaging in vigorous leisure time physical activity for greater than or equal to 20 minutes at a frequency greater than or equal to three times per week."
Reference population: These data refer to the civilian noninstitutionalized population.

SOURCE: "Percentage of Population Age 45 and over Who Reported Engaging in Regular Leisure Time Physical Activity, by Age Group, 1997–2008," in *Older Americans 2010: Key Indicators of Well-Being*, Federal Interagency Forum on Aging-Related Statistics, July 2010, http://www.agingstats.gov/agingstatsdotnet/Main_Site/Data/2010_Documents/Docs/OA_2010.pdf (accessed April 2, 2011)

declined with advancing age—just 11% of adults aged 85 years and older engaged in regular physical activity. (See Figure 7.14.) Increasing evidence suggests that behavior change, even late in life, is beneficial and can improve disease control and enhanced quality of life.

Maintaining a Healthy Weight

The United States is in the throes of an obesity epidemic. Obesity is defined as a body mass index (a number that shows body weight adjusted for height) greater than or equal to 30 kilograms per meters squared. In 2010, 27.6% of adults aged 60 years and older were obese, and the group of adults aged 40 to 59 years that will soon join the ranks of older Americans reported the highest rate of obesity at 32.7%. (See Figure 7.15.) Furthermore, the percentages of older adults who are obese have increased from 1988–94, when just 24% of men and 27% of women aged 65 to 74 years, and 13% of men and 19% of women aged 75 years and older were obese. (See Figure 7.11.) By 2007–08, 40% of men and 35% of women aged 65 to 74 years, and 26% of men and 27% of women aged 75 years and older were obese.

The National Center for Health Statistics notes that overweight and obese individuals are at an increased risk for multiple health problems, including hypertension, high cholesterol, type 2 diabetes, coronary heart disease, congestive heart failure, stroke, arthritis, obstructive sleep apnea, and other serious conditions.

Smoking

According to the Federal Interagency Forum on Aging-Related Statistics, in *Older Americans 2010*, the per capita tobacco consumption declined in the United States during the last decades of the 20th century. By 2008 fewer people over the age of 65 (11% of men and 8% of women) smoked than all other age groups. Data from the National Health Interview Survey reveal that in 2010 adults aged 65 years and older were the least likely to be current smokers—just 9.5% compared to 21.6% each of adults aged 18 to 44 years and 45 to 64 years. (See Figure 7.16.)

The U.S. surgeon general explains that even older adult smokers can realize health benefits from quitting. For example, a smoker's risk of heart disease begins to decline almost immediately after quitting, regardless of how long the person smoked.

Physical Activity

Regular physical activity comes closer to being a fountain of youth than any prescription medicine. Along with helping older adults to remain mobile and independent, exercise can lower the risk of obesity, heart disease, stroke, diabetes, and some cancers. It can also delay osteoporosis and arthritis, reduce symptoms of depression, and improve sleep quality and memory. Despite these demonstrated benefits, in 2010 just 26.7% of adults

FIGURE 7.15

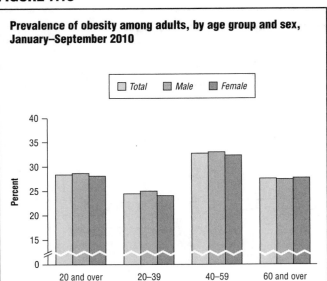

Prevalence of obesity among adults, by age group and sex, January–September 2010

Notes: Obesity is defined as a body mass index (BMI) of 30 kg/m² or more. The measure is based on self-reported height and weight. Estimates of obesity are restricted to adults aged 20 years and over for consistency with the *Healthy People 2010* (3) program. The analyses excluded 836 people (4.1%) with unknown height or weight.

SOURCE: P.M. Barnes et al., "Figure 6.2. Prevalence of Obesity among Adults Aged 20 Years and over, by Age Group and Sex: United States, January–September 2010," in *Early Release of Selected Estimates Based on Data from the January–September 2010 National Health Interview Survey*, Centers for Disease Control and Prevention, National Center for Health Statistics, March 2011, http://www.cdc.gov/nchs/data/nhis/earlyrelease/201103_06.pdf (accessed April 20, 2011)

FIGURE 7.16

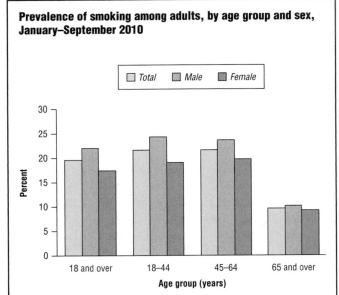

Prevalence of smoking among adults, by age group and sex, January–September 2010

Notes: Current smokers were defined as those who had smoked more than 100 cigarettes in their lifetime and now smoke every day or some days. The analyses excluded 140 persons (0.7%) with unknown smoking status.

SOURCE: P.M. Barnes et al., "Figure 8.3. Prevalence of Current Smoking among Adults Aged 18 Years and over, by Age Group and Sex: United States, January–September 2010," in *Early Release of Selected Estimates Based on Data from the January–September 2010 National Health Interview Survey*, Centers for Disease Control and Prevention, National Center for Health Statistics, March 2011, http://www.cdc.gov/nchs/data/nhis/earlyrelease/201103_08.pdf (accessed April 20, 2011)

aged 65 to 74 years and 17.8% of adults aged 75 years and older engaged in regular leisure-time physical activity. (See Figure 7.17.)

Use of Preventive Health Services

More widespread use of preventive services is a key to preserving and extending the health and quality of life of older Americans. Screening for early detection of selected cancers—such as breast, cervical, and colorectal—as well as diabetes, cardiovascular disease, and glaucoma can save lives and slow the progress of chronic disease. Because people with a regular source of medical care are more likely to receive basic medical services, such as routine checkups, which present the opportunity to receive preventive services, it is not surprising that in 2010, 97% of adults aged 65 years and older reported having a regular source of medical care. (See Figure 7.18.) Given that Medicare covers many preventive services and screenings, it seems unlikely that cost prevents older adults from obtaining these services. Data from the 2010 National Health Interview Survey reveal that just 3.1% of respondents aged 65 years and older reported that they failed to obtain needed medical care because of cost during the 12 months preceding the interview. (See Figure 7.19.)

SEXUALITY IN AGING

Despite the popular belief that sexuality is exclusively for the young, sexual interest, activity, and capabilities are often lifelong. Even though the growing population of older adults will likely spur additional research, to date there are scant data about the levels of sexual activity among older adults. The data that are available are often limited to community-dwelling older adults, so there is nearly no information about the sexual behavior of institutionalized older adults.

After age 50 sexual responses slow; however, very rarely does this natural and gradual diminution cause older adults to end all sexual activity. More important, in terms of curtailing older adults' sexual activity is the lack of available partners, which limits opportunities for sexual expression, especially for older women. Another issue is the greater incidence of illness and progression of chronic diseases that occurs with advancing age. Medical problems with the potential to adversely affect sexual function include diabetes, hypothyroidism (a condition in which the thyroid is underactive—producing too little thyroid hormones), neuropathy (a disease or abnormality of the nervous system), cardiovascular disease, urinary tract infections, prostate cancer, incontinence,

FIGURE 7.17

Percentage of adults aged 18 years and over who engage in regular leisure-time physical activity, by age group and sex, January–September 2010

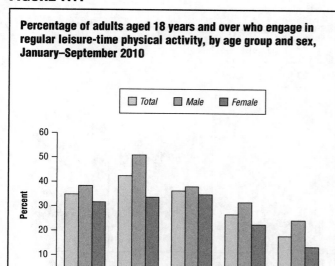

Notes: This measure reflects the definition used for the physical activity Leading Health Indicator in *Healthy People 2010* (3). Regular leisure-time physical activity is defined as engaging in light-moderate leisure-time physical activity for greater than or equal to 30 minutes at a frequency greater than or equal to five times per week or engaging in vigorous leisure-time physical activity for greater than or equal to 20 minutes at a frequency greater than or equal to three times per week. In Early Releases before September 2005 (based on the 2004 National Health Interview Survey), regular physical activity was calculated slightly differently than for *Healthy People 2010*. The earlier early release estimates excluded from the analysis persons with unknown duration of light-moderate or vigorous leisure-time physical activity who were known to have not met the frequency recommendations for lightmoderate or vigorous leisure-time physical activity (i.e., partial unknowns). With the current release, persons who were known to have not met the frequency recommendations are classified as "not regular," regardless of duration. The analyses excluded 361 persons (1.7%) with unknown physical activity participation.

SOURCE: P.M. Barnes et al., "Figure 7.2. Percentage of Adults Aged 18 Years and over Who Engaged in Regular Leisure-Time Physical Activity, by Age Group and Sex: United States, January–September 2010," in *Early Release of Selected Estimates Based on Data from the January–September 2010 National Health Interview Survey*, Centers for Disease Control and Prevention, National Center for Health Statistics, March 2011, http://www.cdc.gov/nchs/data/nhis/earlyrelease/201103_07.pdf (accessed April 20, 2011)

arthritis, depression, and dementia. Many pharmacological treatments for chronic illnesses have sexual side effects that range from diminished libido (sexual desire and drive) to erectile dysfunction. For example, some medications (e.g., antihypertensives, antidepressants, diuretics, steroids, anticonvulsants, and blockers) have high rates of sexual side effects.

One of the biggest recent changes in the sex lives of older adults is older men's use of potency drugs for erectile dysfunction (Viagra, Cialis, and Levitra) to enhance their performance. Since the 1998 debut of Viagra, these pharmaceutical solutions to erectile changes affecting older men have enjoyed tremendous popularity. Concern about the drugs' potential impact on vision arose when a suspected link between Viagra and vision loss led to lawsuits. However, Ernst R. Schwarz et al. of the Cedars-Sinai Medical Center in Los Angeles, California, find in "The Effects of Chronic Phosphodiesterase-5 Inhibitor Use on Different Organ Systems" (*International Journal of Impotence Research*, vol. 19, no. 2, March–April 2007) that occurrence of the vision disorder was similar to that of the general population.

Sexuality Transmitted Diseases

In "Sexual Activity and STDs among Seniors" (*U.S. Pharmacist*, vol. 33, no. 8, August 2008), Mary Ann E. Zagaria of MZ Associates Inc. in Norwich, New York, observes that most adults aged 57 to 85 years are engaged in spousal or other intimate relationships and regard sexuality as an important part of life. Zagaria also reports that older adults are one-sixth less likely to use condoms, which offer considerable protection from sexually transmitted diseases (STDs), than younger adults. Complicating matters, aging is associated with changes that increase the risk of any kind of infection, including STDs.

According to Anupam B. Jena et al., in "Sexually Transmitted Diseases among Users of Erectile Dysfunction Drugs: Analysis of Claims Data" (*Annals of Internal Medicine*, vol. 153, no.1, July 6, 2010), younger adults have many more STDs than older adults; however, the rates of STDs are growing more rapidly among older adults. Furthermore, the rate of STDs in older men taking erectile dysfunction drugs such as Viagra is twice as high as in their nonmedicated peers. The researchers report that the most commonly diagnosed STDs among older men are HIV, chlamydia, syphilis, and gonorrhea.

Data from the 2010 National Health Interview Survey reveal that adults aged 65 years and older were the least likely to have ever had an HIV test of any age group. Just 16% of men and 11.3% of women aged 65 years and older reported having had an HIV test. (See Figure 7.20.)

THE UNITED STATES LACKS SPECIALISTS IN GERIATRIC MEDICINE

In 1909 the American physician Ignatz L. Nascher (1863–1944) coined the term *geriatrics* from the Greek *geras* (old age) and *iatrikos* (physician). Geriatricians are physicians trained in internal medicine or family practice who obtain additional training and medical board certification in the diagnosis and treatment of older adults.

The American Geriatrics Society observes in "Fact Sheet: The American Geriatrics Society (AGS)" (2011, http://www.americangeriatrics.org/about_us/who_we_are/faq_fact_sheet/) that in 2011 board-certified geriatricians numbered 6,000—one for every 5,000 Americans aged 65 years and older—fewer than half of the estimated need. Because of the growth of the older population, this ratio will decrease to one geriatrician for every 7,665 Americans aged 65 years and older by 2030. The shortage of specially trained physicians will intensify as the baby

FIGURE 7.18

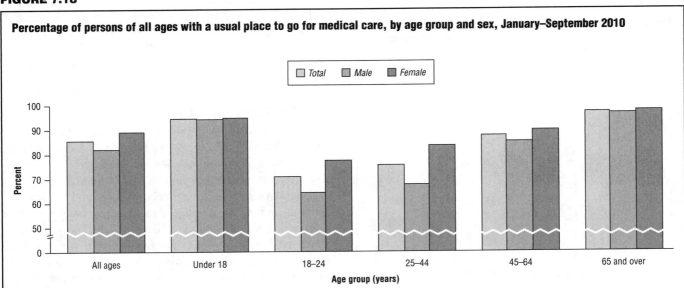

Percentage of persons of all ages with a usual place to go for medical care, by age group and sex, January–September 2010

Notes: The usual place to go for medical care does not include a hospital emergency room. The analyses excluded 225 persons (1.1%) with an unknown usual place to go for medical care.

SOURCE: P.M. Barnes et al., "Figure 2.2. Percentage of Persons of All Ages with a Usual Place to Go for Medical Care, by Age Group and Sex: United States, January–September 2010," in *Early Release of Selected Estimates Based on Data from the January–September 2010 National Health Interview Survey*, Centers for Disease Control and Prevention, National Center for Health Statistics, March 2011, http://www.cdc.gov/nchs/data/nhis/earlyrelease/201103_02.pdf (accessed April 20, 2011)

FIGURE 7.19

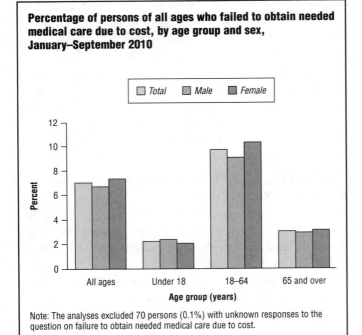

Percentage of persons of all ages who failed to obtain needed medical care due to cost, by age group and sex, January–September 2010

Note: The analyses excluded 70 persons (0.1%) with unknown responses to the question on failure to obtain needed medical care due to cost.

SOURCE: P.M. Barnes et al., "Figure 3.2. Percentage of Persons of All Ages Who Failed to Obtain Needed Medical Care Due to Cost at Some Time during the Past 12 months, by Age Group and Sex: United States, January–September 2010," in *Early Release of Selected Estimates Based on Data from the January–September 2010 National Health Interview Survey*, Centers for Disease Control and Prevention, National Center for Health Statistics, March 2011, http://www.cdc.gov/nchs/data/nhis/earlyrelease/201103_03.pdf (accessed April 20, 2011)

boom generation joins the ranks of older adults. The American Geriatrics Society contends that financial disincentives pose the greatest barrier to new physicians entering geriatrics. Geriatricians are almost entirely dependent on Medicare reimbursement, and low Medicare reimbursement, which directly influences their earning potential, dissuades some physicians from entering the field. Other prospective geriatricians may also be discouraged by having to spend at least part of their workdays in nursing homes.

FIGURE 7.20

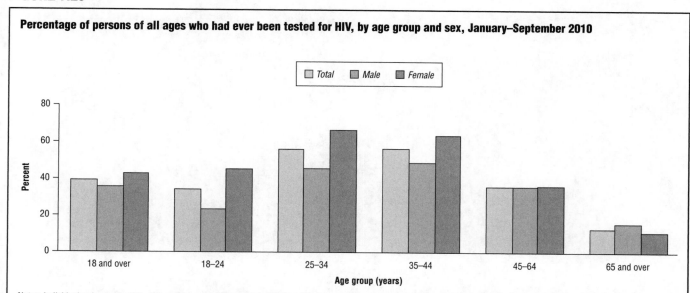

Percentage of persons of all ages who had ever been tested for HIV, by age group and sex, January–September 2010

Notes: Individuals who received the human immunodeficiency virus (HIV) testing solely as a result of blood donation were considered as not having been tested for HIV. The analyses excluded 888 adults (4.2%) with unknown HIV test status.

SOURCE: P.M. Barnes et al., "Figure 10.2. Percentage of Adults Aged 18 Years and over Who Had Ever Been Tested for Human Immunodeficiency Virus (HIV), by Age Group and Sex: United States, January–September 2010," in *Early Release of Selected Estimates Based on Data from the January–September 2010 National Health Interview Survey*, Centers for Disease Control and Prevention, National Center for Health Statistics, March 2011, http://www.cdc.gov/nchs/data/nhis/earlyrelease/201103_10.pdf (accessed April 20, 2011)

CHAPTER 8

MENTAL HEALTH AND MENTAL ILLNESS

Changes in mental capabilities are among the most feared aspects of aging. As Brenda L. Plassman et al. note in "Prevalence of Cognitive Impairment without Dementia in the United States" (*Annals of Internal Medicine*, vol. 148, no. 6, March 18, 2008), mental health problems that impair functioning are among the most common age-related changes—and they are cause for concern because cognitive impairment without dementia (loss of intellectual functioning accompanied by memory loss and personality changes) is associated with increased risk for disability and progression to dementia.

The aging population has spurred interest in age-related problems in cognition (the process of thinking, learning, and remembering). Cognitive difficulties much milder than those that are associated with organic brain diseases, such as Alzheimer's disease or dementia, affect a significant proportion of older adults. Organic brain diseases, often referred to as organic brain syndromes, refer to physical disorders of the brain that produce mental health problems as opposed to psychiatric conditions, which may also cause mental health problems. A landmark study supported by the National Institute on Aging (NIA) and summarized by Frederick W. Unverzagt et al. in "Prevalence of Cognitive Impairment: Data from the Indianapolis Study of Health and Aging" (*Neurology*, vol. 57, November 13, 2001) estimates that in 2001, 23.4% of community-dwelling older adults and 19.2% of nursing home residents suffered some degree of cognitive impairment, besides those who suffered from much more serious cognitive impairment. The prevalence of this mild cognitive impairment grew significantly with age, with rates increasing by about 10% for every 10 years of age after age 65. Unverzagt et al. conclude that "cognitive impairment short of dementia affects nearly one in four community-dwelling elders and is a major risk factor for later development of dementia."

Plassman et al. state that estimates of the prevalence of cognitive impairment that is not severe enough to be diagnosed as dementia ranges from 3% to 29%. In addition, they state "cognitive impairment that does not reach the threshold for dementia diagnosis is associated with increased risk for progression to dementia in most studies, with progression rates of 10% to 15% per year compared to 1% to 2.5% among cognitively healthy older adults." Cognitive impairment without dementia that results from chronic medical conditions affects a large proportion of older adults in the United States—it accounts for about 24% of all cognitive impairment.

Because the number of people with cognitive impairments and dementia is anticipated to increase as the population ages, and older adults with cognitive impairment are at risk for institutionalization, the financial costs to individuals and to society are expected to escalate. As such, the mental health and illness of older adults is an increasingly important public health issue.

MENTAL HEALTH

Mental health may be measured in terms of an individual's abilities to think and communicate clearly, learn and grow emotionally, deal productively and realistically with change and stress, and form and maintain fulfilling relationships with others. Mental health is a principle component of wellness (self-esteem, resilience, and the ability to cope with adversity), which influences how people feel about themselves.

When mental health is defined and measured in terms of the absence of serious psychological distress, then older adults fare quite well compared to other age groups. The 2010 National Health Interview Survey, which was conducted by the Centers for Disease Control and Prevention, questioned whether respondents had experienced serious psychological distress within the 30 days preceding the interview. Adults aged 65 years and older were the least likely to have experienced serious psychological distress (2.4%) in 2010, compared to adults aged 45 to 64

FIGURE 8.1

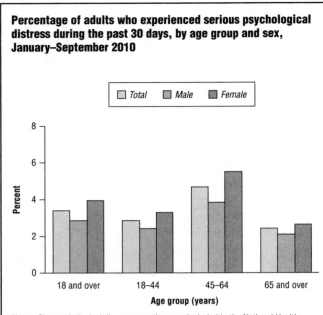

Percentage of adults who experienced serious psychological distress during the past 30 days, by age group and sex, January–September 2010

Notes: Six psychological distress questions are included in the National Health Interview Survey's Sample Adult Core component. These questions ask how often a respondent experienced certain symptoms of psychological distress during the past 30 days. The response codes (0–4) of the six items for each person are summed to yield a scale with a 0–24 range. A value of 13 or more for this scale is used here to define serious psychological distress (16).

SOURCE: P.M. Barnes et al., "Figure 13.2. Percentage of Adults Aged 18 Years and over Who Experienced Serious Psychological Distress during the Past 30 Days, by Age Group and Sex: United States, January–September 2010," in *Early Release of Selected Estimates Based on Data from the January–September 2010 National Health Interview Survey*, Centers for Disease Control and Prevention, National Center for Health Statistics, March 2011, http://www.cdc.gov/nchs/data/nhis/earlyrelease/201103_13.pdf (accessed April 22, 2011).

years (4.7%) and adults aged 18 to 44 years (2.8%). (See Figure 8.1.)

Experience Shapes Mental Health in Old Age

One theory of aging, called continuity theory and explained by Robert C. Atchley in *The Social Forces in Later Life: An Introduction to Social Gerontology* (1985), posits that people who age most successfully are those who carry forward the habits, preferences, lifestyles, and relationships from midlife into late life. This theory has gained credence from research studies that find that traits measured in midlife are strong predictors of outcomes in later life and that many psychological and social characteristics are stable across the lifespan. For most people, old age does not represent a radical departure from the past; changes often occur gradually and sometimes unnoticeably. Most older adults adapt to the challenges and changes associated with later life using well-practiced coping skills that were acquired earlier in life.

Adults who have struggled with mental health problems or mental disorders throughout their life often continue to suffer these same problems in old age. Few personal problems disappear with old age, and many progress and become more acute. Marital problems, which may have been kept at bay because one or both spouses were away at work, may intensify when a couple spends more time together in retirement. Reduced income, illness, and disability in retirement can aggravate an already troubled marriage and can strain even healthy interpersonal, marital, and other family relationships.

Older age can be a period of regrets, which can lead to mutual recriminations. With life expectancy rising, married couples can now expect to spend many years together in retirement. Most older couples manage the transition, but some have problems.

Coping with losses of friends, family, health, and independence may precipitate mental health problems. Hearing loss is common, and close correlations have been found between loss of hearing and depression. Visual impairment limits mobility and the ability to read and watch television. Loss of sight or hearing can cause perceptual disorientation, which in turn may lead to depression, paranoia, fear, and alienation.

A constant awareness of the imminence of death can also become a problem for older adults. Even though most older adults resolve their anxieties and concerns about death, some live in denial and fear. How well older adults accept the inevitability of death is a key determinant of satisfaction and emotional well-being in old age.

Memory

Because memory is a key component of cognitive functioning, declining memory that substantially impairs older adults' functioning is a major risk factor for institutionalization. In "Trends in the Prevalence and Mortality of Cognitive Impairment in the United States: Is There Evidence of a Compression of Cognitive Morbidity?" (*Alzheimer's and Dementia*, vol. 4, no. 2, March 2008), Kenneth M. Langa et al. compare the cognitive health of older adults in 1993 and 2002 and find that rates of cognitive impairment declined from 12.2% to 8.7%. The researchers determine that improvements in cognitive health were associated with higher levels of education and financial status. They hypothesize that improved treatment for conditions such as stroke and heart disease may account for some of this improvement. Langa et al.'s results also support the idea that the brains of more educated people may have more "cognitive reserve," so that they are better able to defend against impairment damage from Alzheimer's or other diseases that compromise memory and cognition.

Brenda L. Plassman et al. estimate in "Incidence of Dementia and Cognitive Impairment, Not Dementia in the United States" (*Annals of Neurology*, March 18, 2011), an eight-year study of 456 adults aged 72 years and older, the national incidence rates (the number of new cases in the population during a specified period of time) for cognitive impairment in the United States. The researchers find that the incidence of cognitive impairment without dementia is greater than the incidence of dementia and that people with cognitive impairment have an increased risk of progressing to dementia.

The MetLife Foundation indicates in "What America Thinks: MetLife Alzheimer's Survey" (February 2011, http://www.metlife.com/assets/cao/contributions/foundation/alzheimers-2011.pdf) that Americans' fear of developing Alzheimer's is only exceeded by their fear of developing cancer. Even though nearly two-thirds (62%) of survey participants admitted that they do not know very much about Alzheimer's, 31% said they fear it. In contrast, just 8% of participants said they are afraid of heart disease and stroke and only 6% said they are most fearful of developing diabetes. Despite the high level of fear about the disease, few survey participants (18%) said they have made any plans to prepare for the possibility of developing it: 21% said they have made financial arrangements, 33% have investigated options for care, and 44% have designated who will care for them.

ORGANIC BRAIN DISEASES—DEMENTIAS

Dementia refers to a range of mental and behavioral changes caused by cerebrovascular or neurological diseases that permanently damage the brain, impairing the activity of brain cells. These changes can affect memory, speech, and the ability to perform the activities of daily living.

Occasional forgetfulness and memory lapses are not signs of dementia. Dementia is caused by disease and is not the inevitable result of growing older. Many disorders may cause or simulate dementia, which is not a single disorder—dementia refers to a condition that is caused by a variety of diseases and disorders, a small proportion of which are potentially reversible.

Furthermore, research suggests that even though people with cognitive impairment have an increased risk for dementia, not all people with mild cognitive impairment will progress over time to dementia. Alex J. Mitchell and Mojtaba Shiri-Feshki conducted a large meta-analysis (a review that looks at the findings of many studies) and published their findings in "Rate of Progression of Mild Cognitive Impairment to Dementia—Meta-analysis of 41 Robust Inception Cohort Studies" (*Acta Psychiatrica Scandinavica*, vol. 119, no. 4, April 2009). The researchers show that only a minority (20% to 40%) of people developed dementia even after long-term follow-up and that the risk appeared to decrease slightly with time. The analysis also suggests that mild cognitive impairment is not necessarily a transitional state between normal age-related changes and dementia. Mitchell and Shiri-Feshki find that some patients do not progress and others actually improve.

Multi-infarct Dementia

The National Institute of Neurological Disorders and Stroke indicates in "NINDS Multi-infarct Dementia Information Page" (November 19, 2010, http://www.ninds.nih.gov/disorders/multi_infarct_dementia/multi_infarct_dementia.htm) that multi-infarct dementia is a common cause of memory loss and progressive dementia. Multi-infarct dementia is caused by a series of small strokes that disrupt blood flow and damage or destroy brain tissue. Sometimes these small strokes are "silent"—meaning that they produce no obvious symptoms and are detected only on imaging studies, such as computed tomography (CT) or magnetic resonance imaging (MRI) scans of the brain. An older adult may have a number of small strokes before experiencing noticeable changes in memory, reasoning, or other signs of multi-infarct dementia.

Because strokes occur suddenly, the loss of cognitive skills and memory present quickly, although some affected individuals may appear to improve for short periods of time, then decline again after having more strokes. Establishing the diagnosis of multi-infarct dementia is challenging because its symptoms are difficult to distinguish from those of Alzheimer's disease. Treatment cannot reverse the damage already done to the brain. Instead, it focuses on preventing further damage by reducing the risk of additional strokes. This entails treating the underlying causes of stroke, such as hypertension, diabetes, high cholesterol, and heart disease. Surgical procedures to improve blood flow to the brain, such as carotid endarterectomy (a surgical procedure that removes blockages from the carotid arteries, which supply blood to the brain), angioplasty (a procedure to open narrowed or blocked blood vessels of the heart), or stenting (using wire scaffolds that hold arteries open), as well as medications to reduce the risk of stroke are used to treat this condition.

PEOPLE WITH DIABETES MAY BE AT INCREASED RISK. Rachel A. Whitmer et al. reveal in "Hypoglycemic Episodes and Risk of Dementia in Older Patients with Type 2 Diabetes Mellitus" (*Journal of the American Medical Association*, vol. 301, no. 15, April 15, 2009) that people with type 2 diabetes may be at an increased risk for developing dementia. The researchers find that just two episodes of dangerously low blood sugar, called hypoglycemia, which is caused by excess insulin, increased the risk by 80%, and people who had three or more episodes had a 94% increase in risk—meaning they had nearly twice the risk of developing dementia as people with normal blood sugar levels.

In "Uncontrolled Diabetes Increases the Risk of Alzheimer's Disease: A Population-Based Cohort Study" (*Diabetologia*, vol. 52, no. 6, June 2009), a long-term study of 1,248 adults aged 75 years and older, Weili Xu et al. confirm that uncontrolled diabetes increases the risk of developing Alzheimer's disease and vascular dementia.

Alzheimer's Disease

Alzheimer's disease (AD) is the most common form of dementia among older adults. It is characterized by severely compromised thinking, reasoning, behavior, and memory, and it may be among the most fearsome of age-related disorders because it challenges older adults' ability to live independently. The disease was named after Alois Alzheimer (1864–1915), the German neurologist who first described the anatomical changes in the brain—the plaques and tangles that are the characteristic markers of this progressive, degenerative disease.

According to the Alzheimer's Association, in *2011 Alzheimer's Disease Facts and Figures* (2011, http://www.alz.org/downloads/Facts_Figures_2011.pdf), an estimated 5.4 million Americans were afflicted with AD in 2011. The overwhelming majority of AD sufferers (5.2 million) were aged 65 years and older. Women have a higher lifetime risk of developing the disease because, on average, they live longer than men.

The Alzheimer's Association projects that the number of people aged 65 years and older with AD will reach 7.7 million in 2030 and that new AD cases each year will likely increase from 454,000 in 2010, to 615,000 in 2030, to 959,000 in 2050. The association asserts that if a cure or preventive measure is not found by 2050, then the number of Americans aged 65 years and older with AD will range from 11 million to 16 million.

SYMPTOMS AND STAGES. In general, AD has a slow onset, with symptoms such as mild memory lapses and disorientation that may not be identified as problematical beginning between the ages of 55 and 80. As the disease progresses, memory loss increases and mood swings are frequent, accompanied by confusion, irritability, restlessness, and problems communicating. AD patients may experience trouble finding words, impaired judgment, difficulty performing familiar tasks, and changes in behavior and personality.

In "Stages of Alzheimer's" (June 1, 2011, http://www.alz.org/alzheimers_disease_stages_of_alzheimers.asp), the Alzheimer's Association describes the seven stages of how AD progresses. The stages range from the first and second, in which there is no and then little apparent cognitive decline, to stage 3, which is marked by mild lapses and is often discernable to family, friends, and coworkers. Stage 4 is called mild or early stage AD, and during this stage moderate cognitive decline is observed. For example, AD patients may have diminished recall of recent activities or current events and compromised ability to perform tasks such as paying bills or shopping for groceries. In stages 5 and 6 memory impairment continues along with personality changes, sleep disturbances, and, if left unsupervised, a dangerous tendency to wander off and become lost.

Ultimately, the disease progresses to stage 7, when patients are entirely unable to care for themselves. In their terminal stages, AD victims require round-the-clock care and supervision. They no longer recognize family members, other caregivers, or themselves, and they require assistance with daily activities such as eating, dressing, bathing, and using the toilet. Eventually, they may become incontinent, blind, completely unable to communicate, and have difficulty swallowing.

According to the Alzheimer's Association, in *2011 Alzheimer's Disease Facts and Figures*, in 2007 AD claimed 74,632 lives and was the sixth-leading cause of death in people of all ages and the fifth-leading cause of death among adults aged 65 years and older.

GENETIC ORIGINS OF AD. AD is not a normal consequence of growing older. It is a disease of the brain that develops in response to genetic predisposition and nongenetic causative factors. Scientists have identified some genetic components of the disease and have observed the different patterns of inheritance, ages of onset, genes, chromosomes, and proteins that are linked to the development of AD.

In "The *mec*-4 Gene Is a Member of a Family of *Caenorhabditis elegans* Genes That Can Mutate to Induce Neuronal Degeneration" (*Nature*, February 14, 1991), Monica Driscoll and Martin Chalfie of Columbia University reported their discovery that a mutation in a single gene could cause AD. The defect was in the gene that directs cells to produce a substance called amyloid protein. The researchers also found that low levels of acetylcholine, a neurotransmitter that is involved in learning and memory, contribute to the formation of hard deposits of amyloid protein that accumulate in the brains of AD patients. In healthy people, the protein fragments are broken down and excreted by the body.

In 1995 three more genes linked to AD were identified. Two genes appear to be involved with forms of early onset AD, which can begin as early as age 30. The third gene, known as apolipoprotein E (apoE), is involved in important physiological functions throughout the body. It regulates lipid metabolism and helps redistribute cholesterol. In the brain, apoE participates in repairing nerve tissue that has been injured. According to the NIA, in the press release "Cortex Area Thinner in Youth with Alzheimer's-Related Gene" (April 24, 2007, http://www.nimh.nih.gov/science-news/2007/cortex-area-thinner-in-youth-with-alzheimers-related-gene.shtml), 40% of late-onset AD patients have at least one apoE-4 gene, whereas only 10% to 25% of the general population has an apoE-4 gene. The NIA notes in "Alzheimer's Disease Fact Sheet" (February 19, 2010, http://www.nia.nih.gov/Alzheimers/Publications/adfact.htm) that several studies have confirmed that the apoE-4 gene increases the risk of developing AD, but it is not yet known how it acts to increase this risk. The NIA points out that inheriting the apoE-4 gene does not necessarily mean that a person will develop AD and that the absence of the gene does not ensure that an individual will not develop AD. The NIA also suggests that additional genes related to AD risk may be identified by a genome-wide association study, which rapidly scans markers across the genomes (complete sets of deoxyribonucleic acid [DNA]) of many people to detect genetic variations that are associated with a particular disease.

In April 2011 two studies published in *Nature Genetics* (vol. 43, no. 5)—Adam C. Naj et al.'s "Common Variants at MS4A4/MS4A6E, CD2AP, CD33, and EPHA1 Are Associated with Late-Onset Alzheimer's Disease" and Paul Hollingworth et al.'s "Common Variants at ABCA7, MS4A6A/MS4A4E, EPHA1, CD33, and CD2AP Are Associated with Alzheimer's Disease"—identified five additional genes that are implicated in increasing the risk of developing the disease and the course of the disease. However, it should be noted that none of the recently identified genes play as important a role as apoE—the newly identified genes increase risk by just 10% to 15%, compared to apoE, which confers a 400-fold increase in risk of developing AD.

As of June 2011, there were two ongoing, long-term NIA initiatives: the Alzheimer's Disease Genetics Study, which began in 2003 and collects blood samples and DNA for researchers to use, and the Alzheimer's Disease Genetics Consortium, which began in 2007 and aims to compare genetic material from 10,000 people with AD to genetic material from 10,000 people without the disease. The NIA also supports the National Cell Repository for Alzheimer's Disease, a national repository of clinical information and DNA that is available to researchers.

DIAGNOSTIC TESTING. Historically, the only sure way to diagnose AD was to examine brain tissue under a microscope, during an autopsy. Examining the brain of a patient who has died of AD reveals a characteristic pattern that is the hallmark of the disease: tangles of fibers (neurofibrillary tangles) and clusters of degenerated nerve endings (neuritic plaques) in areas of the brain that are crucial for memory and intellect.

Evaluation of people with cognitive changes always involves obtaining a thorough medical history and a physical examination to rule out cognitive changes that may result from an underlying illness such as diabetes, a psychiatric disorder such as depression, or a reaction to medication. Physicians will also ask patients a series of questions to assess their memory, thinking, reasoning, and problem-solving capabilities. Even though a complete medical history, physical examination, and psychiatric and neurological assessment do not provide as definitive a diagnosis of AD as an examination of the brain, they can usually produce an accurate diagnosis by ruling out other potential causes of cognitive impairment and decline. Diagnostic tests for AD

may also include analysis of blood and spinal fluid as well as the use of brain scans (CT and MRI) to detect strokes or tumors and to measure the volume of brain tissue in areas of the brain that are used for memory and cognition. Such brain scans assist to accurately identify people with AD and to predict who may develop AD in the future.

In "Alzheimer-Signature MRI Biomarker Predicts AD Dementia in Cognitively Normal Adults" (*Neurology*, vol. 76, no. 16, April 19, 2011), Brad C. Dickerson et al. used MRI to measure the thickness of the cerebral cortex (the outer portion of the brain that is responsible for higher-order functions such as information processing and language) to help predict which cognitively normal people would develop AD. The researchers hypothesized that the cortical thinning observed in patients with mild AD dementia might be present in cognitively normal adults who will develop AD before they have any symptoms of the disease. Dickerson et al. find that cognitively normal adults who went on to develop AD had thinner cortical areas and those in the highest third of cortical thickness never developed AD. The researchers conclude that "this measure [is] a potentially important imaging biomarker of early neurodegeneration."

The NIA explains in "Alzheimer's Disease Fact Sheet" that apoE testing is used as a research tool to identify research subjects who may have an increased risk of developing AD. Investigators are then able to look for early brain changes in research subjects and compare the effectiveness of treatments for people with different apoE profiles. Because the apoE test does not accurately predict who will or will not develop AD, it is useful for studying AD risk in populations but not for determining any one individual's specific risk.

Leslie M. Shaw et al. describe in "Cerebrospinal Fluid Biomarker Signature in Alzheimer's Disease Neuroimaging Initiative Subjects" (*Annals of Neurology*, vol. 65, no. 4, April 2009) a test that can accurately detect AD in its earliest stages, before dementia symptoms begin. The test measures the concentration of specific biomarkers, in this case proteins (tau protein and amyloid beta42 polypeptide) in spinal fluid, which can indicate AD. Shaw et al. note that subjects with low concentrations of amyloid beta42 and high levels of tau in their spinal fluid were more likely to develop AD. The test had an 87% accuracy rate when predicting which subjects with early memory problems and other symptoms of cognitive impairment would ultimately be diagnosed with AD.

In "Identification of a Blood-Based Biomarker Panel for Classification of Alzheimer's Disease" (*International Journal of Neuropharmacology*, April 5, 2011), Christoph Laske et al. of the University of Tübingen recount their efforts to identify blood biomarkers for AD. The researchers collected 155 serum samples from people with early AD and age-matched healthy controls and measured the levels of 24 biomarkers. They found that three specific biomarkers enabled them to distinguish the AD patients from the healthy controls more than 80% of the time. Laske et al. suggest that these and other blood-based biomarkers may be useful for distinguishing AD from other forms of dementia.

A simple and accurate test, such as the blood-based biomarkers identified by Laske et al., that distinguishes people with AD from those with cognitive problems or dementias arising from other causes will prove useful for scientists, physicians, and other clinical researchers. An accurate test would not only identify those at risk of developing AD and allow the detection of AD early enough for the use of experimental medications to slow the progress of the disease but also monitor the progress of treatments aimed at preventing AD or slowing its progression. However, the availability of tests to predict who may develop AD raises ethical and practical questions: Do people really want to know their risks of developing AD? Is it helpful to predict a condition that is not yet considered preventable or curable?

NEW DIAGNOSTIC GUIDELINES AND CRITERIA FOR AD. In 2011 the NIA and the Alzheimer's Association tasked a workgroup to establish new guidelines for diagnosing AD, and Guy M. McKhann et al. summarize the details in "The Diagnosis of Dementia Due to Alzheimer's Disease: Recommendations from the National Institute on Aging and the Alzheimer's Association Workgroup" (*Alzheimer's and Dementia*, vol. 7, no. 3, May 2011). The new guidelines update diagnostic criteria that were developed in 1984 and aim to detect and treat the disease earlier than ever before. They are intended for use by physicians in practice settings without access to advanced diagnostic testing capabilities, such as imaging studies and analysis of blood and cerebrospinal fluid, and researchers investigating biomarkers for AD. The revised guidelines address the use of imaging and biomarkers in blood and spinal fluid to help determine whether AD is the cause of observed changes in patients. They also acknowledge that imaging and biomarkers should not "be used routinely in clinical diagnosis without further testing and validation."

The new updated guidelines describe AD as a continuum of mental decline that may begin many years before the first symptoms arise. The updated guidance describes three phases: preclinical, which occurs absent symptoms; mild cognitive impairment, which involves noticeable memory problems without loss of ability to function independently; and Alzheimer's dementia, with its characteristic decline in reasoning and function.

The workgroup also created new criteria for determining cognitive impairment caused by AD, and Marilyn S. Albert et al. outline the details in "The Diagnosis of Mild Cognitive Impairment Due to Alzheimer's Disease: Recommendations from the National Institute on Aging

and Alzheimer's Association Workgroup" (*Alzheimer's and Dementia*, vol. 7, no. 3, May 2011). The workgroup established two sets of criteria: one for use by health care providers without access to advanced imaging techniques or blood and cerebrospinal fluid analysis and one for use by clinical researchers. The second set of criteria describe the use of biomarkers that are based on imaging and blood and cerebrospinal fluid measures and establish four levels of confidence, depending on the presence and character of the biomarker findings.

TREATMENT. There is still no cure or prevention for AD, and treatment focuses on managing symptoms. Medication may slow the appearance of some symptoms and can lessen others, such as agitation, anxiety, unpredictable behavior, and depression. Physical exercise and good nutrition are important, as is a calm and highly structured environment. The object is to help the AD patient maintain as much comfort, normalcy, and dignity for as long as possible.

According to the Alzheimer's Association, in "Current Alzheimer's Treatments" (http://www.alz.org/research/science/alzheimers_disease_treatments.asp), in 2011 there were five prescription drugs—Aricept, Razadyne, Namenda, Exelon, and Cognex—for the treatment of AD that had been approved by the U.S. Food and Drug Administration, and National Institutes of Health (NIH) affiliates and pharmaceutical companies were involved in clinical trials of new drugs to treat AD. All the drugs being tested were intended to improve the symptoms of AD and slow its progression, but none was expected to cure AD. The investigational drugs aim to address three aspects of AD: to improve cognitive function in people with early AD, to slow or postpone the progression of the disease, and to control behavioral problems such as wandering, aggression, and agitation of patients with AD.

Even though no new drugs for AD were approved in 2011, a new method of drug delivery, a transdermal patch that delivers the drug through the skin, compared favorably to oral drug administration. The results of a study involving 56 caregivers for patients with AD were presented at the 26th International Conference of Alzheimer's Disease International in Toronto, Canada, in March 2011. Pam Harrison reports in "Transdermal Patch for Alzheimer's Gets Caregiver Thumbs-Up: Delivery Method May Reduce Caregiver Stress, Enhance Patient Response" (*Medscape Medical News*, March 30, 2011) that Pablo Martinez-Lage et al. said that some patient caregivers felt the patch slowed, or even stopped, the deterioration that is the hallmark of AD. They opined that the continuous drug delivery offered by the patch might account for the reported improvement in the patients' behavior. Martinez-Lage et al. also observed that AD caregivers found administering the patch easier and less stressful than administering oral medication to potentially combative or uncooperative patients.

There is also some evidence that a combination of vitamin E and anti-inflammatory drugs play a role in slowing the progress of AD. According to Megan Rauscher, in "Vitamin E May Slow Alzheimer's Disease" (Reuters, May 4, 2009), the findings of an NIH-funded study conducted at the Massachusetts General Hospital Memory Disorders Unit, the Bedford VA Medical Center, and Harvard Medical School were presented at the annual meeting of the American Geriatrics Society in May 2009. The investigators followed a total of 540 AD patients who received traditional treatment as well as either vitamin E but no anti-inflammatory drug, an anti-inflammatory drug but no vitamin E, both vitamin E and an anti-inflammatory drug, or neither. Subjects who took both vitamin E and the anti-inflammatory drug appeared to have a slower decline of mental and physical function over the course of three years of follow-up.

In "High Plasma Levels of Vitamin E Forms and Reduced Alzheimer's Disease Risk in Advanced Age" (*Journal of Alzheimer's Disease*, vol. 20, no. 4, November 2010), a six-year study of 232 adults aged 80 years and older, Francesca Mangialasche et al. confirm a relationship between vitamin E and AD. At the start of the study the researchers measured the subjects' blood levels of the eight naturally occurring components of vitamin E. They found that subjects with higher blood levels of all forms of vitamin E had a reduced risk of developing AD compared to subjects with lower blood levels of the vitamin E components. Mangialasche et al. hypothesize that the combination of different forms of vitamin E confer a protective effect against AD, noting that "our findings need to be confirmed by other studies, but they open up the possibility that the balanced presence of different vitamin E forms can have an important neuroprotective effect."

ADVANCES IN RESEARCH AND TREATMENT. In the press release "New Research Advances from the Alzheimer's Association International Conference on Alzheimer's Disease 2010" (July 14, 2010, http://www.alz.org/Icad/2010_release _advances_071410_1230pm.asp), the Alzheimer's Association notes that at its 2010 International Conference on Alzheimer's Disease in Honolulu, Hawaii, researchers described new advances in research and treatment, including:

- The results of a large-scale study of veterans, which revealed that early detection, diagnosis, and treatment of patients with cognitive impairment and dementia can reduce outpatient costs by nearly 30%.

- A long-term study of older adults that suggests that physical activity and specific nutrients such as tea and vitamin D may help maintain cognitive ability and reduce the risk of developing AD.

- Historically, much AD research has focused on the role of beta amyloid plaque in the development of AD; however, researchers are now also focusing on tau protein, which forms neurofibrillary tangles in the brain.

- FTO, a gene that is associated with obesity, may also increase the risk of developing AD and dementia.

- Imaging studies indicate that the brains of patients with AD contain different shapes of beta amyloid deposits, depending on which version of the apoE gene is present.

- Researchers find that people with AD also have an increased risk of developing other potentially serious medical conditions such as seizures and anemia.

CARING FOR THE AD PATIENT. AD affects members of the patient's family. Even though medication may suppress some symptoms and occasionally slow the progression of the disease, eventually most AD patients require constant care and supervision. In the past, nursing homes and residential care facilities were not equipped to provide this kind of care, and if they accepted AD patients at all, they admitted only those in the earliest stages of the disease. Since 2000 a growing number of nursing homes have welcomed AD patients, even though they are more difficult and costly to care for than older adults without AD. This change is primarily financially motivated, because nursing home occupancy rates have been dropping in response to the growth of alternative housing for older adults. According to Genworth Financial, in *Genworth 2011 Cost of Care Survey: Home Care Providers, Adult Day Health Care Facilities, Assisted Living Facilities, and Nursing Homes* (April 2011, http://www.genworth.com/content/ etc/medialib/genworth_v2/pdf/ltc_cost_of_care.Par.8024 .File.dat/cost_of_care.pdf), these nursing homes offer families with ample financial resources—in 2011 the annual costs ranged from $52,925 to $227,760, depending on the location of the facility in the United States and the intensity of services—an alternative to caring for the AD patient at home.

Many children and other relatives of AD patients care for the affected family member at home as long as possible because they cannot afford institutional care or they feel a moral obligation to do so. No matter how willing and devoted the caregiver, the time, patience, and resources that are required to provide care over a long period are immense, and the task is often overwhelming. As the patient's condition progresses, caregivers often find themselves socially isolated. Caregiving has been linked to increased rates of depression, compromised immune function, and a greater use of medication and psychotropic drugs (medications that are used to improve mood and relieve symptoms of mental distress).

Caregivers who participate in support groups and make use of home health aides, adult day care, and respite care (facilities where patients stay for a limited number of days) not only feel healthier but also are better able to care for AD patients and maintain them at home longer than those who do not.

In *2011 Alzheimer's Disease Facts and Figures*, the Alzheimer's Association describes the growing burden that AD imposes on families, caregivers, and the U.S. health care system. The association states that in 2010 nearly 15 million caregivers provided 17 billion hours of unpaid care to people with AD. The dollar value of that care was estimated to be more than $202 billion. The total cost of health and long-term care for people with AD was an estimated $183 billion in 2011.

MENTAL ILLNESS

Older people with mental illnesses were once considered senile—that is, mentally debilitated as a result of old age. Serious forgetfulness, emotional disturbances, and other behavioral changes do not, however, occur as a normal part of aging. They may be caused by chronic illnesses such as heart disease, thyroid disorders, or anemia; infections, poor diet, or lack of sleep; or prescription drugs, such as narcotic painkillers, sedatives, and antihistamines. Social isolation, loneliness, boredom, or depression may also cause memory lapses. When accurately diagnosed and treated, these types of problems can frequently be reversed.

Mental illness refers to all identifiable mental health disorders and mental health problems. In the landmark study *Mental Health: A Report of the Surgeon General, 1999* (1999, http://www.surgeongeneral.gov/library/mentalhealth/home.html), the U.S. surgeon general defines mental disorders as "health conditions that are characterized by alterations in thinking, mood, or behavior (or some combination thereof) associated with distress and/or impaired functioning." The surgeon general distinguishes mental health disorders from mental health problems, describing the signs and symptoms of mental health problems as less intense and of shorter duration than those of mental health disorders, but it acknowledges that both mental health disorders and problems may be distressing and disabling.

The surgeon general observes that nearly 20% of people aged 55 years and older experience mental disorders that are not part of normal aging. The most common disorders, in order of estimated prevalence rates, are anxiety (11.4%), severe cognitive impairment (6.6%), and mood disorders (4.4%) such as depression. The surgeon general also points out that mental disorders in older adults are frequently unrecognized, underreported, and undertreated.

Diagnosing mental disorders in older adults is challenging because their symptoms and presentation may be different from that of other adults. For example, many older adults complain about physical as opposed to emotional or psychological problems, and they present symptoms that are not typical of depression or anxiety disorders. Accurately identifying, detecting, and diagnosing mental disorders in older adults is also complicated by the following:

- Mental disorders often coexist with other medical problems.

- The symptoms of some chronic diseases may imitate or conceal psychological disorders.

- Older adults are more likely to report physical symptoms than psychological ones, because there is less stigma associated with physical health or medical problems than with mental health problems.

Serious Psychological Distress

Beth Han et al. report in "Serious Psychological Distress and Mental Health Service Use among Community-Dwelling Older U.S. Adults" (*Psychiatric Services*, vol. 62, no. 3, March 2011) that about 4.7% of adults aged 65 years and older experience serious psychological distress (SPD) each year. Examples of SPD include prolonged or intense anxiety, depression, or other emotional stress. Of those aged 50 years and older who reported SPD during the past year, 37.7% received mental health treatment—4.8% received inpatient services, 15.8% received outpatient services, and 32.1% received prescription medications.

Depression

Symptoms of depression are an important indicator of physical and mental health in older adults, because people who experience many symptoms of depression are also more likely to report higher rates of physical illness, disability, and health service utilization.

The prevalence of clinically relevant depressive symptoms (as distinguished from brief periods of sadness or depressed mood) increases with advancing age. According to the Federal Interagency Forum on Aging-Related Statistics, in *Older Americans 2010: Key Indicators of Well-Being* (July 2011, http://www.agingstats.gov/agingstatsdotnet/Main_Site/Data/2010_Documents/Docs/OA_2010.pdf), between 1998 and 2006, 19% of adults aged 85 years and older experienced these symptoms, compared to 14% of those aged 65 to 69 years. (See Figure 8.2.) Older women aged 65 to 84 years reported depressive symptoms more than older men. For example, 17% of women aged 70 to 74 years reported depressive symptoms, compared to 8% of men the same age.

Often, illness itself can trigger depression in older adults by altering the chemicals in the brain. Examples of illnesses that can touch off depression are diabetes, hypothyroidism (a condition in which the thyroid is underactive—producing too little thyroid hormones), kidney or liver dysfunction, heart disease, and infection. In patients with these ailments, treating the underlying disease usually eliminates the depression. David M. Clarke and Kay C. Currie find in "Depression, Anxiety, and Their Relationship with Chronic Diseases: A Review of the Epidemiology, Risk, and Treatment Evidence" (*Medical Journal of Australia*, vol. 190, no. 7, April 6, 2009) not only strong

FIGURE 8.2

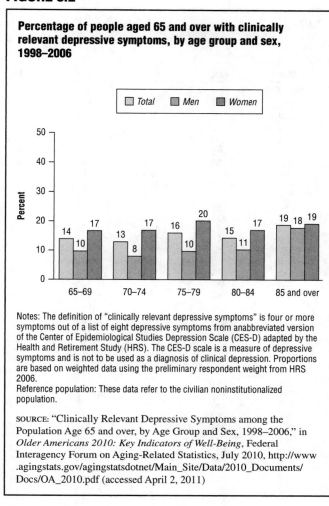

Percentage of people aged 65 and over with clinically relevant depressive symptoms, by age group and sex, 1998–2006

Notes: The definition of "clinically relevant depressive symptoms" is four or more symptoms out of a list of eight depressive symptoms from an abbreviated version of the Center of Epidemiological Studies Depression Scale (CES-D) adapted by the Health and Retirement Study (HRS). The CES-D scale is a measure of depressive symptoms and is not to be used as a diagnosis of clinical depression. Proportions are based on weighted data using the preliminary respondent weight from HRS 2006.
Reference population: These data refer to the civilian noninstitutionalized population.

SOURCE: "Clinically Relevant Depressive Symptoms among the Population Age 65 and over, by Age Group and Sex, 1998–2006," in *Older Americans 2010: Key Indicators of Well-Being*, Federal Interagency Forum on Aging-Related Statistics, July 2010, http://www.agingstats.gov/agingstatsdotnet/Main_Site/Data/2010_Documents/Docs/OA_2010.pdf (accessed April 2, 2011)

evidence for the association of physical illness, depression, and anxiety but also their effects on outcomes (how well patients fare). The researchers indicate that people with disabling chronic illnesses such as arthritis, stroke, and pulmonary diseases are likely to become depressed. Furthermore, Clarke and Currie note that some prescription medications, as well as over-the-counter (nonprescription) drugs, may also cause depression.

Depression causes some older adults to deliberately neglect or disregard their medical needs by eating poorly and failing to take prescribed medication or taking it incorrectly. These may be covert acts of suicide. Actual suicide, which is frequently a consequence of serious depression, is highest among older adults relative to all other age groups. In 2007 the death rate for suicide among people aged 75 to 84 years was 16.3% and among adults aged 85 years and older it was 15.6%. (See Table 8.1.) Older men had the highest rates—34.3% for those aged 75 to 84 years and 41.8% for those aged 85 years and older.

TREATMENT OF DEPRESSION. According to the surgeon general, in *Mental Health*, despite the availability of effective treatments for depression, a substantial fraction of affected older adults do not receive treatment, largely because they either do not seek it or because their depression is not identified or accurately diagnosed. For example, even though older patients respond well to antidepressant medications, some physicians do not prescribe them to older patients already taking many drugs for chronic medical conditions because they do not want to risk drug-drug interactions or add another drug to an already complicated regimen. As a result, only a minority of older adults diagnosed with depression receives the appropriate drug dose and duration of treatment for depression.

Common treatments for depression include psychotherapy, with or without the use of antidepressant medications, and electroconvulsive therapy (ECT). Psychotherapy is most often used to treat mild to moderate depression and is prescribed for a limited, defined period, generally ranging from 10 to 20 weeks. ECT is used for life-threatening depression that does not respond to treatment with antidepressant drugs.

In "The Effect of a Primary Care Practice-Based Depression Intervention on Mortality in Older Adults: A Randomized Trial" (*Annals of Internal Medicine*, vol. 146, no. 10, May 15, 2007), a five-year study of 1,226 older patients, Joseph J. Gallo et al. not only find that depression is independently associated with mortality risk in older adults but also confirm that treatment for depression reduces this risk. Of the total number of subjects, about 600 were determined to be suffering from major or minor depression. During the five-year follow-up, 223 subjects had died. Subjects who received treatment for depression were 33% less likely to die than those who were not treated.

In "Depressive Symptoms in Old Age: Relations among Sociodemographic and Self-Reported Health Variables" (*International Psychogeriatrics*, April 13, 2011), Gloria Teixeira Nicolosi et al. collected data from 303 adults aged 65 years and older to determine the circumstances and factors that are associated with depression. The researchers find that symptoms of depression are associated with a higher number of self-reported health problems, poor perceived health assessment, and lower levels of academic attainment. Among older women, health and financial problems are most closely associated with symptoms of depression.

Magnus Lindwell, Pernilla Larsman, and Martin S. Hagger identify in "The Reciprocal Relationship between Physical Activity and Depression in Older European Adults: A Prospective Cross-Lagged Panel Design Using Share Data" (*Health Psychology*, April 11, 2011) a reciprocal relationship between physical activity and symptoms of depression in older adults. The researchers observe that "regular physical activity may be a valuable tool in the prevention of future depressive symptoms in older adults,

TABLE 8.1

Death rates for suicide, by selected characteristics, selected years 1950–2007

[Data are based on death certificates]

Sex, race, Hispanic origin, and age	1950[a, b]	1960[a, b]	1970[b]	1980[b]	1990[b]	2000[c]	2006[c]	2007[c]
All persons				Deaths per 100,000 resident population				
All ages, age-adjusted[d]	13.2	12.5	13.1	12.2	12.5	10.4	10.9	11.3
All ages, crude	11.4	10.6	11.6	11.9	12.4	10.4	11.1	11.5
Under 1 year	—	—	—	—	—	—	—	—
1–4 years	—	—	—	—	—	—	—	—
5–14 years	0.2	0.3	0.3	0.4	0.8	0.7	0.5	0.5
15–24 years	4.5	5.2	8.8	12.3	13.2	10.2	9.9	9.7
15–19 years	2.7	3.6	5.9	8.5	11.1	8.0	7.3	6.9
20–24 years	6.2	7.1	12.2	16.1	15.1	12.5	12.5	12.6
25–44 years	11.6	12.2	15.4	15.6	15.2	13.4	13.8	14.3
25–34 years	9.1	10.0	14.1	16.0	15.2	12.0	12.3	13.0
35–44 years	14.3	14.2	16.9	15.4	15.3	14.5	15.1	15.6
45–64 years	23.5	22.0	20.6	15.9	15.3	13.5	16.0	16.8
45–54 years	20.9	20.7	20.0	15.9	14.8	14.4	17.2	17.7
55–64 years	26.8	23.7	21.4	15.9	16.0	12.1	14.5	15.5
65 years and over	30.0	24.5	20.8	17.6	20.5	15.2	14.2	14.3
65–74 years	29.6	23.0	20.8	16.9	17.9	12.5	12.6	12.6
75–84 years	31.1	27.9	21.2	19.1	24.9	17.6	15.9	16.3
85 years and over	28.8	26.0	19.0	19.2	22.2	19.6	15.9	15.6
Male								
All ages, age-adjusted[d]	21.2	20.0	19.8	19.9	21.5	17.7	18.0	18.4
All ages, crude	17.8	16.5	16.8	18.6	20.4	17.1	17.8	18.3
Under 1 year	—	—	—	—	—	—	—	—
1–4 years	—	—	—	—	—	—	—	—
5–14 years	0.3	0.4	0.5	0.6	1.1	1.2	0.7	0.6
15–24 years	6.5	8.2	13.5	20.2	22.0	17.1	16.2	15.9
15–19 years	3.5	5.6	8.8	13.8	18.1	13.0	11.5	11.1
20–24 years	9.3	11.5	19.3	26.8	25.7	21.4	20.8	20.8
25–44 years	17.2	17.9	20.9	24.0	24.4	21.3	21.5	22.3
25–34 years	13.4	14.7	19.8	25.0	24.8	19.6	19.7	20.7
35–44 years	21.3	21.0	22.1	22.5	23.9	22.8	23.2	23.8
45–64 years	37.1	34.4	30.0	23.7	24.3	21.3	24.8	25.8
45–54 years	32.0	31.6	27.9	22.9	23.2	22.4	26.2	27.0
55–64 years	43.6	38.1	32.7	24.5	25.7	19.4	22.7	24.3
65 years and over	52.8	44.0	38.4	35.0	41.6	31.1	28.5	28.6
65–74 years	50.5	39.6	36.0	30.4	32.2	22.7	22.7	22.5
75–84 years	58.3	52.5	42.8	42.3	56.1	38.6	33.3	34.3
85 years and over	58.3	57.4	42.4	50.6	65.9	57.5	43.2	41.8
Female								
All ages, age-adjusted[d]	5.6	5.6	7.4	5.7	4.8	4.0	4.5	4.7
All ages, crude	5.1	4.9	6.6	5.5	4.8	4.0	4.6	4.8
Under 1 year	—	—	—	—	—	—	—	—
1–4 years	—	—	—	—	—	—	—	—
5–14 years	0.1	0.1	0.2	0.2	0.4	0.3	0.3	0.3
15–24 years	2.6	2.2	4.2	4.3	3.9	3.0	3.2	3.2
15–19 years	1.8	1.6	2.9	3.0	3.7	2.7	2.8	2.5
20–24 years	3.3	2.9	5.7	5.5	4.1	3.2	3.6	3.9
25–44 years	6.2	6.6	10.2	7.7	6.2	5.4	5.9	6.2
25–34 years	4.9	5.5	8.6	7.1	5.6	4.3	4.7	5.0
35–44 years	7.5	7.7	11.9	8.5	6.8	6.4	7.0	7.3
45–64 years	9.9	10.2	12.0	8.9	7.1	6.2	7.7	8.2
45–54 years	9.9	10.2	12.6	9.4	6.9	6.7	8.4	8.8
55–64 years	9.9	10.2	11.4	8.4	7.3	5.4	6.8	7.3
65 years and over	9.4	8.4	8.1	6.1	6.4	4.0	3.9	3.9
65–74 years	10.1	8.4	9.0	6.5	6.7	4.0	4.1	4.2
75–84 years	8.1	8.9	7.0	5.5	6.3	4.0	4.0	3.8
85 years and over	8.2	6.0	5.9	5.5	5.4	4.2	3.1	3.1

and depressive symptoms may also prevent older adults from engaging in regular physical activity."

Anxiety Disorders

Anxiety disorders (extreme nervousness and apprehension or sudden attacks of anxiety without apparent external causes) can be debilitating and destructive. Symptoms may include fear, a "knot" in the stomach, sweating, or elevated blood pressure. If the anxiety is severe and long lasting, more serious problems may develop. People suffering from anxiety over an extended period may have headaches, ulcers, irritable bowel syndrome, insomnia, or depression. Because anxiety tends to create various other emotional and physical symptoms, a

TABLE 8.2

Death rates for suicide, by selected characteristics, selected years 1950–2007 [CONTINUED]

[Data are based on death certificates]

Sex, race, Hispanic origin, and age	1950[a, b]	1960[a, b]	1970[b]	1980[b]	1990[b]	2000[c]	2006[c]	2007[c]
White male[e]				Deaths per 100,000 resident population				
All ages, age-adjusted[d]	22.3	21.1	20.8	20.9	22.8	19.1	19.6	20.2
All ages, crude	19.0	17.6	18.0	19.9	22.0	18.8	19.8	20.5
15–24 years	6.6	8.6	13.9	21.4	23.2	17.9	17.1	16.9
25–44 years	17.9	18.5	21.5	24.6	25.4	22.9	23.5	24.5
45–64 years	39.3	36.5	31.9	25.0	26.0	23.2	27.4	28.8
65 years and over	55.8	46.7	41.1	37.2	44.2	33.3	30.9	31.1
65–74 years	53.2	42.0	38.7	32.5	34.2	24.3	24.7	24.7
75–84 years	61.9	55.7	45.5	45.5	60.2	41.1	36.0	36.9
85 years and over	61.9	61.3	45.8	52.8	70.3	61.6	46.1	45.4

—Category not applicable.

[a]Includes deaths of persons who were not residents of the 50 states and the District of Columbia (D.C.).

[b]Underlying cause of death was coded according to the 6th revision of the *International Classification of Diseases* (ICD) in 1950, 7th revision in 1960, 8th revision in 1970, and 9th revision in 1980–1998.

[c]Starting with 1999 data, cause of death is coded according to ICD-10.

[d]Age-adjusted rates are calculated using the year 2000 standard population. Prior to 2003, age-adjusted rates were calculated using standard million proportions based on rounded population numbers. Starting with 2003 data, unrounded population numbers are used to calculate age-adjusted rates.

[e]The race groups, white, black, Asian or Pacific Islander, and American Indian or Alaska Native, include persons of Hispanic and non-Hispanic origin. Persons of Hispanic origin may be of any race. Death rates for the American Indian or Alaska Native and Asian or Pacific Islander populations are known to be underestimated.

Notes: Starting with *Health, United States, 2003*, rates for 1991–1999 were revised using intercensal population estimates based on the 2000 census. Rates for 2000 were revised based on 2000 census counts. Rates for 2001 and later years were computed using 2000-based postcensal estimates. Figures for 2001 include September 11-related deaths for which death certificates were filed as of October 24, 2002. Age groups were selected to minimize the presentation of unstable age-specific death rates based on small numbers of deaths and for consistency among comparison groups. Starting with 2003 data, some states allowed the reporting of more than one race on the death certificate. The multiple-race data for these states were bridged to the single-race categories of the 1977 Office of Management and Budget standards for comparability with other states. Data for additional years are available.

SOURCE: Adapted from "Table 39. Death Rates for Suicide, by Sex, Race, Hispanic Origin, and Age: United States, Selected Years 1950–2007," in *Health, United States 2010: With Special Feature on Death and Dying*, National Center for Health Statistics, 2011, http://www.cdc.gov/nchs/data/hus/hus10.pdf (accessed April 8, 2011)

---

cascade effect can occur in which these new or additional problems produce even more anxiety.

Unrelenting anxiety that appears unrelated to specific environments or situations is called generalized anxiety disorder. People suffering from this disorder worry excessively about the events of daily life and the future. They are also more likely to experience physical symptoms such as shortness of breath, dizziness, rapid heart rate, nausea, stomach pains, and muscle tension than people who are afflicted with other panic disorders, social phobias, or agoraphobia (fear of being in an open space or a place where escape is difficult).

The surgeon general estimates in *Mental Health* the prevalence of anxiety disorder as about 11.4% of adults aged 55 years and older. Phobic anxiety disorders such as social phobia, which causes extreme discomfort in social settings, are among the most common mental disturbances in late life. In contrast, some disorders have low rates of prevalence among older adults, such as panic disorder (0.5%) and obsessive-compulsive disorder (1.5%). Generalized anxiety disorder, rather than specific anxiety syndromes, may be more prevalent in older people.

Effective treatment for anxiety involves medication, primarily benzodiazepines, such as Valium, Librium, and Xanax, as well as psychotherapy. Like other medications, the effects of benzodiazepines may last longer in older adults, and their side effects may include drowsiness, fatigue, physical impairment, memory or other cognitive impairment, confusion, depression, respiratory problems, abuse or dependence problems, and withdrawal reactions.

Nondrug treatment may also be effective for older adults suffering from debilitating anxiety. Melinda A. Stanley et al. compared cognitive behavioral therapy (CBT; goal-oriented treatment that focuses on changing thoughts to solve psychological problems) to enhanced usual care (treatment that consists of biweekly telephone calls to ensure patient safety and provide minimal support) for treatment of generalized anxiety disorder in older adults and reported their findings in "Cognitive Behavior Therapy for Generalized Anxiety Disorder among Older Adults in Primary Care: A Randomized Clinical Trial" (*Journal of the American Medical Association*, vol. 301, no. 14, April 8, 2009). The researchers find that the CBT, which consisted of education and awareness, motivational interviewing, relaxation training, cognitive therapy, problem-solving skills training, and behavioral sleep management, resulted in greater relief from worry and depressive symptoms and improved general mental health for older patients with general anxiety disorder than the enhanced usual care.

Stanley et al. also conducted a study of 66 adults aged 55 years and older who suffered from anxiety and/or depression to determine whether they had a preference for therapy that incorporates religion and/or spirituality.

In "Older Adults' Preferences for Religion/Spirituality in Treatment for Anxiety and Depression" (*Aging Mental Health*, vol. 15, no. 3, April 2011), the researchers report that the majority of participants said it was important to include religion and spirituality in therapy. Furthermore, Stanley et al. conclude that "participants who thought it was important to include religion or spirituality in therapy reported more positive religious-based coping, greater strength of religious faith, and greater collaborative and less self-directed problem-solving styles than participants who did not think it was important."

Schizophrenia

Schizophrenia is an extremely disabling form of mental illness. Its symptoms include hallucinations, paranoia, delusions, and social isolation. People suffering from schizophrenia "hear voices," and over time the voices take over in the schizophrenic's mind, obliterating reality and directing all kinds of erratic behaviors. Suicide attempts and violent attacks are common in the lives of schizophrenics. In an attempt to escape the torment inflicted by their brains, many schizophrenics turn to drugs. The National Institute of Mental Health indicates in *Schizophrenia* (2009, http://www.nimh.nih.gov/health/publications/schizophrenia/schizophrenia-booket-2009.pdf) that most symptoms of schizophrenia emerge early in life—the late teens or 20s and rarely begin after age 45.

In *Mental Health*, the surgeon general notes that the prevalence of schizophrenia among adults aged 65 years and older is estimated to be 0.6%, less than half of the 1.3% that is estimated for the population aged 18 to 54 years. However, the economic burden of late-life schizophrenia is high. Even though the use of nursing homes and state hospitals for patients with all mental disorders has declined over the past two decades, this decline is small for older patients with schizophrenia.

Drug treatment of schizophrenia in older adults is complicated. The medications that are used to treat schizophrenia, such as Haldol, effectively reduce symptoms (e.g., delusions and hallucinations) of many older patients, but they also have a high risk of disabling side effects, such as tardive dyskinesias (involuntary, rhythmic movements of the face, jaw, mouth, tongue, and trunk). Even newer atypical antipsychotic medications that are used to treat the symptoms of schizophrenia, such as Abilify, can produce troubling side effects including tremors, restlessness, shakes, muscle stiffness, or other involuntary movements.

MISUSE OF ALCOHOL AND PRESCRIPTION DRUGS

The surgeon general observes in *Mental Health* that older adults are more likely to misuse, as opposed to abuse, alcohol and prescription drugs. The surgeon general estimates that the prevalence of heavy drinking

(12 to 21 drinks per week) in the cohort (a group of individuals that shares a common characteristic such as birth years and is studied over time) of older adults is 3% to 9%. The prevalence rates are expected to rise as the baby boomer (people born between 1946 and 1964) cohort, with its history of alcohol and illegal drug use, joins the ranks of older adults. In "Substance Use Disorder among Older Adults in the United States in 2020" (*Addiction*, vol. 104, no. 1, January 2009), Beth Han et al. forecast that the number of adults aged 50 years and older with substance use disorder (alcohol/illicit drug dependence or abuse) is projected to double from an average of 2.8 million per year in 2006 to 5.7 million in 2020. The current group of older adults is more likely to suffer substance misuse problems, such as drug dependence, arising from underuse, overuse, or erratic use of prescription and over-the-counter medications.

Figure 8.3 shows that in 2010 adults aged 65 years and older had the lowest rate of excessive alcohol consumption—just 5.4%—of all age groups. Older men (10.2%) were much more likely than older women (1.8%) to have met the National Health Interview Survey criteria for excessive alcohol consumption (five or more drinks in one day at least once in the past year).

FIGURE 8.3

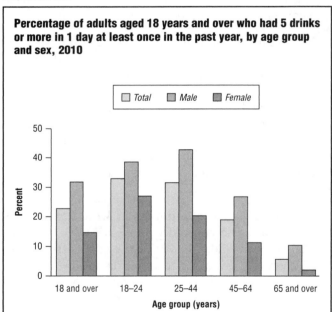

Percentage of adults aged 18 years and over who had 5 drinks or more in 1 day at least once in the past year, by age group and sex, 2010

Note: The analyses excluded 245 adults (1.2%) with unknown alcohol consumption.

SOURCE: P.M. Barnes et al., "Figure 9.2. Percentage of Adults Aged 18 Years and over Who Had 5 or More Drinks in 1 Day at Least Once in the Past Year, by Age Group and Sex: United States, January–September 2010," in *Early Release of Selected Estimates Based on Data from the January–September 2010 National Health Interview Survey*, Centers for Disease Control and Prevention, National Center for Health Statistics, March 2011, http://www.cdc.gov/nchs/data/nhis/earlyrelease/201103_09.pdf (accessed April 22, 2011)

Prevalence of Types of Older Problem Drinkers

In *Module 10C: Older Adults and Alcohol Problems* (March 2005, http://pubs.niaaa.nih.gov/publications/Social/Module10COlderAdults/Module10C.html), the National Institute on Alcohol Abuse and Alcoholism (NIAAA) describes the prevalence of three types of problem drinkers: at-risk drinkers, problem drinkers, and alcohol-dependent drinkers.

- At-risk drinking is alcohol use that increases the risk of developing alcohol-related problems and complications. People over the age of 65 years who drink more than seven drinks per week (one per day) are considered at risk of developing health, social, or emotional problems caused by alcohol.

- Problem drinkers have already suffered medical, psychological, family, financial, self-care, legal, or social consequences of alcohol abuse.

- Alcohol-dependent drinkers suffer from a medical disorder that is characterized by a loss of control over consumption, preoccupation with alcohol, and continued use despite adverse health, social, legal, and financial consequences.

Figure 8.4 shows the estimated prevalence rates of these different types of drinkers as well as the majority (65%) of older adults that abstains from alcohol consumption.

FIGURE 8.4

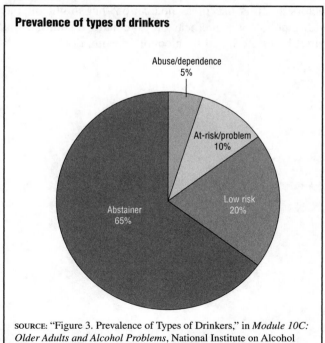

Prevalence of types of drinkers

Abuse/dependence 5%

At-risk/problem 10%

Low risk 20%

Abstainer 65%

SOURCE: "Figure 3. Prevalence of Types of Drinkers," in *Module 10C: Older Adults and Alcohol Problems*, National Institute on Alcohol Abuse and Alcoholism, March 2005, http://pubs.niaaa.nih.gov/publications/Social/Module10COlderAdults/Module10C.html (accessed April 29, 2011)

Types of Older Problem Drinkers

Another way to characterize older problem drinkers is by the duration and the patterns of their drinking histories. The first group consists of those over the age of 60 years who have been drinking for most of their life. The members of this group are called survivors or early onset problem drinkers. They have beaten the statistical odds by living to old age despite heavy drinking. These are the people most likely to suffer medical problems such as cirrhosis of the liver (a chronic degenerative disease of the liver marked by scarring of liver tissue and eventually liver failure) and mental health disorders such as depression.

The second group, intermittents, has historically engaged in binges or bout drinking interspersed with periods of relative sobriety. These drinkers are at risk for alcohol abuse because they are more likely than others to self-medicate with alcohol to relieve physical pain and emotional distress or to assuage loneliness and social isolation.

Reactors or late-onset problem drinkers make up the third group. The stresses of later life, particularly the loss of work or a spouse, may precipitate heavy drinking. These people show few of the physical consequences of prolonged drinking and fewer disruptions in their life.

Alcohol-Related Issues Unique to Older Adults

Older adults generally have a decreased tolerance to alcohol. Consumption of a given amount of alcohol by older adults usually produces higher blood-alcohol levels than it would in a younger population. Chronic medical problems such as cirrhosis may be present, but older adults are less likely to require detoxification and treatment of alcohol-withdrawal problems. One possible explanation is that few lifelong alcohol abusers survive to old age.

Because older adults usually take more medication than people in other age groups, they are more susceptible to drug-alcohol interactions. Alcohol reduces the safety and efficacy (the ability of an intervention to produce the intended diagnostic or therapeutic effect in optimal circumstances) of many medications and, in combination with some drugs, may produce coma or death. Adverse consequences of alcohol consumption in older adults are not limited to problem drinkers. Older adults with medical problems, including diabetes, heart disease, liver disease, and central nervous system degeneration, may also suffer adverse reactions from alcohol consumption.

SCREENING, DIAGNOSIS, AND TREATMENT. The NIAAA advocates screening to identify at-risk drinkers, problem drinkers, and dependent drinkers to determine the need for further diagnostic evaluation and treatment. Furthermore, in *Module 10C* it provides a screening protocol that recommends:

- All adults aged 60 years and older should be screened for alcohol and prescription drug use/abuse as part of any medical examination or application for health or social services.

- Annual rescreening should be performed if certain physical symptoms emerge or if the individual is undergoing major life changes, stresses, or transitions.

- These screening criteria apply to any health, social, work, or recreation setting that serves older adults and are not limited to medical care and substance treatment settings.

Diagnosis of problem drinking in the older population is complicated by the fact that many psychological, behavioral, and physical symptoms of problem drinking also occur in people who do not have drinking problems. For example, brain damage, heart disease, and gastrointestinal disorders often develop in older adults independent of alcohol use, but may also occur with drinking. In addition, mood disorders, depression, and changes in employment, economic, or marital status often accompany aging but can also be symptoms of alcoholism. Alcohol-induced organic brain syndrome is characterized by cognitive impairment (memory lapses, confusion, and disorientation). As a result, some older alcoholics may be incorrectly diagnosed as suffering from dementia or other mental illness.

Older problem drinkers make up a relatively small proportion of the total number of clients seen by most agencies for treatment of alcohol abuse. Little data about the effectiveness of intervention and treatment, which usually consists of some combination of counseling and education, in the older population exist. Nonetheless, the chances for recovery among older drinkers are considered good because older clients tend to complete the full course of therapy more often than younger clients.

Simon Coulton et al. assert in "The Effectiveness and Cost-Effectiveness of Opportunistic Screening and Stepped Care Interventions for Older Hazardous Alcohol Users in Primary Care (AESOPS): A Randomised Control Trial Protocol" (*BMC Health Services Research*, vol. 8, June 2008) that even though the prevalence of harmful alcohol consumption in adults aged 55 years and older is generally lower than in the general population, because it is associated with a wide range of physical, psychological, and social problems, it merits attention and effective treatment. Coulton et al. note that there is an association between increased alcohol consumption and increased risk of falls, heart disease, hypertension, stroke, alcohol-related liver disease, and many cancers. Alcohol consumption can contribute to the development of dementia and other age-related cognitive deficits as well as to psychological problems including depression, anxiety, and suicide.

Even though alcohol use can pose risks for older adults, few physicians inquire about it with their older patients. O. Kenrik Duru et al. surveyed 31 physicians and 3,305 patients aged 60 years and older to find out whether the patients had discussed alcohol use in the year before the survey. In "Correlates of Alcohol-Related Discussions between Older Adults and Their Physicians" (*Journal of the American Geriatrics Society*, vol. 58, no. 12, December 2010), Duru et al. report that the likelihood of physicians discussing alcohol use declined with patient age despite the presence of clinically relevant factors such as use of a medication that might interact with alcohol or a medical or psychiatric condition that might be exacerbated by alcohol consumption.

CHAPTER 9
CARING FOR OLDER ADULTS: CAREGIVERS

In the United States most long-term care of older adults continues to be provided by families as opposed to nursing homes, assisted living facilities, social service agencies, or government programs. This continuing commitment to family care of older adults in the community is remarkable in view of relatively recent changes in the fabric of American society. American family life has undergone significant changes in the past three decades. Most households require two incomes, and greater numbers of women have entered the workforce. Delayed marriage and childbearing has produced a so-called sandwich generation of family caregivers that is simultaneously caring for two generations: their children and their parents. For the first time in U.S. history, adults may spend more years caring for a parent than for a child. Increased geographic separation of families further compounds the difficulties of family caregiving.

Another challenge is that the supply of caregivers is not keeping pace with the growth in the older population. The number of older adults for every 100 adults of working age (aged 20 to 64 years) is called the dependency ratio. Laura B. Shrestha of the Congressional Research Service notes in *Age Dependency Ratios and Social Security Solvency* (October 27, 2006, http://aging.senate .gov/crs/ss4.pdf) that in 2012 there will be an estimated 21.7 older adults for every 100 working-age adults. (See Table 9.1.) When the youngest members of the baby boomer generation (those born between 1946 and 1964) begin approaching retirement age in 2025, there will be 31.2 older adults for every 100 people of working age.

In *Retooling for an Aging America: Building the Health Care Workforce* (2008, http://www.nap.edu/openbook.php? record_id=12089&page=R1), the Institute of Medicine's Committee on the Future Health Care Workforce for Older Americans reports that an increasing number of Americans are hiring caregivers to assist with older relatives. About 3 million workers were employed in direct caregiving for older

adults in 2006, and the need for these caregivers is expected to outpace supply, largely because of the aging population but also because the number of women aged 26 to 54 years, the group that typically provides home care and personal care services, is not expected to grow.

Ike Wilson reports in "Health Care Field Needs Employees Other Than Nurses" (*Frederick [MD] News-Post*, April 20, 2011) that home health care services are booming, with one industry executive anticipating that 100,000 professional in-home caregivers would be hired nationally in 2011.

Furthermore, the Committee on the Future Health Care Workforce for Older Americans observes that about 80% of older adults rely exclusively on unpaid help from family and friends for assistance at home and that less than 10% receive all their care from paid workers. An estimated 29 million to 52 million Americans—as many as 31% of all U.S. adults—provide some kind of unpaid help or care.

FAMILY CAREGIVERS

According to the Family Caregiver Alliance, in "Selected Caregiver Statistics" (2011, http://www.caregiver .org/caregiver/jsp/content_node.jsp?nodeid=439), the majority of adults who received long-term care at home in 2011 relied exclusively on informal caregivers—family and friends. Every year, approximately 52 million Americans devote billions of hours providing this care, which includes help with tasks such as bathing, meal preparation, and managing medications, for adult family members aged 20 years and older. Thirty-four million caregivers provide care for adults aged 50 years and older, and of this group 8.9 million care for an older adult suffering from dementia (loss of intellectual functioning accompanied by memory loss and personality changes). Between 5.8 million and 7 million people provide care for adults aged 65 years and older, enabling them to remain in the community and age in place (remain in their own home rather than relocating to assisted living facilities or other supportive housing).

TABLE 9.1

Age dependency ratios, 2010–30

Year	Population (in thousands)				Dependency ratio (number of dependents per 100 persons of working age)		
	Total	Children (0–19)	Working age (20–64)	Older persons (65–65+)	All dependents	Children (0–19)	Older persons (65–65+)
2012	319,718	85,087	192,733	41,898	65.9	44.1	21.7
2013	322,215	85,283	193,681	43,251	66.4	44.0	22.3
2014	324,710	85,525	194,629	44,556	66.8	43.9	22.9
2015	327,202	85,796	195,496	45,910	67.4	43.9	23.5
2016	329,662	86,106	196,245	47,311	68.0	43.9	24.1
2017	332,086	86,466	196,874	48,746	68.7	43.9	24.8
2018	334,497	86,859	197,405	50,233	69.4	44.0	25.4
2019	336,892	87,247	197,826	51,819	70.3	44.1	26.2
2020	339,270	87,547	198,213	53,510	71.2	44.2	27.0
2021	341,626	87,736	198,642	55,248	72.0	44.2	27.8
2022	343,958	87,883	199,059	57,016	72.8	44.1	28.6
2023	346,255	88,003	199,475	58,777	73.6	44.1	29.5
2024	348,514	88,233	199,736	60,545	74.5	44.2	30.3
2025	350,729	88,597	199,789	62,343	75.5	44.3	31.2
2026	352,871	88,942	199,847	64,082	76.6	44.5	32.1
2027	354,936	89,266	199,965	65,705	77.5	44.6	32.9
2028	356,946	89,574	200,139	67,233	78.3	44.8	33.6
2029	358,898	89,863	200,347	68,688	79.1	44.9	34.3
2030	360,794	90,133	200,644	70,017	79.8	44.9	34.9

SOURCE: Adapted from Laura B. Shrestha, "Appendix Table 1. Age Dependency Ratios, United States, 1950–2080," in *Age Dependency Ratios and Social Security Solvency*, Congressional Research Service, The Library of Congress, October 27, 2006, http://aging.senate.gov/crs/ss4.pdf (accessed May 2, 2011)

The Family Caregiver Alliance also predicts that these volunteer family caregivers will remain the principal source of long-term home care services and that by 2050 an estimated 37 million unpaid caregivers will provide care for older adults in the United states. This figure represents an 85% increase from 2000.

Caregiving in the United States

In the fact sheet "Selected Caregiver Statistics" (2011, http://www.caregiver.org/caregiver/jsp/content_node.jsp?nodeid=439), the Family Caregiver Alliance describes the average caregiver as a middle-aged (35 to 64 years old) working woman who spends an average of 4.3 years caring for a parent who lives about 20 minutes away. One-fifth of caregivers provide 40 hours of care per week and more than 40% of caregivers have provided care for five years or longer and 20% for more than 10 years. Many caregivers are older adults themselves: the average age of caregivers caring for adults aged 50 years and older is 47 and the average age of caregivers caring for adults aged 65 years and older is 63. Older caregivers (aged 50 years and older) are more likely than younger ones to have been caregiving for more than 10 years.

Caregiving can take a toll on physical and mental health and well-being. Research reveals that caregivers may suffer a range of health problems including:

- Elevated blood pressure and insulin levels, which in turn increase the risk of developing cardiovascular disease

- High levels of physical and emotional stress and impaired immune function, which renders them less able to defend against illness

- Depression, anxiety, anger, and other emotional problems

The Economics of Caregiving

Most of the costs and responsibility for long-term care for older adults rest with family caregivers in the community. The shift toward increasing reliance on this informal system of care was spurred by changes in the health care delivery financing system that resulted in shorter hospital stays, rising costs of nursing home care, older adults preferring home care over institutional care, and a shortage of workers in all long-term care settings. Taken together, these factors continue to increase the likelihood that frail, disabled, and ill older adults will be cared for by relatives in the community.

During the next few decades, as the number of older people who need assistance to remain independent increases dramatically, the burden and cost of providing care to an ill or disabled relative will affect almost every U.S. household. UnitedHealthcare and the National Alliance for Caregiving observe in *Evercare Survey of the Economic Downturn and Its Impact on Family Caregiving* (April 28, 2009, http://www.caregiving.org/data/EVC_Caregivers_Economy_Report%20FINAL_4-28-09.pdf) that if the services of family caregivers for older adults were replaced by paid home health care staff, the cost would be $375 billion per year, more than the combined costs of home health care and nursing home care.

The Economic Downturn Affects Informal Caregiving

To assess the impact of the economic recession (which lasted from late December 2007 to mid-2009) and its lingering effects on caregivers and the people they care for, UnitedHealthcare and the National Alliance for Caregiving surveyed more than 1,000 family caregivers in 2009 and reported their findings in *Evercare Survey of the Economic Downturn and Its Impact on Family Caregiving*. The survey finds that the economic downturn placed additional pressure on caregivers, forcing many to change their living situation, use savings, or take on additional debt to pay for expenses that were associated with caregiving. Among the survey's key findings are:

- Forty-three percent reported the economic downturn resulted in a pay cut or reduction in their work hours, and 15% said they had been laid off.

- Nearly six out of 10 (59%) working caregivers said they were less comfortable taking time off from work to provide care, and just over one-third (35%) reported working additional hours or taking an additional job.

- About half (51%) of caregivers said the economic downturn increased their stress about their ability to continue to provide caregiving services.

- During the 12 months before the survey, 21% of caregivers had moved in with the person for whom they provided care. Caregivers with household incomes of less than $50,000 (27%) were nearly twice as likely as those with higher incomes (14%) to make such a move.

- Almost two-thirds (63%) of caregivers said they were saving less for retirement.

- Nearly a quarter (24%) of caregivers said they had cut back on spending that was associated with caregiving, and 13% said the economy had caused them to spend more on expenses that were associated with caregiving.

Furthermore, 65% of the caregivers who were spending more on the people they cared for in response to the economic downturn said this additional spending was a hardship, causing them difficulties in paying for their own basic necessities and bills. Other financial consequences of the downturn included being unable to sell a home or place a relative in a facility as planned and increased credit card debt.

The caregivers surveyed also reported emotional consequences of the economic downturn. More caregivers under the age of 65 years said they felt additional stress than their older counterparts, 54% and 31%, respectively. Fourteen percent of caregivers said the economy forced them to spend less time caregiving, and 27% reported that outside assistance from government agencies and nonprofit organizations had been cut back. Nearly two out of 10 (19%) caregivers said the quality of care their relative was receiving had declined as a result of the economy. Caregivers with the lowest household income (less than $25,000) were more likely to report a negative effect on the quality of care (27%) than those with higher incomes (14%).

The Effects of Health Care Reform Legislation on Informal Caregivers

In March 2010 President Barack Obama (1961–) signed the Patient Protection and Affordable Care Act into law. The law, which reformed health care delivery to improve access to care in the United States, will be fully implemented in 2014. The Family Caregiver Alliance explains in "Health Care Reform and Family Caregivers" (2010, http://www.caregiver.org/content/pdfs/HCR%20 provisions%20for%20caregivers-2010.pdf) that the law acknowledges the need for home care services and provides incentives for the states to provide these services through Medicaid (a federal and state health care program for people below the poverty level) for older adults with low incomes—up to 300% of the maximum Supplemental Security Income payment. Beginning in 2010 the law also allocated $10 million per year for five years to support Aging and Disability Resource Center initiatives, which serve as entry points for older adults in need of long-term care services. Furthermore, the law requires federally funded geriatric education centers to offer free or low-cost training to family caregivers.

The Effects of Health Care Reform Legislation on Paid Caregivers

The Patient Protection and Affordable Care Act redirects health care reimbursement to incentivize health professionals to care for people with chronic conditions in the community rather than in hospitals. It created the Independence at Home Medical Practice Pilot Program that beginning in January 2012 will provide coordinated, primary care services to Medicare beneficiaries with multiple chronic conditions in their home. It also created the Community-Based Care Transitions Program to assist Medicare beneficiaries to return to their home following hospital discharge.

Furthermore, the health care reform legislation aims to increase the numbers of health care workers by:

- Offering grant funding and other incentives to encourage students and health professionals to train in primary care, geriatrics, chronic care, and long-term care

- Providing funding to train health care workers who are direct-service providers such as home health aides and other providers of long-term and community-based services

- Establishing the Personal Care Attendants Workforce Advisory Panel to assess and advise on issues involving direct-care workers including salaries, wages, and benefits. It will also consider the total numbers of direct-care workers needed and the issues related to accessing services

- Instituting the National Health Care Workforce Commission to advise on ways to better meet the growing need for health care workers

In the press release "Home Care and Hospice Community Encouraged by CMS' Proposed 2012 Hospice Wage Index"

(April 29, 2011, http://www.nahc.org/media/mediaPR_042911.html), the National Association for Home Care and Hospice (NAHC) asserts that the increase in home care and hospice workers' wages proposed in Medicare's 2012 wage index (http://www.gpo.gov/fdsys/pkg/FR-2011-05-16/html/C1-2011-10689.htm) will improve access to these valuable services for older adults. Val J. Halamandaris, the president of the NAHC, opines, "While these changes begin to move us in the right direction, we need to build on this momentum and continue to find ways to advance and improve care, not stifle it."

THE CONTINUUM OF FORMAL SERVICES

As the older population increases, the segment of the population that is available to provide unpaid care, generally consisting of family members, has decreased. Because the availability of caregivers has diminished, increasing numbers of older adults in need of assistance will have to rely on a combination of family caregiving and paid professional services or on professional services alone.

Home Health Care

Home health care agencies provide a wide variety of services. Services range from helping with activities of daily living, such as bathing, light housekeeping, and meals, to skilled nursing care. Home health agencies employ registered nurses, licensed practical nurses, and nursing or home health aides to deliver the bulk of home care services. Other personnel involved in home health care include physical therapists, social workers, and speech-language pathologists.

Home health care grew faster during the early 1990s than any other segment of health services. Its growth may be attributable to the observation that in many cases caring for patients at home is preferable to and more cost effective than care that is provided in a hospital, nursing home, or some other residential facility.

Before 2000 Medicare coverage for home health care was limited to patients immediately following discharge from the hospital. By 2000 Medicare covered beneficiaries' home health care services with no requirement for prior hospitalization. There were also no limits to the number of professional visits or to the length of coverage. As long as the patient's condition warranted it, the following services were provided:

- Part-time or intermittent skilled nursing and home health aide services

- Speech-language pathology services

- Physical and occupational therapy

- Medical social services

- Medical supplies

- Durable medical equipment (with a 20% co-payment)

Since 2000 the population receiving home care services has changed. Even though the health reform legislation enacted in 2010 contains provisions to increase community-based chronic and long-term care, as of June 2011 much of home health care was associated with rehabilitation from critical illnesses, and fewer users were long-term patients with chronic (long-term) conditions. This changing pattern of use reflects a shift from longer-term care for chronic conditions to short-term postacute care. Compared to postacute care users, the long-term patients are older, more functionally disabled, more likely to be incontinent, and more expensive to serve.

According to the NAHC, in *Basic Statistics about Home Care* (2010, http://www.nahc.org/facts/10HC_Stats.pdf), approximately 12 million people received home care services from more than 33,000 providers of home care services, and annual expenditures for home health care services were an estimated $72.2 billion in 2009.

Respite Care and Adult Day Care

Respite care enables caregivers to take much-needed breaks from the demands of caregiving. It offers relief for families who may be overwhelmed and exhausted by the demands of caregiving and may be neglecting their own needs for rest and relaxation.

Respite care takes many forms. In some cases the respite worker comes to the home to take care of the older adult so that the caregiver can take a few hours off for personal needs, relaxation, or rest. Inpatient respite care, which is offered by some nursing homes and board-and-care facilities, provides an alternative to in-home care. Respite care is also available for longer periods, so that caregivers can recuperate from their own illnesses or even take vacations.

Adult day care programs, which are freestanding or based in hospitals, provide structured daytime programs where older adults may receive the social, health, and recreational services they need to restore or maintain optimal functioning. Even though they are not specifically intended to provide respite for caregivers, adult day care programs temporarily relieve families of the physical and emotional stress of caregiving.

Community Services

Besides home health care services, many communities offer a variety of services to help older adults and their caregivers:

- Home care aides to assist with chores such as housecleaning, grocery shopping, or laundry, as well as to help with the activities of daily living

- Repair services to help with basic home maintenance, as well as minor changes to make homes secure and safe, such as the installation of grab bars in bathrooms, special seats in the shower, or ramps for wheelchairs

- Home-delivered meal programs offering nutritious meals to those who can no longer cook or shop for groceries

- Companion and telephone reassurance services to keep in touch with older adults living alone (volunteers make regular visits or phone calls to check on and maintain contact with isolated older adults)

- Trained postal or utility workers to spot signs of trouble at the homes of older people

- Personal Emergency Response Systems devices that allow older adults to summon help in emergencies (when the user pushes the button on the wearable device, it sends a message to a response center or police station)

- Senior centers offering recreation programs, social activities, educational programs, health screenings, and meals

- Communities providing transportation to help older adults run errands, attend medical appointments, and make related trips (such services are often subsidized or free of charge)

- Adult day care centers providing care for older adults who need supervised assistance (services may include health care, recreation, meals, rehabilitative therapy, and respite care)

Home and Community-Based Services

Home and community-based services refer to the entire array of supportive services that help older people live independently in their home and community. In 1981 federal law implemented the Medicaid Home and Community-Based Services (HCBS) waiver program. Before the passage of this legislation, Medicaid long-term care benefits were primarily limited to nursing homes. The HCBS legislation provided a vehicle for states to offer services not otherwise available through their Medicaid programs to serve people in their own home and community, thereby preserving their independence and ties to family and friends at a cost no higher than that of institutional care. States have the flexibility to design HCBS waiver programs to meet the specific needs of defined groups.

Seven specific services may be provided under HCBS waivers:

- Case management services

- Homemaker services

- Home health aide services

- Personal care services

- Adult day care/health care services

- Respite care services

- Rehabilitation services

Other services may be provided at the request of the state if approved by the federal government. Services must be cost effective and necessary for the prevention of institutionalization. Further services may be provided to older adults and people with disabilities, people with developmental disabilities or mental retardation, and people with physical or mental illness. States have flexibility in designing their waiver programs; this allows them to tailor their programs to the specific needs of the populations they want to serve.

The HCBS waiver program has experienced tremendous growth since its enactment in 1981. According to the Centers for Medicare and Medicaid Services, in "HCBS Waivers—Section 1915 (c)" (April 11, 2011, http://www.cms.hhs.gov/MedicaidStWaivProgDemoPGI/05_HCBS Waivers-Section1915(c).asp), 48 states and the District of Columbia offered 287 of these programs in 2011.

The National Aging Network

The National Aging Network (September 20, 2010, http://www.eldercare.gov/ELDERCARE.NET/Public/About/Aging_Network/Index.aspx), which is funded by the Older Americans Act (OAA), provides funds for supportive home and community-based services to 629 area agencies on aging, 246 Native American organizations, 56 state units on aging, and over 29,000 service providers. It also awards funds for disease prevention/health promotion services, elder rights programs, the National Family Caregiver Support Program, and the Native American Caregiver Support Program. All older Americans may receive services through the OAA, but it specifically targets vulnerable older populations—those older adults who are disadvantaged by social or health disparities.

Eldercare Locator

The U.S. Administration on Aging sponsors the Eldercare Locator Directory (http://www.eldercare.gov/Eldercare.NET/Public/Index.aspx), a nationwide toll-free service that helps older adults and their caregivers find local services. The Eldercare Locator program connects those who contact it to an information specialist who has access to multiple databases, including the National Aging Network.

BenefitsCheckUp

The National Council on Aging offers the online BenefitsCheckUp program (http://www.benefitscheckup.org), which examines a database of more than 2,000 programs to determine older adults' eligibility for federal, state, and local private and public benefits and programs. Users respond to a few confidential questions and then the program lists which federal, state, and local programs they might be eligible for and how to apply. It is the first Internet-based service that is designed to help older Americans, their families, caregivers, and community organizations determine quickly and easily which benefits they qualify for and how to claim them.

In each state, there are approximately 70 programs available to individuals. Among the programs included are those that help older adults find income support, prescription drug savings, government health programs, energy assistance, property tax relief, nutrition programs, in-home services, veteran's programs, and volunteer, educational, and training programs. As of June 2011, the BenefitsCheckUp program had helped over 2.8 million people find benefits worth $10.1 billion to which they were entitled.

Geriatric Care Managers Help Older Adults Age in Place

The increasing complexity of arranging care for older adults, especially when families live at a distance from the older adults in need of care, has given rise to a relatively new service profession: geriatric care management. Geriatric care managers have varied educational backgrounds and professional credentials. They may be gerontologists (professionals who study the social, psychological, and biological aspects of aging), nurses, or social workers who specialize in issues that are related to aging and services for older adults. Geriatric care managers generally work with a formal or informal network of social workers, nurses, psychologists, elder law attorneys, advocates, and agencies that serve older adults.

Geriatric care managers work with families and increasingly with corporations wishing to assist employees to create flexible plans of care to meet the needs of older adults. They oversee home health staffing needs, monitor the quality of in-home services and equipment,

and serve as liaisons for families at a distance from their older relatives. In "Why Your Aging Parent Needs a Geriatric Care Manager" (Reuters, April 26, 2011), Toddi Gutner reports that fees for geriatric care management range from $60 to $300 per hour for follow-up, monitoring, and communicating with the family.

Hired homemakers/caregivers, transportation services, home modifications, and other services are also available. The total monthly cost of aging in place varies. An older adult who needs light housekeeping or companionship for three hours twice a week might spend around $300 per month, whereas someone who needs 24-hour-per-day supervision might pay $5,000 per month or more—much more if care from a certified home health aide or licensed vocational nurse is required.

Geriatric care management is especially important for older adults with dementia. In "Case Management Considerations of Progressive Dementia in a Home Setting" (*Professional Case Management*, vol. 15, no. 2, March–April 2010), Mary Ellen Pierce of Care Management Associates Inc. in Vancouver, Washington, explains that geriatric care managers can develop effective and individualized care plans for older adults with progressive dementia who prefer to live at home. Pierce concludes that "progressive dementia presents multiple challenges in the home care setting. Comprehensive, holistic assessment, preliminary discussions to eliminate barriers, and the creation of an individualized, specific care plan serve to create positive outcomes. The involvement of a professional case or case manager enhances this process by providing the knowledge, oversight, and guidance needed to successfully achieve patient and family goals."

CHAPTER 10

HEALTH CARE USE, EXPENDITURES, AND FINANCING

Health care use and expenditures tend to be concentrated among older adults. Because older adults often suffer multiple chronic conditions, they are hospitalized more frequently, use the most prescription and over-the-counter (nonprescription) drugs, make the highest number of physician visits, and require care from more physician-specialists and other health care providers—such as podiatrists and physical therapists—than any other age group.

Nearly all older Americans have health insurance through Medicare, which covers inpatient hospitalization, outpatient care, physician services, home health care, short-term skilled nursing facility care, hospice (end-of-life care) services, and prescription drugs. Historically, older adults' use of health care services has changed in response to physician practice patterns, advances in medical technology, and Medicare reimbursement for services. For example, advances in medical technology and physician practice patterns have shifted many medical procedures once performed in hospitals to outpatient settings such as ambulatory surgery centers.

Another example of changes in utilization occurred during the 1980s, when the average lengths of stay (ALOS) in hospitals for Medicare patients declined in response to the introduction of prospective payment and diagnostic-related groups—methods that are used to reimburse various providers for services performed. Even though the ALOS decreased between 1992 and 2007, the hospitalization rate increased from 306 to 365 hospital stays per 1,000 Medicare enrollees. (See Figure 10.1.)

Older adults are responsible for disproportionate health care expenditures. For example, the Centers for Medicare and Medicaid Services (CMS) notes in "NHE Fact Sheet" (June 14, 2011, https://www.cms.gov/NationalHealthExpend Data/25_NHE_Fact_Sheet.asp) that in 2004 older adults consisted of just 12% of the U.S. population, yet they accounted for 34% of health care expenditures. That same year personal health care spending for people aged 65 years and older was $14,797, which was 5.6 times higher than health care spending per child and 3.3 times higher than spending for working-aged adults. In "Healthy Aging: Helping People to Live Long and Productive Lives and Enjoy a Good Quality of Life—At a Glance 2011" (May 11, 2011, http://www.cdc.gov/chronic disease/resources/publications/AAG/aging.htm), the Centers for Disease Control and Prevention explains that these disproportionate expenses are in part attributable to the fact that 80% of older adults have one chronic health condition, and 50% have at least two chronic conditions. The CMS projects that the national health expenditure will grow to $4.6 trillion by 2019. (See Table 10.1; note that because these numbers are projections, they differ from numbers presented in other tables and figures.) Medicare is projected to reach $891.4 billion by 2019, accounting for more than 19% of all health care expenditures.

FINANCING HEALTH CARE FOR OLDER ADULTS

Until the March 2010 enactment of the Patient Protection and Affordable Care Act (PPACA), the United States was the only industrialized nation that did not have a national health care program. Nearly all other developed countries have national medical care programs that cover almost all health-related costs, from birth to long-term care.

The PPACA aims to ensure that all Americans have access to quality, affordable health care. Besides access to care, it addresses key components of health care reform including:

- Improving the quality and efficiency of health care—there will be special emphasis placed on improving clinical outcomes (how patients fare as a result of treatment) for people receiving care through government entitlement programs

- Prevention of chronic disease and improving public health—the PPACA created a new interagency council

FIGURE 10.1

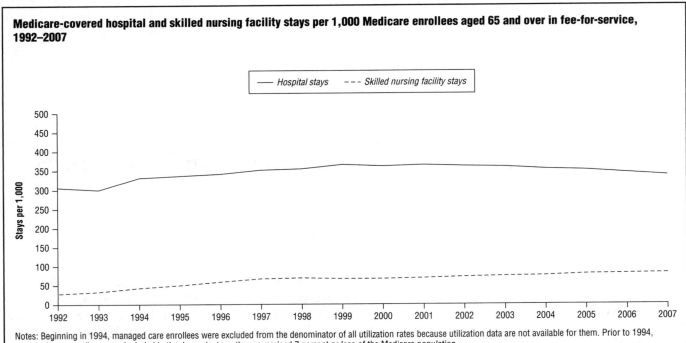

Medicare-covered hospital and skilled nursing facility stays per 1,000 Medicare enrollees aged 65 and over in fee-for-service, 1992–2007

Notes: Beginning in 1994, managed care enrollees were excluded from the denominator of all utilization rates because utilization data are not available for them. Prior to 1994, managed care enrollees were included in the denominators; they comprised 7 percent or less of the Medicare population.
Reference population: These data refer to Medicare enrollees in fee-for-service.

SOURCE: "Medicare-Covered Hospital and Skilled Nursing Facility Stays per 1,000 Medicare Enrollees Age 65 and over in Fee-for-Service, 1992–2007," in *Older Americans 2010: Key Indicators of Well-Being*, Federal Interagency Forum on Aging-Related Statistics, July 2010, http://www.agingstats.gov/agingstatsdotnet/Main_Site/Data/2010_Documents/Docs/OA_2010.pdf (accessed April 2, 2011)

to promote healthy policies and to establish a national prevention and health promotion strategy; it also established the Prevention and Public Health Investment Fund to expand and support continuing national investment in prevention and public health

• Health care workforce—increasing the supply, training, and quality of health care workers

• Transparency and program integrity—providing public information and combatting fraud and abuse

• Community living assistance services and supports (CLASS)—the PPACA instituted the CLASS Independence Benefit Plan, a voluntary, self-funded long-term care insurance program, to help older adults and others pay for community living assistance services

Of the many changes resulting from enactment of this health care reform legislation, several are particularly relevant to older adults. For example, the PPACA eliminates lifetime and unreasonable limits on benefits, prohibits cancellation of health insurance policies, and enables people with preexisting conditions to acquire insurance coverage. The act increases Medicare provider fees in rural areas and extends Medicare bonus payments for ground and air ambulance services in rural and other areas. It also created the independent, 15-member Medicare Advisory Board to present Congress with proposals to reduce costs and improve quality for Medicare beneficiaries.

The Health Care and Education Affordability Reconciliation Act of 2010 amends the PPACA. It contains a number of provisions that are important for older adults, including closing the Medicare prescription drug benefit known as the "doughnut hole." The U.S. Department of Health and Human Services explains in "What Is the Medicare Doughnut Hole?" (2011, http://answers.hhs.gov/questions/6136) that the doughnut hole is a coverage gap in the Medicare Part D program that requires Medicare beneficiaries to pay 100% of their prescription drug costs from the time when their total annual drug costs reach $2,830 until their total prescription costs reach $6,440. The PPACA retroactively provides a $250 rebate to each Medicare beneficiary who reached the doughnut hole by January 1, 2010. After January 1, 2011, the PPACA began decreasing the doughnut hole by reducing beneficiaries' co-payments, with the intention of completely closing the hole by 2020.

In the United States the major government health care entitlement programs are Medicare and Medicaid. They provide financial assistance for people aged 65 years and older, the poor, and people with disabilities. Before the existence of these programs, many older Americans could not afford adequate medical care. For older adults who are beneficiaries, the Medicare program provides reimbursement for hospital and physician care, whereas Medicaid pays for the cost of nursing home care.

TABLE 10.1

National health expenditures by source of funds, selected years 2004–19

Amount in billions

Year	Total	Out-of-pocket payments	Third-party payments Total	Private health insurance Total	Employer-Sponsored PHI	Exchanges	Other PHI	Other private funds	Public Total	Federal[a]	State and local[a]	Medicare[b]	Medicaid & CHIP[c]
Historical estimates													
2004	$1,855.4	$234.8	$1,620.6	$646.1				$134.5	$839.9	$599.8	$240.2	$311.3	$297.5
2005	1,982.5	247.5	1,735.0	691.0				144.3	899.8	641.4	258.4	339.8	319.1
2006	2,112.5	254.9	1,857.6	727.6				154.3	975.7	709.6	266.1	403.4	318.4
2007	2,239.7	270.3	1,969.4	759.7				171.0	1,038.7	755.3	283.4	432.2	337.9
2008	2,338.7	277.8	2,061.0	783.2				171.1	1,106.7	816.9	289.8	469.2	354.5
Projected													
2009	2,473.3	283.2	2,190.1	810.2	770.8	—	39.4	176.5	1,203.4	918.6	284.8	507.1	390.0
2010	2,600.2	288.4	2,311.8	844.9	802.4	—	42.6	182.5	1,284.4	982.9	301.5	534.4	427.3
2011	2,709.8	297.5	2,412.4	863.9	822.2	—	41.8	190.7	1,357.7	989.6	368.1	548.9	466.0
2012	2,851.6	309.3	2,542.3	895.4	852.6	—	42.8	201.0	1,445.9	1,058.2	387.8	585.7	501.5
2013	3,024.8	325.4	2,699.3	943.6	899.4	—	44.2	214.5	1,541.2	1,130.1	411.2	619.8	540.0
2014	3,302.4	321.8	2,980.6	1,064.7	971.7	84.4	8.7	224.5	1,691.4	1,248.6	442.8	655.8	634.1
2015	3,538.2	337.9	3,200.4	1,161.4	1,051.6	100.8	9.0	243.9	1,795.0	1,324.3	470.7	684.5	683.8
2016	3,795.9	353.8	3,442.1	1,257.6	1,102.2	146.1	9.3	266.0	1,918.5	1,417.6	501.0	723.1	737.5
2017	4,044.8	374.2	3,670.5	1,345.8	1,149.7	186.7	9.5	285.9	2,038.8	1,502.5	536.3	770.9	780.1
2018	4,297.6	410.2	3,887.4	1,397.5	1,182.5	205.6	9.4	306.3	2,183.6	1,611.3	572.4	828.0	835.5
2019	4,571.5	438.8	4,132.7	1,467.3	1,240.7	217.3	9.2	325.5	2,339.9	1,729.5	610.4	891.4	896.2

Per capita amount

Year	Total	Out-of-pocket payments	Third-party payments Total	Private health insurance Total	Employer-Sponsored PHI	Exchanges	Other PHI	Other private funds	Public Total	Federal[a]	State and local[a]	Medicare[b]	Medicaid & CHIP[c]
Historical estimates													
2004	$6,327	$801	$5,527	$2,204				$459	$2,864	$2,045	$819	d	d
2005	6,701	837	5,865	2,336				488	3,041	2,168	873	d	d
2006	7,071	853	6,218	2,435				517	3,266	2,375	891	d	d
2007	7,423	896	6,527	2,518				567	3,443	2,503	939	d	d
2008	7,681	912	6,768	2,572				562	3,635	2,683	952	d	d
Projected													
2009	8,050	922	7,129	2,637	2,509	—	128	574	3,917	2,990	927	d	d
2010	8,389	930	7,458	2,726	2,589	—	137	589	4,144	3,171	973	d	d
2011	8,666	951	7,714	2,763	2,629	—	134	610	4,342	3,165	1,177	d	d
2012	9,040	980	8,059	2,838	2,703	—	136	637	4,584	3,354	1,229	d	d
2013	9,505	1,023	8,483	2,965	2,826	—	139	674	4,843	3,551	1,292	d	d
2014	10,288	1,003	9,286	3,317	3,027	263	27	699	5,269	3,890	1,380	d	d
2015	10,928	1,044	9,885	3,587	3,248	311	28	753	5,544	4,090	1,454	d	d
2016	11,625	1,083	10,541	3,851	3,376	447	28	814	5,875	4,341	1,534	d	d
2017	12,282	1,136	11,146	4,087	3,491	567	29	868	6,191	4,563	1,629	d	d
2018	12,941	1,235	11,706	4,208	3,561	619	28	922	6,576	4,852	1,724	d	d
2019	13,652	1,311	12,342	4,382	3,705	649	27	972	6,988	5,165	1,823	d	d

Percent distribution

Year	Total	Out-of-pocket payments	Third-party payments Total	Private health insurance Total	Other private funds	Public Total	Federal[a]	State and local[a]	Medicare[b]	Medicaid & CHIP[c]
Historical estimates										
2004	100.0	12.7	87.3	34.8	7.2	45.3	32.3	12.9	16.8	16.0
2005	100.0	12.5	87.5	34.9	7.3	45.4	32.4	13.0	17.1	16.1
2006	100.0	12.1	87.9	34.4	7.3	46.2	33.6	12.6	19.1	15.1
2007	100.0	12.1	87.9	33.9	7.6	46.4	33.7	12.7	19.3	15.1
2008	100.0	11.9	88.1	33.5	7.3	47.3	34.9	12.4	20.1	15.2

TABLE 10.1

National health expenditures by source of funds, selected years 2004–19 [CONTINUED]

			Third-party payments									
			Private health insurance					Public				
Year	Total	Out-of-pocket payments	Total	Employer-Sponsored PHI	Exchanges	Other PHI	Other private funds	Total	Federal[a]	State and local[a]	Medicare[b]	Medicaid & CHIP[a]
Projected												
2009	100.0	11.4	32.8	31.2	—	1.6	7.1	48.7	37.1	11.5	20.5	15.8
2010	100.0	11.1	32.5	30.9	—	1.6	7.0	49.4	37.8	11.6	20.6	16.4
2011	100.0	11.0	31.9	30.3	—	1.5	7.0	50.1	36.5	13.6	20.3	17.2
2012	100.0	10.8	31.4	29.9	—	1.5	7.0	50.7	37.1	13.6	20.5	17.6
2013	100.0	10.8	31.2	29.7	—	1.5	7.1	51.0	37.4	13.6	20.5	17.9
2014	100.0	9.7	32.2	29.4	2.6	0.3	6.8	51.2	37.8	13.4	19.9	19.2
2015	100.0	9.5	32.8	29.7	2.8	0.3	6.9	50.7	37.4	13.3	19.3	19.3
2016	100.0	9.3	33.1	29.0	3.8	0.2	7.0	50.5	37.3	13.2	19.0	19.4
2017	100.0	9.3	33.3	28.4	4.6	0.2	7.1	50.4	37.1	13.3	19.1	19.3
2018	100.0	9.5	32.5	27.5	4.8	0.2	7.1	50.8	37.5	13.3	19.3	19.4
2019	100.0	9.6	32.1	27.1	4.8	0.2	7.1	51.2	37.8	13.4	19.5	19.6
Annual percent change from previous year shown												
Historical estimates												
2004	—	—	—	—	—	—	—	—	—	—	—	—
2005	6.9	5.4	6.9	—	—	—	7.3	7.1	6.9	7.6	9.2	7.2
2006	6.6	3.0	5.3	—	—	—	7.0	8.4	10.6	3.0	18.7	-0.2
2007	6.0	6.0	4.4	—	—	—	10.8	6.5	6.4	6.5	7.1	6.2
2008	4.4	2.8	3.1	—	—	—	0.1	6.5	8.2	2.2	8.6	4.9
Projected												
2009	5.8	1.9	3.5	—	—	—	3.2	8.7	12.4	-1.7	8.1	10.0
2010	5.1	1.9	4.3	4.1	—	8.1	3.4	6.7	7.0	5.8	5.4	9.6
2011	4.2	3.1	2.2	2.5	—	-1.9	4.5	5.7	0.7	22.1	2.7	9.0
2012	5.2	4.0	3.6	3.7	—	2.6	5.4	6.5	6.9	5.3	6.7	7.6
2013	6.1	5.2	5.4	5.5	—	3.1	6.7	6.6	6.8	6.0	5.8	7.7
2014	9.2	-1.1	12.8	8.0	—	-80.4	4.6	9.7	10.5	7.7	4.4	17.4
2015	7.1	5.0	9.1	8.2	19.5	4.4	8.7	6.1	6.1	6.3	5.6	7.8
2016	7.3	4.7	8.3	4.8	44.9	2.6	9.0	6.9	7.0	6.4	6.6	7.8
2017	6.6	5.8	7.0	4.3	27.8	2.0	7.5	6.3	6.0	7.0	7.4	5.8
2018	6.3	9.6	3.8	2.9	10.1	-3.0	7.1	7.1	7.2	6.7	7.7	7.1
2019	6.4	7.0	5.0	4.9	5.7	-2.5	6.3	7.2	7.3	6.7	7.7	7.3

PHI = Private Health Insurance.

CHIP = Children's Health Insurance Program.

Notes: Per capita amounts based on July 1 Census resident based population estimates. Numbers and percents may not add to totals because of rounding. The health spending projections were based on the 2008 version of the National Health Expenditures released in January 2010, updated to take into account the impact of health reform and other relevant legislation and regulatory changes.

[a] Includes CHIP.

[b] Subset of federal funds.

[c] Subset of federal and State and local funds.

[d] Calculation of per capita estimates is inappropriate.

SOURCE: "Table 2. National Health Expenditures; Aggregate and per Capita Amounts, Percent Distribution and Annual Percent Change by Source of Funds: Calendar Years 2004–2019," in *National Health Expenditures Projections 2009–2019*, Centers for Medicare and Medicaid Services, Office of the Actuary, 2010, https://www.cms.gov/NationalHealthExpendData/downloads/NHEProjections2009to2019.pdf (accessed May 3, 2011)

FIGURE 10.2

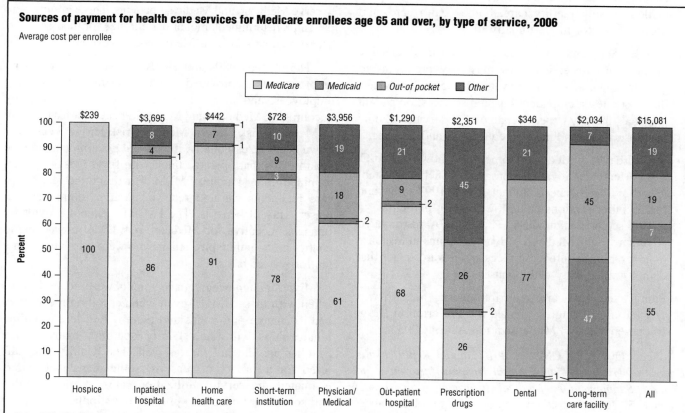

Sources of payment for health care services for Medicare enrollees age 65 and over, by type of service, 2006

Average cost per enrollee

Notes: "Other" refers to private insurance, Department of Veterans Affairs, and other public programs.
Reference population: These data refer to Medicare enrollees.

SOURCE: "Sources of Payment for Health Care Services for Medicare Enrollees Age 65 and over, by Type of Service, 2006," in *Older Americans 2010: Key Indicators of Well-Being*, Federal Interagency Forum on Aging-Related Statistics, July 2010, http://www.agingstats.gov/agingstatsdotnet/Main_Site/Data/2010_Documents/Docs/OA_2010.pdf (accessed April 2, 2011)

MEDICARE

The spirit in which this law is written draws deeply upon the ancient dreams of all mankind. In Leviticus, it is written, "Thou shall rise up before the hoary head, and honor the face of an old man."

—Senator Russell B. Long (D-LA) at the original vote for Medicare in 1965

The Medicare program, which was enacted under Title XVIII ("Health Insurance for the Aged") of the Social Security Act, was signed into law by President Lyndon B. Johnson (1908–1973) and went into effect on July 1, 1966. That year 19 million older adults entered the program. Michelle M. Megellas of Novartis Pharmaceuticals in Colleyville, Texas, forecasts in "Medicare Modernization: The New Prescription Drug Benefit and Redesigned Part B and Part C" (*Proceedings Baylor University Medical Center*, vol. 19, no. 1, January 2006) that by 2030 the number of Americans insured by Medicare will exceed 78 million.

The establishment of the Medicare program in 1966 served to improve equity in health care. Before the creation of Medicare about half of the older population was uninsured, and the insured population was often limited

to benefits of just $10 per day. Furthermore, because poverty rates among older adults hovered at about 30%, the older population could not be expected to pay for private health insurance. The Medicare program extended health care coverage to a population with growing health needs and little income.

In 2006, 40 years after its inception, the Medicare program covered 55% of the health care costs of older Americans. (See Figure 10.2.) Medicaid covered 7% and other payers, primarily private health insurers, covered 19%. Older adults paid 19% of their health care costs out of pocket. Historically, Medicare has focused almost exclusively on acute (short-term) care services such as hospitals, physicians, and short-term rehabilitation and home health care, but in 2006 Medicare offered its first prescription drug benefits. Other public and private payers finance long-term care.

The Medicare program is composed of several parts:

- Part A provides hospital insurance. Coverage includes physicians' fees, nursing services, meals, semiprivate rooms, special care units, operating room costs, laboratory tests, and some drugs and supplies. Part A also covers rehabilitation services, limited posthospital skilled nursing facility care, home health care, and hospice care for the terminally ill.

- Part B (Supplemental Medical Insurance) is elective medical insurance; enrollees must pay premiums to get coverage. It covers private physicians' services, diagnostic tests, outpatient hospital services, outpatient physical therapy, speech pathology services, home health services, and medical equipment and supplies.

- The third part of Medicare, sometimes known as Part C, is the Medicare Advantage program, which was established by the Balanced Budget Act of 1997 to expand beneficiaries' options and allow them to participate in private-sector health plans. The PPACA restructured payments to the Medicare Advantage plans in response to geographic differences in fees and rewards plans that demonstrate quality with bonuses.

- Part D, the Medicare prescription drug benefit, was enacted after Congress passed the Prescription Drug, Improvement, and Modernization Act of 2003.

According to the CMS, in *2010 Annual Report of the Boards of Trustees of the Federal Hospital Insurance and Federal Supplementary Medical Insurance Trust Funds* (August 5, 2010, https://www.cms.gov/ReportsTrustFunds/downloads/tr2010.pdf), in 2009, $502 million was spent to provide coverage for the 46.3 million people who were enrolled in Medicare. The majority (38.7 million or 84%) of Medicare recipients were aged 65 years and older and 7.6 million were people with disabilities. The CMS estimates that 92.7 million people will be eligible for Medicare by 2050. The CMS concludes that "the financial outlook for the Medicare program is substantially improved as a result of the far-reaching changes in the Patient Protection and Affordable Care Act."

Reimbursement under Medicare

Historically, Medicare reimbursed physicians on a fee-for-service basis (paid for each visit, procedure, or treatment delivered), as opposed to per capita (per head) or per member per month (PMPM). In response to the increasing administrative burden of paperwork, reduced compensation, and delays in reimbursements, some physicians opt out of Medicare participation—they do not provide services under the Medicare program and choose not to accept Medicare patients into their practice. Others continue to provide services to Medicare beneficiaries, but they do not "accept assignment"—that is, their patients must pay out of pocket for services and then seek reimbursement from Medicare.

The Tax Equity and Fiscal Responsibility Act of 1982 authorized a "risk managed care" option for Medicare, based on agreed-on prepayments. Beginning in 1985 CMS could contract to pay health care providers, such as health maintenance organizations (HMOs) or other prepaid plans, to serve Medicare and Medicaid patients. These groups were paid a predetermined amount per enrollee for their services. These became known as Medicare-risk HMOs.

During the 1980s and 1990s the federal government, employers that provided health coverage for retiring employees, and many states sought to control costs by encouraging Medicare and Medicaid beneficiaries to enroll in Medicare-risk HMOs. Medicare-risk HMOs kept costs down because, essentially, the federal government paid the health plans that operated them with fixed fees—a predetermined dollar amount PMPM. For this fixed fee, Medicare recipients were to receive a fairly comprehensive, preset array of benefits. The PMPM payment provided a financial incentive for Medicare-risk HMO physicians to control costs, unlike physicians who were reimbursed on a fee-for-service basis.

Even though Medicare recipients were generally satisfied with these HMOs (even when enrolling meant they had to change physicians and thereby end long-standing relationships with their family doctors), many of the health plans did not fare as well. The health plans suffered for a variety of reasons: some plans had underestimated the service utilization rates of older adults, and some were unable to provide the stipulated range of services as effectively as they were intended. For other plans, the PMPM payment was simply not sufficient to enable them to cover all the clinical services and administrative overhead.

Regardless, the health plans providing these "senior HMOs" competed fiercely to market to and enroll older adults. Some health plans feared that closing their Medicare-risk programs would be viewed negatively by employer groups, which, when faced with the choice of plans that offered coverage for both younger workers and retirees or one that only covered the younger workers, would choose the plans that covered both. Despite losing money, most health plans maintained their Medicare-risk programs to avoid alienating the employers they depended on to enroll workers who were younger, healthier, and less expensive to serve than the older adults.

Approximately 10 years into operations, some Medicare-risk programs faced a challenge that proved insurmountable. Their enrollees had aged and required even more health care services than they had previously. For example, a senior HMO member who had joined as a healthy 65-year-old could now be a frail 75-year-old with multiple chronic health conditions requiring many costly health care services. The PMPM had increased over the years, but for some health plans it was simply insufficient to cover their costs. Many health plans, especially the smaller ones, were forced to end their Medicare-risk programs abruptly, leaving thousands of older adults scrambling to join other health plans. Others have endured, offering older adults comprehensive care and generating substantial cost savings for employers and the federal government.

Medicare Advantage

The Balanced Budget Act of 1997 replaced the Medicare-risk plans with Medicare+Choice, which later became known as Medicare Advantage. These plans offer Medicare beneficiaries a wider range of managed care plan options than just HMOs—older adults can join preferred provider organizations and provider-sponsored organizations that generally offer greater freedom of choice of providers (physicians and hospitals) than is available through HMO membership. Figure 10.3 shows the two ways to obtain Medicare coverage: through traditional, or original, Medicare or through a Medicare Advantage plan.

When older adults join the Medicare Advantage plans that have entered into contracts with the CMS, the plans are paid a fixed amount PMPM, which represents Medicare's

share of the cost of the services. The attraction of these plans is that members no longer have to pay the regular Medicare deductibles and co-payments for Medicare-covered services. Some plans charge modest monthly premiums, and/or nominal co-payments as services are used, but there are no other charges by the plan for physician visits, hospitalization, or use of other covered services. However, members of the Medicare Advantage plans must continue to pay the Medicare Part B monthly premium. According to the CMS, in "Will Premiums for Medicare Advantage Plans Go up in 2011?" (2011, http://www.medicare.com/advantage-plans/will-premiums-for-medicare-advantage-plans-go-up-in-2011.html), 11.8 million Medicare beneficiaries were enrolled in the Medicare Advantage plans in 2010.

In *Reaching for the Stars: Quality Ratings of Medicare Advantage Plans, 2011* (February 2011, http://www.kff.org/medicare/upload/8151.pdf), the Kaiser Family Foundation observes that the 2010 health care reform legislation stipulates that by 2012 all Medicare Advantage plans' quality ratings, which assign one to five stars (one star indicates poor performance and five stars denote excellent performance), will be used to calculate payments. Plans that receive four-star ratings or better will receive bonus payments.

The Kaiser Family Foundation reports that in 2011 nearly one-quarter (24%) of all Medicare Advantage members were in plans that received ratings of four or more stars. Nonetheless, six out of 10 (60%) Medicare Advantage members were in plans that received 3 to 3.5 stars, which the CMS defines as average performance, and 7% were in plans that earned fewer than 3 stars. In 2011 the average Medicare Advantage rating was 3.47 stars.

Insurance to Supplement Medicare Benefits

In 2008, 12 million (32.7%) older adults had private insurance obtained through the workplace to supplement their Medicare coverage. (See Table 10.2.) The most popular private insurance is supplemental insurance known as Medigap insurance. Federal regulations mandate that all Medigap policies sold offer a standard minimum set of benefits, but there are 10 standard variations that offer additional coverage and benefits. As Table 10.2 shows, the percentage of older adults with Medigap insurance has declined from 32.5% in 1995 to 21.5% in 2008, and the percentage with only Medicare or another public plan has risen from 10.5% in 1995 to 14.9% in 2008.

Besides Medigap policies, older adults may also purchase Medicare supplement health insurance called Medicare SELECT, which offers essentially the same coverage as Medigap policies, but it requires use of preferred providers (specific hospitals and in some cases plan physicians) to receive full benefits. Even though Medicare SELECT policies restrict older adults' choices, they are generally less expensive than Medigap policies.

FIGURE 10.3

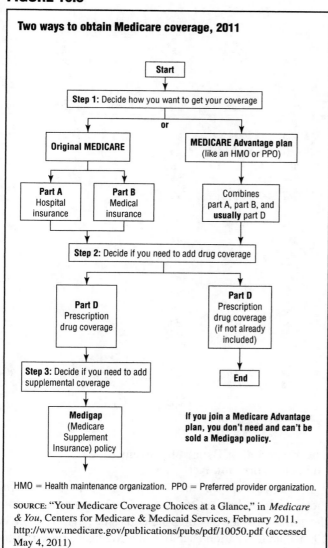

Two ways to obtain Medicare coverage, 2011

HMO = Health maintenance organization. PPO = Preferred provider organization.

SOURCE: "Your Medicare Coverage Choices at a Glance," in *Medicare & You*, Centers for Medicare & Medicaid Services, February 2011, http://www.medicare.gov/publications/pubs/pdf/10050.pdf (accessed May 4, 2011)

TABLE 10.2

Health insurance coverage for persons aged 65 and over, according to type of coverage and selected characteristics, selected years 1992–2008

[Data are based on household interviews of a sample of noninstitutionalized Medicare beneficiaries]

Characteristic	Medicare Health Maintenance Organization[a]					Medicaid[b]				
	1992	1995	2000	2007	2008	1992	1995	2000	2007	2008
Age					Number in millions					
65 years and over	1.1	2.6	5.9	7.3	8.1	2.7	2.8	2.7	3.3	3.2
					Percent of population					
65 years and over	3.9	8.9	19.3	20.4	22.1	9.4	9.6	9.0	9.2	8.8
65–74 years	4.2	9.5	20.6	21.0	22.9	7.9	8.8	8.5	8.8	8.2
75–84 years	3.7	8.3	18.5	20.8	23.0	10.6	9.6	8.9	9.3	9.1
85 years and over	*	7.3	16.3	17.0	16.5	16.6	13.6	11.2	11.4	10.3
Sex										
Male	4.6	9.2	19.3	21.9	23.6	6.3	6.2	6.3	6.6	5.8
Female	3.4	8.6	19.3	19.2	20.9	11.6	12.0	10.9	11.4	11.2
Race and Hispanic origin										
White, not Hispanic or Latino	3.6	8.4	18.4	18.5	20.2	5.6	5.4	5.1	5.7	5.4
Black, not Hispanic or Latino	*	7.9	20.7	27.9	28.5	28.5	30.3	23.6	18.8	20.0
Hispanic	*	15.5	27.5	36.7	37.5	39.0	40.5	28.7	24.4	21.1
Percent of poverty level[c]										
Below 100%	3.6	7.7	18.4	—	—	22.3	17.2	15.9	—	—
100%–less than 200%	3.7	9.5	23.4	—	—	6.7	6.3	8.4	—	—
200% or more	4.2	10.1	18.0	—	—	*	*	*	—	—
Marital status										
Married	4.6	9.5	18.7	22.2	24.2	4.0	4.3	4.3	4.1	4.0
Widowed	2.3	7.7	19.4	15.8	17.1	14.9	15.0	13.6	14.3	13.9
Divorced	*	9.7	24.4	24.5	25.5	23.4	24.5	20.2	18.0	16.8
Never married	*	*	15.8	21.1	20.7	19.2	19.0	17.0	22.1	18.2

Characteristic	Employer-sponsored plan[d]					Medigap[e]				
	1992	1995	2000	2007	2008	1992	1995	2000	2007	2008
Age					Number in millions					
65 years and over	12.5	11.3	10.7	12.1	12.0	9.9	9.5	7.6	7.9	7.9
					Percent of population					
65 years and over	42.8	38.6	35.2	33.8	32.7	33.9	32.5	25.0	22.0	21.5
65–74 years	46.9	41.1	36.6	35.1	34.0	31.4	29.9	21.7	20.4	19.6
75–84 years	38.2	37.1	35.0	33.1	31.2	37.5	35.2	27.8	22.9	22.7
85 years and over	31.6	30.2	29.4	30.2	31.1	38.3	37.6	31.1	26.2	26.3
Sex										
Male	46.3	42.1	37.7	36.5	35.3	30.6	30.0	23.4	20.2	20.1
Female	40.4	36.0	33.4	31.6	30.7	36.2	34.4	26.2	23.4	22.7
Race and Hispanic origin										
White, not Hispanic or Latino	45.9	41.3	38.6	36.8	35.4	37.2	36.2	28.3	25.3	24.9
Black, not Hispanic or Latino	25.9	26.7	22.0	25.8	23.2	13.6	10.2	7.5	7.3	6.5
Hispanic	20.7	16.9	15.8	16.2	19.7	15.8	10.1	11.3	7.7	7.8
Percent of poverty level[c]										
Below 100%	29.0	32.1	28.1	—	—	30.8	29.8	22.6	—	—
100%–less than 200%	37.5	32.0	27.0	—	—	39.3	39.1	28.4	—	—
200% or more	58.4	52.8	49.0	—	—	32.8	32.2	26.2	—	—
Marital status										
Married	49.9	44.6	41.0	39.1	38.3	33.0	32.6	25.6	22.1	21.4
Widowed	34.1	30.3	28.7	28.7	27.6	37.5	35.2	26.7	24.3	23.6
Divorced	27.3	26.6	22.4	22.3	19.3	27.9	24.1	16.9	16.1	18.5
Never married	38.0	35.1	28.5	28.1	28.9	29.1	26.2	21.9	17.4	14.6

A less popular option is hospital indemnity coverage—insurance that pays a fixed cash amount for each day of hospitalization up to a designated number of days. Some coverage may have added benefits such as surgical benefits or skilled nursing home benefits. Most policies have a maximum annual number of days or a lifetime maximum payment amount.

The Prescription Drug, Improvement, and Modernization Act

Congress passed the Prescription Drug, Improvement, and Modernization Act of 2003, which represents the largest expansion of Medicare since its creation in 1965. The legislation established a Medicare prescription drug benefit. The benefit was phased in and took full

TABLE 10.2

Health insurance coverage for persons aged 65 and over, according to type of coverage and selected characteristics, selected years 1992–2008 [CONTINUED]

[Data are based on household interviews of a sample of noninstitutionalized Medicare beneficiaries]

Characteristic	Medicare fee-for-service only or other[f]				
	1992	1995	2000	2007	2008
Age			Number in millions		
65 years and over	2.9	3.1	3.5	5.2	5.5
			Percent of population		
65 years and over	9.9	10.5	11.5	14.6	14.9
65–74 years	9.7	10.7	12.6	14.8	15.2
75–84 years	10.1	9.9	9.9	14.0	14.0
85 years and over	10.8	11.3	12.1	15.2	15.8
Sex					
Male	12.2	12.6	13.3	14.8	15.1
Female	8.3	8.9	10.2	14.4	14.7
Race and Hispanic origin					
White, not Hispanic or Latino	7.7	8.7	9.6	13.7	14.1
Black, not Hispanic or Latino	26.7	25.0	26.1	20.2	21.7
Hispanic	18.3	17.1	16.7	15.0	13.9
Percent of poverty level[c]					
Below 100%	14.3	13.3	15.1	—	—
100%–less than 200%	12.9	13.1	12.7	—	—
200% or more	4.0	4.5	6.3	—	—
Marital status					
Married	8.5	9.0	10.5	12.6	12.1
Widowed	11.2	11.9	11.6	16.8	17.7
Divorced	15.7	15.1	16.1	19.1	20.0
Never married	*	13.1	16.8	11.4	17.7

*Estimates are considered unreliable if the sample cell size is 50 or fewer.
—Data not available.
[a]Enrollee has Medicare Health Maintenance Organization (HMO) regardless of other insurance.
[b]Enrolled in Medicaid and not enrolled in a Medicare risk HMO.
[c]Percent of poverty level is based on family income and family size and composition using U.S. Census Bureau poverty thresholds.
[d]Private insurance plans purchased through employers (own, current, or former employer, family business, union, or former employer or union of spouse) and not enrolled in a Medicare risk HMO or Medicaid.
[e]Supplemental insurance purchased privately or through organizations such as Association of American Retired Persons (AARP) or professional organizations, and not enrolled in a Medicare risk HMO, Medicaid, employer-sponsored plan.
[f]Medicare fee-for-service only or other public plans (except Medicaid).
Notes: Data for noninstitutionalized Medicare beneficiaries. Insurance categories are mutually exclusive. Persons with more than one type of coverage are categorized according to the order in which the health insurance categories appear. Data for additional years are available.

SOURCE: "Table 139. Health Insurance Coverage of Medicare Beneficiaries 65 Years of Age and over, by Type of Coverage and Selected Characteristics: United States, Selected Years 1992–2008," in *Health, United States 2010: With Special Feature on Death and Dying*, National Center for Health Statistics, 2011, http://www.cdc.gov/nchs/data/hus/hus10.pdf (accessed April 8, 2011).

effect in January 2006. Among other things, it provides help for low-income beneficiaries and those with the highest drug costs.

Medicare Prescription Drug Coverage

Enrollees in the Medicare prescription drug program, called Part D, pay a monthly premium, which varies by plan, and a yearly deductible that in 2011 was no more than $310. They also pay a part of the cost of their prescriptions, including a co-payment or coinsurance. Table 10.3 shows how the prescription drug plan works for Ms. Smith, a hypothetical Medicare drug plan member in 2011. Costs vary among the different drug plans— some plans offer more coverage and access to a wider range of drugs for a higher monthly premium. According to the Kaiser Family Foundation, in "Income-Relating

Medicare Part B and Part D Premiums: How Many Medicare Beneficiaries Will Be Affected?" (December 2010, http://www.kff.org/medicare/upload/8126.pdf), in 2011 the monthly Part D premiums ranged from $32.34 to $126.82. Older adults with limited incomes may not have to pay premiums or deductibles for the drug coverage.

Medicare Faces Challenges

Like Social Security, the Medicare program's continuing financial viability is in jeopardy. The Social Security and Medicare trust funds are examined annually by the Social Security and Medicare Boards of Trustees, who publish an annual report on the current and projected financial status of the two programs. This section reviews the origins of the challenges Medicare faces and the Trustees' findings in *The 2010 Annual Report of the Board of*

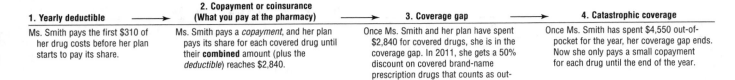

TABLE 10.3

How Medicare Part D provides prescription drug benefits, 2011

Monthly premium—Ms. Smith pays a monthly premium throughout the year.

1. Yearly deductible	2. Copayment or coinsurance (What you pay at the pharmacy)	3. Coverage gap	4. Catastrophic coverage
Ms. Smith pays the first $310 of her drug costs before her plan starts to pay its share.	Ms. Smith pays a *copayment*, and her plan pays its share for each covered drug until their **combined** amount (plus the *deductible*) reaches $2,840.	Once Ms. Smith and her plan have spent $2,840 for covered drugs, she is in the coverage gap. In 2011, she gets a 50% discount on covered brand-name prescription drugs that counts as out-of-pocket spending, and helps her get out of the coverage gap.	Once Ms. Smith has spent $4,550 out-of-pocket for the year, her coverage gap ends. Now she only pays a small copayment for each drug until the end of the year.

SOURCE: "Monthly Premium—Ms. Smith Pays a Monthly Premium throughout the Year," in *Medicare & You*, Centers for Medicare & Medicaid Services, February 2011, http://www.medicare.gov/ publications/pubs/pdf/10050.pdf (accessed May 4, 2011)

FIGURE 10.4

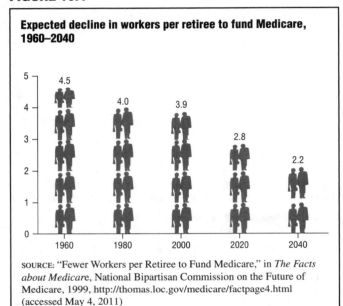

Expected decline in workers per retiree to fund Medicare, 1960–2040

SOURCE: "Fewer Workers per Retiree to Fund Medicare," in *The Facts about Medicare*, National Bipartisan Commission on the Future of Medicare, 1999, http://thomas.loc.gov/medicare/factpage4.html (accessed May 4, 2011)

FIGURE 10.5

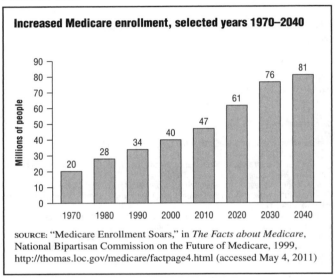

Increased Medicare enrollment, selected years 1970–2040

SOURCE: "Medicare Enrollment Soars," in *The Facts about Medicare*, National Bipartisan Commission on the Future of Medicare, 1999, http://thomas.loc.gov/medicare/factpage4.html (accessed May 4, 2011)

Trustees of the Federal Old-Age and Survivors Insurance and Federal Disability Insurance Trust Funds (August 9, 2010, http://www.ssa.gov/oact/TR/2010/tr2010.pdf).

A NATIONAL BIPARTISAN COMMISSION CONSIDERS THE FUTURE OF MEDICARE. The National Bipartisan Commission on the Future of Medicare was created by Congress in the Balanced Budget Act of 1997. The commission was charged with examining the Medicare program and drafting recommendations to avert a future financial crisis and reinforce the program in anticipation of the retirement of the baby boomers (people born between 1946 and 1964).

The commission observed that like Social Security, Medicare would suffer because there would be fewer workers per retiree to fund it. (See Figure 10.4.) It predicted that beneficiaries' out-of-pocket costs would rise and forecasted soaring Medicare enrollment. (See

Figure 10.5.) Perhaps the commission's direst prediction was the determination that, without reform, the Medicare Part A fund would become bankrupt by 2008.

When the commission disbanded in March 1999, it was unable to forward an official recommendation to Congress because the plan it proposed fell one vote short of the required majority needed to authorize an official recommendation. The plan would have changed Medicare into a premium system, where instead of Medicare directly covering beneficiaries, the beneficiaries would be given a fixed amount of money to purchase private health insurance. The plan would have also raised the age of eligibility from 65 to 67, as has already been done with Social Security, and provided prescription drug coverage for low-income beneficiaries, much like the Medicare Prescription Drug, Improvement, and Modernization Act of 2003.

THE MEDICARE PRESCRIPTION DRUG, IMPROVEMENT, AND MODERNIZATION ACT AIMS TO REFORM MEDICARE. The Medicare Prescription Drug, Improvement, and Modernization Act of 2003 is a measure intended to introduce private-sector enterprise into a Medicare model in urgent need of reform. Under the act, premiums and deductibles may rise quickly because they are indexed to the growth in per capita Medicare expenditures.

Older adults with substantial incomes face increasing premium costs. According to the CMS, in "2011 Part B Premium Amounts for Persons with Higher Income Levels" (November 5, 2010, https://questions.medicare.gov/app/answers/detail/a_id/2306/session/L2F2LzEvc2lkL3hFMXYtN3Rr), in 2011 older adults with annual incomes of $85,000 or less or couples earning $170,000 or less paid the standard premium. Individuals and couples with higher incomes paid additional income-adjusted amounts monthly, ranging from $96.40 to $369.10 per month.

The act also expanded coverage of preventive medical services. According to the CMS, new beneficiaries receive a free physical examination along with laboratory tests to screen for heart disease and diabetes. The act also provided employers with $89 billion in subsidies and tax breaks to help offset the costs that are associated with maintaining retiree health benefits.

Medicare's Problems May Be More Urgent Than Those of Social Security

Forecasts of Medicare costs show them outpacing Social Security costs because it is anticipated that per capita health care costs will continue to grow faster than the per capita gross domestic product (GDP; the total value of goods and services produced by the United States) in the future. In *Status of the Social Security and Medicare Programs: A Summary of the 2011 Annual Reports* (May 5, 2011, http://www.ssa.gov/oact/TRSUM/index.html), the Social Security and Medicare Boards of Trustees project that Medicare expenditures will increase from 3.6% of the GDP in 2010, to 5.6% in 2035, to 6.2% by 2085. (See Figure 10.6.) According to the Trustees, Medicare paid out more in benefits than it collected in 2011 and that by 2024 it will be insolvent (incapable of meeting financial obligations). The Trustees observe that the 2010 health care reform legislation improved the financial outlook for Medicare. The 2010 projections for Medicare consider the cost reductions that were mandated by the health care reform legislation. Nonetheless, the Trustees caution that "projected long-run program costs for both Medicare and Social Security are not sustainable under currently scheduled financing, and will require legislative corrections if disruptive consequences for beneficiaries and taxpayers are to be avoided." The Trustees call for prompt action to address the financial imbalances for Medicare and Social Security.

MEDICAID

Congress enacted Medicaid in 1965 under Title XIX ("Grants to States for Medical Assistance Programs") of the Social Security Act. It is a joint federal-state program

FIGURE 10.6

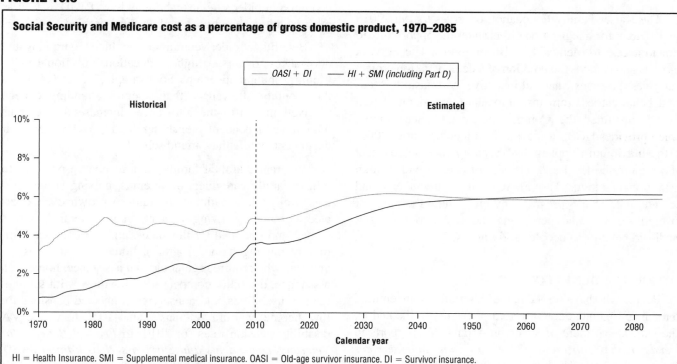

Social Security and Medicare cost as a percentage of gross domestic product, 1970–2085

HI = Health Insurance. SMI = Supplemental medical insurance. OASI = Old-age survivor insurance. DI = Survivor insurance.

SOURCE: "Chart A. Social Security and Medicare Cost as a Percentage of GDP," in *Status of the Social Security and Medicare Programs: A Summary of the 2011 Annual Reports*, U.S. Social Security Administration, Office of the Chief Actuary, May 5, 2011, http://www.socialsecurity.gov/OACT/TRSUM/ (accessed June 23, 2011)

that provides medical assistance to selected categories of low-income Americans: the aged, people who are blind and/or disabled, and families with dependent children. Medicaid covers hospitalization, physicians' fees, laboratory and radiology fees, and long-term care in nursing homes. It is the largest source of funds for medical and health-related services for the United States' poorest people and the second-largest public payer of health care costs, after Medicare. In 2006 Medicaid provided coverage for 7% of adults aged 65 years and older. (See Figure 10.2.)

The Kaiser Family Foundation reports in "Medicaid and Long-Term Care Services and Supports" (March 2011, http://www.kff.org/medicaid/upload/2186-08.pdf) that Medicaid long-term care expenditures in fiscal year 2009 totaled $122 billion, with 43% of Medicaid being spent on home and community-based services (HCBS). More than 3 million Americans (7% of people covered by Medicaid) used long-term care services paid for by Medicaid. Between fiscal years 2006 and 2009 long-term care expenditures increased by $13 billion, from $109 billion to $122 billion. The percentage of Medicaid spending for institutional long-term care (e.g., nursing homes and intermediate care facilities) decreased from 59% in 2006 to 57% in 2009, whereas the percentage of expenditures for HCBS increased from 41% to 43% during this same period. This trend is expected to persist as Medicaid programs continue to invest more resources in alternatives to institutional services.

The Kaiser Family Foundation observes that the 2010 health care reform legislation offers states the opportunity to expand access to Medicaid HCBS programs. The PPACA supports and extends the duration of a demonstration project that gives the states financial incentives to transition Medicaid beneficiaries from institutional to community-based care. It instituted the Community First Choice Option, which provides HCBS to people with incomes up to 300% of the maximum Supplemental Security Income payment who require the level and intensity of care provided in an institutional setting. The PPACA also strengthens and expands state HCBS programs by broadening the range of covered services and permitting the states to offer full Medicaid benefits to people receiving HCBS.

VETERANS' BENEFITS

People who have served in the U.S. military are entitled to medical treatment at any veterans' facility in the nation. The U.S. Department of Veterans Affairs (VA) reports in *Trends in the Utilization of VA Programs and Services* (December 2010, http://www.va.gov/vetdata/docs/quick facts/utilizationslideshow.pdf) that in fiscal year 2009 approximately 5.3 million veterans received nearly $40 billion in health services.

The Veterans Millennium Health Care and Benefits Act of 1999 extended benefits and services for veterans. It enhanced access to and availability of an expanded range of health care programs and improved housing programs. Among the health care programs that were stipulated by the act, the requirement to provide extended and long-term care and a pilot program related to assisted living are especially relevant for older veterans.

The number of veterans aged 65 years and older who received health care from the Veterans Health Administration (VHA) increased steadily between 1990 and 2008. (See Figure 10.7.) This increase may be attributable in part to the fact that VHA benefits cover services that are not covered by Medicare, such as prescription drugs (Medicare coverage began in 2006), mental health care, long-term care (nursing home and community-based care), and specialized services for people with disabilities. In 2008 approximately 2.2 million veterans aged 65 years and older received health care from the VHA. An additional 1.2 million older veterans were enrolled to receive health care but did not use the services in 2008.

The VA offers a number of health services that are designed to meet older veterans' unique health care needs, such as posttraumatic stress disorder (PTSD; a mental health condition that is marked by severe anxiety, uncontrollable thoughts, and nightmares that are triggered by a terrifying event such as violence). Its National Center for PTSD (http://www.ptsd.va.gov/professional/) offers training to practitioners about how to diagnose and effectively treat this condition in older veterans who may have PTSD as well as other cognitive, emotional, and physical problems.

Benefits for older veterans also include job training and allowances to pursue higher education, vocational skills training, or apprenticeships. For example, Table 10.4 shows the monthly allowances that veterans attending college received in 2010—the allowances increase for veterans who have dependents, enabling them to care for their dependents while they attend school.

Veterans and their families can receive respite care to relieve family caregivers of veterans, nursing home services through three national programs (VA owned and operated community living centers, state veterans' homes owned and operated by the states, and the contract community nursing home program), home care services for veterans who require regular aid and assistance, home loan assistance, disability compensation for those with service-related disabilities, and nonservice-connected pensions for low-income, war-era veterans. Table 10.5 shows the VA disability pension rates for 2010. In *Federal Benefits for Veterans, Dependents and Survivors 2010 Edition* (2010, http://www.va.gov/opa/publications/benefits_book/federal _benefits.pdf), the VA explains that veterans and their dependents may qualify for education and training programs and that there is a college fee waiver for eligible

FIGURE 10.7

Total number of veterans aged 65 and over who are enrolled in or receiving care from the Veterans Health Administration, 1990–2008

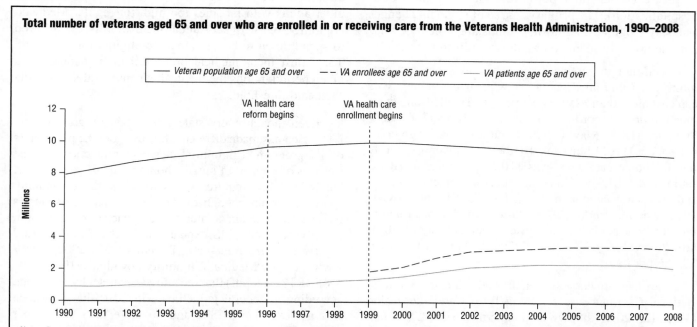

Notes: Department of Veterans Affairs (VA) enrollees are veterans who have signed up to receive health care from the Veterans Health Administration (VHA). VA patients are veterans who have received care each year through VHA. The methods used to calculate VA patients differ from those used in *Older Americans 2004* and *Older Americans Update 2006*. Veterans who received care but were not enrolled in VA are now included in patient counts. VHA Vital Status files from the Social Security Administration (SSA) are now used to ascertain veteran deaths.
Reference population: These data refer to the total veteran population, VHA enrollment population, and VHA patient population.

SOURCE: "Veterans Age 65 and over Enrolled in or Receiving Care from the Veterans Health Administration, 1990–2008," in *Older Americans 2010: Key Indicators of Well-Being*, Federal Interagency Forum on Aging-Related Statistics, July 2010, http://www.agingstats.gov/agingstatsdotnet/Main_Site/Data/2010_Documents/Docs/OA_2010.pdf (accessed April 2, 2011).

TABLE 10.4

Monthly allowance for veterans pursuing higher education, 2010

Training time	Veterans with no dependents	Veterans with one dependent	Veterans with two dependents	Additional dependent
Full-time	$547.54	$679.18	$800.36	$58.34
3/4-time	$411.41	$510.12	$598.38	$44.86
1/2-time	$275.28	$341.07	$400.92	$29.93

SOURCE: "Subsistence allowance is paid at the following monthly rates for training in an institution of higher learning," in *Federal Benefits for Veterans, Dependents and Survivors 2010 Edition*, U.S. Department of Veterans Affairs, 2010, http://www.va.gov/opa/publications/benefits_book/federal_benefits.pdf (accessed May 5, 2011)

TABLE 10.5

Veterans' disability pension rates, 2010

Status of veteran's family situation and caretaking needs	Maximum annual rate
Veteran without dependents	$11,830
Veteran with one dependent	$15,493
Veteran permanently housebound, no dependents	$14,457
Veteran permanently housebound, one dependent	$18,120
Veteran needing regular aid and attendance, no dependents	$19,736
Veteran needing regular aid and attendance, one dependent	$23,396
Two veterans married to one another	$15,493
Increase for each additional dependent child	$2,020

SOURCE: "2010 VA Improved Disability Pension Rates," in *Federal Benefits for Veterans, Dependents and Survivors 2010 Edition*, U.S. Department of Veterans Affairs, 2010, http://www.va.gov/opa/publications/benefits_book/federal_benefits.pdf (accessed May 5, 2011)

---

dependents. In addition, surviving families of veterans who served during times of war may be helped by burial cost reimbursement and death pensions.

LONG-TERM HEALTH CARE

The options for quality, affordable long-term care (LTC) in the United States are limited but improving. Nursing home costs range from $50,000 to more than $200,000 per year, depending on services and location. In *Market Survey of Long-Term Care Costs: The 2010 MetLife Market Survey of Nursing Home, Assisted Living, Adult Day Services, and*

Home Care Costs (October 2010, http://www.metlife.com/assets/cao/mmi/publications/studies/2010/mmi-2010-market-survey-long-term-care-costs.pdf), the MetLife Mature Market Institute notes that in 2010 nursing home care cost an average of $83,585 per year for a private room. Many nursing home residents rely on Medicaid to pay these fees. In 2006 Medicaid covered 47% of LTC facility costs for older Americans. (See Figure 10.2.) The second-most common source of payment at admission is private insurance, the prospective resident's own income, or family support, followed by

Medicare (which only pays for short-term stays after hospitalization). The primary source of payment changes as a stay lengthens. After their funds are "spent down," nursing home residents on Medicare shift to Medicaid.

Even though nursing home care may seem cost prohibitive, an untrained caregiver who makes home visits can cost more than $25,000 per year, and skilled care costs much more. According to the U.S. Bureau of Labor Statistics (BLS; May 17, 2011, http://www.bls.gov/oes/current/oes311011.htm), in 2010 the mean (average) hourly rate for home care aides was $10.25 per hour. In HCBS settings, the BLS indicates that licensed practical nurses and licensed vocational nurses (May 17, 2011, http://www.bls.gov/oes/current/oes292061.htm) earned a mean hourly rate of $19.88 per hour and registered nurses (May 17, 2011, http://www.bls.gov/oes/current/oes291111.htm) earned $32.56 per hour.

The Department of Health and Human Services' National Clearinghouse for Long-Term Care Information (May 12, 2010, http://www.longtermcare.gov/LTC/Main_Site/Paying_LTC/Costs_Of_Care/Costs_Of_Care.aspx) reports an even higher average cost for homemaker and home health aide services: $21 and $19 per hour, respectively, in 2009. As a result, many older adults cannot afford this expense and may exhaust their lifetime savings long before the need for care ends.

Who Pays for Long-Term Care?

Payment for LTC is derived from three major sources: Medicaid, private insurance (LTC insurance), and out-of-pocket spending. In the issue brief *Medicaid Long-Term Care: The Ticking Time Bomb* (2010, http://www.deloitte.com/assets/Dcom-UnitedStates/Local%20Assets/Documents/US_CHS_2010LTCinMedicaid_062910.pdf), the Deloitte Center for Health Solutions describes Medicaid as the "primary [payer] for LTC services and support to the elderly and disabled in the U.S." In 2010 Medicaid financed 34% of total home health care costs and 43% of nursing home costs.

Medicare, Medicaid, and Long-Term Care

Medicare does not cover custodial or long-term nursing home care but, under specific conditions, it will pay for short-term rehabilitative stays in nursing homes and for some home health care. (Custodial care is nonmedical care that helps individuals with their activities of daily living.) Medicaid is the only public program with LTC coverage.

Medicaid, however, does not work like private insurance, which offers protection from catastrophic expense. Medicaid is a means-tested program, so middle-income people needing nursing home care become eligible for Medicaid only after they spend down their own personal income and assets.

Even then, Medicaid will not necessarily pay the entire nursing home bill. Nursing home residents must also meet income eligibility standards. In some states older adults with incomes too high for regular Medicaid eligibility, but with substantial medical bills, are allowed to spend down to become income-eligible for Medicaid. They must incur medical bills until their income for a given period, minus the medical expenses, falls below the Medicaid threshold.

Even though every state's Medicaid program covers LTC, each has made different choices about the parameters of its program. Eligibility rules and protection for the finances of spouses of nursing home residents vary widely, but federal law requires states to allow the community spouse to retain enough of the institutionalized spouse's income to maintain a monthly allowance for minimum living costs. The CMS explains in *2010 SSI and Spousal Impoverishment Standards* (December 30, 2009, http://www.cms.gov/MedicaidEligibility/downloads/1998-2010SSIFBR122909.pdf) that the allowance is set by each state according to federal guidelines—in 2010 the allowance was no less than $1,821 and no more than $2,739 per month. The community spouse is also allowed to retain joint assets—an amount equal to half of the couple's resources at the time the spouse enters the institution, up to a federally specified maximum ($109,560 in 2010).

Figure 10.2 shows the breakdown of LTC expenditures for older adults by the source of payment. In 2006 Medicaid paid the largest proportion of institutional expenses (47%), but nearly the same proportion (45%) was paid out of pocket. Medicare made the largest contribution (91%) toward home care services, whereas 1% of services were covered by Medicaid and 7% were paid out of pocket.

Private Long-Term Care Insurance

Another source of financing is LTC insurance. Private LTC insurance policies typically cover some portion of the cost of nursing home care and home health care services. Jesse Slome of the American Association for Long-Term Care Insurance (AALTCI; personal communication with author, May 10, 2011) reports that approximately 400,000 people purchased LTC insurance in 2010, bringing the total number of Americans with LTC insurance to 8 million. Slome notes that the LTC insurance industry paid out $6.1 billion in benefits to about 200,000 Americans in 2010. Forty-nine percent of claims were for home care services, 24% were for assisted living, and 27% were for nursing home care.

In "New Report Examines What Consumers Really Pay for Long-Term Care Insurance" (December 1, 2010, http://longtermcareinsuranceinfo.blogspot.com/2010/12/new-report-examines-what-consumers.html), Slome states that in 2009 the average age of a new purchaser of LTC insurance was 57 and that 80.5% of new buyers were younger than age 65 when they applied for LTC insurance. According to Slome, purchasers under the age of 61 years pay less than $1,000 per year for LTC insurance.

Sandra Block reports in "Long-Term Care Insurance Worries Baby Boomers" (*USA Today*, November 22, 2010) that the average premium for people aged 55 to 64 years is $2,200 per year. The average premiums for people aged 65 years and older are $3,250. Few policies are available to people in their mid-70s and older, and those that are available are prohibitively expensive.

The National Clearinghouse for Long-Term Care Information (April 8, 2011, http://www.longtermcare.gov/LTC/Main_Site/Paying_LTC/Private_Programs/LTC_Insurance/index.aspx) observes that in addition to the age of the purchaser, the extent of coverage determines the premium. For example, basic coverage that includes $150 per day for care in a facility, $112 per day for home health care, and a lifetime maximum equivalent to five years of care could cost a person who is age 75 at the time of the purchase $520 per month. To reduce monthly premiums, purchasers can opt for lower levels of benefits and coverage and a longer waiting period before coverage begins, but as Table 10.6 reveals, at age 75 the lowest possible premium is still $299 per month, or $3,588 per year.

The premiums for private LTC insurance are tax deductible. The AALTCI explains in the press release "2011 Tax Deduction Limits for Long-Term Care Insurance"

TABLE 10.6

Long-term care insurance costs by age and extent of benefits

Age at purchase	Plan A	Plan B	Plan C	Plan D	Plan E
40	$90	$79	$74	$60	$24
45	$108	$95	$89	$72	$32
50	$130	$114	$107	$86	$43
55	$159	$140	$131	$106	$59
60	$195	$170	$160	$130	$83
65	$248	$216	$204	$165	$120
70	$324	$282	$267	$216	$179
75	$520	$299	$427	$347	$327

The basic coverage design depicted in Plan A is as follows:
• Comprehensive coverage (facility and at-home and community care)
• Facility care daily benefit of $150/day
• Home health care benefits paid at $112/day (75% of the facility care amount).
• Elimination period of 30 days
• Lifetime coverage maximum equivalent to 5 years (or just under $275,000 for a policy paying $150/day)
• Automatic compound annual inflation protection

Plans B through E show you different ways to reduce your premium costs compared to the coverage described in Plan A. You should examine how the compared to the coverage described in Plan A. You should examine how the premium changes for Plans B through Plans E based on the Plan A (base plan).
Plan B: Same as Plan A, except the elimination period is 90 days instead of 30 days.
Plan C: Same as Plan A, except the lifetime maximum is equal to 3 years, or just under $165,000
Plan D: Pays benefits at $100/day for facility care and, correspondingly, $75/day. All other elements remain the same.
Plan E: Same as Plan A, except it does not include compound annual inflation protection. Instead, each year you can elect to increase your coverage by a set amount (generally 5% of the prior years' benefit amount) and you would pay for that additional amount at the time you elect it.

SOURCE: "Designing Coverage to Best Meet Your Needs," in *What is Long Term Care Insurance?* U.S. Department of Health and Human Services, National Clearinghouse for Long Term Care Information, 2011, http://www.longtermcare.gov/LTC/Main_Site/Paying_LTC/Private_Programs/LTC_Insurance/index.aspx (accessed May 5, 2011)

(November 2, 2010, http://www.aaltci.org/news/long-term-care-association-news/2011-tax-deduction-limits-for-long-term-care-insurance) that in 2011 the Internal Revenue Service increased deductibility levels to encourage the purchase of LTC insurance. The amount that may be deducted increases with advancing age. For example, people up to age 40 may deduct $340, whereas older adults aged 60 to 70 years can deduct up to $3,390 and adults aged 70 years and older can deduct $4,240.

HEALTH CARE REFORM LEGISLATION MAY INCREASE ACCESS TO LONG-TERM CARE INSURANCE. The health care reform legislation enacted in 2010 contains the Community Living Assistance Services and Supports (CLASS) Act, which aims to help people remain in their home rather than enter an LTC facility. The CLASS Act went into effect on January 1, 2011, but the PPACA requires the Department of Health and Human Services to provide guidance no later than October 2012. In "Community Living Assistance Services and Supports (CLASS) Provisions in the Patient Protection and Affordable Care Act (PPACA)" (June 4, 2010, http://scphi.org/pdf/Workgroups/LTC%20Work group/Community%20Living%20Assistance%20Services%20and%20Supports%20%28CLASS%29%20Provisions%20in%20PPACA.pdf), Janemarie Mulvey and Kirsten J. Colello explain that the CLASS Act establishes a federally administered voluntary LTC insurance program. Employers can choose to participate in the program and automatically enroll their employees who do not opt out. Employees whose employers do not choose to participate and people who are self-employed will also be able to participate in the program. To be eligible for benefits, employees must pay into the program for at least five years and work three of those five years. The program will provide funds that may be used to pay for HCBS or help cover the costs of assisted living or nursing home care. Mulvey and Colello report that the initial average premium would be about $240 per month for an average benefit of $50 per day, which is about one-third the daily benefit provided by most private LTC insurance policies.

HOME HEALTH CARE

In *National Home and Hospice Care Survey (NHHCS): Home Health—Data Highlights* (January 15, 2010, http://www.cdc.gov/nchs/nhhcs/nhhcs_home_highlights.htm), the National Center for Health Statistics describes home health care as "provided to individuals and families in their places of residence for the purpose of promoting, maintaining, or restoring health or for maximizing the level of independence while minimizing the effects of disability and illness, including terminal illness."

Andrea Sisko et al. observe in "Health Spending Projections through 2018: Recession Effects Add Uncertainty to the Outlook" (*Health Affairs*, vol. 28, no. 2, March–April 2009) that home health care grew by an estimated 9.1% in 2008, down from 11.3% growth in

2007. This slowdown is expected to continue through 2011. Between 2013 and 2018 home health care spending growth is expected to remain steady, averaging 7.9% per year and reaching $134.9 billion in the next decade. Even though Medicare has been the principal payer for home health care, Medicaid became the largest payer of these services in 2010, as care continued to be redirected from institutions to HCBS settings.

Community Housing with Home Care Services

Some older adults have access to a variety of home care services through their place of residence. Assisted living facilities, retirement communities, and continuing care retirement communities are community housing alternatives that often provide services such as meal preparation, laundry and cleaning services, transportation, and assistance adhering to prescribed medication regimens.

In 2007 just 2% of Medicare recipients aged 65 years and older lived in community housing that offered at least one home care service and an additional 4% lived in LTC facilities. (See Figure 10.8.) The percentage of people residing in community housing that offered home care services was higher in the older age groups. Among people aged 85 years and older, 7% lived in community housing with services and 15% lived in LTC facilities.

Older adults living in community housing with support services had more functional limitations than those living in the community but fewer than residents of LTC facilities. Fourteen percent of older adults living in community housing with services had three or more activities of daily living limitations, compared to 7% of older adults living in the community and 67% of older adults in LTC facilities. (See Figure 10.9.)

FIGURE 10.8

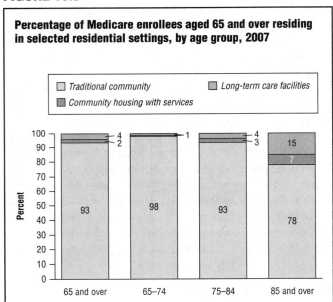

Percentage of Medicare enrollees aged 65 and over residing in selected residential settings, by age group, 2007

Notes: Community housing with services applies to respondents who reported they lived in retirement communities or apartments, senior citizen housing, continuing care retirement facilities, assisted living facilities, staged living communities, board and care facilities/homes, and other similar situations, and who reported they had access to one or more of the following services through their place of residence: meal preparation; cleaning or housekeeping services; laundry services; help with medications. Respondents were asked about access to these services, but not whether they actually used the services. A residence (or unit) is considered a long-term care facility if it is certified by Medicare or Medicaid; or has three or more beds and is licensed as a nursing home or other long term care facility and provides at least one personal care service; or provides 24-hour, seven-day-a-week supervision by a non-family, paid caregiver.
Reference population: These data refer to Medicare enrollees.

SOURCE: "Percentage of Medicare Enrollees Age 65 and over in Selected Residential Settings, by Age Group, 2007," in *Older Americans 2010: Key Indicators of Well-Being*, Federal Interagency Forum on Aging-Related Statistics, July 2010, http://www.agingstats.gov/agingstatsdotnet/Main_Site/Data/2010_Documents/Docs/OA_2010.pdf (accessed April 2, 2011)

FIGURE 10.9

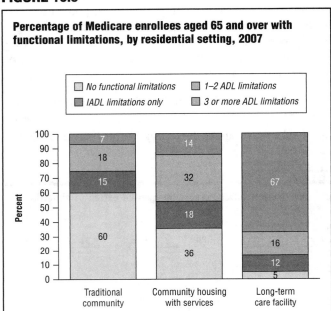

Percentage of Medicare enrollees aged 65 and over with functional limitations, by residential setting, 2007

ADL = Activities of daily living. IADL = Instrumental activities of daily living.
Notes: Community housing with services applies to respondents who reported they lived in retirement communities or apartments, senior citizen housing, continuing care retirement facilities, assisted living facilities, staged living communities, board and care facilities/homes, and other similar situations, AND who reported they had access to one or more of the following services through their place of residence: meal preparation; cleaning or housekeeping services; laundry services; help with medications. Respondents were asked about access to these services, but not whether they actually used the services. A residence (or unit) is considered a long-term care facility if it is certified by Medicare or Medicaid; or has three or more beds and is licensed as a nursing home or other long term care facility and provides at least one personal care service; or provides 24-hour, seven-day-a-week supervision by a non-family, paid caregiver. Instrumental activities of daily living (IADL) limitations refer to difficulty performing (or inability to perform for a health reason) one or more of the following tasks: using the telephone; light housework; heavy housework; meal preparation; shopping; managing money. Activities of daily living (ADL) limitations refer to difficulty performing (or inability to perform for a health reason) the following tasks: bathing; dressing; eating; getting in/out of chairs; walking; using the toilet. Long-term care facility residents with no limitations may include individuals with limitations in certain IADLs: doing light or heavy housework or meal preparation. These questions were not asked of facility residents.
Reference population: These data refer to Medicare enrollees.

SOURCE: "Percentage of Medicare Enrollees Age 65 and over with Functional Limitations, by Residential Setting, 2007," in *Older Americans 2010: Key Indicators of Well-Being*, Federal Interagency Forum on Aging-Related Statistics, July 2010, http://www.agingstats.gov/agingstatsdotnet/Main_Site/Data/2010_Documents/Docs/OA_2010.pdf (accessed April 2, 2011)

CHAPTER 11

CRIME AND ABUSE OF OLDER ADULTS

Elder financial abuse is a crime growing in intensity and, especially now, with the plummeting economy, elders will be unable to recover from such losses.

—Pamela Teaster, quoted in *Broken Trust: Elders, Family, and Finances* (March 2009)

Elder abuse comes in many different forms—physical abuse, emotional abuse, or financial abuse. Each one is devastating in its own right.... I know because it happened to me. My money was taken and misused. When I asked for information, I was told that I couldn't have any of my own information. I was told it was "for my own good" and that "it was none of my business." I was literally left powerless.

— Mickey Rooney, testimony before the U.S. Senate, Special Committee on Aging (March 2, 2011)

Professionals against Confidence Crimes (PACC), a nonprofit, nonpartisan organization of law enforcement professionals, states in "Fear of Crime" (August 28, 2008, http://stopcon.org/Fear%20of%20Crime.htm) that older adults believe they are most susceptible to crimes such as murder, rape and aggravated assault, armed robbery, theft from their person, burglary, and fraud. Their fears are not, however, entirely consistent with reality. Older adults are the least likely to become victims of violent crimes. The crimes more often committed against older adults are purse snatching and pocket picking (theft of their purses or wallets), fraud and confidence crimes, mail theft, vandalism, and burglary.

PACC attributes older adults' misplaced fears in part to sensational media reports that do not correctly convey the real crime risks for older adults. As a result, older adults do not have an accurate understanding about the crimes that affect them. PACC contends that unless older adults understand the real risks, they will not take the proper steps to protect themselves.

CRIME AGAINST OLDER ADULTS

Older adults have lower rates of violent crime than other age groups, and the number of homicides of older adults decreased between 1976 and 2000 and has remained relatively stable since then. Jennifer L. Truman and Michael R. Rand of the Bureau of Justice Statistics (BJS) indicate in *Criminal Victimization, 2009* (October 2010, http://vrc.poe.house.gov/UploadedFiles/BJA_Criminal_Victimization_2009.pdf) that in 2009 victimization rates for violent crime declined with the advancing age of the victim, consistent with data that were reported in previous years. In 2009 the rate of violent victimizations of people aged 65 years and older was 3.2 per 1,000 people aged 12 years and older. (See Table 11.1.)

Michael R. Rand and Jayne E. Robinson of the BJS report *Criminal Victimization in the United States, 2008 Statistical Tables* (May 12, 2011, http://bjs.ojp.usdoj.gov/content/pub/pdf/cvus08.pdf) that among adults aged 65 years and older in 2008, African-Americans (10.7 per 1,000 population) were much more likely to be the victims of violent crime than whites (2.4 per 1,000 population). (See Table 11.2.) For example, the rate of attempted or threatened violence was 8.4 per 1,000 population for older African-Americans, compared to 2 per 1,000 population for older whites.

According to Rand and Robinson, in 2008 older adults were as likely to be assaulted by a stranger as by someone well known. Table 11.3 shows that people aged 65 years and older were only slightly more likely to experience violent victimization by a stranger (1.1 per 1,000 people aged 12 years and older) than by someone well known (1 per 1,000 people aged 12 years and older).

Older adults also experienced low rates of property crimes in 2008. For example, adults aged 65 years and older had the lowest rates of vehicle theft (3.1 per 1,000 households), compared to those aged 20 to 34 years (8.8 per 1,000 households). (See Table 11.4.) Rand and Robinson indicate that the rates of household burglary and theft also declined with advancing age.

TABLE 11.1

Violent crime rates, by gender, race, Hispanic origin, and age of victim, 2009

Demographic characteristics of victim	Population	Total	Violent victimizations per 1,000 persons age 12 or older				
			Rape/sexual assault	Robbery	Total assault	Aggravated assault	Simple assault
Gender							
Male	124,041,190	18.4	0.2^	2.7	15.6	4.3	11.3
Female	130,064,420	15.8	0.8	1.6	13.5	2.3	11.2
Race							
White	206,331,920	15.8	0.4	1.6	13.7	2.7	11.0
Black	31,046,560	26.8	1.2	5.6	19.9	6.8	13.0
Other race*	13,982,530	9.8	—^	0.5^	9.3	1.9^	7.4
Two or more race	2,744,600	42.1	—^	5.2^	36.9	9.3^	27.5
Hispanic origin							
Hispanic	35,375,280	18.1	0.5^	3.4	14.2	3.2	11.0
Non-Hispanic	218,238,010	17.0	0.5	1.9	14.6	3.3	11.3
Age							
12–15	16,230,740	36.8	0.9^	3.1	32.8	6.9	25.9
16–19	17,203,070	30.3	0.6^	5.2	24.6	5.3	19.3
20–24	20,620,150	28.1	0.8^	3.5	23.8	7.5	16.3
25–34	41,073,240	21.5	0.8^	2.8	17.9	4.5	13.4
35–49	64,323,190	16.1	0.4^	2.0	13.7	2.6	11.1
50–64	56,651,170	10.7	0.3^	1.1	9.3	1.9	7.5
65 or older	38,004,060	3.2	0.2^	0.4^	2.5	0.3^	2.2

Note: Violent crimes measured by the National Crime Victimization Survey (NCVS) include rape, sexual assault, robbery, aggravated assault, and simple assault. Because the NCVS interviews persons about their victimizations, murder and manslaughter cannot be included.
—Rounds to less than 0.05 violent victimizations per 1,000 persons age 12 or older.
^Based on 10 or fewer sample cases.
*Includes American Indians, Alaska Natives, Asians, Native Hawaiians, and other Pacific Islanders.

source: Jennifer L. Truman and Michael R. Rand, "Table 5. Rates of Violent Crime, by Gender, Race, Hispanic Origin, and Age of Victim, 2009," in *Criminal Victimization, 2009* , U.S. Department of Justice, Bureau of Justice Statistics, October 2010, http://vrc.poe.house.gov/UploadedFiles/BJA_Criminal_Victimization_2009.pdf (accessed May 17, 2011)

The Physical and Emotional Impact of Crime

According to the BJS, most older Americans who are the victims of violent crime are not physically injured. However, physical injuries do not tell the whole story. Victimization and fear of victimization can have far more serious effects on the quality of older adults' lives than they might for younger people.

Older adults are often less resilient than younger people. Even so-called nonviolent crimes, such as purse snatching, vandalism, or burglary, can be devastating. Stolen or damaged articles and property are often irreplaceable because of their sentimental or monetary value. Furthermore, nonviolent crimes leave victims with a sense of violation and heightened vulnerability.

Older People Are Considered Easy Prey

Because of their physical limitations, older adults are often considered easy prey. They are less likely than younger victims to resist criminal attacks. Their reluctance to resist may be based on awareness that they lack the strength to repel a younger aggressor and that they are physically frail and at risk of injuries that could permanently disable them. The U.S. Bureau of Justice reports that crime victims over the age of 65 years who try to protect themselves most often use nonphysical actions, such as arguing, reasoning, or screaming. Younger victims are more likely to use physical action, such as attacking, resisting, or running from or chasing offenders.

FRAUD

Older adults are also considered easy prey for fraud, deception, and exploitation. They are more readily accessible to con artists than other age groups because they are likely to be at home to receive visits from door-to-door salespeople or calls from telemarketers. Older adults who are homebound or otherwise isolated may not have regular contact with others who might help them to identify possible schemes or frauds. Law enforcement officials and consumer advocates assert that older people are targeted because:

- They are more likely than younger people to have substantial financial savings, home equity, or credit, all of which are tempting to fraud perpetrators.

- They are often reluctant to be rude to others, so they may be more likely to hear out a con's story. They may also be overly trusting.

- Older adults are less likely to report fraud because they are embarrassed, they do not know how or to whom to report the crime, or they fear appearing incapable of handling their personal finances.

TABLE 11.2

Victimization rates by age, race, and type of crime, 2008

| | | | | | | Rate per 1,000 persons in each age group | | | | | | |
| | | | | | | Robbery | | | Assault | | | |
Race and age	Total population	Crimes of violence	Completed violence	Attempted/ threatened violence	Rape/ sexual assault[a]	Total	With injury	Without injury	Total	Aggravated	Simple	Purse snatching/ pocket picking
White only												
12–15	12,624,200	40.3	9.9	30.4	2.0*	3.8	1.4*	2.4*	34.4	6.2	28.3	0.4*
16–19	13,080,920	38.9	12.2	26.7	2.2*	2.9	1.7*	1.2*	33.8	6.5	27.2	0.6*
20–24	16,185,710	35.0	12.6	22.5	1.1*	4.1	0.9*	3.2	29.8	8.2	21.6	0.5*
25–34	31,710,270	22.6	5.4	17.2	0.2*	1.5	0.6*	0.9*	20.9	3.5	17.4	0.5*
35–49	52,429,400	16.4	3.9	12.4	0.8	1.8	0.6*	1.2	13.8	2.4	11.4	0.7*
50–64	46,192,590	10.1	1.5	8.6	0.1*	0.6*	0.1*	0.5*	9.5	1.7	7.8	0.4*
65 or older	32,460,400	2.4	0.3*	2.0	0.2*	0.1*	0.1*	0.0*	2.1	0.3*	1.8	0.5*
Black only												
12–15	2,579,390	56.0	23.5	32.5	0.0*	12.7*	4.6*	8.1*	43.3	8.8*	34.5	4.3*
16–19	2,780,180	30.2	14.4	15.8	3.4*	12.5*	3.7*	8.7*	14.3	3.8*	10.5*	0.0*
20–24	2,714,240	52.6	28.6	23.9	5.9*	11.2*	3.3*	7.9*	35.5	8.4*	27.1	1.8*
25–34	5,388,590	32.3	11.0	21.3	3.0*	5.4*	3.1*	2.2*	24.0	8.5	15.4	0.0*
35–49	8,165,110	17.9	5.3	12.6	0.6*	2.8*	0.0*	2.8*	14.5	4.8	9.7	0.9*
50–64	5,952,610	11.6	3.8*	7.9	1.2*	2.5*	0.6*	1.9*	7.9	2.0*	6.0*	0.0*
65 or older	3,129,740	10.7*	2.3*	8.4*	1.0*	1.3*	0.0*	1.3*	8.4*	1.7*	6.7*	0.0*

Note: Detail may not add to total shown because of rounding. Excludes data on persons of "other" races.

*Estimate is based on 10 or fewer sample cases.

[a]Includes verbal threats of rape and threats of sexual assault.

SOURCE: Michael R. Rand and Jayne E. Robinson, "Table 9. Personal Crimes, 2008: Victimization Rates for Persons Age 12 or Older, by Race and Age of Victims and Type of Crime," in *Criminal Victimization in the United States, 2008 Statistical Tables*, U.S. Department of Justice, Bureau of Justice Statistics, May 12, 2011, http://bjs.ojp.usdoj.gov/content/pub/pdf/cvus08.pdf (accessed May 17, 2011)

TABLE 11.3

Victimization rate by victim-offender relationship, type of crime, and selected victim characteristics, 2008

Rate per 1,000 persons age 12 or older

Characteristic	Total population	Crimes of violence[a]				Assault				Aggravated assault				Simple assault			
		Relatives	Well-known	Casual acquaintances	Strangers	Relatives	Well-known	Casual acquaintances	Strangers	Relatives	Well-known	Casual acquaintances	Strangers	Relatives	Well-known	Casual acquaintances	Strangers
Sex																	
Male	123,071,020	1.0	3.7	3.2	9.5	1.0	3.1	3.0	7.8	0.3	0.6	0.5	1.7	0.7	2.5	2.5	6.2
Female	129,171,510	3.0	5.9	2.1	4.6	2.6	5.0	1.9	3.4	0.3	1.0	0.4	0.8	2.3	4.0	1.5	2.6
Race																	
White only	204,683,500	2.0	4.7	2.6	6.1	1.8	4.0	2.4	5.2	0.3	0.8	0.4	1.1	1.6	3.3	2.0	4.1
Black only	30,709,860	1.5	4.7	3.6	12.0	1.4	3.5	3.1	7.6	0.7*	1.2*	0.8*	1.6	0.7*	2.3	2.3	6.0
Other race only[d]	13,952,240	1.9*	3.5	0.8*	7.2	1.9*	2.6*	0.8*	4.7	0.5*	0.3*	0.3*	1.7*	1.5*	2.3*	0.5*	3.0
Two or more races[e]	2,896,930	6.1*	21.6	3.9*	14.0	4.4*	21.6	2.0*	11.2*	0.0*	2.6*	1.4*	1.4*	4.4*	19.0	0.6*	9.8*
Age																	
12–15	16,414,550	1.5*	12.2	7.9	12.8	1.2*	10.1	6.9	10.1	0.0*	2.2*	1.7*	1.5*	1.2*	7.9	5.2	8.6
16–19	17,280,270	1.3*	12.5	5.6	11.7	1.3*	9.9	4.8	8.7	0.1*	1.3*	0.6*	2.6	1.2*	8.6	4.1	6.1
20–24	20,547,620	4.9	9.6	4.2	14.1	4.4	7.4	3.8	10.2	1.0*	3.3	0.0*	3.1	3.4	4.2	3.8	7.1
25–34	40,649,500	3.2	4.9	1.7	10.3	2.7	4.7	1.7	8.7	0.6*	0.8*	0.3*	1.5	2.1	3.8	1.4	7.2
35–49	65,123,030	2.5	4.0	2.5	6.0	2.2	3.5	2.3	4.7	0.4*	0.5*	0.4*	1.1	1.9	3.0	1.9	3.6
50–64	55,116,320	1.3	2.1	2.0	3.7	1.2	1.8	1.9	3.4	0.2*	0.3*	0.6*	0.6*	1.0	1.5	1.3	2.8
65 or older	37,111,240	0.0*	1.0*	0.4*	1.1	0.0*	0.8*	0.4*	0.8*	0.0*	0.0*	0.1*	0.3*	0.0*	0.8*	0.4*	0.6*
Marital status[b]																	
Married	126,540,850	1.1	1.3	1.1	4.0	1.0	1.2	1.0	3.5	0.3	0.1*	0.1*	0.8	0.7	1.1	0.9	2.6
Widowed	13,992,180	0.6*	1.8*	1.3*	1.1*	0.6*	1.6*	1.3*	1.1*	0.0*	0.5*	0.7*	0.0*	0.6*	1.1*	0.6*	1.1*
Divorced or separated	27,712,690	7.7	8.4	3.8	8.1	6.8	7.5	3.5	6.2	0.6*	1.1*	1.1*	1.3*	6.2	6.4	2.4	4.9
Never married	81,999,560	1.7	9.7	5.1	12.3	1.4	7.9	4.5	9.5	0.3*	1.9	0.8	2.1	1.2	6.0	3.7	7.4
Family income[c]																	
Less than $7,500	6,760,710	5.6	15.5	4.2*	10.1	4.8*	11.7	3.4*	6.5	1.2*	3.6*	1.4*	2.0*	3.6*	8.1	2.0*	4.5*
$7,500–$14,999	10,261,320	3.1*	9.3	7.2	14.3	3.1*	7.3	6.7	10.5	0.5*	1.3*	2.6*	2.7*	2.6*	5.9	4.0	7.9
$15,000–$24,999	17,538,250	3.5	7.7	3.6	8.3	3.0	6.6	3.3	6.9	0.3*	1.9*	0.8*	1.6*	2.7	4.6	2.5	5.2
$25,000–$34,999	19,522,830	4.4	6.4	3.4	7.5	3.9	5.5	3.1	5.6	0.3*	0.4*	1.1*	1.0*	3.6	5.0	2.0	4.6
$35,000–$49,999	28,963,880	2.6	6.1	3.2	8.3	2.3	5.5	3.1	6.7	0.3*	1.0*	0.4*	1.4	1.9	4.5	2.7	5.3
$50,000–$74,999	33,797,170	0.5*	1.8	2.6	7.7	0.5*	1.6	2.4	7.0	0.3*	0.5*	0.2*	1.6	0.3*	1.2	2.2	5.4
$75,000 or more	59,992,830	1.1	2.9	1.7	5.2	0.9	2.3	1.4	4.5	0.3*	0.4*	0.1*	0.9	0.6*	1.9	1.3	3.5

*Estimate is based on 10 or fewer sample cases.

aIncludes data on rape, sexual assault, and robbery (not shown separately).

bExcludes data on persons whose marital status was not ascertained.

cExcludes data on persons whose family income was not ascertained.

dIncludes American Indian, Alaskan Native, Asian, Hawaiian/Pacific Islander if only one of these races if given.

eIncludes all persons indicating two or more races.

SOURCE: Michael R. Rand and Jayne E. Robinson, "Table 35. Family Violence, 2008: Victimization Rate by Victim-Offender Relationship, by Type of Crime and Selected Victim Characteristics," in *Criminal Victimization in the United States, 2008 Statistical Tables,* U.S. Department of Justice, Bureau of Justice Statistics, May 12, 2011, http://bjs.ojp.usdoj.gov/content/pub/pdf/cvus/current/cv0835.pdf (accessed May 17, 2011)

TABLE 11.4

Number of victimizations and victimization rates of vehicle theft, by selected household characteristics, 2008

Characteristic	Based on households			Based on vehicles owned		
	Number of households	Number of thefts	Rate per 1,000	Number of vehicles owned	Number of thefts	Rate per 1,000
Race of head of household						
All races	121,141,060	795,160	6.6	228,757,090	853,690	3.7
White only	98,421,450	529,820	5.4	192,819,050	563,140	2.9
Black only	15,538,060	196,100	12.6	22,923,710	216,000	9.4
Other race only	5,926,740	46,080	7.8	10,719,990	51,390	4.8
Two or more races	1,254,810	23,160*	18.5*	2,294,340	23,160*	10.1*
Age of head of household						
12–19	1,267,680	21,210*	16.7*	1,981,200	21,210*	10.7*
20–34	26,940,670	236,500	8.8	46,921,420	253,440	5.4
35–49	36,190,160	254,310	7.0	75,789,720	283,330	3.7
50–64	32,253,420	207,710	6.4	67,409,070	220,270	3.3
65 or older	24,489,120	75,440	3.1	36,655,670	75,440	2.1
Form of tenure						
Owned or being bought	82,681,000	444,740	5.4	177,855,220	485,320	2.7
Rented	38,460,060	350,410	9.1	50,901,870	368,370	7.2
Locality of residence						
Urban[a]	37,542,470	375,320	10.0	59,624,290	402,150	6.7
Suburban[b]	54,774,340	356,820	6.5	110,210,830	376,820	3.4
Rural[c]	28,824,260	63,020	2.2	58,921,970	74,720	1.3

Note: Detail may not add to total shown because of rounding. The number of thefts based on vehicles owned is equal to or higher than the corresponding figure based on households because the former includes all completed or attempted vehicle thefts, regardless of the final classification of the event. Personal crimes of contact and burglary occurring in conjunction with motor vehicle thefts take precedence in determining the final classification based on the number of households.
*Estimate is based on 10 or fewer sample cases.
[a]Denotes principal cities.
[b]Denotes communities outside principal cities.
[c]Denotes nonmetropolitan areas.

SOURCE: Michael R. Rand and Jayne E. Robinson, "Table 18. Motor Vehicle Theft, 2008: Number of Victimizations and Victimization Rates on the Basis of Thefts per 1,000 Households and of Thefts per 1,000 Vehicles Owned, by Selected Household Characteristics," in *Criminal Victimization in the United States, 2008 Statistical Tables*, U.S. Department of Justice, Bureau of Justice Statistics, May 12, 2011, http://www.bjs.gov/content/pub/pdf/cvus/current/cv0818.pdf (accessed May 17, 2011)

• Older adults who do report fraud may not make good witnesses. Their memories may fade over the often protracted span of time between the crime and the trial, and on the witness stand they may be unable to provide detailed enough information to lead to a conviction.

In "The Effects of Loneliness on Telemarketing Fraud Vulnerability among Older Adults" (*Journal of Elder Abuse and Neglect*, vol. 20, no. 1, February 2008), Linda M. Alves and Steve R. Wilson indicate that the typical telemarketing fraud victim is a male between the ages of 60 and 70 years who is divorced or separated and is college educated. The researchers suggest that loneliness and social isolation may increase an older adult's vulnerability to telemarketing fraud.

Liz Pulliam Weston reports in "Help Seniors Hang up on Telemarketing Scams" (MSN.com, May 20, 2009) that the AARP has taken action to help prevent older adults from falling victim to telemarketing fraud. One approach involves a kind of reverse telemarketing in which trained peer counselors telephone older adults to caution them about the dangers of responding to

unscrupulous telemarketers. The AARP explains that this educational approach works because it respects rather than chastises older adults; victims and potential victims are not made to feel foolish because they have considered or fallen for a telemarketing scam.

The Federal Trade Commission (FTC) is the federal government's lead consumer protection agency. FTC authority extends over practically the entire economy, including business and consumer transactions via telephone and the Internet. The FTC's consumer mission includes prohibiting unfair or deceptive acts or practices.

The U.S. Food and Drug Administration (FDA) and the FTC actively work to prevent health fraud and scams. These agencies identify products with substandard or entirely useless ingredients as well as those with fraudulent or misleading advertising to prevent the dissemination of unsubstantiated or deceptive claims about the health benefits of particular products or services.

The FTC acts not only to prevent consumer fraud but also to monitor its occurrence. In *Consumer Fraud in the United States: The Second FTC Survey* (October 2007, http://www.ftc.gov/opa/2007/10/fraud.pdf), the most recent survey for which data were available as of June 2011, the FTC reports the results of a 2005 survey. The FTC indicates that older consumers were significantly less likely to be victims of specific kinds of fraud such as weight-loss products, prize promotions, foreign lotteries, work-at-home programs, credit repair, and unauthorized billing for Internet services. Whereas 15.4% of adults aged 35 to 44 years were victims of fraud in 2005, just 11% of adults aged 55 to 64 years and 5.6% of those aged 75 years and older were victims of fraud.

Health Fraud

Older adults may be particularly susceptible to false or misleading claims about the safety and/or efficacy (the ability of an intervention to produce the intended diagnostic or therapeutic effect in optimal circumstances) of over-the-counter (nonprescription) drugs, devices, foods, dietary supplements, and health care services because the marketing of such products and services often relates to conditions that are associated with aging. Also, many of these unproven treatments promise false hope and offer immediate cures for chronic (long-term) diseases or complete relief from pain. It is easy to understand how older adults who are frightened or in pain might be seduced by false promises of quick cures.

Working together, the FDA and the FTC combat deceptive advertising for health services such as false and unsubstantiated claims for dietary supplements. One example of their joint effort can be seen in their letter to Tennessee Scientific Inc. and Scientific Formulations LLC (February 1, 2011, http://www.fda.gov/ICECI/EnforcementActions/ WarningLetters/ucm241970.htm). The letter warned Tennessee Scientific and Scientific Formulations that advertising on their websites, which made medical claims for the treatment of specific diseases with nutritional supplements, violated Section 201(g)(1)(B) of the Federal Food, Drug, and Cosmetic Act. The letter also contained a threat of potential action by the FTC. The FDA and the FTC warn consumers to be wary of Internet sites and other promotions for products that claim to diagnose, prevent, mitigate, treat, or cure diseases.

Financial Fraud, Abuse, and Exploitation

Financial crimes against older adults are largely underrecognized, underreported, and underprosecuted but are estimated to total losses of at least $2.6 billion each year. This section describes findings from *Broken Trust: Elders, Family, and Finances* (March 2009, http://www.metlife .com/assets/cao/mmi/publications/studies/mmi-study-broken-trust-elders-family-finances.pdf), a study about preventing financial abuse of older adults that was conducted by the MetLife Mature Market Institute, the National Committee for the Prevention of Elder Abuse, and the Center for Gerontology at the Virginia Polytechnic Institute and State University. The study considers elder financial abuse as "the

unauthorized use or illegal taking of funds or property of people aged 60 and older."

The study's principal findings include:

- Older adults' larger net worth (adults over the age of 50 years control 70% of the net worth of U.S. households) and vulnerabilities, such as impaired cognitive abilities, loneliness, and social isolation, make them prime targets for financial abuse.

- Aging of the population coupled with social changes such as families living at a distance and technological advances such as virtual social networks will act to sharply increase opportunities for financial abuse of older adults.

- Financial abuse generally occurs at the hands of someone the older adults trust—business and service professionals including paid caregivers, neighbors, and family members—rather than strangers.

- Financial abuse of older adults occurs among men and women of every race and ethnicity.

- A typical victim is a white woman aged 70 to 89 years, who is frail, cognitively impaired, and trusting, lonely, or isolated.

Financial abuse is considered the third-most common type of abuse of older adults, following neglect and emotional/psychological abuse.

Medicare Fraud

Every year Medicare loses millions of dollars because of fraud and abuse. *Broken Trust* reports that Medicare and Medicaid fraud totaled $121.4 million in a three-month period (April to June 2008), during which researchers monitored Newsfeed media reports. The most common forms of Medicare fraud were:

- Billing for services not furnished

- Misrepresenting a diagnosis to justify a higher payment

- Soliciting, offering, or receiving a kickback

- Charging Medicare higher fees than normal for certain procedures

- Falsifying certificates of medical necessity, plans of treatment, and medical records to justify payment

- Billing for a service not furnished as billed

The Health Insurance Portability and Accountability Act of 1996 allocated funds to protect Medicare's integrity and prevent fraud. In one of the largest efforts in the history of Medicare, the program has undertaken a major campaign to help eliminate Medicare fraud, waste, and abuse.

To combat Medicare fraud at the beneficiary level, the Administration on Aging (AoA) provides grants to local organizations to help older Americans become more vigilant health care consumers so that they can identify and prevent fraudulent health care practices. The Senior Medicare Patrol, now known as the SMP program, trains community volunteers, many of whom are retired professionals, such as doctors, nurses, accountants, investigators, law enforcement personnel, attorneys, and teachers, to help Medicare beneficiaries become better health care consumers. In "Performance Data for the Senior Medicare Patrol Projects" (May 19, 2010, http://oig.hhs.gov/oei/reports/oei-02-10-00100.pdf), Stuart E. Wright of the U.S. Department of Health and Human Services (HHS) indicates that despite having fewer volunteers than in previous years, in 2009 the SMP program had recouped nearly $300,000. Since its inception in 1997, the program's volunteers have recovered nearly $4.6 million in Medicare funds and saved Medicare beneficiaries and taxpayers approximately $101 million. According to the AoA, in *FY 2011 Online Performance Appendix* (February 2011, http://www.aoa.gov/aoaroot/about/Budget/DOCS/OPA_AoA_FY2012.pdf), the number of SMP-trained volunteers fell from 36,479 in 2008 to 26,600 in 2009. Despite decreasing manpower, the program has ambitious goals and aims to recover $5 million by September 2012.

ABUSE AND MISTREATMENT OF OLDER ADULTS

Domestic violence against older adults is a phenomenon that first gained publicity during the late 1970s, when Representative Claude Denson Pepper (1900–1989; D-FL) held widely publicized hearings about the mistreatment of older adults. In the three decades since those hearings, policy makers, health professionals, social service personnel, and advocates for older Americans have sought ways to protect the older population from physical, psychological, and financial abuse.

Magnitude of the Problem

It is difficult to determine exactly how many older adults are the victims of abuse or mistreatment. As with child abuse and domestic violence among younger adults, the number of actual cases is larger than the number of reported cases. There is consensus among professionals and agencies that deal with issues of elder abuse that it is far less likely to be reported than child or spousal abuse. The challenge of estimating the incidence and prevalence of this problem is further compounded by the varying definitions of abuse and reporting practices used by the voluntary, state, and federal agencies, as well as the fact that comprehensive national data are not collected. Furthermore, research suggests that abuse often occurs over long periods of time and that only when it reaches a critical juncture, such as instances of severe injury, will the neglect

or abuse become evident to health, social service, or legal professionals.

Even though the magnitude of the problem of abuse of older adults is unknown, its social and moral importance is obvious. Abuse and neglect of older individuals in society violate a sacred trust and moral commitment to protect vulnerable individuals and groups from harm and to ensure their well-being and security.

High-profile cases of elder abuse and the media's spotlight on the problem have helped increase Americans' awareness that it is a pervasive problem that occurs among people of all races, ethnicities, incomes, and educational attainment. For example, in 2009 the media chronicled the trial of Anthony D. Marshall, the son of the wealthy socialite and philanthropist Brooke Astor (1902–2007), who was charged with stealing millions of dollars from his mother's estate. In October 2009 the 85-year-old Marshall was found guilty of draining his mother's fortune as she suffered from Alzheimer's disease and was sentenced to up to three years in prison.

Greater Efforts Are Needed to Combat Elder Abuse

In her testimony *Elder Justice: Stronger Federal Leadership Could Help Improve Response to Elder Abuse* (March 2, 2011, http://www.gao.gov/new.items/d11384t.pdf) before the U.S. Senate's Special Committee on Aging, Kay E. Brown of the U.S. Government Accountability Office (GAO) stated that in 2009 the prevalence of elder abuse was approximately 14.1% among noninstitutionalized older Americans (people who are not in the U.S. military, school, jail, or mental health facilities) and suggested that this was probably a low estimate of prevalence. During the same committee hearing Mark Lachs (March 2, 2011, http://aging.senate.gov/events/hr230ml.pdf) of Cornell University noted that a study conducted in New York state revealed that for every reported instance of elder abuse as many as 24 remain unreported. The committee was advised that even though family members and staff are largely responsible for abuse and neglect of older adults in nursing homes and other facilities, older adults might also be victimized by fellow nursing home residents.

The committee also heard testimony from Mickey Rooney (1920–; http://aging.senate.gov/events/hr230mr.pdf), an American actor and veteran of World War II (1939–1945), who suffered from elder abuse. Rooney described the loss of control he experienced:

> In my case, I was eventually and completely stripped of the ability to make even the most basic decisions in my own life. Over the course of time, my daily life became unbearable. Worse, it seemed to happen out of nowhere. At first, it was something small, something I could control. But then it became something sinister that was completely out of control. I felt trapped, scared, used, and frustrated. But above all, I felt helpless. For years I suffered silently. I couldn't muster the courage to seek the

help I knew I needed. Even when I tried to speak up, I was told to be quiet. It seemed like no one believed me.

His testimony underscored the observation that any older adult can fall victim to abuse and that this problem is not limited exclusively to older adults in nursing homes or those who suffer from cognitive impairments.

Brown concluded in her testimony that many state adult protective service programs that are charged with addressing elder abuse have struggled to keep pace with growing caseloads because they lack the funding and leadership to effectively fulfill their responsibilities. She recounted that in fiscal year 2009 a total of $11.9 million of federal funds were directed to elder justice activities. Figure 11.1 shows the allocation of these funds to the HHS's and the U.S. Department of Justice's institutes and centers that are concerned with preventing and investigating elder abuse.

Furthermore, Brown called for stronger and more effective federal guidance for adult protective service programs. Among the many actions to combat such abuse, she recommended that the HHS develop an effective method for national surveillance of elder abuse and the collection of data as well as a system for compiling and disseminating these data nationwide.

Types of Mistreatment

Federal definitions of elder abuse, neglect, and exploitation appeared for the first time in the Older Americans Act Amendments of 1987. Broadly defined, there are three basic categories of abuse: domestic elder abuse, institutional elder abuse, and self-neglect or self-abuse.

Most documented instances of elder abuse refer to a form of maltreatment of an older person by someone who has a special relationship with the older adult, such as a spouse, sibling, child, friend, or caregiver. Until recently, most data indicated that adult children were the most common abusers of older family members, but Pamela B. Teaster of the University of Kentucky indicates in *A Response to the Abuse of Vulnerable Adults: The 2000 Survey of State Adult Protective Services* (March 7, 2003, http://www.ncea.aoa. gov/ncearoot/Main_Site/pdf/research/apsreport030703.pdf) that the landmark 2000 National Center on Elder Abuse (NCEA) survey found that spouses are the most common perpetrators of abuse and mistreatment. The major types of elder abuse and mistreatment include:

- Physical abuse—inflicting physical pain or bodily injury

- Sexual abuse—nonconsensual sexual contact of any kind with an older person

- Emotional or psychological abuse—inflicting mental anguish by, for example, name calling, humiliation, threats, or isolation

- Neglect—willful or unintentional failure to provide basic necessities, such as food and medical care, as a result of caregiver indifference, inability, or ignorance

- Material or financial abuse—exploiting or misusing an older person's funds or assets

- Abandonment—the desertion of an older adult by an individual who has physical custody of the elder or who has assumed responsibility for providing care for the older person

- Self-neglect—behaviors of an older person that threaten his or her own health or safety

Reporting Abuse

Like child abuse and sexual assault crimes, many crimes against older adults are not reported because the victims are physically or mentally unable to summon help or because they are reluctant or afraid to publicly accuse relatives or caregivers. Loneliness or dependency prevents many victims from reporting the crimes, even when they are aware of them, simply because they are afraid to lose the companionship and care of the perpetrator. When financial abuse is reported, the source of the

FIGURE 11.1

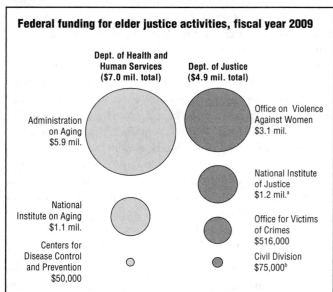

Federal funding for elder justice activities, fiscal year 2009

Dept. of Health and Human Services ($7.0 mil. total)

Dept. of Justice ($4.9 mil. total)

Administration on Aging $5.9 mil.

Office on Violence Against Women $3.1 mil.

National Institute of Justice $1.2 mil.[a]

National Institute on Aging $1.1 mil.

Office for Victims of Crimes $516,000

Centers for Disease Control and Prevention $50,000

Civil Division $75,000[b]

Note: Size of the circles are proportional to amount of funding by agency in fiscal year 2009. While the Office of the Assistant Secretary for Planning and Evaluation completed elder justice-related work in fiscal year 2009, funding for this work was provided in fiscal year 2006.
[a]Of this amount, $650,000 came from the Civil Division's funding for elder abuse research.
[b]The Civil Division also expended $361,000 in fiscal year 2009 for hiring staff to provide legal and law enforcement support for cases of elder abuse in institutions, although this was outside the scope of our study.

SOURCE: Kay E. Brown, "Figure 2. Amount of Federal Funding Expended on Elder Justice Activities in Fiscal Year 2009, by Department and Agency," in *Elder Justice: Stronger Federal Leadership Could Help Improve Response to Elder Abuse*, U.S. Government Accountability Office, March 2, 2011, http://www.gao .gov/new.items/d11384t.pdf (accessed May 17, 2011)

information is likely to be someone other than the victim: a police officer, an ambulance attendant, a bank teller, a neighbor, or other family member.

In "Elder Abuse and Neglect: When Home Is Not Safe" (*Clinics in Geriatric Medicine*, vol. 25, no. 1, February 2009), Linda Abbey of the Virginia Commonwealth University reports that all 50 states require physicians and other social service professionals to report evidence of abuse, neglect, and exploitation when an older adult is in an institution and most also require reporting when abuse occurs in a private home. Abbey notes that according to a 2004 study of state programs funded by the AoA, the most common reporters for older adults were family members (17%), social services (10.6%), friends/neighbors (8%), the older adults themselves (6.3%), long-term care staff (5.5%), law enforcement (5.3%), and nurses/aides (3.8%). Physicians represented just 1.4% of reporters. Abbey asserts that low physician reporting may be attributable to lack of awareness of the problem, lack of training about how to identify abuse, denial that the family may be abusing a loved one, concern about compromising relationships with the family, reluctance to become involved with legal proceedings, and time pressures that prevent the identification of instances of abuse. She also opines that physician discomfort with the problem may impede case finding and observes that "family violence does not fit neatly within the traditional medical paradigm of symptoms, diagnoses and treatment."

Causes of Elder Abuse

According to the NCEA, no single theory can explain why older people are abused. The causes of abuse are diverse and complicated. Some relate to the personality of the abuser, some reflect the relationship between the abuser and the abused, and some are reactions to stressful situations. Even though some children truly dislike their parents and the role of caregiver, many others want to care for their parents or feel it is the right thing to do but may be emotionally or financially unable to meet the challenges of caregiving.

STRESS. Meeting the daily needs of a frail and dependent older adult is demanding and may be overwhelming for some family members who serve as caregivers. When the older person lives in the same household as the caregiver, crowding, differences of opinion, and constant demands often add to the strain of providing physical care. When the older person lives in a different house, the pressure of commuting and managing two households may be stressful.

Stress may be a reality in the life of caregivers, but research does not support its role as the most significant contributing factor in abuse of older adults. Instead, Namkee G. Choi, Jinseok Kim, and Joan Asseff note in "Self-Neglect and Neglect of Vulnerable Older Adults:

Reexamination of Etiology" (*Journal of Gerontological Social Work*, vol. 52, no. 2, February–March 2009) that research points to social and financial problems, such as frail older adults' and their families' lack of resources to pay for essential goods and services, and to inadequate health care and other formal support programs for older adults and their caregivers. Choi, Kim, and Asseff assert that inadequate public policy and supportive services rather than individual and family risk factors need to be considered as a significant cause of elder abuse.

FINANCIAL BURDEN. Caring for an older adult often places a financial strain on a family. Older parents may need financial assistance at the same time that their children are raising their own family. Instead of an occasional night out, a long-awaited vacation, or a badly needed newer car, families may find themselves paying for ever-increasing medical care, prescription drugs, special dietary supplements, extra food and clothing, or therapy. Saving for their children's college education, for a daughter's wedding, or for retirement may be difficult or impossible. Choi, Kim, and Asseff observe that financial strain may be a contributor to mistreatment of older adults.

In "Worsening Economy Increases Risk Factors for Elder Abuse" (*New Jersey Jewish Standard* [Teaneck, New Jersey], July 17, 2009), Lois Goldrich observes that the economic recession, which lasted from late 2007 to mid-2009, and its lasting effects have forced many families to live under the same roof and that economic pressures may be implicated in the uptick in elder abuse cases. Adult children who have lost their jobs may feel frustrated by their inability to care for aging parents. Compounding the economic pressures are cuts to many of the social services older adults and their caregivers depend on and underfunded state adult protective services programs.

CYCLE OF ABUSE. One theory of the causation of abuse of older adults posits that people who abuse an older parent or relative were themselves abused as children. Suzanne K. Steinmetz, the director of the Family Research Center at Indiana University and a recognized expert on domestic violence, finds support for this hypothesis in her landmark study of abusers, *Duty Bound: Elder Abuse and Family Care* (1988). She finds that only one out of 400 adult children who were treated nonviolently when they were children attacked their older parents; by contrast, one out of two adult children who were violently mistreated as children abused their older parents.

The National Council on Child Abuse and Family Violence confirms this pattern of abuse in "Elder Abuse Information" (June 1, 2011, http://www.nccafv.org/elder.htm), stating that "in a family where there is a tendency to physically harm members who are weak or dependent, the aging members of society, who are among the most vulnerable, become the next victims in the cycle of intergenerational family violence." The council cautions that "it is important to remember that violence and its related behaviors are learned and often passed from one generation to the next. A child who is abused by a parent may become an adult who uses violence toward a spouse or child then, as caretaker for an aging parent, extends the abuse to his/her parent or relative."

INVASION OF PRIVACY. Monique I. Sellas and Laurel H. Krouse indicate in "Elder Abuse" (June 8, 2011, http:// emedicine.medscape.com/article/805727-overview) that a shared living arrangement is a major risk factor for mistreatment of older adults, with older people living alone at the lowest risk for abuse. A shared residence increases the opportunities for contact, conflict, and mistreatment. When the home must be shared, there is an inevitable loss of a certain amount of control and privacy. Movement may be restricted, habits may need to change, and rivalries between generations may follow. Frustration and anxiety may result as both older parent and supporting child try to suppress anger, with varying degrees of success.

SOCIAL ISOLATION. Sellas and Krouse note that social isolation is linked to abuse and the mistreatment of older adults. It may be that socially isolated families are better able to hide unacceptable behaviors from friends and neighbors who might report the abuse. Even though there are no data that support the corollary to this finding, it is hypothesized that mistreatment is less likely in families that are rooted in strong social networks.

ALZHEIMER'S DISEASE OR OTHER DEMENTIA. Claudia Cooper et al. assert in "Abuse of People with Dementia by Family Carers: Representative Cross Sectional Survey" (*BMJ*, vol. 338, January 22, 2009) that the diagnosis of Alzheimer's disease (a progressive disease that is characterized by memory loss, impaired thinking, and declining ability to function) or other dementia (loss of intellectual functioning accompanied by memory loss and personality changes) is a risk factor for the physical abuse of older adults. Cooper et al. researched the prevalence of psychological and physical abuse by family caregivers of older adults with Alzheimer's or another dementia. They find that more than half (52%) of caregivers reported some abusive behavior, with verbal abuse reported most frequently. Only 1.4% of caregivers reported physical abuse.

According to Randy R. Gainey and Brian K. Payne, in "Caregiver Burden, Elder Abuse, and Alzheimer's Disease: Testing the Relationship" (*Journal of Health and Human Services Administration*, vol. 29, no. 2, fall 2006), "caregiver burden" (the stress that is associated with caring for older adults with dementia with limited community support services) is the most frequently cited explanation for the observation that people suffering from dementia are at a greater risk for mistreatment. The researchers looked at instances of mistreatment of older adults with Alzheimer's and those who were not cognitively impaired and found

almost no difference in caregiver burden among those caring for older adults with or without dementia. Research has not pinpointed the relationship between dementia and the risk for abuse; however, it may be that dementia itself is not the risk factor but instead it is the disruptive behaviors that result from dementia. This hypothesis is consistent with research that shows that the disruptive behavior of Alzheimer's patients is an especially strong predictor and cause of caregiver stress.

REVERSE DEPENDENCY. Some sources believe that abusers may be quite dependent, emotionally and financially, on their victims for housing, financial assistance, and transportation than are nonabusing caregivers. They appear to have fewer resources and are frequently unable to meet their own basic needs. Rather than having power in the relationship, they are relatively powerless. From these observations, some researchers speculate that abusing caregivers may not always be driven to violence by the physical and emotional burden of caring for a seriously disabled older person but may have mental health problems of their own that can lead to violent behavior. Several studies specifically point to depression as a characteristic of perpetrators of elder mistreatment.

The Abusive Spouse

Edward O. Laumann, Sara A. Leitsch, and Linda J. Waite of the University of Chicago estimate in "Elder Mistreatment in the United States: Prevalence Estimates from a Nationally Representative Study" (*Journal of Gerontology, Series B: Psychological Sciences and Social Sciences*, vol. 63, no. 4, July 2008) the prevalence of mistreatment of older adults using data from the National Social Life, Health, and Aging Project—the first population-based, nationally representative study to ask older adults about their recent experience of mistreatment. The researchers find that approximately 13% of older Americans had been abused and 26% identified a spouse or romantic partner as the abuser.

The high rate of spousal abuse among the older population is possibly because many older adults live with their spouse, so the opportunity for spousal violence is great. Violence against an older spouse may be the continuation of an abusive relationship that began years earlier—abuse does not end simply because a couple ages. Sometimes, however, the abuse may not begin until later years, in which case it is often associated with mental illness, alcohol abuse, unemployment, postretirement depression, and/or loss of self-esteem.

The problem of spousal abuse among older adults may be underestimated and underreported. In "Perceptions of Intimate Partner Violence, Age, and Self-Enhancement Bias" (*Journal of Elder Abuse and Neglect*, vol. 23, no. 1, January 2011), Michael N. Kane, Diane Green, and Robin J. Jacobs find that students preparing for careers in human services such as social work, psychology, and criminal justice were less likely to take allegations of domestic violence between older adults seriously. The students mistakenly assumed that a 30-year-old couple was more likely to engage in conflict and violence than a 75-year-old couple. They also felt that the 30-year-old couple was more likely to change its circumstances than the older couple. Kane, Green, and Jacobs opine that these are ageist beliefs and call for increased awareness and sensitivity to the issue, stating that "raising awareness may help students to identify the possibility of intimate partner abuse when the bruises on the 70-year-old face of Aunt Rose are not attributable to being clumsy but are attributable to 72-year-old Uncle Frank."

Intervention and Prevention

All 50 states and the District of Columbia have laws addressing abuse of older adults, but like laws aiming to prevent and reduce child abuse and domestic violence among younger people, they are often ineffective. The effectiveness of these laws varies from state to state and even from county to county within a given state. No standard definition of abuse exists among enforcement agencies. In many cases authorities cannot legally intervene and terminate an abusive condition unless a report is filed, the abuse is verified, and the victim files a formal complaint. An older adult could understandably be reluctant, physically unable, or too fearful to accuse or prosecute an abuser.

Clearly, the best way to stop elder abuse is to prevent its occurrence. Older people who know that they will eventually need outside help should carefully analyze the potential challenges of living with their family and, if necessary and possible, make alternate arrangements. Furthermore, older adults should take action to protect their money and assets to ensure that their valuables cannot be easily taken from them.

Families or individuals who must serve as caregivers for older adults, voluntarily or otherwise, must be helped to realize that their frustration and despair do not have to result in abuse. Health and social service agencies offer myriad interventions including group support programs and counseling to help caregivers and their families. Many communities allocate resources to assist families to offset the financial burden of elder care, for example, through tax deductions or subsidies for respite care.

INSTITUTIONAL ABUSE: A FORGOTTEN POPULATION?

Abuse of the older population can and does occur in the institutions (nursing homes, board-and-care facilities, and retirement homes) that are charged with, and compensated for, caring for the nation's older population. The term *institutional abuse* generally refers to the same forms of abuse as domestic abuse crimes but is perpetrated by

people who have legal or contractual obligations to provide older adults with care and protection. Even though the Omnibus Budget Reconciliation Act of 1987 states that nursing homes must take steps to attain or maintain the "highest practicable physical, mental, and psychosocial well-being of each resident," too many residents are the victims of neglect or abuse by these facilities or their employees.

Older adult residents of long-term care facilities or supportive housing are thought to be at higher risk for abuse and neglect than community-dwelling older adults. They are particularly vulnerable because most suffer from one or more chronic diseases that impair their physical and cognitive functioning, rendering them dependent on others. Furthermore, many are either unable to report abuse or neglect, or they are fearful that reporting may generate reprisals from the facility staff or otherwise adversely affect their life. Others are unaware of the availability of help.

There are federal laws and regulations that govern nursing homes, but there are no federal standards that oversee or regulate residential care facilities, such as personal care homes, adult congregate living facilities, residential care homes, homes for the aged, domiciliary care homes, board-and-care homes, and assisted living facilities. As a result, it is much more difficult than with nursing homes to estimate the prevalence or nature of abuse or neglect in these facilities. Despite reports in recent years that have raised the specter of widespread and serious abuse of institutionalized older people, as of June 2011 there had never been a systematic study of the prevalence of abuse in nursing homes or other residential facilities.

However, Gerald J. Jogerst, Jeannette M. Daly, and Arthur J. Hartz of the University of Iowa identify in "State Policies and Nursing Home Characteristics Associated with Rates of Resident Mistreatment" (*Journal of the American Medical Directors Association*, vol. 9, no. 9, November 2008) state and nursing home characteristics that are associated with rates of nursing home resident mistreatment. The researchers indicate that in 2004, 1.6% of the nursing home population was reported to be mistreated. There was an average rate of 16 reports per 1,000 residents, but rates varied widely between states. Incident report rates per 1,000 residents ranged from 0.04 in Virginia to 46 in Alabama and complaint report rates ranged from 0.42 in Hawaii to 52 in New Mexico. Higher rates of complaint and reports were associated with lower levels of staffing.

Several studies of elder abuse in long-term care facilities—such as Linda R. Phillips and Guifang Gao's "Mistreatment in Assisted Living Facilities: Complaints, Substantiations, and Risk Factors" (*Gerontologist*, vol. 51, no. 3, January 2011) and Radka Buzgová and Katerina Ivanová's "Violation of Ethical Principles in Institutional Care for Older People" (*Nursing Ethics*, vol. 18, no. 1, January 2011)—find that it is associated with high staff turnover, which in turn may reflect unsatisfactory working conditions or other organizational problems as well as the use of unlicensed or poorly trained personnel.

Types of Abuse and Neglect

Nursing home neglect and abuse can take many forms, including:

- Failure to provide proper diet and hydration
- Failure to assist with personal hygiene
- Over- or undermedication
- Failure to answer call lights promptly
- Failure to turn residents in their beds to promote circulation and prevent decubitus ulcers (bedsores)
- Slapping or other physical abuse
- Leaving residents in soiled garments or beds or failure to take them to the toilet
- Use of unwarranted restraints
- Emotional or verbal abuse
- Retaliation for making a complaint
- Failure to provide appropriate medical care
- Sexual assault, unwanted touching, indecent exposure, or rape
- Theft of the resident's property or money

Surveys conducted with certified nursing assistants (CNAs) who work in long-term care facilities are summarized in "Preventing Abuse and Neglect in Nursing Homes: The Role of Staffing and Training" (November 23, 2003, http://sp.srph.tamhsc.edu/centers/moved_SRHRC/PPT/nh2_gsa03.ppt) by Catherine Hawes, the former director of the Southwest Rural Health Research Center at Texas A&M University. Hawes reveals that more than one-third of the CNAs had witnessed abuses, including incidents of physical and verbal or psychological abuse, such as:

- Aggressiveness with a resident and rough handling
- Pulling too hard on a resident
- Yelling in anger
- Threatening behavior
- Punching, slapping, kicking, or hitting
- Speaking in a harsh tone, cursing at a resident, or saying harsh or mean things to a resident

The CNAs also offered examples of neglect, which is often more difficult to detect and measure, including:

- Neglecting oral/dental care
- Failing to perform prescribed range of motion exercises

- Failing to change residents after an episode of incontinence
- Ignoring residents who are bedfast, such as by not offering activities to them
- Not performing prescribed wound care
- Failing to bathe residents regularly
- Performing a one-person transfer (move from bed to chair or wheelchair) when the resident requires a two-person transfer
- Not providing cuing or task segmentation to residents who need that kind of assistance to maximize their independence
- Failing to perform scheduled toileting or helping residents when they ask
- Not keeping residents hydrated
- Turning off a call light and taking no action on the resident's request

Resident Risk Factors

Even though there has been scant research describing the factors that contribute to risk for abuse of institutionalized older adults, some studies indicate that the risk for abuse increases in direct relationship to the older resident's dependence on the facility's staff for safety, protection, and care. For example, Diana K. Harris and Michael L. Benson, in *Maltreatment of Patients in Nursing Homes: There Is No Safe Place* (2006), and Andrew C. Coyne of the University of Medicine and Dentistry of New Jersey, in "The Relationship between Dementia and Elder Abuse" (*Geriatric Times*, vol. 2, no. 4, July–August 2001), suggest that a resident with a diagnosis of Alzheimer's disease, another dementia, or some type of memory loss or confusion is at greater risk for abuse in the average nursing home population. In "Elder Abuse and Neglect in Long-Term Care" (*Elder Abuse and Neglect in Long-Term Care Clinics in Geriatric Medicine*, vol. 21, no. 2, May 2005), Seema Joshi and Joseph H. Flaherty of the St. Louis Veterans Administration Medical Center suggest that residents with behavioral symptoms, such as physical aggressiveness, appear to be at higher risk for abuse by staff; this finding is supported by interviews with the CNAs.

Social isolation may also increase the risk for abuse. Residents who have no visitors are especially vulnerable because they lack family or friends who could oversee their care, bear witness to and report any abuses, and advocate on their behalf.

Efforts to Identify and Reduce Abuse

In an effort to improve the quality of care and eliminate abuse in nursing homes, government regulations and laws have been enacted that require greater supervision and scrutiny of nursing homes. President

TABLE 11.5

Actual and projected results of ombudsman program, 2008–2011

Indicator	Most recent result	Fiscal year 2010 projection	Fiscal year 2011 projection	Fiscal year 2011 +/− fiscal year 2010
Output Q: Number of complaints (*output*)	FY 2008: 271,650	270,000	265,000	−5,000
Output R: Number of ombudsman consultations (*output*)	FY 2008: 455,423	411,000	455,000	+44,000
Output S: Facilities regularly visited not in response to a complaint (*output*)	FY 2008: 37,706	35,000	37,000	+2,000
Output U: Elder abuse prevention non-OAA service expenditures ($ thousand) (*output*)	FY 2008: $19,936	$17,992	$19,950	+$1,958

OAA = Older Americans Act

SOURCE: Adapted from "Protection of Vulnerable Older Americans Outcomes and Outputs," in *Department of Health and Human Services Fiscal Year 2011 Justification of Estimates for Appropriations Committees*, Department of Health and Human Services, Administration on Aging, 2011, http://www.aoa.gov/aoaroot/about/Budget/DOCS/AoA_CJ_FY_2011.pdf (accessed May 17, 2011)

Ronald Reagan (1911–2004) signed the Omnibus Budget Reconciliation Act of 1987, which included protections for patient rights and treatment. The law went into effect in October 1990, but compliance with the law varies from state to state and from one nursing facility to another.

In 1987 the AoA established the Prevention of Elder Abuse, Neglect, and Exploitation program. This program trains law enforcement officers, health care workers, and other professionals about how to identify and respond to elder abuse and supports education campaigns to increase public awareness of elder abuse and how to prevent it.

Many states have adopted additional legislation to help stem instances of institutional abuse and neglect. For example, in 1998 the state of New York enacted Kathy's Law, which created the new felony-level crime of "abuse of a vulnerable elderly person." At the state level there are many agencies involved in identifying and investigating cases of abuse and neglect. These agencies differ across states but may include ombudsmen (offices that assist patients who have complaints), adult protective services, the state survey agency responsible for licensing nursing homes, the state agency responsible for the operation of the nurse aide registry, Medicaid fraud units in the attorney general's office, and professional licensing boards.

The NCEA (December 2010, http://www.ncea.aoa.gov/NCEAroot/Main_Site/Resources/Newsletter/2010/december.pdf) asserts that raising public awareness of the problem is vital for preventing it. It encourages adult children to discuss mistreatment, abuse, and exploitation with their parents and other older adults and to take specific steps to reduce the risk of abuse, such as by carefully screening prospective caregivers.

LONG-TERM CARE OMBUDSMAN PROGRAM. Long-term care ombudsmen are advocates for residents of nursing homes, board-and-care homes, assisted living facilities, and other adult care facilities. The Long-Term Care Ombudsman Program was established under the Older Americans Act, which is administered by the AoA.

In "Long-Term Care Ombudsman Program" (March 9, 2011, http://www.aoa.gov/AoARoot/AoA_Programs/Elder_Rights/Ombudsman/index.aspx), the AoA reports that in fiscal year 2009, 8,661 volunteers and 1,203 paid ombudsmen worked to resolve 233,025 complaints. More than three-quarters (81%) of all nursing homes and nearly half (45%) of all board-and-care, assisted living, and similar homes were visited regularly by state and local ombudsmen. Table 11.5 shows the actual numbers of complaints that were at least partially resolved by ombudsmen in fiscal year 2008 as well as the number of ombudsman consultations, facility visits in response to complaints, and expenditures for prevention. It also projects these measures through fiscal year 2011.

IMPORTANT NAMES
AND ADDRESSES

AARP (formerly American Association of Retired Persons)
601 E St. NW
Washington, DC 20049
1-888-687-2277
URL: http://www.aarp.org/

Administration on Aging
One Massachusetts Ave. NW
Washington, DC 20001
(202) 619-0724
FAX: (202) 357-3555
E-mail: aoainfo@aoa.hhs.gov
URL: http://www.aoa.gov/

Alliance for Aging Research
750 17th St. NW, Ste. 1100
Washington, DC 20006
(202) 293-2856
FAX: (202) 255-8394
E-mail: info@agingresearch.org
URL: http://www.agingresearch.org/

Alzheimer's Association
225 N. Michigan Ave., 17th Floor
Chicago, IL 60601-7633
(312) 335-8700
1-800-272-3900
FAX: 1-866-699-1246
E-mail: info@alz.org
URL: http://www.alz.org/

American Association for Geriatric Psychiatry
7910 Woodmont Ave., Ste. 1050
Bethesda, MD 20814-3004
(301) 654-7850
FAX: (301) 654-4137
E-mail: main@aagponline.org
URL: http://www.aagponline.org/

American Geriatrics Society
40 Fulton St., 18th Floor
New York, NY 10038
(212) 308-1414
FAX: (212) 832-8646

E-mail: info@americangeriatrics.org
URL: http://www.americangeriatrics.org/

American Heart Association
7272 Greenville Ave.
Dallas, TX 75231
1-800-242-8721
URL: http://www.americanheart.org/

Arthritis Foundation
PO Box 7669
Atlanta, GA 30357-0669
1-800-283-7800
URL: http://www.arthritis.org/

Assisted Living Federation of America
1650 King St., Ste. 602
Alexandria, VA 22314-2747
(703) 894-1805
FAX: (703) 894-1831
E-mail: info@alfa.org
URL: http://www.alfa.org/

Boomer Project
2601 Floyd Ave.
Richmond, VA 23220
(804) 358-8981
FAX: (804) 342-1790
E-mail: matt@boomerproject.com
URL: http://www.boomerproject.com/

Centers for Disease Control and Prevention
1600 Clifton Rd.
Atlanta, GA 30333
1-800-232-4636
E-mail: cdcinfo@cdc.gov
URL: http://www.cdc.gov/

Centers for Medicare and Medicaid Services
7500 Security Blvd.
Baltimore, MD 21244
(410) 786-3000
1-877-267-2323
URL: http://www.cms.gov/

Children of Aging Parents
PO Box 167
Richboro, PA 18954
(215) 355-6611
1-800-227-7294
URL: http://www.caps4caregivers.org/

Civic Ventures
114 Sansome St., Ste. 850
San Francisco, CA 94104
(415) 430-0141
FAX: (415) 430-0144
URL: http://www.civicventures.org/

Eldercare Locator Directory
1-800-677-1116
URL: http://www.eldercare.gov/

Family Caregiver Alliance
180 Montgomery St., Ste. 900
San Francisco, CA 94104
(415) 434-3388
1-800-445-8106
E-mail: info@caregiver.org
URL: http://www.caregiver.org/

Gerontological Society of America
1220 L St. NW, Ste. 901
Washington, DC 20005
(202) 842-1275
FAX: (202) 842-1150
URL: http://www.geron.org/

Gray Panthers
1612 K St. NW, Ste. 300
Washington, DC 20006
(202) 737-6637
1-800-280-5362
URL: http://www.graypanthers.org/

Insurance Institute for Highway Safety
1005 N. Glebe Rd., Ste. 800
Arlington, VA 22201
(703) 247-1500
FAX: (703) 247-1588
URL: http://www.highwaysafety.org/

LeadingAge (formerly the American Association of Homes and Services for the Aging)
2519 Connecticut Ave. NW
Washington, DC 20008-1520
(202) 783-2242
FAX: (202) 783-2255
E-mail: info@LeadingAge.org
URL: http://leadingage.org/

Mature Workers Employment Alliance
826 Euclid Ave.
Syracuse, NY 13210
(315) 446-3587
E-mail: mwea4cny@mwea-cny.com
URL: http://mwea-cny.com/index.php

Medicare Rights Center
1224 M St. NW, Ste. 100
Washington, DC 20005
(202) 637-0961
1-800-333-4114
FAX: (202) 637-0962
URL: http://www.medicarerights.org/

National Academy of Elder Law Attorneys
1577 Spring Hill Rd., Ste. 220
Vienna, VA 22182
(703) 942-5711
FAX: (703) 563-9504
URL: http://www.naela.org/

National Alliance for Caregiving
4720 Montgomery Ln., Second Floor
Bethesda, MD 20814
URL: http://www.caregiving.org/

National Association for Home Care and Hospice
228 Seventh St. SE
Washington, DC 20003
(202) 547-7424
FAX: (202) 547-3540
URL: http://www.nahc.org/

National Caregiving Foundation
801 N. Pitt St., Ste. 116
Alexandria, VA 22314
(800) 930-1357
E-mail: info@caregivingfoundation.org
URL: http://www.caregivingfoundation.org/

National Caucus and Center on Black Aged
1220 L St. NW, Ste. 800
Washington, DC 20005
(202) 637-8400
FAX: (202) 347-0895
E-mail: support@ncba-aged.org
URL: http://www.ncba-aged.org/

National Center on Elder Abuse Center for Community Research and Services University of Delaware
297 Graham Hall
Newark, DE 19716

(302) 831-3525
FAX: (302) 831-4225
URL: http://www.ncea.aoa.gov/ncearoot/Main_Site/index.aspx

National Center for Health Statistics Division of Data Services
3311 Toledo Rd.
Hyattsville, MD 20782
1-800-232-4636
URL: http://www.cdc.gov/nchs

National Consumer Voice for Quality Long-Term Care (formerly the National Citizens' Coalition for Nursing Home Reform)
1001 Connecticut Ave. NW, Ste. 425
Washington, DC 20036
(202) 332-2275
FAX: (202) 332-2949
E-mail: info@theconsumervoice.org
URL: http://www.theconsumervoice.org/

National Family Caregivers Association
10400 Connecticut Ave., Ste. 500
Kensington, MD 20895-3944
(301) 942-6430
1-800-896-3650
FAX: (301) 942-2302
E-mail: info@thefamilycaregiver.org
URL: http://www.thefamilycaregiver.org/

National Hispanic Council on Aging
Walker Bldg.
734 15th St. NW, Ste. 1050
Washington, DC 20005
(202) 347-9733
FAX: (202) 347-9735
E-mail: nhcoa@nhcoa.org
URL: http://www.nhcoa.org/

National Hospice and Palliative Care Organization
1731 King St., Ste. 100
Alexandria, VA 22314
(703) 837-1500
FAX: (703) 837-1233
E-mail: nhpco_info@nhpco.org
URL: http://www.nhpco.org/

National Indian Council on Aging
10501 Montgomery Blvd. NE, Ste. 210
Albuquerque, NM 87111
(505) 292-2001
FAX: (505) 292-1922
E-mail: info@nicoa.org
URL: http://www.nicoa.org/

National Institute on Aging
Bldg. 31, Rm. 5C27
31 Center Dr., MSC 2292
Bethesda, MD 20892
(301) 496-1752
FAX: (301) 496-1072
URL: http://www.nih.gov/nia

National Osteoporosis Foundation
1150 17th St. NW
Washington, DC 20036
(202) 223-2226
1-800-231-4222
FAX: (202) 223-2237
URL: http://www.nof.org/

National PACE Association
801 N. Fairfax St., Ste. 309
Alexandria, VA 22314
(703) 535-1565
FAX: (703) 535-1566
E-mail: info@npaonline.org
URL: http://www.npaonline.org/

National Respite Locator Service Chapel Hill Training-Outreach Project
800 Eastowne Dr., Ste. 105
Chapel Hill, NC 27514
(919) 490-5577
FAX: (919) 490-4905
E-mail: info@respitelocator.org
URL: http://www.respitelocator.org/

National Senior Citizens Law Center
1444 Eye St. NW, Ste. 1100
Washington, DC 20005
(202) 289-6976
FAX: (202) 289-7224
URL: http://www.nsclc.org/

National Society for American Indian Elderly
200 E. Fillmore St., Ste. 151
Phoenix, AZ 85004
(602) 424-0542
E-mail: info@nsaie.org
URL: http://www.nsaie.org/

National Urban League
120 Wall St.
New York, NY 10005
(212) 558-5300
FAX: (212) 344-5332
URL: http://www.nul.org/

Older Women's League
1025 Connecticut Ave. NW, Ste. 701
Washington, DC 20036
1-877-653-7966
FAX: (202) 833-3472
E-mail: Info@owl-national.org
URL: http://www.owl-national.org/

Pension Benefit Guaranty Corporation
1200 K St. NW, Ste. 9429
Washington, DC 20005-4026
(202) 326-4000
1-800-400-7242
URL: http://www.pbgc.gov/

Pension Rights Center
1350 Connecticut Ave. NW, Ste. 206
Washington, DC 20036-1739
(202) 296-3776
FAX: (202) 833-2472
URL: http://www.pensionrights.org/

SeniorNet
12801 Worldgate Dr., Ste. 500
Herndon, VA 20170
(571) 203-7100
FAX: (703) 871-3901
URL: http://www.seniornet.org/

Service Corps of Retired Executives
409 Third St. SW, Sixth Floor
Washington, DC 20024

1-800-634-0245
URL: http://www.score.org/

U.S. Census Bureau
4600 Silver Hill Rd.
Washington, DC 20233
URL: http://www.census.gov/

U.S. Department of Veterans Affairs
Washington, DC 20011

1-800-827-1000
URL: http://www.va.gov/

U.S. Social Security Administration
Office of Public Inquiries
Windsor Park Building
6401 Security Blvd.
Baltimore, MD 21235
1-800-772-1213
http://www.ssa.gov/

RESOURCES

Many of the demographic data cited in this text were drawn from U.S. Census Bureau and U.S. Bureau of Labor Statistics publications, including "Older Americans Month: May 2011" (March 2011), *The Next Four Decades—The Older Population in the United States: 2010 to 2050* (Grayson K. Vincent and Victoria A. Velkoff, May 2010), and the 2009 American Community Survey. The Guinness World Records and the National Centenarian Awareness Project provided information about the growing number of centenarians in the United States.

The reports *A Profile of Older Americans: 2010* (Saadia Greenberg, 2011) by the Administration on Aging and *Older Americans 2010: Key Indicators of Well-Being* (July 2011) by the Federal Interagency Forum on Aging-Related Statistics provided useful data about older adults. Additional population data were drawn from *The World Factbook* (2011) by the Central Intelligence Agency.

The *The 2011 Retirement Confidence Survey: Confidence Drops to Record Lows, Reflecting "the New Normal"* (Ruth Helman et al., March 2011) by the Employee Benefit Research Institute and Matthew Greenwald & Associates provided information about pension plans and other employee benefits. The U.S. Department of Labor and the National Economic Council Interagency Working Group on Social Security described trends in labor force participation. The "Modest Increase in 2010 Funded Status as a Result of Record Employer Contributions" (John W. Ehrhardt and Paul C. Morgan, March 2011) provided information about pensions. The Equal Employment Opportunity Commission offered information about age discrimination issues and claims. Peter Shapiro's *A History of National Service in America* (1994) detailed the establishment of a national senior service during the administration of President John F. Kennedy.

The American Association of Community Colleges (AACC) reported on students at the nation's community colleges. The Pew Internet and American Life Project

report *Generations 2010* (Kathryn Zickuhr, December 2010) tracked Internet use by age.

The National Highway Traffic Safety Administration, in *Enhancing the Effectiveness of Safety Warning Systems for Older Drivers: Project Report* (December 2010), documented the increasing numbers of older drivers. The U.S. Government Accountability Office (GAO) publication *Transportation-Disadvantaged Seniors: Efforts to Enhance Senior Mobility Could Benefit from Additional Guidance and Information* (August 2004) and Rhianna JoIris Babka, Jill F. Cooper, and David R. Ragland's *Evaluation of Urban Travel Training for Older Adults* (November 2008) explored ways to improve transportation options for older adults. The Insurance Institute for Highway Safety publication "Fatality Facts 2009: Older People" (December 2010) reported that even though the oldest and youngest drivers have the highest fatality rates on a per-mile-driven basis, older drivers involved in crashes are less likely than younger drivers to hurt others. In "Realizing Dignified Transportation for Seniors" (April 2009), Philanthropy New York reported that each year more than 1 million older adults stop driving because of declines in their fitness level, vision, and ability to think clearly. The American Medical Association and the National Highway Traffic Safety Administration developed the *Physician's Guide to Assessing and Counseling Older Drivers* (February 2010), which details medical conditions and their potential effects on driving skills. The U.S. Department of Transportation, in *Older Driver Program: Five-Year Strategic Plan* (December 2010), aims to help the states prepare for the more than 40 million drivers aged 65 years and older who will take to the roads in the coming decade.

The U.S. Department of Housing and Urban Development's Office of Community Planning and Development described in *The Third Annual Homeless Assessment Report to Congress* (July 2008) the plight of homeless older Americans. The National Low Income Housing Coalition report *Out of Reach 2010: Renters in the Great Recession, the Crisis*

Continues (Megan DeCrappeo et al., June 2010) documented rental housing cost data. *Assessing the Impact of Severe Economic Recession on the Elderly: Summary of a Workshop* (Malay Majmundar, 2011), a report of the National Research Council of the National Academies, described how older adults are responding to economic uncertainty.

The U.S. Social Security Administration provided information about the history and future of Social Security as well as benefits and eligibility in publications such as *Fast Facts and Figures about Social Security, 2010* (August 2010), "Social Security Basic Facts" (May 2011), and *The 2010 Annual Report of the Board of Trustees of the Federal Old-Age and Survivors Insurance and Federal Disability Insurance Trust Funds* (August 2010).

The Centers for Medicare and Medicaid Services (CMS) coordinates Medicare and Medicaid. The CMS provided information about the history, the beneficiaries, and the future of these entitlement programs. The Centers for Disease Control and Prevention (CDC) provided vital health statistics in publications such as *Health, United States, 2010* (February 2011), "Births: Preliminary Data for 2009" (Brady E. Hamilton, Joyce A. Martin, and Stephanie J. Ventura, December 2010), and the 2010 National Health Interview Survey. The Kaiser Family Foundation report "Medicaid and Long-Term Care Services and Supports" (March 2011) detailed long-term care expenditures. The U.S. Department of Veterans Affairs reported in *Federal Benefits for Veterans, Dependents and Survivors 2010 Edition* (2010) on the benefits and services that are used by U.S. veterans.

In *Market Survey of Long-Term Care Costs: The 2010 MetLife Market Survey of Nursing Home, Assisted Living, Adult Day Services, and Home Care Costs* (October 2010), the MetLife Mature Market Institute reported on the costs that are associated with nursing homes and assisted living. *Retooling for an Aging America: Building the Health Care Workforce* (2008) by the Institute of Medicine's Committee on the Future Health Care Workforce for Older Americans reported that an increasing number of Americans are hiring caregivers to assist with older relatives.

The AARP underwrites research about older Americans. One example of its research cited in this text is the AARP Public Policy Institute report *The Mortgage Crisis: Older Americans Are Feeling the Pain* (February 2009), which offered insight into older homeowners' experiences with foreclosure.

Many organizations and publications provide information on specific health and medical problems of older adults. Among the many publications cited in this text are the American Heart Association's "Understand Your Risk of Heart Attack" (2011), the American Cancer Society's *Cancer Facts and Figures, 2010* (2010), the CDC's "Falls among Older Adults: An Overview" (December 2010), and the Alzheimer's Association's *2011 Alzheimer's Disease Facts and Figures* (2011). The Department of Veterans

Affairs provided demographic projections of the health and other needs of older veterans.

Similarly, many agencies, organizations, and professional organizations, notably LeadingAge (formerly the American Association of Homes and Services for the Aging), the National Center for Education Statistics, the Mature Workers Employment Alliance, and the American Geriatrics Society, offered data and analyses of myriad issues of importance to older Americans.

Professional medical journals offered research findings and information about health and disease among older adults as well as health service utilization and financing. Articles from the following journals were cited in this text: *Acta Psychiatrica Scandinavica, Addiction, Aging, Neuropsychology, and Cognition, Alzheimer's and Dementia, American Journal of Geriatric Psychiatry, Annals of Internal Medicine, Annals of Neurology, Annual Review of Public Health, Archives of Ophthalmology, BMC Health Services Research, BMJ, Clinics in Geriatric Medicine, Demography, Gerontologist, Health Affairs, Health Psychology, International Journal of Impotence Research, Journal of the American Medical Association, Journal of the American Medical Directors Association, Journal of the American Geriatrics Society, Journal of Gerontological Social Work, Journal of Gerontology, Journal of Happiness Studies, Journal of Health and Human Services Administration, Journal of Personality and Social Psychology, Medical Clinics of North America, Medical Journal of Australia, Milbank Quarterly, Neurology, Online Journal of Issues in Nursing, Proceedings Baylor University Medical Center, Psychology and Aging, Seminars in Respiratory and Critical Care Medicine, Social Science and Medicine*, and *U.S. Pharmacist*.

Because the aging population affects nearly every aspect of society, from employment and housing to health care and politics, consumer publications frequently feature articles about and of interest to older adults. Articles cited in this volume were drawn from *Newsweek, New York Times, USA Today, U.S. News & World Report*, and *Wall Street Journal*.

Information about abuse and mistreatment of older adults was found in *Broken Trust: Elders, Family, and Finances* (March 2009) by the MetLife Mature Market Institute, the National Committee for the Prevention of Elder Abuse, and the Center for Gerontology at the Virginia Polytechnic Institute and State University; and in *Consumer Fraud in the United States: The Second FTC Survey* (October 2007) by the Federal Trade Commission. The Bureau of Justice Statistics' *Criminal Victimization, 2009* (Jennifer L. Truman and Michael R. Rand, October 2010) and *Criminal Victimization in the United States, 2008 Statistical Tables* (Michael R. Rand and Jayne E. Robinson, May 2011) and the *Journal of Elder Abuse and Neglect* provided data about fraud, abuse, and violent victimization of older adults.

We are very grateful to the Gallup Organization for permitting us to present the results of its renowned opinion polls and graphics.

INDEX

Page references in italics refer to photographs. References with the letter t following them indicate the presence of a table. The letter f indicates a figure. If more than one table or figure appears on a particular page, the exact item number for the table or figure being referenced is provided.

A

AALTCI (American Association for Long-Term Care Insurance), 165

AARP
  age for membership eligibility, 4
  on aging U.S. population, 20
  contact information, 181
  on older workers, 69–70
  political power of, 85–86
  telemarketing fraud and, 171
  transportation initiatives, 89
  transportation surveys by, 87

AARP Bulletin Today, 33

AARP Driver Safety Program, 95

"AARP Driver Safety Program History and Facts" (AARP), 95

AARP Global Network, 37, 61

AARP Public Policy Institute, 29–30

Abbey, Linda, 175

Abilify (drug), 142

"About AARP" (AARP), 85

Absenteeism
  absences from work, by age/sex, 71t
  myth about older workers, 69

"Abuse of People with Dementia by Family Caregivers: Representative Cross Sectional Survey" (Cooper et al.), 176

Abuse/mistreatment of older adults
  at board-and-care facilities, 57
  causes of, 175–176
  efforts to combat, 173–174
  federal funding for elder justice activities, 174f

institutional abuse, 177–179
  magnitude of problem, 173
  ombudsman program, actual/projected results of, 179t
  reporting, 174–175
  spousal abuse, 176–177
  types of, 174

Accessory apartments, 58

Acetylcholine, 134

ACTION agency, 76

Activities of daily living (ADLs)
  chronic conditions that limited, 99
  Medicare enrollees aged 65 and older unable to perform activities of daily living, 103f

AD. *See* Alzheimer's disease

Addresses/names, of organizations, 181–183

ADEA. *See* Age Discrimination in Employment Act

ADEA Amendments of 1978, 66

Adherence, to prescription drugs, 120

Adler, Nancy E., 5

ADLs. *See* Activities of daily living

Administration on Aging (AoA)
  on alternative transportation for older adults, 96, 97
  contact information, 181
  Eldercare Locator Directory, 149
  on living arrangements of older adults, 47
  Medicare fraud and, 172–173
  Prevention of Elder Abuse, Neglect, and Exploitation program, 179

Adult congregate living facilities, 52

Adult day care
  centers, 149
  description of, 148

Adult education
  educational attainment of population aged 65 and over, 80(f5.1)
  educational attainment of population aged 65 and over, by race/Hispanic origin, 80(f5.2)

Elderhostels, 79, 83
  enrollment in degree-granting institutions by sex, age, attendance status, 81t–82t
  older adults' participation in, 79

"Adult Education in America" (ETS Policy Information Center), 79

Adult protective service programs, 174, 174f

Adventure programs, 83

African-Americans
  criminal victimization rates for, 167
  educational attainment of older Americans, 79
  health ratings of Americans, 99
  living arrangements of older adults, 47–48
  median household income of, 22
  multigenerational households of, 48
  net worth of households, 29
  older Americans, 8, 10

Age
  absences from work, by age/sex, 71t
  age-related changes, skills of older drivers and, 91–96
  aging labor force, 66–67, 69
  aging population of U.S., 1–3
  average annual expenditures/ characteristics by, 34t–36t
  birth rates, by age of mother, 65t
  boomers' attitudes about, 37
  of caregivers, 146
  children/older adults as percentage of global population, 2f
  death, leading causes of, numbers of deaths, by age, 111(t7.5)
  discrimination and work, 71–72, 74
  economic changes and, 65–66
  of entrepreneurs, 71
  foreign-born population by sex, age, region of birth, 13t–15t
  of fraud victims, 172
  health ratings and, 99

sexuality and, 126–127

urinary incontinence, 109

vision changes, 113

CIA. *See* Central Intelligence Agency

Cialis, 127

Cigarettes

percentage of adults aged 65 and older who smoke, 124*f*

smoking among older adults, 123

Circulatory problems, 107

City of Jackson, Smith v., 72, 74

Civic Ventures, 74–75, 181

Clark, Robert F., 57

Clarke, David M., 138–139

CLASS Independence Benefit Plan, 152

CMS. *See* Centers for Medicare and Medicaid Services

CNAs (certified nursing assistants), 178

"Cognitive Behavior Therapy for Generalized Anxiety Disorder among Older Adults in Primary Care: A Randomized Clinical Trial" (Stanley et al.), 141

Cognitive behavioral therapy (CBT), 141

Cognitive decline

hearing loss and, 112

oral health problems and, 115

Cognitive impairment

caused by Alzheimer's disease, 136

dementia and, 133

memory decline, 132–133

prevalence of, 138

rates of, 131

Cognitive skills, of older adult drivers, 94

Cohousing, 57–58

Cohousing Association of the United States, 58

COLAs (cost-of-living adjustments), 38–39

Colello, Kirsten J., 165

College

degrees earned by older Americans, 79

enrollment in degree-granting institutions by sex, age, attendance status, 81*t*–82*t*

older adults attending, 64, 79

older adults in technology classes, 70–71

veterans' benefits for, 162

veterans pursuing higher education, monthly allowance for, 163(*t*10.4)

Collins, Nick, 17

Comarow, Avery, 54

Committee on the Future Health Care Workforce for Older Americans, 145

"Common Variants at ABCA7, MS4A6A/MS4A4E, EPHA1, CD33, and CD2AP Are Associated with Alzheimer's Disease" (Hollingworth et al.), 135

"Common Variants at MS4A4/MS4A6E, CD2AP, CD33, and EPHA1 Are Associated with Late-Onset Alzheimer's Disease" (Naj et al.), 135

Community First Choice Option, 162

Community housing

with home care services, 166

percentage of Medicare enrollees aged 65 and over residing in selected residential settings, by age group, 166(*f*10.8)

percentage of Medicare enrollees aged 65 and over with functional limitations, 166(*f*10.9)

Community Living Assistance Services and Supports (CLASS) Act, 165

"Community Living Assistance Services and Supports (CLASS) Provisions in the Patient Protection and Affordable Care Act (PPACA)" (Mulvey & Colello), 165

Community services, 148–149

Community Services Block Grant Programs, 96

Community-Based Care Transitions Program, 147

Compellent Technologies, 71

Computer, 83–84

"Congress Passes Sections 811 and 202 Legislation, President Expected to Sign Bills into Law" (National Low Income Housing Coalition), 62

Consumer expenses

average annual expenditures and characteristics, by age, 34*t*–36*t*

average annual expenditures of all consumer units, 89*t*

car ownership costs, 87–88

overview of, 33

See also Costs; Expenditures

Consumer Fraud in the United States: The Second FTC Survey (Federal Trade Commission), 171–172

Consumer Price Index (CPI), 30

Consumers, aging

baby boomers, 37

effect on consumer sectors, 33, 35

Contact information, for organizations, 181–183

Continuing care retirement communities (CCRCs)

decline in applications to, 59

description of, 52, 57

with home care services, 166

Continuity theory, 132

Cooper, Claudia, 176

Cooper, Jill F., 87, 88

Cornwell, Benjamin, 12

"Correlates of Alcohol-Related Discussions between Older Adults and Their Physicians" (Duru et al.), 144

"Cortex Area Thinner in Youth with Alzheimer's-Related Gene" (National Institute on Aging), 134

Cost-of-living adjustments (COLAs), 38–39

Costs

of age discrimination suit, 72

of assisted living, 57

of car ownership, 87–88

of care for AD patients, 138

of caregiving, 146, 147

of CCRCs, 57

of health care, legislation on, 152

of health care for older adults, 151

of hiring older workers, 69–70

of long-term care, 163–164, 165*t*

of Medicare, 161

national health expenditures by source of funds, 153*t*–154*t*

of prescription drugs, 119, 119*f*

pressure on employees to retire, 72

Social Security/Medicare cost as percentage of GDP, 161*f*

See also Expenditures

Coulton, Simon, 144

Council of Large Public Housing Authorities, 61–62

Court cases

Gross v. FBL Financial Services, Inc., 74

Meacham et al. v. Knolls Atomic Power Laboratory, 74

Smith v. City of Jackson, 72, 74

Coyne, Andrew C., 178

CPI (Consumer Price Index), 30

Crime

federal funding for elder justice activities, 174*f*

fraud, 168, 171–173

against older adults, 167–168

victimization number/rates for vehicle theft, 171*t*

victimization rate by victim-offender relationship, type of crime, victim characteristics, 170*t*

victimization rates by age, race, type of crime, 169*t*

violent crime rates, by gender, race, Hispanic origin, age of victim, 168*t*

Criminal Victimization, 2009 (Truman & Rand), 167

Criminal Victimization in the United States, 2008 Statistical Tables (Rand & Robinson), 167

CT scan, 135

Culture change, 55

"Current Alzheimer's Treatments" (Alzheimer's Association), 136

Currie, Kay C., 138–139

Cycle of abuse, 175–176

D

Daly, Jeannette M., 177

De Tocqueville, Alexis, 86

Death, awareness of imminence of, 132

Death rates

aging of population and, 3

for cerebrovascular disease, 123*t*–124*t*

for malignant neoplasms, 121*t*–122*t*

for motor vehicle accidents, 90

E

Financing, health care for older adults, 151–152
First Solar, 71
Fixed route and scheduled services transportation, 96
Flaherty, Joseph H., 178
Flinders, Abigail, 120
Florida, older adult population in, 12
FMR (fair market rent), 61
Food
  malnutrition, 110, 112
  poverty rates based on food budget, 30
Food and Drug Administration (FDA), 171, 172
"For Nursing Homes, 'It's Diversify or Die'" (Sedensky), 54
"Forecasting Age-Related Macular Degeneration through the Year 2050: The Potential Impact of New Treatments" (Rein et al.), 114–115
Foreclosures
  rate of for older adults, 30
  strategic defaults, 59
Foreign-born population
  by sex, age, region of birth, 13t–15t
  statistics on, 12
Foster Grandparent Program, 75–76
401(k) plan, 25
Fram, Alan, 64
Franklin, Benjamin, 63
Fraud
  at board-and-care facilities, 57
  financial fraud, 172
  health fraud, 172
  Medicare fraud, 172–173
  against older adults, 168, 171–172
  pension fraud, 28
Freedman, Marc, 74
FTC (Federal Trade Commission), 171–172
FTO gene, 137
Full-time work, 69
Funding
  for caregiving, 147
  for elder justice activities, 174, 174f
FY 2011 Online Performance Appendix (Administration on Aging), 173

G

Gainey, Randy R., 176
Gallo, Joseph J., 139
Gallup Organization
  public opinion on Social Security, 42
  ratings of past presidents, 85
Gandhi, Mohandas, 79
GAO. *See* U.S. Government Accountability Office
Gao, Guifang, 177
Gaudiosi, John, 84
"GDC 2011: Game Developers Focus on New Baby Boomer Casual Gamers" (Gaudiosi), 84

GDP (gross domestic product), 161, 161f
Gender
  absences from work, by age/sex, 71t
  alcohol consumption and, 142
  Alzheimer's disease and, 134
  of caregivers, 146
  chronic conditions, frequency of occurrence by, 99
  chronic conditions, people aged 65 and over who reported having, 111(t7.6)
  depression and, 138
  foreign-born population by, 13t–15t
  hearing loss and, 112
  life expectancy by, 5
  living arrangements of older adults by, 47–48, 51f
  marital status of older Americans and, 11, 11f
  of older adults in labor force, 66–67
  of older adults in U.S., 6
  physical functioning difficulties by, 101
  population, projected, by age/sex, 7t–8t, 9f
  population aged 65 and over, percentage female, by age, 8f
  population aged 65 and over living alone, by age group/sex, 50(t3.3)
  urinary incontinence by, 109
  violent crime rates by, 168t
Generalized anxiety disorder, 141
Generation X, 48
Generations 10 (Zickuhr), 83–84
Genetic origins, of Alzheimer's disease, 134–135
Genworth 2011 Cost of Care Survey: Home Care Providers, Adult Day Health Care Facilities, Assisted Living Facilities, and Nursing Homes (Genworth Financial), 137
Genworth Financial, 137
Geographical distribution
  of older Americans, 12
  percentage increase in population aged 65 and older, 17f
  persons aged 65 and older as percentage of total population, 16f
Georgia, older adult population in, 12
Geriatric care managers, 150
Geriatricians, 127–128
Gerontological Society of America, 181
Gerontology, 4
Gerontology Research Group, 8
Ginzler, Elinor, 54
Glaucoma
  description of, 113
  screening for, 126
Glenn, John, 63
Global life expectancy
  countries with lowest estimated life expectancy at birth, 6t
  estimated life expectancy at birth by country, 5t
  trends in, 5–6

Glucose, 107
God, belief in, 12
"The Golden Age of Innovation" (Theil), 71
Goldrich, Lois, 175
Gout, 104
Grandparents, living with grandchildren, 48–49, 51t
"Grandparents Day 2010: Sept. 12" (U.S. Census Bureau), 48
Granny units, 58
Gray Panthers, 181
"Gray power," 85–86
Great Depression, 38
Green, Diane, 176–177
Green, Steve, 72, 74
Green House Project, 56
Greenberg, Saadia
  on aging U.S. population, 1
  data from *A Profile of Older Americans: 2010*, 2
  on geographic distribution of older Americans, 12
  on income distribution, 22
  on income sources, 24
  on income spent on housing, 59
  on older adults in U.S., 6
  on older adults living in nursing homes, 47
Grieco, Elizabeth M., 12
Gross domestic product (GDP), 161, 161f
Gross v. FBL Financial Services, Inc., 74
"Groundbreaking New Survey Asks American Workers, Ages 44–70, about Longer Working Lives" (Freedman), 74
"Growing Old in America: Expectations vs. Reality" (Pew Research Center), 12, 16
"Guest Opinion: Social Security Lifts U.S. Seniors out of Poverty" (Melcher), 38
Guinness World Records, 8
Gutner, Toddi, 150

H

Hagger, Martin S., 139
Halamandaris, Val J., 147–148
Haldol (drug), 142
Hamilton, Anita, 84
Han, Beth, 138, 142
Hansen, James E., 63
Happiness, among older adults, 16–19
"Happiness Peaks in Our Eighties" (Collins), 17
Hard to Swallow: Older Americans and the High Cost of Prescription Drugs (AFSCME), 119
Harnick, Chris, 84
Harris, Diana K., 178
Harris, Meghan, 115
Harrison, Pam, 136
Hartman-Stein, Paula, 20
Hartz, Arthur J., 177

MetLife Mature Market Institute
  on assisted living, 56
  on cost of nursing home care, 163
  on costs of assisted living, 57
  financial fraud study, 172
Mexico, 5
Middle-old
  definition of, 4
  percent of older adult population, 6
Milbank Memorial Fund, 61–62
Miller, Mark, 59
Miller, Rina, 30
Minnix, Larry, 59
"Mission, Vision and Values" (Pioneer
  Network), 54–55
Mistreatment. See Abuse/mistreatment of
  older adults
"Mistreatment in Assisted Living
  Facilities: Complaints, Substantiations,
  and Risk Factors" (Phillips & Gao),
  177
Mitchell, Alex J., 133
Mobile phones, older adults' use of, 84
Mobility
  injury prevention, 122–123
  limitation of from arthritis, 104
  See also Disability
"Modest Increase in 2010 Funded Status as
  a Result of Record Employer
  Contributions" (Ehrhardt & Morgan), 28
Module 10C: Older Adults and Alcohol
  Problems (NIAAA), 143–144
Montana, older adult population in, 12
Monteverde, Malena, 5
Mood disorders, 138
Moody, Harry R., 20
"More Silver Surfers Are Using Social
  Networking Sites" (Techsling.com), 84
Morgan, Paul C., 28
Morris, Frank C., Jr., 74
Mortality
  depression and, 139
  rates, aging of population and, 3
The Mortgage Crisis: Older Americans Are
  Feeling the Pain (AARP Public Policy
  Institute), 29–30
Mortgages
  mortgage crisis, 29–30
  reverse, 59
  subprime mortgage and loan crisis, 59
Mother, birth rates by age of, 65t
Motor vehicle, ownership costs, 87–88
Motor vehicle accidents
  death rates for motor vehicle-related
    injuries, 91t–92t
  deaths of older adults from, 93
  driver involvement in fatal crashes, by
    age group/sex, 90f
  drivers/pedestrians involved in fatal
    accidents, by age group/BAC, 93t
  fears about older drivers, 94

motor vehicle fatality rates among older
  adults, by age group, 95f
nonfatal injuries, ten leading causes of,
  92t
older adult drivers and, 89–91
"Movement Disorders" (Harris et al.), 115
MRI scan, 135
Multigenerational households, 48–49
Multi-infarct dementia, 133
Mulvey, Janemarie, 22, 165
Murders, of older adults, 167
Musculoskeletal disabilities, 94
Myths, 69–71
"Myths about Older Workers" (North
  Carolina Collaboration on Lifelong
  Learning and Engagement), 69, 70

N

Naj, Adam C., 135
Names/addresses, of organizations, 181–183
Nascher, Ignatz L., 127
National Academy of Elder Law Attorneys,
  182
National Aging Network, 149
National Alliance for Caregiving, 146–147
National Association for Home Care and
  Hospice, 148, 182
National Association of Home Builders,
  58–59
National Bipartisan Commission on the
  Future of Medicare, 160
National Caregiving Foundation, 182
National Caucus and Center on Black Aged,
  182
National Cell Repository for Alzheimer's
  Disease, 135
National Centenarian Awareness Project
  (NCAP), 7–8
National Center for Health Statistics
  on conditions that limit activity, 99
  contact information, 182
  on deaths from strokes, 122
  on home health care, 165
  on life expectancy, 5
  on nursing home residents, 53
  on obesity, 125
National Center for Injury Prevention and
  Control, 90
National Center for PTSD, 162
National Center on Elder Abuse (NCEA)
  on causes of elder abuse, 175
  contact information, 182
  on prevention of institutional abuse, 179
  survey by, 174
National Center on Senior Transportation
  (NCST), 88–89
National Committee for the Prevention of
  Elder Abuse, 172
National Consumer Voice for Quality Long-
  Term Care, 182

National Council for Caregiving, 182
National Council on Aging, 149–150
National Council on Child Abuse and
  Family Violence, 175–176
National Family Caregiver Support
  Program, 149
National Family Caregivers Association,
  182
National Fibromyalgia Association,
  103–104
National Health and Nutrition Survey, 103,
  108
National Health Care Workforce
  Commission, 147
National Health Interview Survey
  on access to medical care, 126
  on alcohol consumption, 142
  data on HIV test, 127
  data on smoking, 125
  on psychological distress, 131–132, 132f
National Highway Traffic Safety
  Administration (NHTSA)
  on older adult drivers, 87
  Physician's Guide to Assessing and
    Counseling Older Drivers, 92–95
National Hispanic Council on Aging, 182
National Home and Hospice Care Survey
  (NHHCS): Home Health—Data
  Highlights (National Center for Health
  Statistics), 165
National Hospice and Palliative Care
  Organization, 182
National Indian Council on Aging, 182
National Institute of Mental Health, 142
National Institute of Neurological Disorders
  and Stroke (NINDS), 133
National Institute on Aging (NIA)
  on age limits for driving, 95
  on apoE-4 gene and AD, 134–135
  cognitive impairment study, 131
  contact information, 182
  diagnostic guidelines for AD, 136
National Institute on Alcohol Abuse and
  Alcoholism, 143–144
National Institute on Drug Abuse, 118
National Institutes of Health (NIH), 109,
  136–137
National Kidney and Urological Diseases
  Information Clearinghouse, 108
National Long-Term Care Surveys, 118
National Low Income Housing Coalition, 62
National Nursing Home Survey, 54
National Osteoporosis Foundation, 104, 182
National PACE Association, 182
National Resource Center on Nutrition,
  Physical Activity, and Aging, 110
National Respite Locator Service, Chapel
  Hill Training-Outreach Project, 182
National Senior Citizens Law Center, 182
National Service Corps, 75
National service organizations, 75–76

Wilson, Steve R., 171

Wireless Internet access, 83

Wolpert, Lewis, 17

Women. *See* Females; Gender

Work

absences from work, by age/sex, 71*t*

accomplished older adults, examples of, 63

age discrimination, 71–72, 74

Age Discrimination in Employment Act charges, 73*t*

aging labor force, 66–67, 69

labor force, projected percentage change in, by age, 69*f*

labor force participation rates for civilian workers, by age group, 68(*f*4.2)

labor force participation rates of women aged 55 and over, by age group, 68(*f*4.3)

median years of tenure with current employer for employed workers, by age/sex, 70*t*

older workers, myths/stereotypes about, 69–71

social/demographic changes, impact on work/retirement, 64–65

unemployment rates for civilian workers, by age group, 67*f*

unemployment statistics, by age group, 67*t*

U.S. economy, changes in, 65–66

volunteers by age groups, 76*t*

volunteers by annual hours volunteered, 77*t*

volunteers by type of organization, 78*t*

Workers. *See* Older workers

Working: People Talk about What They Do All Day and How They Feel about What They Do (Terkel), 63

The World Factbook: United States (Central Intelligence Agency), 3, 5

World Population Prospects: The 2008 Revision (United Nations' Department of Economic and Social Affairs), 6

World War II, fertility rates after, 3

"World's Oldest Man Dies in Montana at 114" (Volz), 8

Worry

about personal savings, 28

of older adults, stereotypes and, 19–20

"Worsening Economy Increases Risk Factors for Elder Abuse" (Goldrich), 175

WPIX-TV/Channel 11, 74

Wright, Stuart E., 173

Wyoming, older adult population in, 12

X

Xu, Jingping, 19

Xu, Weili, 133

Y

Young-old, 4, 6

You're Looking Very Well: The Surprising Nature of Getting Old (Wolpert), 17

Z

Zagaria, Mary Ann E., 127

Zhanel, George G., 117

Zhang, Yuqing, 103

Zickuhr, Kathryn, 83–84